The Second Amendment in Court

The Second Amendment in Court

Defining the Right to Keep and Bear Arms

Donald J. Campbell

BLOOMSBURY ACADEMIC
NEW YORK • LONDON • OXFORD • NEW DELHI • SYDNEY

BLOOMSBURY ACADEMIC
Bloomsbury Publishing Inc, 1359 Broadway, New York, NY 10018, USA
Bloomsbury Publishing Plc, 50 Bedford Square, London, WC1B 3DP, UK
Bloomsbury Publishing Ireland, 29 Earlsfort Terrace, Dublin 2, D02 AY28, Ireland

BLOOMSBURY, BLOOMSBURY ACADEMIC and the Diana logo are trademarks of Bloomsbury Publishing Plc

First published in the United States of America 2025

Cover image: Juan Ruiz Paramo, iStock/Getty Images Plus

A catalog record for this book is available from the Library of Congress.

Library of Congress Cataloging-in-Publication Data
Names: Campbell, Donald J., 1948– author.
Title: The Second Amendment in court : defining the right to keep and bear arms / Donald J. Campbell.
Description: New York : Bloomsbury Academic, 2025. |
Includes bibliographical references and index.
Identifiers: LCCN 2025008901 | ISBN 9798765137284 (hardback) |
ISBN 9798765137321 (paperback) | ISBN 9798765137307 (epub) |
ISBN 9798765137291 (pdf)
Subjects: LCSH: United States. Constitution. 2nd Amendment. |
United States. Constitution. 2nd Amendment–Cases. | Firearms–Law and legislation–United States. | Gun control–United States.
Classification: LCC KF3941 .C367 2025 | DDC 344.7305/33–dc23/eng/20250616
LC record available at https://lccn.loc.gov/2025008901

ISBN: HB: 979-8-7651-3728-4
ePDF: 979-8-7651-3729-1
eBook: 979-8-7651-3730-7

Typeset by Newgen KnowledgeWorks Pvt. Ltd., Chennai, India

For product safety related questions contact productsafety@bloomsbury.com.

To find out more about our authors and books visit www.bloomsbury.com and sign up for our newsletters.

To my son Andrew who never got to read this book.
He probably would have enjoyed it.

Contents

1

An Iconic Right in Dispute

A well regulated militia, being necessary to the security of a free state, the right of the people to keep and bear arms shall not be infringed.

Second Amendment of the United States Constitution

The Second Amendment of the federal Bill of Rights consists of only twenty-seven words in two clauses. Despite this brevity—perhaps because of it—this amendment has long been the most fiercely contested right of the Constitution's ten enumerated rights, with its meaning and interpretation subject to exhaustive deliberation. In popular media, in scholarly journals, and in state and federal courts, intense debate has revolved around whether the amendment's handful of words refers to a personal, individual right or to a collective, state's right. This book is an attempt to provide—at least on the judicial level—insight into the forces that gave rise to such markedly different understandings of the amendment, and to the influences that fueled such heated disagreements.

The causes of these dissimilar interpretations are not just attributable to the amendment's words, as the words are fairly clear-cut. Any engaged citizen—a subscriber to the *New York Times* or the *Washington Post*—could likely expound knowingly on the Second Amendment's meaning. Similarly, citizens of a more conservative bent—readers of the *Washington Times* or members of the National Rifle Association—could also elaborate insightfully on the amendment and its interpretation. The problem is that the knowing construal of the *New York Times* subscriber and the insightful construal of the *American Rifleman* reader will almost certainly differ, quite radically.

The structure of the amendment itself—having two clauses each focused on a different idea—contributes to this fundamental dispute over the amendment's true nature. Depending on the clause emphasized, the meaning of the amendment shifts. Focus on the first clause, and the amendment revolves around the collective state, and its security and well-being. Focus on the second clause, and the amendment revolves around the people, and the individual's right to keep and carry firearms. These two contrasting ideas have dominated the interpretative clashes surrounding the amendment, and their influence is evident in the many scholarly treatises, law reviews, serious essays, and academic publications that have examined and dissected the amendment's history.

Additionally, the very abundance of relevant historical documents has also contributed to these interpretive conflicts. In parsing the voluminous congressional records, political debates, and legal commentaries contemporaneous with the amendment's construction and enactment, scholars and experts of quite different interpretative orientations have easily found convincing arguments and passages buttressing their preferred perspective.

Other forces are also at work. The Second Amendment has long been a flashpoint in America's gun culture war,[1] and advocacy groups have not been above presenting partisan interpretations as the amendment's "only" possible interpretation. Some noteworthy gun rights supporters,[2] for instance, have maintained that the amendment's "shall not be infringed" assertion means precisely that: an absolute prohibition against any and all firearms restrictions. No regulation is constitutional. Similarly, notable gun control advocates[3] have argued that the true meaning of the Second Amendment has always centered on state security, and the amendment has never been viewed as protecting individual gun ownership. That notion, they claim, is simply a lie created by the gun lobby. These politicized views, presented passionately by both camps, have also significantly complicated the chance of arriving at a common understanding of the amendment.

Even outside the politicized camps, disagreements exist concerning the nature of the amendment. Accepting that the average law-abiding citizen likely sees the Second Amendment as conforming to the other enumerated rights in the Bill of Rights—affirming an individual right, specifically in this instance to own and use a personal firearm—that average citizen would also likely acknowledge that mere common sense demands *some* restrictions on firearm ownership and use. Without reasonable regulations, how could a community protect itself from a drunken reveler celebrating the New Year by carelessly firing a revolver into the sky or prevent a paranoid troublemaker from periodically brandishing and terrorizing neighbors with a high-caliber hunting rifle? But while these average citizens might allow that the amendment permits some reasonable, presumably minor restrictions, actually specifying the nature and degree of such permissible regulation—determining in essence what the amendment practically means—differs extensively even among such individuals.

Another contributing factor to interpretive confusion is the very arena in which interpretive clarity is expected to emerge: the court system. Firearms have been part of the American experience since before the country's founding, and legal disputes over firearms and the Second Amendment date back almost as far, with court cases easily tallying in the tens of thousands. Given that background, one might anticipate some judicial consensus around the amendment's interpretation. Such is not the case. Perhaps the highly specific circumstances of individual adjudications have stymied such judicial convergence, but for whatever reason, court decisions also show much disagreement regarding the nature of the amendment, with these decisions reflecting substantially different understandings.

The hierarchical nature of the judicial system itself—with higher-level courts having the power to review and overturn lower-court decisions—may also inadvertently contribute to judicial disagreement about the amendment. Within the federal structure's three levels, the lowest level—ninety-four US District Courts dispersed across the fifty states—are the trial courts that handle all disputes involving federal laws and regulations. At the next level, each of the thirteen US Circuit Courts (covering twelve regional areas and Washington, DC) review all the district court trial cases appealed in their specific region. At the highest level stands the Supreme Court of the United States, addressing all issues disputed (or even created) in the circuit courts.

Within this hierarchy, a US District Court might encounter, review, and adjudicate a specific Second Amendment issue, with that court's ruling offering some interpretation of the amendment's meaning. But that court's ruling (and whatever Second Amendment insight it might provide) has no "reach." The ruling applies only to that case. It does not bind other federal court to follow the ruling or its Second Amendment interpretation. Other federal courts may continue to adhere to substantially contrary interpretations.

Further, should the case move to the next judicial level, the US Circuit Court of Appeals may reject the district court's analysis, overturn that court's ruling, and provide a different interpretation of the issue and the amendment. At this level, whatever the case disposition, the circuit court's ruling sets precedent, and its analysis is binding in that circuit. All future district court decisions within the circuit's specific regional area must follow that interpretation. However, the decision and interpretation of that circuit court is *not* binding on any of the other US Circuit Courts or their geographic regions. The other circuits remain free to adjudicate and interpret as they see fit. Thus, even at this level, the "meaning" of the Second Amendment—what it guarantees and protects—is not truly established.

Moreover, a party to an unfavorable decision at the circuit level may still appeal for reconsideration to the US Supreme Court. If the court accepts the case, the Justices are likely to provide additional analysis, exploring alternative views of the legal issues and probing the amendment's nature and implications further. Since appeal beyond the US Supreme Court is not possible, and Supreme Court decisions bind *all* the courts of the United States, one might think that in these analyses the amendment's "true" meaning would finally emerge. One would again be disappointed. Historically, the Supreme Court has directly addressed the nature of the Second Amendment in only a handful of cases, and the court's analyses—as perhaps best seen in the iconic and pivotal *United States v. Miller* 1939 decision[4] (discussed in Chapter 3)—were usually characterized by a focused narrowness (or by a distinct lack of clarity) and until recently were disappointingly unhelpful.

At the state level, judicial matters are just as complex and unhelpful. While most state constitutions contain provisions similar to the Second Amendment guaranteeing the right to keep and bear arms, the state analogues are not identical to the federal amendment. For instance, Pennsylvania's analogue, enacted in its 1790 constitution, simply affirms that "the right of the citizens to bear arms in defense of themselves and the State shall not be questioned." Vermont's analogue, enacted in its 1777 constitution, is more expansive. The provision not only notes a right for self-defense and common defense, it also specifically subordinates the military to civil authority: "That the people have a right to bear arms for the defense of themselves and the State—and as standing armies in times of peace are dangerous to liberty, they ought not to be kept up; and that the military should be under strict subordination to and governed by the civil power." In contrast, Arkansas' analogue, enacted in its 1868 constitution, mentions neither self-defense nor the military: "The citizens of this state shall have the right to keep and bear arms for their common defense." These variations in wordings and emphases are characteristic of virtually all the states' Second Amendment analogues,[5] and thus they permit only limited constitutional generalizations to the federal amendment.

Additionally, state judicial systems have the same hierarchical structure as the federal system, with state decisions within each system exhibiting the same disagreements and divergent interpretations of the Second Amendment as found in federal courts. Further, judicial decisions across states are independent, and analyses accepted in one state are not necessarily endorsed even in bordering states. Thus, neither the federal nor state judicial system has offered a consistently agreed-upon interpretation of the amendment's meaning and guaranteed protections. Even currently, despite the clarifications provided by several twenty-first century US Supreme Court gun case opinions, the Second Amendment continues to engender disagreement, legal push-back, and judicial wrangling.

For all these reasons, the controversies besetting the amendment—what it covers and protects, what it permits, and what it prohibits—are understandable. Because court decisions have advanced contrasting views, these conflicts are not surprising. Despite some widely aired assertions[6] that the Second Amendment was "settled law" with its constitutional meaning firmly established, past court decisions have demonstrated precisely the opposite. The pattern of opinions across numerous state and federal "gun" cases shows that judicial understandings of the right to keep and bear arms varied considerably in different states and in different periods, and were much more ambiguous than "settled law." These gun-related cases reveal sharp and ongoing judicial arguments over the Second Amendment's right to arms. Courts disagreed about *whether* the amendment provided any gun-rights protection for individuals, and, even when affirming such protection, about *what* guarantees the amendment offered.

Despite this diversity in Second Amendment rulings, court decisions still remain the "gold standard" for defining what "the right to keep and bear arms" means in practice. Other relevant documents and sources certainly offer historical insights and particular understandings of the amendment, but insights and understandings gleaned from law reviews, congressional debates, and scholarly analyses have practical impact only to the degree they shape a court's findings. In this light, the Second Amendment means only what federal and state courts have said it means, with rulings presumably influenced by the historical record and prior legal commentaries.

Thus, by examining the actual court decisions of notable state and federal firearms cases—by exploring the reasoning justices have used in arriving at their conclusions—this book traces the conflicting legal opinions that have made the amendment so controversial. This tracing illustrates how different courts have made sense of the amendment's twenty-seven words and shows how different emphases placed on these words allowed disagreements to develop and emerge.

The Amendment's Clashing Interpretations

Courts at different times and in different jurisdictions have offered at least three general interpretations of the right to keep and bear arms. One interpretation simply reflected the popular idea that the Second Amendment protects a personal, individual right to arms. Commentators and legal scholars have often referred to this view as the "individual right" interpretation, or the "standard model." In 2008, the US Supreme Court finally adopted this view in the landmark *Heller v. District of Columbia*[7] opinion, discussed in Chapter 4.

Some earlier courts interpreted the Second Amendment as merely protecting the right of the people (acting through their state legislatures) to maintain an effective state militia. In this view, the amendment secured a *state's* right to form and arm a militia, but it offered no necessary constitutional protection for *individuals* to keep and bear arms. Labeled the "collective right" model, critics of the standard model (and of the *Heller* decision) have subscribed to this view. They have asserted that the collective interpretation was actually the accepted and agreed-upon meaning of the Second Amendment, at least until the *Heller* decision apparently overturned "settled law."

Still other courts have interpreted the Second Amendment using a variation of the collective right model. These courts have suggested that the amendment protects an individual's right to possess arms, but only militia-type arms and only when engaged in collective defense or training. In this view, the amendment protected an individual right to possess arms but limited that protection to militia activities and involvement. This partial acknowledgment of an individual right is sometimes referred to as the "sophisticated collective right" model, but its legal implications are virtually identical to the more general "collective right" interpretation.

These differing understandings reflect the particular emphases various courts have placed on the two clauses of the amendment. The individual interpretation attends to the second clause and its prohibition on infringement; the collective interpretations attend to the first clause and its call for a well-regulated militia. Court decisions throughout the nineteenth and twentieth centuries have revolved around these opposed perspectives. The early chapters of the book examine representative cases that wrestled with whether the Second Amendment supports a person's right—or a state's right—to keep and bear arms. The cases illustrate the reasoning used to support the various arguments and judicial determinations.

Because the *Heller* decision has already upheld the standard model and has asserted that the Second Amendment confers an *individual* right to keep and bear arms, examination of these cases might initially seem unnecessary and digressive. But given the many judges and prosecutors who have long endorsed the militia-linked, collective view, simply taking the *Heller* decision at face value is actually not sufficient. As one commentator[8] has noted, "For more than a hundred years … the Supreme Court, and the lower courts as well, [held that] the amendment conferred on state militias a right to bear arms—but did not give individuals a right to own or carry a weapon." Following the judicial path illuminating how this perspective developed is crucial for assessing the reasoning in *Heller* that invalidated it.

Additionally, examination of pre-*Heller* court cases provides other useful benefits. If *Heller's* interpretation of the Second Amendment is a "mistake"—if the amendment only protects some type of militia-linked, collective right, as the "settled law" argument asserts—then a future Supreme Court opinion may overturn it. Conversely, if the collective right interpretation is the legal "mistake"—and the meaning of the Second Amendment was never "settled" law—then an examination of how this faulty interpretation came to be is important. The examination may offer an indication of how the country views and interprets the Second Amendment in some future period. More broadly, the exploration of these past court cases also offers some useful understanding and insight into the country's gun culture, indirectly attesting to how it arose and how it evolved.

Organization of the Book

The first five chapters examine the nature of the Second Amendment, that is, the degree to which the amendment protects an individual or collective right to arms. Cases in each of these chapters follow chronologically and present the judiciary's treatment of Second Amendment issues as these issues arose over time. Chapter 2 covers nineteenth-century state court opinions—federal gun legislation is a twentieth-century development. These early state cases generally reflect an "individual right" interpretation of the amendment. In the adjudications, courts typically acknowledge that individuals had a Second Amendment right to arms, but a right revolving around militia-related concerns. Judges extended Second Amendment protection to guns and other weapons when the weapon had a logical relationship to the type of arms an early citizen-soldier might have owned and carried. If, instead, the firearm was of a different character than a militia arm—a small and easily concealable "pocket" gun, for example—Second Amendment protections were usually not extended, with rulings that allowed restrictions and prohibitions to stand.

In other early cases, legal questions centered on the *degree* of protection the amendment afforded a certain gun-related behavior. Under what circumstances was a specific type of restriction—a prohibition on concealed carry, for example—reasonable and permissible? When does such a prohibition go too far and become unconstitutional? These state adjudications present the arguments courts used to justify or reject different Second Amendment limitations, and they highlight the degree of consensus (or its lack) that existed across particular states and jurisdictions regarding these limitations.

Chapter 3 covers the twentieth century, and the cases examined reflect the significant shift that occurred in the judiciary's view of the Second Amendment. Particularly on the federal level, judicial opinions began to reflect a collective orientation toward the amendment. Spurred on by the Supreme Court's 1939 *Miller* opinion, and perhaps by the changing nature of the country, federal courts started to interpret the Second Amendment as a guarantee of a state's right to arm and maintain a militia, rather than as a protection of a personal right to own and carry a firearm.

Chapter 4 examines the twenty-first-century cases that overturned this collective right interpretation, including the two Supreme Court opinions (*Heller* in 2008 and *McDonald*[9] in 2010) that brought the judiciary's understanding of the amendment full circle, as an individual right, with certain limits. While the opinions in this chapter usefully clarified the fundamental nature of the Second Amendment, they left to future courts the associated task of determining the kinds of "reasonable regulation" the amendment allowed.

With Chapter 5, the book begins its examination of court cases exploring the nature of "reasonable" regulation. Primarily centered on firearm permit requirements and the constitutionality of "may-issue/proper cause" licensing schemes, the cases covered in the chapter trace the judiciary's treatment of gun permitting and culminates in a consideration of another landmark firearms adjudication, the Supreme Court's 2022 decision in *New York State Rifle & Pistol Assn. v. Bruen*.[10] The *Bruen* opinion highlights the constitutional problems of a firearms regulatory practice dating back over a hundred years, addressing these concerns.

Despite its seemingly limited focus on the constitutionality of gun licenses and permitting, the *Bruen* decision is a pivotal firearms adjudication, serving both to reinforce the Supreme Court's interpretation of the Second Amendment offered in *Heller* and *McDonald*, and to implicitly call into question—with its interpretative emphasis on "text, history, and tradition"—many previously enacted gun control laws. These laws, upheld in past court rulings that typically applied the interpretative standard of "intermediate scrutiny" and "interest-balancing," were now opened to challenge and re-litigation by gun rights advocates who saw in *Bruen's* new historical standard a more appropriate—and favorable—criterion.

Thus, the next three chapters examine cases where courts have often rejected Second Amendment protections in light of apparent general safety concerns. These cases center on the perceived dangerousness of a particular type of weapon or the specific character of an individual or the abnormal nature of a behavior. Using these concerns, courts have justified limited infringements on the right to keep or bear arms. Chapter 6, for instance, involves court opinions analyzing the constitutionality of restrictions on certain types of weapons. These restrictions involved prohibitions not only on the ownership or possession of modern military armaments (e.g., machine guns) but also on certain commonly owned revolvers, semi-automatic rifles, and handguns deemed especially dangerous or hazardous.

The cases in Chapter 7 center on the constitutionality of restricting the Second Amendment rights of individuals considered especially dangerous (or potentially dangerous) to the community. This category includes convicted felons (violent and non-violent) and domestic abusers. Chapter 8 continues this theme, examining challenges to statutes prohibiting individuals considered risky or irresponsible from possessing firearms (i.e., drug addicts, minors, and the mentally unstable). These adjudications examine the conditions under which courts have deprived these categories of individuals of their gun rights in the past and whether courts applying "text, history, and tradition" will continue to uphold these Second Amendment limitations.

Chapter 9 ends the book with a reconsideration of the question that opened the book: what does the Second Amendment actually mean? What do these court opinions—frequently conflicting and contradictory—allow us to conclude about the constitutional right to keep and bear arms? The cases make apparent that the courts (like the public generally) have long struggled to reconcile an individual's right to possess arms with the community's need to control criminal and negligent gun misuse. In various time periods, in attempting to resolve these conflicting demands, judicial outcomes favored one perspective over the other and employed different evaluative standards in determining permissible limitations on the amendment. What does this struggle imply about the judiciary's role as an honest broker? What does it imply about the Constitution as a document that provides a fixed standard to judge if a statute is legal?

Along these lines, this last chapter also considers American society's growing tendency to see the judiciary as a political entity rather than as a neutral constitutional arbiter. The implications for the Second Amendment (and the Bill of Rights in general) of such a potential shift are substantial and warrant attention. Finally, the chapter looks to the future and considers the types of Second Amendment gun issues judges will likely encounter as they continue to clarify the right to keep and bear arms.

Chapter Format

Within each chapter, the presentation follows a generally similar pattern, consisting of some brief case background, an identification of the legal issues involved, and any noteworthy ancillary information. The examination then delves into the court's analysis, highlighting the court's approach to the case and the arguments framing the legal concerns. In an effort to avoid presenting a possibly subjective and biased interpretation, the presentation draws heavily on the presiding judge's actual wording and uses extensive, direct quotes from the opinion's most relevant sections.

Further, because it is frequently difficult to distinguish judicial comments that are not essential for rendering a decision (i.e., "dicta") from statements representing the court's actual "holding" (i.e., the findings that are central and determine the court's actual decision), the presentation errs on quoting more of the court's reasoning than less. The case discussion typically ends with some short commentary on the opinion's significance and implications for understanding the Second Amendment.

Finally, it is worthwhile to remember that the outcome of many gun challenges determined an individual's fate and freedom. In these circumstances, defense attorneys often presented several legal arguments to buttress their clients' position. In these cases, the court's opinion necessarily addressed multiple constitutional or regulatory arguments in addition to Second Amendment claims. In those instances, unless the "secondary" arguments influenced the case's Second Amendment interpretation, the presentation concentrates on the Second Amendment issues and only briefly considers (or ignores) the other constitutional or statutory issues raised.

Case Selection

In choosing court cases from the extensive number of Second Amendment gun adjudications available, several considerations shaped selection. First, those cases often discussed and cited in prior analyses of the Second Amendment, as found in law reviews, scholarly works, and legal writings, typically made the list. Citations from these cases suggested other cases to examine, and if a Second Amendment citation appeared across a number of cases, that case was also considered.

A second consideration was the judicial level of the case. Since federal cases have more impact and greater legal implications than state cases, those cases received preference. Within the federal judiciary, Supreme Court and Circuit Court of Appeal cases took precedence over district court cases, especially if a circuit court eventually reconsidered a district court's adjudication. As a result of this selection approach, and also because of the historical development of firearms legislation—federal laws regulating firearms did not exist until 1934—the selected cases broadly separated into two chronological groups, with federal cases typically the most recent.

Prior to federal legislation, gun regulation was usually a reaction to violent criminal activity and handled at the state and municipal levels. Thus, challenges to these firearm regulations occurred in state courts, and the majority of the nineteenth- and early-twentieth-century cases discussed in the book are state adjudications. This chronological artifact does not imply that these cases have only minor relevance to an understanding of the Second Amendment. Arguments and considerations appearing in these earlier cases resurface and influence the outcomes of later federal cases, even though state adjudications do not bind federal courts. Thus, full appreciation of the Second Amendment requires a consideration of these state-level opinions.

In an effort to highlight the evolution of judicial reasoning, cases within each chapter are examined chronologically, but the chronology in the book's later topical chapters necessarily overlaps. Historically, Second Amendment adjudications have wrestled with at least four general issues. Beginning in the 1800s, the earliest gun cases centered on the kinds of restrictions the amendment permitted, or if it even permitted any at all—the *permissible restrictions* issue. A bit later in the century, courts addressed whether the amendment pertained to the states, or whether it just constrained the federal government—the *incorporation* issue.

Still later in the century, and continuing into the 1900s, some courts began to suggest that the amendment merely codified a state's right to maintain a militia, while others maintained that the amendment protected an individual right—the *individual versus collective right* issue. This controversy extended into the twenty-first century and, as noted, culminated in several landmark Supreme Court decisions. These decisions established that the Second Amendment protected an individual right, *but* one subject to reasonable regulation. Thus, the fourth issue brought the evolution of judicial gun concerns full circle, once again revolving around the nature and type of *permissible limitations.*

Of course, since the cases considered in the book are only a subset of relevant gun adjudications, this effort to discern a "pattern" in judicial thinking may at first seem ill-advised. After all, might not a set of omitted cases suggest a different emphasis and pattern? Probably not. Given the nature of firearms litigation—with virtually all important gun issues raised in multiple courts in multiple jurisdictions—it seems unlikely that the examined court adjudications have overlooked possible controversial positions and findings in unexamined cases. Arguments raised in omitted cases would have surfaced in the cases considered. The range of opinions in such cases would not differ substantially from the range of rulings in the explored cases, thus leaving unaltered the overall thrust and conclusions presented.

Legal Concepts and Conventions

Some court opinions have pivoted on particular legal concepts or conventions that make a judicial analysis of the case's Second Amendment issues inappropriate (e.g., lack of "standing") or make a substantive analysis unnecessary (e.g., "*stare decisis*"). Other firearms cases have pivoted on conventions that significantly influence the court's eventual determination (e.g., the level of "scrutiny" used). Familiarity with these terms help clarify a number of adjudications examined in the book. These concepts are grouped into three broad categories: grounds for judicial intervention, adjudication frameworks and standards, and procedural concepts and processes.

Grounds for Judicial Intervention

Three legal concepts—incorporation, standing, and pre-enforcement challenge—deal with the feasibility of a substantive judicial response to a case brought before the court. "Incorporation" refers to whether a right enumerated in the Bill of Rights applies to state legislation; "standing" examines whether an individual has a basis for bringing a court action; and "pre-enforcement challenge" seeks to prevent the enforcement of a law before it is applied. Questions of incorporation and standing can short-circuit a court's consideration of a case before addressing the case's substantive issues; while a pre-enforcement challenge allows an individual to establish standing in situations where standing might otherwise be denied. Each of these concepts has impacted gun adjudications discussed in the book.

Incorporation. This constitutional doctrine makes the federal Bill of Rights applicable to the states; it binds state governments to recognize and uphold the freedoms guaranteed in the federal Constitution's first ten amendments at the state and municipal level. Historically, prior to incorporation, the Bill of Rights limited only the power of the federal government. State governments were not constrained to honor or protect those federally enumerated rights. During the first century or so of the nation's founding, courts adjudicating Second Amendment challenges sometimes dismissed such cases by noting that the amendment's protections extended only to the actions of the national government, not the actions of state governments. Thus, the absence of incorporation might permit a court to resolve a gun case without substantively addressing the Second Amendment issue underlying the case.

As a legal doctrine, incorporation was a reaction to Chief Justice John Marshall's conclusion (in the 1833 case of *Barron v. Mayor and City Council of Baltimore*[11]) that the federal Bill of Rights restrained only the powers of the federal government and did not limit or apply to the powers of the states. Evolving over a period of decades, the incorporation process started with the passage of the Fourteenth Amendment in 1868, and followed a piecemeal and fragmentary legal course thereafter. The process did not include the Second Amendment until the twenty-first century, when the Supreme Court's *McDonald* opinion incorporated the amendment. Thus, in many early gun cases, many state courts resolved potential Second Amendment violations by noting that the amendment was not applicable to the states. Some such cases are examined in Chapter 2, including the controversial 1875 *United States v. Cruikshank*[12] case.

Standing. This concept refers to an entity's ability to initiate a legal action and bring a case to court. In the gun adjudications considered, individuals wishing to engage the judicial system must first show that they are in some way affected by and are actually injured by a firearms statute or restriction. They must also show that some court action can rectify their injury. If either of these conditions are absent—if the injury is only hypothetical or speculative, or if the court is unable to provide a legal remedy—then those individuals have no basis for initiating (or participating in) a legal action: they have no "standing" to address the court.

The District of Columbia's civil lawsuit against the January 6, 2021, demonstrators involved in the US Capitol Building clashes offers a non-firearms illustration of the importance of standing. Defense attorneys filed a motion to dismiss the case, arguing that the District did not have standing to bring the case to court. They contended that the incidents occurred on federal land, not on District of Columbia ground; and since the District had suffered no injury for the court to redress, they argued that the District had no standing to sue.[13]

Similarly, *Hickman v. Block*,[14] a 1996 Ninth Circuit US Appeals Court adjudication, reflects the importance of standing in a firearms case. Douglas Hickman had applied for and been denied a concealed weapons permit by both the County of Los Angeles and the City of San Fernando. California at that time had a "may issue" gun licensing approach. "May issue" jurisdictions do not obligate the licensing authority (e.g., the county sheriff) to issue a firearms permit, even if an individual meets all statutory requirements. In Hickman's case, both jurisdictions had a "good cause" provision in their issuing policy, and both determined that Hickman did not meet this standard.

Hickman appealed the district court's summary dismissal of his case, arguing that the Second Amendment obliged the states to regulate firearm possession and use in a "reasonable" manner. Judge Cynthia Hall summarized Hickman's appeal as a question of whether the amendment gave individual citizens "standing to enforce the right to keep and bear arms." She answered this way: "We follow our sister circuits in holding that the Second Amendment is a right held by the states, and does not protect the possession of a weapon by a private citizen. We conclude that Hickman can show no legal injury, and therefore lacks standing to bring this action."[15]

Standing was also a central issue in *Seegars v. Gonzales*,[16] a 2005 District of Columbia case. The plaintiffs—Sandra Seegars and others—challenged on Second Amendment grounds the district's statute that barred them from registering and lawfully possessing handguns in the district. The district court rejected the plaintiffs' challenge, holding that they lacked standing to bring suit, and the circuit court affirmed their lack of standing.

Senior Circuit Judge Stephen Williams wrote the court's opinion for this case. He acknowledged that the District of Columbia statute made it impossible for pistols not already registered to now be registered; and as a result, it was no longer possible in the District to purchase and lawfully possess a new pistol, or any pistol not registered three decades ago. However, the judge went on to note, "No plaintiff in this case has been arrested and prosecuted for violating the disputed provisions of the Code, so plaintiffs' case constitutes a 'preenforcement' challenge. ... The district court held that the pistol plaintiffs lacked standing because they faced no credible threat of imminent prosecution under the District's gun laws."[17]

Williams continued, "We agree with the district court ... that the pistol plaintiffs have not shown a threat of prosecution reaching the level of imminence required. ... plaintiffs allege no prior threats against them or any characteristics indicating an especially high probability of enforcement against them. ... therefore, we affirm the decision of the district court"[18] denying standing and dismissing the challenge.

Standing also featured prominently in the 2007 *Parker v. District of Columbia*[19] case, which, on appeal to the Supreme Court, later became the landmark *Heller* adjudication. Of the six petitioners in *Parker*, only one of them—Dick Heller—had actually applied for, and been denied, a firearms permit by the District. His co-petitioners had neither applied for nor been denied a permit. At best, they suffered only a "hypothetical injury" but Heller's denial was an objective "legal injury," and that gave him standing to pursue the case.

Pre-enforcement challenges. As noted above, in order to have standing to bring a court action, a plaintiff must have suffered an actual—not hypothetical—legal injury. But in some circumstances, the mere *threat* of enforcement is enough to provide a plaintiff grounds to challenge a purported unconstitutional statute—even before actually violating it. This is accomplished through a court's "pre-enforcement review" of the statute. For instance, in a case where the Bureau of Alcohol, Tobacco, Firearms and Explosives (BATFE) had criminalized the manufacture and sales of a specific type of trigger, the trigger manufacturer challenged the regulation as exceeding the agency's regulatory authority.

BATFE responded by arguing that the plaintiff had no standing to challenge the regulation, in that the agency had not enforced the regulation against this manufacturer. In a pre-enforcement review, the court noted that a plaintiff did not have to first expose himself to actual arrest or prosecution in order to challenge a law allegedly deterring the exercise of a constitution right. Dismissing BATFE's objections, the court determined that, based on the pre-enforcement review, the manufacturer had standing, and analyzed the case on its merits.[20]

Adjudication Frameworks and Standards

The judicial lens that a court brings to a gun case, and the assessment standard used for evaluating the constitutionality of a challenged regulation, greatly influence the case's eventual outcome. Four concepts are especially important. Two notions—constitutional rights versus common law rights and "stare decisis"—are essential for understanding gun cases generally. Two other concepts—"means—end analysis" (i.e., levels of scrutiny) and "text, history, and tradition"—are contrasting assessment standards that both state and federal courts have used to judge a specific statute's constitutionality.

Common Law Rights/Constitutional Rights. In some gun cases, courts have noted a distinction between a constitutionally based right and a common-law based right. For instance, in his dissent in the *Heller* opinion, Justice John Paul Stevens observed that the right to keep arms and bear arms for self-defense is enshrined in a common-law principle preceding (and independent of) the Second Amendment. This distinction suggests that, in a practical sense, arguments over the meaning and nature of the amendment are perhaps largely academic. If individuals maintain a right to arms rooted in the common law (i.e., in case law derived from past judicial opinions and decisions rather than in legislated statutes or constitutional protections), perhaps the Second Amendment guarantee of a right to arms is mostly redundant and unnecessary; and concerns about its infringement are judicially not that important.

The implication that a common-law based right makes a constitutionally based protection unnecessary is questionable. Because common law is unwritten and relies on precedents that individual judges can select and modify (or even overturn), rights anchored in common law are less protected and more fragile than rights based on constitutional grounds. Further, legislated statutes typically supersede common law, and a right grounded only in common law is potentially subject to statutory modifications and requirements.

In contrast, a right secured by constitutional fiat (such as those enumerated in the federal Bill of Rights) possesses the strongest protection against possible government erosion. Thus, regardless of common law support, the Second Amendment remains pivotal in defining an individual right to arms. This importance probably explains the intense significance both pro- and anti-gun advocates place on the amendment.

Stare Decisis/Precedent. The concept of "stare decisis" (literally meaning "to stand by things decided") is the legal principle that future courts should follow a previous court's ruling when adjudicating an identical or highly similar issue. While stare decisis is not quite as sweeping as it initially appears, the concept is at the heart of "binding precedent." It generally demands that judges apply the findings and conclusions in similar past cases to support and justify decisions in current cases.

This convention attempts to insure that all individuals receive fair and consistent treatment. As prior court rulings accumulate around a particular legal issue, the rulings of future judges are largely constrained, presumably producing a high degree of stability and predictability in judicial findings and verdicts. Since past courts have already examined and adjudicated the issue (or ones highly similar), precedent and stare decisis direct the findings of the present court. The issue becomes "settled law," and offers the predictability and stability required for consistent legal treatment across similar cases.

Stare decisis has played a prominent role in the judicial analysis of many of the gun-related cases discussed in Chapter 3. In these cases, courts often dismissed arguments based on an "individual right" interpretation of the Second Amendment simply by citing a multitude of prior court adjudications affirming the amendment's "collective" nature. These precedents justified a cursory analysis of the underlying Second Amendment issue.

Stare decisis also figured prominently in *Seegars v. Gonzales*, discussed above. Before determining that the plaintiffs had no standing to challenge the District of Columbia's gun statutes, Judge Williams observed that under more relaxed non-firearm judicial precedents, the plaintiffs' pre-enforcement challenge might have succeeded, and might have given them standing. But at that time, the only firearms circuit case dealing with a pre-enforcement challenge – *Navegar, Inc. v. United States*[21]—used more stringent assessment criteria, and he was obligated to follow that approach.

Means-Ends Analysis (Levels of Scrutiny). This evaluative process examines the fit between the objectives a gun statute is designed to achieve and the statute's "reasonableness" in achieving those objectives. Specifically, the procedure determines a gun law's constitutionality by weighing the law's expected societal benefits against its degree of infringement on an individual's right to arms. Sometimes referred to as an "interest-balancing" approach, courts in conducting means-end analysis have used three increasingly stringent levels in assessing reasonableness of fit. The first and most relaxed level—the rational basis level—upholds a law or regulation as constitutional so long as the regulation has some rational relationship to a legitimate governmental purpose. Since virtually every law or statute has *some* connection to a legitimate government interest—Congress or the legislature would not have passed it otherwise—this standard sets a fairly low bar for assessing constitutionality.

While courts hardly ever applied rational basis review in adjudicating Second Amendment matters, there are exceptions. For instance, in the 2002 case of *Silveira v. Lockyer*,[22] the plaintiffs challenging California's "assault weapons" ban argued that any statute allowing some people (in this case, active and retired peace officers) to exercise a fundamental right (such as the Second Amendment) differently from others (e.g., the plaintiffs) should be subject to "heightened scrutiny"—that is, a strict level of examination. The court, concluding the plaintiffs had no constitutional right to possess weapons to begin with, and thus had no basis for a Second Amendment challenge, determined that heightened scrutiny did not apply and instead used rational-basis review to determine the constitutionality of the statute.

A more stringent gauge, and one frequently used in Second Amendment rulings, is "intermediate scrutiny." This level of examination deemed a statute constitutional if it met two requirements. First, the statute had to further an important governmental interest (e.g., reduction in violent crime). Second, it had to achieve this interest in a way "substantially related" to that end (e.g., imposing additional penalties on individuals carrying firearms during the execution of a crime). Determining whether a specific law "substantially" relates to the governmental end in question obviously involves a degree of subjective judgment and judicial interpretation. While the fit between the means and the end has to be evident, it is not necessary that the means (i.e., the specific law) be the "best" or least intrusive way of achieving the government's desired objective.

Under this standard, even if a statute or regulation impinged in some limited way on Second Amendment protections, the court might uphold the statute's constitutionality as a reasonable balance between the rights of the individual and the security and safety needs of the public. Intermediate scrutiny had a central role in many of the adjudications leading up to the Supreme Court's 2022 opinion in the *Bruen* case, discussed in Chapter 5.

Until the Supreme Court's *Bruen* opinion, "strict scrutiny" was the most rigorous assessment level for determining the constitutionality of a law. To pass constitutional muster under this standard, a gun statute must further a *compelling* governmental interest, and the statute must be narrowly tailored to achieve that interest. Courts reserved this level of analysis for statutes that substantially intruded on core American rights, such as those enumerated in the federal Bill of Rights.

As an enumerated right, one might expect that courts typically used strict scrutiny when examining Second Amendment cases. However, as implied above, some subjectivity almost always exists in determining the appropriate evaluative standard to use. Judgment is involved in assessing whether a *compelling* governmental interest is at stake and in deciding whether a law poses a *substantial* infringement. Thus, determining an appropriate assessment standard for a firearms case was not always clear-cut, but the choice always impacted the case's outcome.

Text, History, and Tradition. The Supreme Court, in the 2022 *Bruen* opinion, rejected means-ends analysis and the "levels of scrutiny" approach for evaluating Second Amendment constitutional questions. Instead, the court endorsed a method that emphasizes an examination of the actual text of the amendment informed by a consideration of the historical understandings and American traditions at the time of the amendment's adoption. Associate Justice Brett Kavanaugh first proposed this approach when he served on the District of Columbia Circuit Court.[23]

Arguing that courts should look to "text, history, and tradition" in assessing gun regulations and potential infringements on the Second Amendment, Kavanaugh asserted that the "text, history, and tradition" evaluation standard is more likely to reveal the intentions of the amendment's framers and thus more likely to capture the original meaning of the Constitution.

Supporters of this approach have stressed that this standard centers Second Amendment constitutional analysis on what the amendment says and how it was understood.[24]

Similarly, gun rights advocates have championed this approach to assessing challenges to gun laws, contending that it is a more appropriate standard than the intermediate scrutiny framework that many federal circuit courts have favored in the past. Nonetheless, some legal scholars have criticized the new standard as vague and unusual, and one that may encourage judicial policymaking by potentially concealing a judge's personal preferences in a cloak of questionable or speculative historical contentions.[25] Despite these concerns, the Supreme Court's affirmation of this new standard insures that it will shape all future Second Amendment legal challenges and court adjudications.

Procedural Concepts and Processes

In several of the gun cases discussed, the adjudication refers to less common legal processes that may require clarification. This section provides a brief explanation of several procedural concepts encountered in the book: the notion of a "demurrer"; the relationship between an appellate court's "panel" decision and its "en banc" decision; the concept of "de novo"; the notion of a "writ of certiorari"; and "facial" versus "as-applied" constitutional challenges.

Demurrer. A defendant's written motion asserting that, even if the facts alleged in the violation were true, they do not provide a legal basis for a prosecution. Since the facts are not sufficient as a cause of action, the demurrer asks the court to dismiss charges. The judge reviews the demurrer's arguments to determine their validity. Typically in gun cases, the demurrer questions the sufficiency of the allegations in light of Second Amendment guarantees and the specifics of the laws presumably violated. The court may agree with the demurrer and dismiss the prosecution, or it may disagree and proceed with the case. (The federal judiciary has replaced demurrers with "motions to dismiss," but some state courts continue to use them.)

Panel and En Banc Appellate Decisions. At the appellate level, the review of a trial court's opinion typically consists of a hearing before a panel of three judges randomly chosen from the complete set of judges making up the entire appellate circuit. Sometimes, after a panel has rendered a decision in an appeal, an en banc proceeding—a court session consisting of the circuit's entire complement of judges—may sit and undertake a review of the panel's opinion.

This usually only occurs when the legal issue is particularly important and disagreement exists regarding the correctness of the panel's determination. For instance, in 2014, after a Fourth Circuit panel opinion reversed a district court's ruling upholding California's "good cause" handgun permit requirement, the panel ruling was itself reversed by an en banc hearing in 2016. (See Chapter 5 for the details of this case—*Peruta v. County of San Diego*.[26])

De Novo. A Latin term meaning "anew," a de novo judicial review indicates that the reviewing court examines the legal issues as if the case was being heard for the first time, without giving any deference or weight to the lower court's prior decision. De novo reviews often occur when an appeal raises questions about the trial court's interpretation or application of the law.

Writ of Certiorari. The US Supreme Court represents the last hope for parties dissatisfied with a federal circuit opinion, and this last level of appeal requires a petition—a "writ of certiorari." The writ essentially asks the Supreme Court to instruct the appeals court to send up the case for a review of its ruling. Because writ petitions are heard as a matter of discretion, the court is not obligated to grant certiorari and review any specific case; the Supreme Court does so only with a small fraction of the total cases requesting certiorari. Cases chosen typically involve significant constitutional questions or resolve disputing opinions among the federal judiciary or, as with several of the landmark Second Amendment cases, do both.

"Facial" versus "As-applied" Constitutional Challenges. Plaintiffs asserting that a specific law violates the Constitution can make two types of arguments. The first claims that the statute is unconstitutional "facially"—unconstitutional in *all* cases and in *every* set of circumstances. A successful facial challenge invalidates the statute for everyone, not just the plaintiff bringing the case. In contrast, an "as-applied" challenge claims that, because of special factors or unique circumstances, the statute is unconstitutional as applied to that specific individual. The court would then examine the statute focusing on the individual circumstances that allegedly make the statute inapplicable in that specific case.

The distinction between the two types of challenges has significant practical implications. To rebut a facial challenge, the government must only present constitutional applications where the statute would be upheld—even if these applications are completely unrelated to the plaintiff's specific situation. Two cases in Chapter 8 vividly illustrate these distinctions and their practical impact. In the first case, Patrick Daniels—a drug addict in possession of a firearm—challenged the relevant statute as applied to him, and prevailed.[27] In the second case, Devonte Veasley—also a drug addict found in possession of a firearm—similarly challenged the constitutionality of the statute. For legal reasons, he could only mount a facial challenge. That challenge failed.[28]

These different legal constructs and conventions generally influenced only a small number of the adjudications examined in the book, but the impact of a particular construct on a specific case was frequently substantial. For example, the Second Amendment's lack of incorporation played a pivotal role in many gun cases shortly after the US Supreme Court's 1833 *Barron* opinion asserted that the Bill of Rights did not bind the states. Several of the nineteenth-century cases considered in the next chapter demonstrate this point.

One Last Note

Before turning to the nineteenth-century cases in the next chapter, one further organizational detail needs mentioning: case chapters all end with a "Some Observations" passage. This chapter section attempts to highlight some broader implications or significant aspects of the cases considered. It is hoped that these comments may also further an understanding of the Second Amendment. In some ways, such additional commentary may seem out of place in a book whose purpose is to let the judicial opinions "speak for themselves" in defining the right to keep and bear arms.

But as suggested earlier in the chapter, wide diversity exists in the reasoning and rulings of judges addressing Second Amendment gun issues, with individual details and contradictory decisions possibly obscuring the broader implications of the cases. Also, the narrow focus of specific adjudications may sometimes mask more general principles or existing contradictions. Like the proverbial blind men trying to "see" the elephant by touching only one of its appendages, a similar problem might exist with the cases in the absence of some brief observations. These observations provide one way of looking at specific aspects of each set of opinions, and they try to ensure that interesting implications are not missed.

Of course, the viewpoint offered in the commentary represents just a single perspective on the cases and what they say about the right to arms. In the end, the array of court rulings still represents the ultimate statement for understanding the Second Amendment, and familiarity with the decisions themselves allows readers to construct their own informed perspective.

Notes

1 Donald Campbell, *America's Gun Wars: A Cultural History of Gun Control in the United States* (Santa Barbara, CA: Praeger, 2019).

2 See Larry Pratt, "The Uncompromisable Right to Keep and Bear Arms: Preparing Now for the Battles That Are Sure to Come." *Gun Owners of America*, September 29, 2008. At gunowners.org/op0838-htm/. Also, Vin Suprynowicz, "And Every Other Terrible Instrument." *Las Vegas Review Journal*, March 23, 2008. At reviewjournal.com/opinion/and-every-other-terrible-instrument/.

3 Warren Burger, "Second Amendment Fraud." MacNeil / Lehrer News Hour, December 16, 1991. At youtube.com/watch?v=Eya_k4P-iEo.

4 *United States v. Miller, 307, U.S. 174 (1939*). At https://www.law.cornell.edu/supremecourt/text/307/174.

5 See Eugene Volokh, *State Constitutional Right to Keep and Bear Arms Provisions*, 2006. At https://www2.law.ucla.edu/Volokh/beararms/statecon.htm.
See also David Kopel, *What State Constitutions Teach about the Second Amendment*, 2002. At https://davekopel.org/2A/LawRev/WhatStateConstitutionsTeach.htm. For speculations regarding the implications of state constitutions for recent gun cases, see Quinn Yeargain, *The State Constitutional Rights to Bear Arms After Rahimi*, State Court Report, August 5, 2004. At https://statecourtreport.org/our-work/analysis-opinion/state-constitutional-rights-bear-arms-after-rahimi.

6 See John Paul Stevens, *District of Columbia v Heller* Dissent, June 29, 2008. Legal Information Institute. At law.cornell.edu/supct/html/07-290.ZD.html.
Also, Juliet Leftwich, "D.C. Gun Case: Second Amendment on Trial." Law.Com, March 14, 2008. At law.com/therecorder/aimID900005505835/sireturn=20220329170845Also, Saul Cornell, "Guns Have Always Been Regulated." *Atlantic*, December 17, 2015. At theatlantic.com/politics/archive/2015/12/guns-have-always-been-regulated/420531.

7 *District of Columbia v. Heller, 554 U.S. 570 (2008).* At https://supreme.justia.com/cases/federal/us/554/570/.

8 Jeffrey Toobin, "So You Think You Know the Second Amendment?," *New Yorker*, December 17, 2012. At newyorker.com/news/daily-comment/so-you-think-you-know-the-second-amendment.

9 *McDonald v. City of Chicago, 561 U.S. 742 (2010).* At https://supreme.justia.com/cases/federal/us/561/742/.

10 *New York State Rifle & Pistol Assn., INC. v. Bruen* 597 U. S. *(2022).* At https://www.supremecourt.gov/opinions/21pdf/20-843_7j80.pdf.

11 *Barron v. Mayor & City Council of Baltimore, 32 U.S. 243 (1833).* At https://supreme.justia.com/cases/federal/us/32/243/.

12 *United States v. Cruikshank, 92 U.S. 542 (1875).* At https://supreme.justia.com/cases/federal/us/92/542/.

13 Joseph Hanneman, "District of Columbia Lacks Standing to Sue Oath Keepers and Proud Boys for Jan. 6, Defense Attorney Says," *Epoch Times*, April 5, 2022. At theepochtimes.com/district-of-columbia-lacks-standing-to-sue-oath-keepers-and-proud-boys-for-jan-6-defense-attorney-says_4382529.html.

14 *Hickman v. Block 81 F.3d 98 (9th Cir. 1996).* At https://casetext.com/case/hickman-v-block.

15 Ibid.

16 *Seegars v. Gonzales, 396 F. 3d 1248—Court of Appeals, Dist. of Columbia Circuit, (2005).* At https://scholar.google.com/scholar_case?case=1840873585690820786l&q=seegars+v.+gonzales&hl=en&as_sdt=4006&as_vis=1.

17 Ibid.

18 Ibid. Although lack of standing prevented the Seegars plaintiffs from prevailing against DC's gun laws, a highly similar challenge to those laws would occur two years later in 2007. This case would eventually end up in the Supreme Court, and the court would rule in *Heller v. District of Columbia* that the DC statute was an unconstitutional violation of the Second Amendment.

19 *Parker v. District of Columbia, 478 F.3d 370 (2007).* At https://scholar.google.com/scholar_case?case=11156910755936011541&hl=en&as_sdt=6&as_vis=1&oi=scholarr.

20 *National Association of Gun Rights v. Garland et al., 4:23-cv-00830-O (U.S. District Court of Texas) (2024).* At https://fingfx.thomsonreuters.com/gfx/legaldocs/zdvxxkmdjvx/NAGR%20v%20Garland%20decision%207-23.pdf. Chapter 9 discusses this case in more detail.

21 *Navegar, Inc. v. United States, 103 F.3d 994 (D.C. Cir. 1997).* At https://casetext.com/case/navegar-incorporated-v-united-states.

22 *Silveira v. Lockyer 312 F.3d 1052 (9th Cir.* 2002*).* At https://casetext.com/case/silveira-v-lockyer-2.

23 Dru Stevenson, "'Text, History, and Tradition' as a Three-Part Test." *Second Thoughts*, March 11, 2020. At sites.law.duke.edu/secondthoughts/2020/03/11/text-history-and-tradition-as-a-three-part-test/ #:~:text=Jake%20Charles%20discussed%20here%20that,among%20the%20federal%20circuit%20 courts

24 Joseph Greenlee, "Text, History, and Tradition: A Workable Test that Stays True to the Constitution," Duke Center for Firearms Law, May 4, 2022. At https://firearmslaw.duke.edu/2022/05/text-history-and-tradition-a-workable-test-that-stays-true-to-the-constitution/.

25 Stevenson, "'Text, History, and Tradition' as a Three-Part Test." *Second Thoughts,* March 11, 2020.

26 *Peruta v. County of San Diego, 11-16255 (9th Cir. 2016).* At https://law.justia.com/cases/federal/appellate-courts/ca9/10-56971/10-56971-2016-06-09.html.
27 *United States v. Daniels, 22-60596 (Fifth Circuit) (2023).* At https://www.ca5.uscourts.gov/opinions/pub/22/22-60596-CR0.pdf.
28 *United States v. Veasley, 23-1114 (Eighth Circuit) (2024).* At https://caselaw.findlaw.com/court/us-8th-circuit/116062347.html.

2

The Nineteenth Century: Permissible Limits on an Individual Right

But to prohibit the citizen from wearing or carrying a war arm ... is an unwarranted restriction upon his constitutional right to keep and bear arms.

Chief Justice Elbert English, Arkansas Supreme Court[1]

Not long after Congress enacted the federal Bill of Rights in 1791, American courts began to address constitutional challenges to firearms-related arrests and convictions. Brought by individuals charged with some sort of firearms offense—typically, the carrying of a small concealed "pocket" pistol in violation of a state or municipal statute—the defendant's contention usually revolved around whether the particular statute violated the Second Amendment of the federal constitution or the Second Amendment equivalent contained in the state's constitution. In resolving these challenges, judges essentially had to determine the practical meaning of the Second Amendment: what limitations on the right to keep and bear arms might it allow, and what limitations might it prohibit.

However, as suggested in Chapter 1, judicial determinations are not universally compelling. Judges often came to different conclusions about the statutory restrictions the amendment permitted and forbade. Even when a seeming judicial consensus arose, this consensus varied across time periods. Such is the case with nineteenth- and twentieth-century gun opinions. Two conflicting patterns are evident across the two centuries. For nineteenth-century America, the majority of opinions either implicitly or explicitly reflect an "individual right" orientation to the Second Amendment. The opinions generally make clear that the Second Amendment (or its state analogue) guaranteed a personal right to arms—but with reasonable restrictions on that right. For these jurists, the issue was not so much in determining if the right to arms was individual or collective but in determining whether a challenged restriction and perceived infringement on this right was reasonable and justified. Most of the cases examined in this chapter wrestle with this precise problem.

As the next chapter illustrates, a different judicial trend emerged in the latter half of the twentieth century. Many courts during that century—particularly on the federal level—adopted the alternative "collective right" perspective. These two conflicting judicial interpretations shared an uneasy coexistence for decades, until late-twentieth- and twenty-first-century cases—and ultimately Supreme Court intervention—resolved the conflict.

Focused on nineteenth-century opinions, this chapter divides the examined cases into three time periods. Spanning the years 1822 through 1846, the first period explores opinions that generally overruled Second Amendment objections to state and municipal restrictions on an individual's weapon-carrying behavior. Authored by justices of various state Supreme Courts, this period includes the *Bliss* case (1822)—the first state Supreme Court ruling on the Second Amendment—and the *Buzzard* case (1842)—the earliest case to suggest that the right to keep and bear arms may not be an individual right.

The second period covers the years 1871 through 1876. Several cases during this period illustrate the impact of the US Supreme Court's 1833 *Barron* decision—Chief Justice John Marshall's conclusion that the federal Bill of Rights did not apply to the states—on the right to keep and bear arms. This period also includes the US Supreme Court's controversial *Cruikshank* (1875) decision and its impact on gun cases. The last period, covering 1881 through 1894, contains several cases that continued to examine both the constitutionality of carry prohibitions and the Second Amendment's lack of incorporation on gun rights. This period also produced two other rulings—the *Presser* case (1886) and the *Miller* (1894) case—both cases notable principally because they represent US Supreme Court opinions.

1822–46: Individual Rights and Concealed Weapons

The five cases considered in this section originated in five different states—Kentucky, Tennessee, Alabama, Arkansas, and Georgia—but they all centered on the same constitutional question: Does the Second Amendment permit a state legislature to determine the kind of arms an individual can own and carry or to limit the way the individual carries such arms? One court, in *Bliss v. Commonwealth of Kentucky*, concluded in 1822 that a statute imposing *any* restrictions on an individual's right to keep or bear arms violated the amendment. Faced with the same issue, four later courts—*Aymette v. State of Tennessee*, *State of Alabama v. Reid*, *State of Arkansas v. Buzzard*, and *Nunn v. State of Georgia*—all concluded that *some* statutory restrictions on weapons and weapons-wearing did *not* conflict with the Second Amendment and were well within the authority of their legislatures to enact.

The reasoning behind these opinions is instructive. With the exception of *Bliss*, which simply dismissed *any* infringement on the right to arms for *any* reason as constitutionally forbidden, the other four cases provided quite differing rationales for the constitutionality of regulatory gun statutes. In the *Aymette* case, the justification revolved around the purpose of Tennessee's second amendment equivalent. Since the analogue was meant to insure an effective *common* defense, the court concluded that the amendment protected only firearms used in "civilized" warfare, not the pocket guns employed in private quarrels. In the *Reid* case, the court's justification noted that while the Alabama constitution guaranteed the right to keep and bear arms, it did not expressly or implicitly deny the legislature power to regulate arms for public safety.

In the *Buzzard* case, the justification centered on logic. The court reasoned that some restrictions on personal rights were obviously necessary if citizens wanted the benefits of civil governance, and if arms went unregulated, civil society would suffer. Finally, in the *Nunn* case, the court justified a ban on the carrying of firearms *secretly* by noting that individuals could still bear their arms openly, thus maintaining their Second Amendment right to arms. The discussions below elaborate on these points.

Bliss v. Commonwealth of Kentucky (1822): Challenging a Concealed-Carry Statute

Considered the first state Supreme Court opinion to examine the Second Amendment,[2] the Bliss case centered on a defendant found guilty of violating a Kentucky statute prohibiting the wearing of concealed arms. The statute provided that "any person in this commonwealth who shall hereafter wear a pocket pistol, dirk, large knife, or sword in a cane, concealed as a weapon, unless when traveling on a journey, shall be fined any sum not less than one hundred dollars."[3] Bliss was indicted and convicted of having worn a sword concealed in a cane as a weapon. He appealed his conviction to Kentucky's highest court at that time, arguing that his indictment conflicted with the tenth article of the state constitution, which held "that the right of the citizens to bear arms in defense of themselves and the state, shall not be questioned."[4]

The state's attorney acknowledged that the state constitution prohibited the legislature from passing laws that would completely prevent the citizens from bearing arms but argued that "a distinction [exists] between a law prohibiting the exercise of the right, and a law merely regulating the manner of exercising that right; and whilst the former was ... incompatible with the constitution ... the latter is not so."[5]

In evaluating the state's position, the court observed,

> That the provisions of the act in question do not import an entire destruction of the right of the citizens to bear arms in defense of themselves and the state, will not be controverted by the court; for though the citizens are forbid wearing weapons concealed ... they may, nevertheless, bear arms in any other admissible form. But to be in conflict with the constitution, it is not essential that the act should contain a prohibition against bearing arms in every possible form—it is the *right* to bear arms ... that is secured by the constitution, and whatever restrains the full and complete exercise of that right, though not an entire destruction of it, is forbidden by the explicit language of the constitution.[6]

The court went on to note,

> The right [to bear arms] existed at the adoption of the constitution; it had then no limits short of the moral power of the citizens to exercise it ... if any portion of that right be impaired, immaterial how small the part may be ... it is equally forbidden

> by the constitution. … Whether or not an act of the legislature conflicts with the constitution is … a question of great delicacy and deserves the most mature and deliberate consideration. … The court should never, on slight implication or vague conjecture, pronounce the legislature to have transcended its authority … but when a strong and clear conviction is entertained that an act is incompatible with the constitution, there is no alternative … [but to] pronounce the act inoperative and *void.*[7]

In many respects, the *Bliss* opinion and its resounding endorsement of an unfettered individual right to arms is a judicial outlier. Future courts often took a more moderate stance on the legislature's authority to regulate arms; and even Kentucky repudiated *Bliss's* stance in 1850 with a new constitution that specifically permitted the legislature to prohibit the carrying of concealed weapons. Nevertheless, *Bliss* suggests how early courts implicitly viewed the Second Amendment and state analogues—as an *individual* protection and guarantee—just a few decades after ratification of the federal Bill of Rights.

Aymette v. State of Tennessee (1840): Challenging a Concealed-Carry Violation

Like *Bliss*, the *Aymette* case revolved around the constitutionality of a statute that prohibited the carrying of a concealed weapon. In this instance, the statute barred "any person from wearing any bowie knife, or Arkansas toothpick, or other knife or weapon in form, shape or size resembling a bowie knife or Arkansas tooth pick under his clothes or concealed about his person."[8] But unlike *Bliss*, the Tennessee Supreme Court concluded that the legislature *had* the power to enact such a prohibition, despite the state's bill of rights and its guarantee of a citizen's right to keep and bear arms.

Indicted for wearing a Bowie knife concealed under his clothes in violation of the statute, William Aymette in circuit court had pled not guilty. But during the trial, the state established that Aymette had argued with an individual named Hamilton, and later went in search of him, "swearing he would have his life's blood."[9] The state also established that Aymette, in his search for Hamilton, occasionally took out and brandished a Bowie knife which he had concealed under his vest. The jury found him guilty. Sentenced to three months' imprisonment and fined two hundred dollars, Aymette appealed to the Tennessee Supreme Court, arguing that the statute under which he was convicted was unconstitutional.

Justice Nathan T. Green (who later held a full professorship in Cumberland University's Department of Law) authored the Supreme Court opinion. Green began by acknowledging that the first article of the Tennessee state constitution declared "that the free white men of this State, have a right to keep and bear arms for their common defense." Aymette's argument, he then noted, is that this article

> gives to every man the right to arm himself in any manner he may choose, however unusual or dangerous the weapon he may employ; and thus armed, to appear

> wherever he may think proper, without molestation or hindrance, and that any law regulating his social conduct, by restraining the use of any weapon or regulating the manner in which it shall be carried, is beyond legislative competency to enact, and is void.[10]

In assessing Aymette's argument, Justice Green observed that while both the Second Amendment of the federal constitution and the first article of the state constitution have roots in early English acts and declarations, the right protected by the American declarations is much broader than its English precedents: with Americans,

> every free white man is of suitable condition; and, therefore every free white man may *keep and bear arms.* But to keep and bear arms for what? ... It is declared that they may keep and *bear* arms for their *common defense.* ... The object then, for which the right of keeping and bearing arms is secured, is the defence of the *public.* The free white men may keep arms to protect the public liberty, to keep in awe those who are in power, and to maintain the supremacy of the laws and the constitution.[11]

Green continued,

> The words "bear arms" too have reference to their military use, and were not employed to mean wearing them about the person as part of the dress. As the object for which the right to keep and bear arms is secured, is of general and public nature, ... for [people's] common defence, so the arms ... are such as usually employed in civilized warfare .... If the citizens have these arms ... they are prepared ... to repel any encroachment upon their rights by those in authority. They need not ... the use of those weapons which are usually employed in private broils, and which are efficient only in the hands of the robber and the assassin. These weapons would be useless in war. They could not be employed advantageously in the common defence of the citizens. The right to keep and bear them, is not, therefore, secured by the constitution.[12]

A bit later in the opinion, Green observed,

> The legislature, therefore, have a right to prohibit the wearing, or keeping weapons dangerous to the peace and safety of the citizens, and which are *not* usual in civilized warfare, or would not contribute to the common defence. ... And although this right [to keep and bear arms for the common defence] must be inviolably preserved, yet, it does not follow that the legislature is prohibited altogether from passing laws regulating the manner in which these arms may be deployed. ... [While] it is somewhat difficult to draw the precise line where legislation must cease ... it is *not* difficult to state a case where the right of the legislature would exist. The citizens have the unqualified right to *keep* the weapon, it being of the character before described .... But the right to *bear arms* is not of

> that unqualified character. The citizens may bear them for the *common defence*; but it does not follow, that they may be borne by an individual, merely to terrify the people, or for purposes of private assassination. ... the legislature may prohibit such manner of wearing as would never be resorted to by persons engaged in the common defence.[13]

Justice Green then acknowledged that Kentucky's Court of Appeals in a similar case—the *Bliss* case—concluded that such prohibitions were unconstitutional. Green noted that the *Bliss* opinion saw no difference between a law banning the wearing of concealed weapons, and one prohibiting the wearing of them openly. On this point he disagreed. He argued, "if [citizens] were not allowed to bear arms openly, they could not bear them in defense of the state at all. To bear arms in defense of the State [means they] must necessarily be borne openly; so that a prohibition to bear them openly, would be a denial of the right altogether."[14]

Justice Green also rejected dicta in an earlier 1833 Tennessee Supreme Court opinion, *Simpson v. The State of Tennessee*. This case centered on William Simpson, indicted for "being arrayed in a warlike manner [on] a public street ... to the great terror and disturbance"[15] of the community. In determining whether Simpson's action actually constituted an indictable offense, the judge—Justice Whyte—cited the same Second Amendment analogue considered in *Aymette*. However, Whyte interpreted the clause more in line with *Bliss*, "By this clause ... an express power is given to all the free citizens of the State to keep and bear arms for their defence, without any qualification whatever as to their kind or nature."[16]

Despite having concurred on this opinion (and even quoting it in *Aymette*), Green nevertheless dismissed Whyte's interpretation as "only an incidental remark of the judge ... and, therefore is entitled to no weight."[17] Thus, while professing great respect for the Kentucky court, he nonetheless rejected the *Bliss* decision (i.e., "we cannot concur in their reasoning"[18]) and affirmed Aymette's conviction.

Aside from its jarring historical reminder that constitutional protections often applied only to free white citizens in pre-Civil War decades, the *Aymette* opinion is notable from a number of judicial perspectives. First, while not endorsing a completely unfettered right to keep and bear arms, the opinion recognized an individual citizen's unqualified right to *keep* arms of a military character, and a more limited right to *bear* such arms openly. Further, the opinion also identified (perhaps with only arguable success) the type of arms a legislature might constitutionally restrict: arms not usual in civilized warfare; arms that would not contribute to the common defense; and arms dangerous to citizens' peace and safety. Finally, the opinion foreshadowed (with its emphasis on common defense and military-type arms) the reasoning other jurists would use in the next century in interpreting the Second Amendment as a collective right.

State of Alabama v. Reid (1840): Challenging a Concealed-Carry Statute

In the same year that Justice Green decided the fate of William Aymette in Tennessee, Chief Justice Henry Collier of the Alabama Supreme Court wrestled with a similar concealed-carry issue. Alabama's legislature had recently enacted a statute meant "to suppress the evil practice of carrying weapons secretly" and this statute prohibited the concealed carry of "any species of firearms, or any Bowie knife, Arkansas tooth pick, or any other knife of like kind, dirk, or any other deadly weapon."[19] The defendant—Reid, a sheriff no less—was indicted and convicted under this statute. Reid challenged his conviction, arguing that the statute violated a provision of the Alabama state constitution, which held that "every citizen has a right to bear arms, in defence of himself and the State."[20]

After a brief background review of English laws thought to have influenced the American Bill of Rights, Chief Justice Collier observed,

> Does the act, "To suppress the evil practice of carrying weapons secretly" trench upon the constitutional rights of the citizen? We think not. The constitution in declaring that "Every citizen has the right to bear arms in defence of himself and the State" has neither expressly or by implication, denied to the Legislature, the right to enact laws in regard to the manner in which arms shall be borne. The right guaranteed to the citizen, is not to bear arms upon all occasions and in all places, but merely "in defence of himself and the State." The terms in which this provision is phrased seems to us, necessarily to leave with the Legislature the authority to adopt such regulations of police, as may be dictated by the safety of the people and the advancement of public morals.[21]

Collier qualified this position by noting that the authority of the legislature was not unlimited. He noted:

> A statute which, under the pretense of regulating, amounts to a destruction of the right, or which requires arms to be borne as to render them wholly useless for the purpose of defence, would be clearly unconstitutional. But a law which is intended merely to promote personal security, and to put down lawless aggression and violence, and to that end inhibits the wearing of certain weapons … does not come into collision with the constitution.[22]

As Justice Green did in *Aymette*, Chief Justice Collier then discussed and quoted extensively from Kentucky's *Bliss* opinion, acknowledging that *Bliss* contradicted his position. Addressing the question raised in *Bliss* concerning the possibility of one legislature prohibiting concealed carry, and a subsequent legislature barring open carry—which of the enactments would be unconstitutional, if both are not?—Collier observed, "Under the provisions of our constitution, we incline to the opinion that the Legislature cannot inhibit the citizen from bearing arms openly, because it authorizes him to bear them for purposes of defending himself and the State, and it is only when carried openly that they can be efficiently used for defence."[23]

Collier also noted that *Bliss* was a split decision, with one of the three justices dissenting, and that in Indiana—a state having a Second Amendment analogue in its constitution similar to Alabama's analogue—the state supreme court upheld a concealed-carry prohibition almost identical to the Alabama prohibition. Given these conflicting judicial opinions, Collier argued that "it is our duty to maintain [the statute's] validity. It has received the assent of the two houses of the General Assembly and the Governor, under a solemn pledge to support the constitution; and their opinion is at least, prima facie evidence, that they have not overstepped the limits of legislative competency."[24]

As for Reid, the court held, "There was no evidence adduced, tending to show that the defendant could not have defended himself as successfully, by carrying the pistol openly as by secreting it about his person. … If the emergency is pressing, there can be no necessity for concealing the weapon, and if the threatened violence will allow it, the individual may be arrested and constrained to find sureties to keep the peace, or committed to jail."[25] The circuit court's judgment was therefore affirmed.

Reid and *Aymette* share some important similarities. For instance, unlike *Bliss*, both agree that regulation is not the equivalent of prohibition; and both argue that the legislature has the authority to enact statutes that insure the safety and peace of the community. But key differences—significant from a Second Amendment perspective—also characterize the two opinions. While both decisions affirm that the states' Second Amendment analogues do not block their legislatures from barring hidden and unusual weapons, the justifications for upholding the constitutionality of such prohibitions differ.

Where *Aymette* argues that Bowie knives, easily concealed weapons (presumably including small firearms), and other items not used in "civilized warfare" are not military equipment, and cannot contribute to the common defense, *Reid* heavily emphasizes the police power of the state to insure public safety and morals, and stresses the deference owed to the legislature and the governor in determining constitutionally acceptable regulation. Further, where *Aymette* only implicitly upholds the constitutionality of open carry for individual self-protection, *Reid* explicitly endorses this right, noting that the defendant could have just as easily defended himself with openly carrying a pistol as with carrying it hidden.

State of Arkansas v. Buzzard (1842): Challenging a Concealed-Carry Statute

The statute challenged in *State v. Buzzard* declared that "every person who shall wear any pistol, dirk, butcher or large knife, or a sword in a cane, concealed as a weapon, unless upon a journey, shall be adjudged guilty of a misdemeanor."[26] Originally charged with violating this prohibition, defendant Buzzard appealed his district court conviction to the circuit court, where Judge Euclid Johnson quashed Buzzard's indictment, ruling that the statute was an unconstitutional breach of the federal constitution's Second Amendment. The state then appealed to the Arkansas Supreme Court, where Chief Justice Daniel Ringo (whom President Zachary Taylor would later appoint to the federal judiciary) determined that Johnson had erred in quashing the indictment, and that the prohibition on concealed carry was indeed constitutional. He reversed Johnson's ruling.[27]

In supporting the court's opinion, Ringo first reviewed the reasons why governments are instituted. He noted that citizens must obviously accept *some* voluntary restrictions on their personal rights, if they are to reap the benefits and security of effective civil governance. In this light, if the right to bear and keep arms were subject to no legal regulation or limitation, their use "would tend to unhinge society and ... would surely defeat every object for which the government was formed."[28] He then argued that, in any case, the objective of the Second Amendment was not

> to protect ... such rights as are merely private and individual [but] to provide an additional security for the public liberty and the free institutions of the State .... And it is equally apparent [that] a well regulated militia [is] the best security a free state could have .... [To] enable the militia to discharge this most important trust, for this purpose only, ... the right to keep and bear arms was retained.[29]

In a concurring opinion, Ringo's colleague on the court, Justice Dickinson, observed that "when arms are not kept or used for the defense of the State or Federal Government, the manner of carrying them and mode of using them are subject to the control and authority of the State Legislature."[30]

Thus was born the novel militia-based interpretation of the Second Amendment. The Ringo Court clearly linked the Second Amendment to the country's need for an effective militia, but it was ambiguous regarding the amendment's implications for individuals. Chief Justice Ringo noted that Arkansas's State Constitution gave "every citizen the right to bear arms in defense of himself and the State" but that none of the federal courts had considered the type of right the Second Amendment secures. He further observed that, with state courts in disagreement, "it may therefore be considered as an open question [requiring an adjudication of] the Supreme Court of the United States [before] the extent of the right may be distinctly ascertained and definitively settled."[31] In this regard, Chief Justice Ringo was perhaps especially discerning.

Nunn v. State of Georgia (1846): Challenging a Statute Banning Small Pistols

As with Biss, Aymette, Reid, and Buzzard, Hawkins Nunn also ran afoul of a state's concealed-carry statute. In this instance, Section One of the Georgia regulation stipulated

> that it shall not be lawful for any merchant ... or any other person ... to sell ... or to keep or to have about their persons any of [these] weapons, to wit: Bowie or any other kinds of knives manufactured ... as arms of offence or defence; pistols, dirks, sword-canes, spears, &c., shall also be [unlawful], save such pistols as are known and used as horsemen's pistols.[32]

Nunn was convicted for "having and keeping about his person" a "breast" pistol (i.e., a smaller and more easily concealable pistol than a horseman's saddle pistol); and he appealed his conviction to the state Supreme Court, arguing (among other objections) that the Georgia statute violated the Second Amendment of the federal Constitution and contradicted the state Constitution of Georgia.

Chief Justice Joseph Lumpkin, who later would be instrumental in creating the University of Georgia School of Law, wrote the court's opinion. In some preliminary observations, he argued that a law should never be found unconstitutional in doubtful cases: "The presumption is in favor of every legislative act."[33] But with the statute in question, he noted a number of ambiguities in several of its sections, and concluded, "There is great vagueness in the wording of this statute. … Were we disposed to criticize language, an ample field is here spread out before us."[34]

Because of these ambiguities, Lumpkin then attempted to deduce the Legislature's purpose in enacting the statute based on the act as a whole, but "deviating a little … from the literal meaning of the language, and looking to … the reason and spirit of the act."[35] He concluded that the statute's essential purpose was to prohibit concealed weapons kept secretly about the person. Lumpkin noted that Nunn was indicted and convicted of "having and keeping about his person … a pistol, the same not being … a horseman's pistol"[36] but that it was not alleged that Nunn had carried his pistol *secretly*. Lumpkin then asked rhetorically, "Is it competent for the Legislature to deny one of its citizens this privilege? *We think not.*"[37] More explicitly, Lumpkin asserted,

> so far as the act of 1837 seeks to suppress the practice of carrying certain weapons *secretly*, that it is valid, inasmuch as it does not deprive the citizen of his *natural* right of self-defence, or his constitutional right to keep and bear arms. But … as it contains a provision against bearing arms *openly*, it is in conflict with the Constitution and *void*.[38]

In supporting his argument, Chief Justice Lumpkin reviewed opinions from several other state courts, citing and discussing both *Bliss* and *Reid* in some depth. He repeated their conclusions that a legislature may constitutionally regulate the *manner* in which arms may be borne, and their arguments that a statute that functions to destroy the right is clearly not permitted. He acknowledged that these prior adjudications all involved clauses in state constitutions, but asserted that the federal Constitution also implicitly buttressed his opinion:

> The Constitution of the United States, in declaring that the right of the people to keep and bear arms, should not be infringed, only reiterated a truth [already known] …. The language of the *second* amendment is broad enough to embrace both Federal and State governments—nor is there anything in its terms which restrict its meaning …. [D]oes it follow that because the people refused to delegate to the general government the power to take from them the right to keep and bear arms, that they designed to rest it in the State governments?[39]

Lumpkin continued,

> We do not believe that, because the people withheld this arbitrary power of disenfranchisement from Congress, they ever intended to confer it on the local legislatures. … The right of the whole people, old and young, men, women and

> boys, and not militia only, to keep and bear arms of every description and not *such* merely as are used by the militia, shall not be infringed, curtailed or broken in upon, in the smallest degree; … Our opinion is, that any law, State or Federal, is repugnant to the Constitution, and void, which contravenes this right.[40]

Thus, noting that Nunn had been convicted for merely carrying a pistol, without charging that it had been carried in a concealed manner, Chief Justice Lumpkin quashed the proceeding against Nunn and reversed the judgment of the lower court.

From a Second Amendment perspective, the significance of the *Nunn* opinion is twofold. First, the decision is a formidable illustration of the amendment unabashedly interpreted as guarding a personal, individual right to arms. It is the first case where a court directly relied on the Second Amendment in overturning a gun control law,[41] and it is an opinion that later receives significant attention in the landmark *Heller* decision of 2008.

But, additionally, the *Nunn* opinion also grappled with an issue that judges and justices adjudicating new gun cases increasingly had to analyze: Was the Second Amendment even relevant to state-enacted gun statutes, or was it simply a potential limitation on federally-enacted gun regulations? Chief Justice Lumpkin, for example, noted: "I am aware that it has been decided, that [the Second Amendment], like other amendments adopted at the same time, is a restriction upon the government of the United States, and does not extend to the individual States."[42] Nonetheless, invoking the opinion of a New York Chief Justice—asserting that the federal Bill of Rights extended to *all* judicial tribunals and was equally applicable to the states—Chief Justice Lumpkin chose to extend the federal amendment to invalidate the state statute. As the next section demonstrates, not all courts followed his lead.

1871–6: A Federal Limitation Only

Before examining the gun cases, a look at the non-gun case that prompted Lumpkin's remark above is in order. The notion that the federal Bill of Rights may not extend to the states arose in a US Supreme Court case in 1833. The case—*Barron v. Mayor & City Council of Baltimore*—involved John Barron, owner of a wharf in the port of Baltimore. Barron had sued the city, alleging that deposits of earth and sand from the city's road construction had made the water around his wharf much shallower, and this had significantly reduced the value of his wharf. The trial court initially awarded him damages, but the state appellate court overturned the award.

Appealed to the United States Supreme Court on the basis of the Fifth Amendment—that no private property shall be taken for public use without just compensation—Chief Justice John Marshall authored the opinion. Marshall argued:

> The Constitution was ordained and established by the people of the United States for themselves, for their own government, and not for the government of the individual States. Each State established a constitution for itself, and in that constitution provided such limitations and restrictions on the powers of its

> particular government as its judgment dictated. ... [T]he fifth amendment must be understood as restraining the powers of the General Government, not as applicable to the States.[43]

Later in the opinion, he argued more broadly, "These amendments [i.e., the Bill of Rights] demanded security against the apprehended encroachment of the General Government—not against those of the local governments. ... These amendments contain no expression indicating an intention to apply them to the State governments. This court cannot so apply them."[44] Thus, indicating that the court had no jurisdiction in the matter, Marshall dismissed Barron's appeal; the four cases in this section reflect the impact of the *Barron* opinion on Second Amendment challenges to gun regulation.

As with the earlier opinions, the cases here examine the kinds of firearms that the Second Amendment protects and the permissible limitations on the manner of carrying such weapons. Again, the reasoning justifying the constitutionality of the statutory prohibitions is instructive. With the federal amendment no longer a primary consideration in determining the scope of gun rights, courts relied on their state's Second Amendment analogues in gauging the limits of an individual right to arms.

In *Andrews*, the Tennessee court continued to link the right to arms to insure individual readiness in time of war. Thus, the arms protected were the ordinary arms of a trained soldier. In *English*, the Texas court echoed this position, noting that both the federal and state constitutions guaranteed individuals the right to keep and bear only those arms used for warfare, not those typically employed in personal quarrels. Similarly, in *Fife*, the Arkansas court also argued that the state constitution protected only firearms effective for warfare.

In *Cruikshank*, the US Supreme Court side-stepped the issue of permissible gun restrictions, noting only that citizens had to look to their states for protection of individual rights. The four cases illustrate the convergence of various courts on the boundaries of the Second Amendment as a personal, individual right and on the judicial implications of dual state and national citizenship.

Andrews v. State of Tennessee (1871): Challenging a Concealed-Carry Statute

Considered by some commentators to be the most important case concerning the right to bear arms in Tennessee,[45] the *Andrews* case centered on the constitutionality of an 1870 statute enacted by the Tennessee legislature "to preserve the peace and prevent homicide."[46] The statute made it unlawful

> for any person to publicly or privately carry a dirk, sword-cane, Spanish stiletto, belt or pocket pistol. Any person guilty of a violation ... shall pay a fine ... and be imprisoned at the discretion of the court ... and shall give bond in sum not exceeding a thousand dollars to keep the peace for the next six months after conviction.[47]

Tried for violating this statute, defendant Andrews (in a demurrer) initially entered a plea of self-defense, arguing that he carried a pistol because a group of neighborhood men were seeking his life. The court denied the demurrer, and Andrews was found guilty. He then appealed his conviction to the state Supreme Court, arguing that the statute violated the Second Amendment of the federal Constitution and the Permissive Clause of the Tennessee State Constitution. Justice Thomas Freeman authored the court's opinion. Elected to the state Supreme Court in 1870, Freeman was a former colonel in the Confederate Army who would later serve as the first dean of the University of Tennessee's Law Department.

Justice Freeman first addressed Andrews's Second Amendment argument. Noting the Attorney General's assertion that the Second Amendment had no application to the States and only limited the power of the federal government, Freeman—citing Chief Justice Marshall's *Barron* opinion in some detail—concurred with the Attorney General. Freeman observed, "The State Legislature is not, then, limited in its powers on this subject by this article of the Constitution of the United States; it is a limitation, whatever be its construction and meaning, upon the powers of the other [i.e., federal] government, ordained and established by the people of the States themselves."[48]

Freeman then turned to the state constitution "to see what restrictions or limitations the sovereign people of Tennessee have chosen to place upon themselves, in reference to this subject, for the general good."[49] He noted that the relevant section of the state constitution specified, "That the *citizens* of this State have a *right* to *keep* and bear arms for their common defense. But the Legislature shall have the power by law to regulate the wearing of arms to *prevent* crime."[50] He argued that the purpose of this clause—similar to the purpose of federal Second Amendment—was to guarantee "the efficiency of the people as soldiers, when called into actual service for the security of the State … and in order to do this, they were allowed to *keep* arms. [Keeping arms] involves the right to purchase and use them in such a way as is usual, or to keep them for the ordinary purposes to which they are adapted; … with a view that the citizens … shall become familiar with their use in times of peace, that they may the more efficiently use them in times of war."[51]

Justice Freeman continued,

> The right to keep arms for this purpose involves the right to practice their use …. [This] right and use are guaranteed to the citizen, to be exercised and enjoyed in times of peace, in subordination to the general ends of civil society; but, as a right, to be maintained in all its fullness. The right [also] involves the right to purchase them [and] to purchase … ammunition suitable to such arms …. But farther than this … the right to keep arms, involves … the right to use such arms for all the ordinary purposes, and in all the ordinary modes usual in the country … limited by the duties of a good citizen in times of peace; that … he shall not use them for violation of the rights of others.[52]

Freeman additionally noted that "a man would have the right to carry [arms] to and from his home, and no one could claim that the Legislature had the right to punish him for it, without violating this clause of the Constitution."[53]

Freeman also specifically addressed the type of arms that the constitution protected:

> Arms in the use of which a soldier should be trained … the rifle of all descriptions, the shot gun, the musket, and the repeater, are such arms; … under the Constitution the right to keep such arms, can not be *infringed* or *forbidden* by the legislature [but] their *use* [can] be subordinated to such regulations and limitations as are or may be authorized by law.[54]

Citing the Tennessee Supreme Court's *Aymette* opinion of thirty years earlier, Freeman noted that the Convention of 1870 had since amended the state constitution, giving the Tennessee legislature explicit authority to regulate the wearing of arms. However, he asserted that the relevant addition—"But the Legislature shall have the power, by law, to regulate the wearing of arms, with a view to prevent crime"—was not absolute (as the state's Attorney General had argued). He observed: "The power to regulate does not fairly mean the power to prohibit … [it means] some check upon … the manner … or time, or circumstances under which [citizens may wear arms] guided by … some well defined relation to the *prevention* of crime."[55] He then turned to the facts of Andrews's case.

In examining the self-defense claim, Justice Freeman first observed that the evidence showed that Andrews

> had been in the habit of carrying a pistol since the war. In such a case, he could not claim that he was really in peril of life or limb, or great bodily harm, so imminent as to present any element of self-defense in justification of his carrying his pistol. The law of the land gave him ample protection, if he had chosen to seek its aid.[56]

Nonetheless, regarding Andrews's constitutional argument, Freeman found grounds for reversal of the circuit court. While acknowledging the constitutionality of the statue's prohibition against the carrying of dirks and other unusual or non-militia-type weapons, Justice Freeman asserted,

> As to the pistol designated as a revolver … we also know that the pistol known as the repeater is a soldier's weapon …. If such is the character of the weapon here designated, then the prohibition of the statute is too broad … in effect [it] is an absolute prohibition against keeping such a weapon, and not a regulation of the use of it.[57]

Because Andrews's indictment only indicated that he carried a pistol—without specifying whether belt, or pocket pistol, or revolver—the charge was too indefinite to sustain and the case was remanded back to the circuit court.

The *Andrews*' opinion is notable not only for its arguments upholding an individual right to arms, but also for its detailed consideration of the permissible boundaries that the legislature might impose on this right—for example, "the manner, time, and circumstances" that may require limitations in order to prevent crime and insure public safety. Of course, because the *Barron* ruling held that the federal Bill of Rights did not apply to the states, Freeman necessarily based his opinion on Tennessee's state constitution and not the Second Amendment. Nevertheless, Justice Freeman explicitly noted that the same principles shaped both documents (i.e., "the same rights, and for similar reasons, were being provided for and being protected in both the Federal and State constitutions; in the one ... against infringement by the Federal Legislature, and in the other by the Legislature of the State"[58]), indicating that he saw his arguments and conclusions applying to both.

English v. State of Texas (1872): Challenging a Wearing / Carrying Statute

In April of 1871, the Texas legislature enacted a statute similar to the Tennessee statute. It also prohibited the carrying of pistols, dirks, and other deadly weapons; and William English, intoxicated at the time, had been charged with violating this prohibition by wearing a pistol in town. In his defense, English had shown in district court that the pistol was unloaded and in need of repair, and that he had been carrying the pistol to get it fixed—all to no avail. Having been found guilty, English appealed his conviction to the Texas Supreme Court. Like Andrews in Tennessee, he argued that the statute under which he was charged violated both the Second Amendment of the federal government and, in his case, the first article of the Texas state constitution. Justice Moses Walker, a former Union military officer recently appointed to the court, authored the court's opinion.

After quoting the Second Amendment's prohibition against infringing on the right to keep and bear arms, Justice Walker posed a question: "Arms of what kind? Certainly such as are useful and proper to an armed militia. The deadly weapons spoken of in the statute are pistols, dirks, daggers, slungshots, sword canes, spears, brass knuckles, and bowie knives. Can it be understood these were contemplated by the framers of our Bill of Rights?"[59]

In answering this question, Walker turned to the legal treatises of Joel Bishop—a highly respected lawyer and scholar of that age. Walker observed that while Bishop thought the Second Amendment applied to States—"this [particular amendment] seems to be of a nature to bind both the State and national legislatures, and doubtless it does"—he also thought that its "provision protects only the right to 'keep' such arms as are used for purposes of war, in distinction from those which are employed in quarrels and broils, and fights between maddened individuals .... In like manner the right to 'bear' arms merely refers to the military way of using them, not to their use in bravado and affray."[60]

Still quoting Bishop, Justice Walker observed, "the Georgia tribunal seems to have held that a statute prohibiting the open wearing of arms ... violates this provision of the Constitution, though a statute against the wearing of the arms concealed does not. And, in accordance with ... this Georgia doctrine, the Louisiana court has laid it down that the statute against carrying concealed does not infringe the [Second Amendment]"[61] Having noted Bishop's legal analysis, Judge Walker then returned to the Texas statute,

> To refer the deadly devices and instruments called in the statute 'deadly weapons,' to the proper or necessary arms of a "well regulated militia," is simply ridiculous. ... The "arms" of the infantry soldier are the musket and the bayonet; of cavalry and dragoons, the saber, holster pistols, and carbine; of the artillery, the field piece, siege gun, and mortar, with side arms.[62]

Thus, in assessing English's Second Amendment argument, Walker concluded,

> The act referred to makes all necessary exceptions, and points out the place, the time, and the manner in which certain deadly weapons may be carried as means of self-defense, and these exceptional cases ... fully cover all the wants of society. There is no abridgement of the personal rights, such as may be regarded as inherent and inalienable to man, nor do we think his political rights are in the least infringed by any part of this law.[63]

Justice Walker then addressed English's appeal to the Texas state constitution. Walker noted that the applicable provision of the constitution proclaims, "Every person shall have the right to keep and bear arms in the lawful defense of himself or the State, under such regulations as the Legislature may prescribe."[64] Pointing to the latter part of the article, Walker observed that the state constitution clearly "confers upon the legislature the power to regulate the privilege. The legislature may regulate it without taking it away;—this has been done in the act under consideration."[65] Judge Walker then upheld the decision of the district court.

Two aspects of the *English* opinion perhaps deserve attention. As with past cases, the opinion affirms that the Second Amendment, as an individual right, still permits reasonable prohibitions on that right. However, the judicial argument allowing such prohibitions is notable. While acknowledging the need to safeguard public safety and security, Walker especially stressed the amendment's connections to warfare and militia-type weapons. Thus, the opinion shares some limited similarities with the analyses of those judges endorsing a collective right interpretation of the amendment.

The other aspect warranting attention is the opinion's treatment of the amendment as an incorporated right. Following in the footsteps of Georgia's Chief Justice Lumpkin, Justice Walker (relying on Joel Bishop's legal treatise) apparently accepted that the Second Amendment applied to the states as well as the federal government. It is unclear whether he was simply unaware of the *Barron* opinion—it is not mentioned or cited in *English*—or whether, like Lumpkin, he just chose to dismiss it. But as the *Andrews* case above suggests, Walker's implication that the Second Amendment applied to the states was premature by 138 years.

United States v. Cruikshank (1875): Challenging a Violation of the 1870 Federal Enforcement Act

Argued before the US Supreme Court after Louisiana's circuit court produced a divided opinion, the controversial *Cruikshank* case involved a conspiracy indictment against Cruikshank and a number of other defendants. All were apparently involved in Louisiana's disputed 1872 gubernatorial election and the ensuing massacre of Black freedmen and militia men in Colfax, Louisiana. The conspiracy indictment revolved around Section 6 of the federal Enforcement Act of 1870. Section 6 made it a felony for two or more individuals

> to band or conspire together, or go in disguise upon the public highway, or upon the premises of another with intent to violate any provision of this act, or to injure, oppress, threaten, or intimidate any citizen, with intent to prevent or hinder his free exercise and enjoyment of any right or privilege granted or secured to him by the Constitution or the laws of the United States.[66]

The indictment consisted of two sets of eight counts, with the second eight counts simply replacing the phrase "band together" with the phrase "combine, conspire, and confederate together."[67] The counts themselves included to band together/conspire together

> to hinder and prevent [two citizens of African descent] of their lawful right and privilege to peaceably assemble; … [to] hinder and prevent [their] exercise … of the "right to bear and keep arms for a lawful purpose" … [with] intent to deprive the same persons "of their respective lives and liberty of person, without due process of law" … [with] intent to hinder and prevent [their] right and privilege to vote at any election.

and so forth.[68] Chief Justice Morrison Waite, a prominent Ohio lawyer nominated to the court by President Ulysses S. Grant in 1874, authored the court's opinion.

Chief Justice Waite first noted:

> The general charge in the first eight counts is that of "banding," and in the second eight that of "conspiring" together to injure, oppress, threaten, and intimidate Levi Nelson and Alexander Tillman, citizens of the United States, of African descent and persons of color, with the intent thereby to hinder and prevent them in their free exercise and enjoyment of rights and privileges "granted and secured" to them "in common with all other good citizens of the United States by the Constitution and laws of the United States."[69]

Waite continued,

> The offenses provided for by the statute … do not consist in the mere "banding" or "conspiring" … but in their banding or conspiring with the intent … specified. To bring this case … it must appear that the right … which the conspirators intended to hinder or prevent, was one granted or secured by the Constitution or laws of the United States. If it does not so appear, the criminal matter charged has not been made indictable by any act of Congress.[70]

He then observed that the federal government is distinct from state governments, and while each "may … and should, exercise all the power it has for the protection of the rights of its citizens … protection is limited always by the power it possesses for that purpose. … [The federal government] can neither grant nor secure to its citizens any right or privilege not expressly or by implication placed under its jurisdiction."[71]

Having thus set the stage, Chief Justice Waite turned to a consideration of the specific counts of the indictment. He noted that

> the right of the people peaceably to assemble for lawful purposes existed long before the adoption of the Constitution of the United States … with the obligation on the part of the States to afford its protection. As no direct power over it was granted to Congress, it remains … subject to State jurisdiction. … The right was not created by the amendment; neither was its continuance guaranteed, except as against congressional interference. For their protection in its enjoyment … the people must look to the States. The power for that purpose was originally placed there, and has never been surrendered to the United States.[72]

Citing *Barron* and other case precedents, he further observed that all the early amendments were "not intended to limit the powers of the State governments in respect to their own citizens, but to operate upon the National Government alone."[73] Regarding the indictment's second count—interference with Second Amendment rights—Waite argued,

> This is not a right granted by the Constitution. Neither is it in any manner dependent upon that instrument for its existence. The second amendment declares that it shall not be infringed, but this … means no more than it shall not be infringed by Congress. This is one of the amendments that has no other effect than to restrict the powers of the national government, leaving the people to look for their protection against any violation … to merely municipal legislation, or … internal police.[74]

In a similar manner, the court found fatal defects in the indictment's other counts. Waite further noted, "We may suspect that race was the cause of the hostility, but it is not so averred. This is material to a description of the offense, and cannot be supplied by implication. Everything essential must be charged positively, and not inferentially. The defect here is not in form but in substance."[75] Thus, finding all the counts of the indictment for one reason or another "so defective that no judgment of conviction should be pronounced upon them,"[76] the court dismissed all charges against the defendants.

The broad historical significance of the *Cruikshank* opinion is the obvious block it placed on the federal government's Fourteenth Amendment efforts to insure the civil rights of recently freed Black citizens. But more narrowly, from a Second Amendment perspective, its significance is the Supreme Court's stand on the amendment. While implicitly recognizing an individual's right to keep and bear arms, the court stressed that this right predated the Constitution, and the amendment protected infringements only from the federal government. For infringements perpetrated by fellow citizens—or even state governments—individuals must seek protection in state legislatures and state constitutions. As noted earlier, some courts would use comparable reasoning to dismiss Second Amendment challenges well into the twenty-first century.

Fife v. State of Arkansas (1876): Challenging a Wearing/Carrying Statute

Not long after *Cruikshank*, the Supreme Court of Arkansas addressed a much less complicated and controversial case. By 1876, Arkansas had a revised statute regulating the wearing or carrying of arms: "That any person who shall wear or carry any pistol of any kind whatever, or any dirk, butcher or Bowie knife ... as a weapon, shall be adjudged guilty of a misdemeanor, etc., etc. *Provided*, that nothing herein contained shall be so construed as to prohibit any person wearing or carrying any weapon aforesaid on his own premises."[77] Alfred Fife had been charged with carrying a pistol as a weapon, violating the statute. Convicted in district court, Fife appealed his case to the circuit court, where he was found guilty again. Finally, he appealed to the Supreme Court of Arkansas, arguing that his conviction violated his Second Amendment rights under both the United States Constitution and Arkansas' state constitution. Chief Justice Elbert English—serving on the court from 1854 to 1864; and then serving again from 1874 to 1884—authored the court's opinion.

In reviewing eye-witness testimony, Chief Justice English determined, "It is probable, from all the evidence, that the plaintiff was carrying a pocket revolver."[78] Turning to Fife's Second Amendment argument, English first quoted Judge Story's comment on the amendment: "The right of the citizens to keep and bear arms has justly been considered as the palladium of the liberties of a republic."[79] But he then noted that the "arms which [the amendment] guarantees ... are such as are needful to, and ordinarily used by a well regulated militia."[80] Further, citing *Barron*, *Andrews*, and others, English concluded that "this [amendment] ... is a restraint upon federal, and not upon State legislation."[81]

Regarding the guarantee in Arkansas' state constitution—"The citizens of this State shall have the right to keep and bear arms for their common defense"—Chief Justice English pointed out that in the earlier *Buzzard* case, the Arkansas Supreme Court concluded that "the act prohibiting the wearing of concealed weapons was in conflict with neither [the Constitution of the United States nor the Bill of Rights of Arkansas' 1836 Constitution]."[82] Additionally, English drew support from the Tennessee judiciary, citing both *Aymette* and *Andrews*. From *Aymette*, English quoted, "The Legislature, therefore, have the right to prohibit the wearing or keeping weapons dangerous to the peace and safety of the citizens, and which are not usual in civilized warfare, and would not contribute to the common defense."[83]

He also quoted from Judge Freeman's *Andrews* opinion,

> Not everything that may be useful for offense or defense ... may properly be included or understood under the title of arms ... the rifle ... the shotgun, the

> musket and the repeater, are such arms [that] under the Constitution, the right to keep such arms cannot be infringed or forbidden .... Their use, however, [can] be subordinated to such regulations and limitations as are ... authorized by the law of the land."[84]

English then provided a definition of "pistol." He observed that

> Pistol is derived from *Pistola*, a town in Italy, where pistols were first made. A pistol is a small fire-arm, or the smallest firearm used, intended to be fired from one hand .... In the act, the pistol is associated, in the prohibited list of weapons, with the dirk, butcher, or Bowie knife .... From the company in which the pistol is placed ... it is manifest that the pistol intended to be proscribed is such as is usually carried in the pocket, or of a size to be concealed about the person, and used in private quarrels and brawls, and not such as is in ordinary use, and effective as a weapon of war, and useful and necessary for the "common defense."[85]

In affirming Fife's conviction, the court concluded, "The indications in the evidence are, that the plaintiff ... was carrying a pistol ... intended to be prohibited by the Legislature, and which we think may be prohibited, in the police power of the State without any infringement of the constitutional right of the citizens of the State to keep and bear arms for their common defense."[86]

As with other cases in this section, the *Fife* opinion reiterated an individual right to keep and bear arms, but only particular types of arms—those in ordinary use and effective in times of war. Firearms and other weapons more commonly used in private conflicts were not protected by the Second Amendment—even ignoring for the moment the amendment's apparent inapplicability to the States—and were within the police power of the state to prohibit or regulate.

Indeed, Chief Justice English reinforced this significant division between pocket pistols and war arms two years later, in *Wilson v. State of Arkansas.* In this case, English quashed the conviction of Chancy Wilson who, like Fife, had been convicted of carrying a pistol as a weapon. But unlike Fife, the firearm he was carrying was a large, army-size .44-caliber revolver with an eight-inch barrel. Noting that the gun was a weapon commonly used in warfare, English asserted, "to prohibit the citizen from wearing or carrying a war arm ... is an unwarranted restriction upon his constitutional right to keep and bear arms."[87]

1881–94: Federal Limitations and Carry Prohibitions Continued

The four cases here concern state and federal appeals covering a range of statutory offenses. Two of the cases—*Wilforth* and *Shelby*—are Missouri Supreme Court opinions that examined the constitutionality of specific carry bans, one involving carrying a firearm in a church, and the other while intoxicated. While both cases affirmed the constitutionality of the statutes in question, their justifications differed. In *Wilforth*, the court observed that the majority of past judicial opinions upheld reasonable gun restrictions and concluded that the Second Amendment also allowed Missouri's similar statute. In *Shelby*, the court dismissed the federal amendment as inapplicable to state authority, and noted that the state's Second Amendment equivalent specifically permitted gun regulation.

The other two cases—*Presser* and *Miller*—are US Supreme Court opinions. *Presser* involved the constitutionality of a state prohibition against private militias parading with arms. The court rejected Presser's Second Amendment challenge, asserting that banning the drilling or parading with arms was not an infringement on the right to keep and bear arms; and that, in any case, the Second Amendment limited only the federal government. *Miller* involved a Second Amendment objection to a murder conviction, and it too was turned away, with the court reiterating that the amendment restricted only the national government.

Despite upholding the questioned gun statutes, an implicit acceptance of a general individual right to keep and bear arms appears to run through all four cases. Additionally, the cases clearly illustrate *Barron's* negative impact on Second Amendment arguments contesting state-level gun prohibitions.

State of Missouri v. Wilforth (1881): Challenging a Statute Banning Firearms in Churches

In an attempt to control the practice of carrying concealed weapons, an 1875 Missouri statute made it a misdemeanor "to go into any church or place where people have assembled for religious worship, having upon or about his person any kind of firearm, bowie knife, dirk, dagger, slung-shot or other deadly weapon."[88] Apparently unaware of this prohibition, defendant Wilforth entered a church house hosting a school exhibition, with a firearm. Indicted, convicted, and fined ten dollars in the circuit court, he appealed to Missouri's Supreme Court. He argued that the circuit court erred by rejecting evidence, by refusing jury instructions he requested, and by refusing to dismiss the conviction based on an unconstitutional statute. Judge Elijah Norton, a major figure who helped craft Missouri's 1875 Constitution, authored the court's opinion.

Judge Norton noted that during the circuit court trial, Wilforth (as a witness in his own defense) "was asked to state whether at the time he entered the house where a school exhibition was in progress, he knew it was contrary to law to carry arms, and whether he believed he had the right to carry arms." Acknowledging that the lower court rejected this evidence, Norton observed, "This evidence was properly refused. *Ignorantia legis excusat neminem*."[89] [Ignorance of the law excuses no one for its violation.] He further noted that Wilforth wanted the court to instruct the jury that "if they believed defendant carried the pistol for the purpose of trade, or … having reasonable cause to believe that he would be in danger of bodily harm … they would acquit."[90] Noting that the lower court rejected this request, Norton concluded, "These instructions were properly refused for the reason (if for no other) that there was not a scintilla of evidence upon which to base them."[91]

Turning to the constitutional question, Judge Norton continued,

> It is also insisted that the statute … is in conflict with the 2nd [Amendment] …. In Kentucky it has been held that any statute which denies to the citizens the right to carry arms, whether openly or concealed, is an infringement of the right guaranteed by the constitution. *Bliss v. Commonwealth, 2 Litt. 90.* The same doctrine prevails in Tennessee. On the other hand, in the states of Georgia, Louisiana, Arkansas, Indiana and Alabama, it has been held that a statute making it a misdemeanor for a person to carry concealed weapons was not obnoxious to said constitutional provision.[92]

Thus, relying on the weight of these authorities, and emphasizing that the statute was really directed against the practice of carrying concealed weapons, the court concluded that the statute "was not an infringement of the constitutional right of the people to keep and bear arms as secured by the *second amendment to the Constitution of the United States*"[93] and affirmed the lower court's judgment.

Notable about the *Wilforth* opinion is the reasoning behind Judge Norton's assessment that Missouri's statute was constitutional. The gun cases he alluded to—e.g., *Bliss, Aymette, Mitchell, Reid, Nunn*, etc.—typically focused their infringement analysis on clauses in *state* constitutions rather than specifically on the federal amendment. While the conclusions of the cited opinions certainly implicitly applied to the Second Amendment, Justice Norton went further. He plainly asserted that Missouri's statute did not infringe that amendment. In doing so, he too ignored *Barron's* restriction on the applicability of the amendment to the states.

***State of Missouri v. Shelby (1886)*: Challenging a Ban on Concealed Firearms While Intoxicated**

Five years after the *Wilforth* case, the Missouri Supreme Court adjudicated another carry challenge involving the Second Amendment. At this point, the state had revised the 1875 statute prohibiting the carrying of concealed weapons to include "the carrying of deadly weapons when intoxicated."[94] The defendant, Shelby, "being then a guest of [the Palace] hotel, took a pistol from his coat pocket, where it was concealed, and laid it upon his lap while seated … in the dining room, and at the time [he] was under the influence of intoxicating drink."[95] Charged and convicted of both carrying a concealed weapon, and carrying a deadly weapon while intoxicated, Shelby appealed on the grounds that the Missouri statute was "in conflict with the second article of the amendments to the constitution of the United States … and section 17, article 2 of the state constitution, which declares, 'that the right of no citizen to keep and bear arms … shall be called into question, but nothing herein contained is intended to justify the practice of wearing concealed weapons.' "[96]

Judge Francis Black, who would become chief justice of the court in 1893 and, later, the first president of the Kansas City School of Law, authored the opinion. In contrast to Judge Norton, he quickly disposed of Shelby's Second Amendment argument, simply noting, "The second amendment to the constitution of the United States is a restriction upon the powers of the national government only, and is not a restriction upon state legislation."[97] In supporting this assertion, he relied on *Cruikshank*, *Fife*, and other gun cases.

Then, turning to the state's Second Amendment analogue, Judge Black observed,

> The right of the legislature to prohibit the wearing of concealed weapons under state constitutions ... is now generally conceded. Indeed, [in] our constitution ... [t]he portions of the act which make it an offense for any one to carry concealed upon his person a dangerous or deadly weapon, is clearly within the legitimate domain of legislative power. Another clause ... makes it an offense for any one to have or carry any such weapon ... when intoxicated, or under the influence of intoxicating drinks. This court held in *State v. Wilforth* that the act of March 13, 1875 ... was valid and not in conflict with the constitution. [If] the legislature may thus regulate the manner in which arms may be borne ... as to time and place, as is done by that act, no good reason is seen why the legislature may not do the same with reference to the condition of the person who carries such weapons. The statute is designed to promote personal security and to check and put down lawlessness, and is thus in perfect harmony with the constitution.[98]

Judge Black went on to note

> that it shall be a good defense to the charge of carrying such weapon, if the defendant shall show that he has been threatened with great bodily harm, or had good reason to carry ... in the necessary defense of his person, home, or property. Conceding that a revolving pistol comes within the description of such arms as one may carry for the purposes designated in the constitution ... still we are of the opinion the act is but a reasonable regulation of the use of such arms ... and a valid exercise of the legislative power.[99]

Having thus upheld the constitutionality of the statute, Black nonetheless concluded that the evidence did not justify Shelby's conviction on *two* distinct counts. He remanded the case, suggesting that the state could take a verdict of guilty for one offense but not both.

As with other cases discussed, lack of incorporation allowed the court to simply dismiss Shelby's Second Amendment argument. Despite this, Black's discussion of Missouri's Second Amendment analogue indicated that the court saw the right to keep and bear arms—while subject to "reasonable" legislative regulation—as an individual right. More generally, determining the "reasonableness" of a particular regulation or statute would continue to claim judicial attention well into the future.

Presser v. Illinois (1886): Challenging a Municipal Prohibition on Drilling with Arms

The same year that the Supreme Court of Missouri decided the *Shelby* case, the Supreme Court of the United States was also wrestling with a Second Amendment challenge, but one significantly different from drunken carry. Herman Presser, a member of "Lehr und Wehr Verein"—a civil society whose stated purpose was member education in American law and the duties of citizenship[100]—was indicted and convicted of unlawfully parading and drilling "in the City of Chicago with an unauthorized body of men with arms who had associated themselves together as a military company [without] a license from the governor, and [without] belonging to 'the regular organized volunteer militia' of the State of Illinois or the troops of the United States."[101]

Presser's behavior—he rode on horseback through city streets at the head of a company of about 400 men armed with rifles—violated Article XI of the Military Code of Illinois, which made it unlawful "for any body of men … other than the regular organized volunteer militia … to associate themselves together as a military company … or to drill or parade with arms … without the license of the governor …."[102] Initially tried by the district court and found guilty, Presser appealed to the Supreme Court of Illinois, which affirmed his conviction. Presser then brought his case to the United States Supreme Court.

His argument was that the Military Code statute under which he was convicted was invalid on three primary grounds: the state statute usurped military powers reserved to the federal government, in violation of Article 1 of the United States Constitution; it violated the "privileges or immunities" clause of the Fourteenth Amendment; and it infringed on the Second Amendment. Justice William Woods, nominated to the court in 1880 by President Rutherford Hayes and the first southerner so appointed since 1853, authored the court's unanimous opinion.

In assessing Presser's first argument, Justice Woods observed,

> We have not found it necessary to consider or decide the question thus raised as to the validity of the entire Military Code of Illinois [because] the sections under which the plaintiff … was convicted may be valid even if the other sections of the act were invalid. … It is plain … that the two sections upon which the indictment … is based may be separated … and stand upon their own independent provisions. … This view disposes of the objection … that the legislation on which the indictment is based is [invalid] by reason of the provisions of the Constitution of the United States which vests Congress with power to raise and support armies, and to provide for calling out, organizing, arming and disciplining the militia.[103]

Turning to Presser's second argument, Woods rhetorically asked,

> What privilege or immunity of a citizen of the United States is abridged by … Article XI of the Military Code of Illinois? … had he a right as a citizen of the United States, in disobedience of the state law, to associate with others as a military company and to drill and parade with arms in the towns and cities of the state? If the plaintiff … has any such privilege, he must be able to point to the provision of the Constitution … by which it is conferred. … We have not been referred to any statute of the United States which confers upon the plaintiff … the privilege which

> he asserts. ... The right voluntarily to associate together as a military company ... or to drill or parade with arms ... is not an attribute of national citizenship."[104]

Regarding the Military Code's potential infringement on the Second Amendment, Justice Woods noted,

> The sections under consideration, which only forbid bodies of men to associate together as military organizations, or to drill or parade with arms ... do not infringe the right of the people to keep and bear arms. But a conclusive answer to the contention that this amendment prohibits the legislation in question lies in the fact that the amendment is a limitation only upon the power of Congress and the national government, and not upon that of the state.[105]

In support of this assertion, Woods cited *Cruikshank*, *Barron*, and others. Thus, having disposed of Presser's major arguments (and dismissing several minor ones), Woods concluded, "All the federal questions presented by the record were rightly decided by the Supreme Court of Illinois. *Judgment affirmed*."[106]

From a Second Amendment perspective, the significance of the *Presser* opinion stems exclusively from its Supreme Court genesis. The finding itself—that the amendment is a limitation on the national government but not the states—simply reconfirmed *Cruikshank* and many lower court, state-level gun case opinions. Nonetheless, as a Supreme Court case, the opinion has general significance because of its implicit endorsement of an individual's right to arms. While *Presser*—again in line with *Cruikshank* and many earlier opinions—upheld a state's right to regulate certain armed behaviors, it also noted that "the states cannot, even laying the constitutional provision in question out of view, prohibit the people from keeping and bearing arms so as to deprive the United States of their rightful resource for maintaining the public security, and disable the people from performing their duty to the general government."[107]

Miller v. Texas (1894): Challenging a Ban on Carrying Firearms on a Public Street

As the nineteenth century drew to close, the US Supreme Court adjudicated another challenge involving the Second Amendment, and once again reiterated that the amendment applied only to the federal government. However, two aspects of this case set it apart from past gun cases: the nature of the defendant's charge—murder—and the unusual resolution of the case. Justice Henry Brown—who later would author the court's *Plessy v. Ferguson* ruling upholding racial segregation—wrote the short *Miller* opinion.

Convicted in the district court of Dallas County and sentenced to death for the murder of a Mr. Riddle, defendant Miller first appealed to the court of last resort in criminal cases, the Court of Criminal Appeals in Texas. That court affirmed Miller's conviction, and overruled his motion for a rehearing. Miller then appealed to the US Supreme Court, arguing that the Texas statute prohibiting the carrying of dangerous weapons on a public street conflicted with the Second Amendment. Miller further argued that the statute—which additionally provided that violators could be arrested without warrant—also violated the Fourth Amendment against unreasonable searches and seizures, the Fifth Amendment guaranteeing each person the due process of law, and the Fourteenth Amendment, prohibiting states from passing or enforcing laws abridging the privileges or immunities of citizens.[108]

After resolving some procedural issues with the case filing, Justice Brown turned to the arguments presented. He noted:

> There is no federal question properly presented by the record in this case, and the writ of error must be dismissed on that ground. The record exhibits nothing of what took place in the court of original jurisdiction, and begins with the assignment of errors in the court of criminal appeals. In this assignment, no claim was made of any ruling ... adverse to any constitutional right claimed by the defendant, nor does any such appear in the opinion of the court .... In his motion for a rehearing, however, defendant claimed that [the Texas statute] forbidding the carrying of weapons and authorizing the arrest without warrant ... was in conflict with the Second and Fourth Amendments .... We have examined the record in vain, however, to find where the defendant was denied the benefit of any of these provisions.[109]

Continuing, Justice Brown observed,

> even if he were, it is well settled that the restrictions of these amendments operate only upon the federal power, and have no reference whatever to proceedings in state courts. *Barron v. Baltimore* ... *United States v. Cruikshank* .... And if the Fourteenth Amendment limited the power of the states as to such rights ... it was fatal to this claim that it was not set up in the trial court.[110]

Brown supported his reasoning with a quote from an earlier Supreme Court case, "If the right was not set up or claimed in the proper court below, the judgment of the highest court of the state in the action is conclusive, so far as the right of review here is concerned."[111] With that, Justice Brown dismissed Miller's appeal.

As with *Presser*, the Second Amendment significance of the *Miller* opinion resides simply in its Supreme Court heritage—one of only a few cases where the court directly addressed (if only to dismiss) a Second Amendment issue. But in the larger context of defining the right to keep and bear arms, the *Miller* opinion with its lack of substantive comment on the amendment is indicative of how two radically different interpretations of the Second Amendment were able to develop judicially.

Some Observations

Several considerations make the opinions in this chapter significant for understanding the Second Amendment. First, the decisions explicitly or implicitly support an individual right to arms. The cases typically ground that right in the need for both personal protection and in the need for an effective common defense, that is, "in defense of self and state." The right to arms for self-defense is perhaps most apparent in the concealed-carry court opinions. In these cases, the courts generally upheld statutes prohibiting concealed-carry while striking down as unconstitutional statutes restricting open-carry. Apparently, the judiciary of that time regarded concealed arms as surprise attack weapons, giving unscrupulous assailants grave and deadly advantages.

The theme of a common defense need is also manifest in these opinions. This is evident particularly in the distinction made between militia arms (e.g., rifles and saddle pistols) and the weapons of thugs and brawlers (e.g., pocket pistols and Bowie knives). Courts extended Second Amendment protection to militia arms, since these weapons had a use in warfare, whether against foreign invaders or tyrannical administrations. The right to keep and bear such arms during peacetime insured citizens' proficiency in their use during wartime. This early emphasis on common defense and militia-type weaponry is especially worth noting. In the absence of any acknowledgment that the opinions also upheld a right to arms for individual self-defense, this stress on common defense and militia arms foreshadows the judicial reasoning (seen in the next chapter) that gives rise to the militia-based "collective right" interpretation of the Second Amendment.

The opinions also foreshadow several other contemporary Second Amendment themes. For example, one court noted that sometimes only a "blurry line" separates the legitimate regulation of firearms from illegitimate prohibitions. Disputes about this distinction between impermissible prohibitions and acceptable regulations continue today, in disagreements (for example) about the legitimacy of many designated "sensitive places," where firearms are statutorily prohibited. Similarly, the courts' separation of arms used in "civilized" warfare from "dangerous and unusual weapons" reflect contemporary arguments about the nature and relative dangerousness of some of today's semi-automatic rifles and pistols.

Finally, these early opinions illustrate that courts, even then, wrestled with finding ways to insure public safety and security, keep guns from the reckless and the criminal, and still preserve citizens' Second Amendment rights.

Notes

1 *Wilson v. State of Arkansas, 33 Ark. 557, 34 Am. Rep. 52 (1878).* At https://guncite.com/court/state/33ar557.html.
2 Clayton Cramer, *For the Defense of Themselves and the State* (Westport, CT: Praeger, 1994, p. 71.
3 *Bliss v. Commonwealth of Kentucky, 12 Littell 90 Ky. (1822).* At https://press-pubs.uchicago.edu/founders/documents/amendIIs8.html.
4 Ibid.
5 Ibid.
6 Ibid.
7 Ibid.

8 *Aymette v. State of Tennessee, 21 Tenn. (2Hump.)154 (1840).* At https://casetext.com/case/aymette-v-state.
9 Ibid.
10 Ibid.
11 Ibid.
12 Ibid.
13 Ibid.
14 Ibid.
15 *Simpson v. State of Tennessee, 13 Tenn. (5 Yer.) 356 (1833).* At https://guncite.com/court/state/13tn356.html.
16 Ibid.
17 *Aymette v. State of Tennessee, 21 Tenn. (2Hump.)154 (1840).* At https://casetext.com/case/aymette-v-state.
18 Ibid.
19 *State of Alabama v. Reid.1 Ala. 612, 35 Am. Dec. 44 (1840).* At https://guncite.com/court/state/1al612.html.
20 Ibid.
21 Ibid.
22 Ibid.
23 Ibid.
24 Ibid.
25 Ibid.
26 *State of Arkansas v. Buzzard, 4 Ark. (2 Pike) 18 (1842).* At https://guncite.com/court/state/4ar18.html.
27 Ibid.
28 Ibid.
29 Ibid.
30 Ibid. Later in his concurrence, Dickinson notes, "this power to keep and bear arms, could not be extended to an unlimited, uncontrolled right to bear any kind of arms or weapons, upon any and every occasion;" a conclusion that Justice Scalia would roughly echo in the landmark *Heller* case more than 150 years in the future.
31 Ibid. See also Hardy, David, (2011). "The Rise and Demise of the Collective Right Interpretation of the Second Amendment." *Cleveland State Law Review, 59, 3,* p. 335. He has characterized Ringo's analysis as "militia-related but not necessarily militia-restricted." At https://engagedscholarship.csuohio.edu/cgi/viewcontent.cgi?article=1044&context=clevstlrev.
32 *Nunn v. State, 1 Ga. 243 (1846).* At https://cite.case.law/ga/1/243/.
33 Ibid.
34 Ibid.
35 Ibid.
36 Ibid.
37 Ibid.
38 Ibid.
39 Ibid.
40 Ibid.
41 See David Kopel, "Nunn v. State of Georgia (1846)," in Greg Lee Carter (ed.), *Guns in American Society* (Santa Barbara, CA: ABC-Clio, 2002), p. 450.
42 *Nunn v. State, 1 Ga. 243 (1846).* At https://cite.case.law/ga/1/243/.

43 *Barron v. Mayor & City Council of Baltimore, 32 U.S. 243 (1833).* At https://supreme.justia.com/cases/federal/us/32/243/.
44 Ibid.
45 Glenn Reynolds, *Andrews v. State* (2018), Tennessee Historical Society. At http://tennesseeencyclopedia.net/entries/andrews-v-state/.
46 *Andrews v. State, 50 Tenn. (3 Heisk.) 165, 8 Am. Rep. 8 (1871).* At https://guncite.com/court/state/50tn165.html.
47 Ibid.
48 Ibid.
49 Ibid.
50 Ibid.
51 Ibid.
52 Ibid.
53 Ibid.
54 Ibid.
55 Ibid.
56 Ibid.
57 Ibid.
58 Ibid.
59 *English v. State, 35 Tex. 473, 14 Am. Rep. 374 (1872).* At https://guncite.com/court/state/35tx473.html.
60 Ibid.
61 Ibid.
62 Ibid.
63 Ibid.
64 Ibid.
65 Ibid.
66 *United States v. Cruikshank, 92 U.S. 542 (1875).* At https://supreme.justia.com/cases/federal/us/92/542/.
67 Ibid. Despite the Court Syllabus indicating that the indictment included thirty-two counts, the court opinion itself notes that the indictment contains sixteen counts, divided into two sets of eight; the opinion discusses just sixteen counts.
68 Ibid.
69 Ibid.
70 Ibid.
71 Ibid.
72 Ibid.
73 Ibid.
74 Ibid.
75 Ibid.
76 Ibid.
77 *Fife v. State, 31 Ark. 455 (1876).* At https://cite.case.law/ark/31/455/.
78 Ibid.
79 Ibid.
80 Ibid.
81 Ibid.
82 Ibid.
83 Ibid.

84 Ibid.
85 Ibid.
86 Ibid.
87 *Wilson v. State, 33 Ark. 557, 34 Am. Rep. 52 (1878).* At https://guncite.com/court/state/33ar557.html.
88 *State v. Wilforth, 74 Mo. 528, 41 Am. Rep. 330 (1881).* At https://guncite.com/court/state/74mo528.html.
89 Ibid.
90 Ibid.
91 Ibid.
92 Ibid.
93 Ibid.
94 *State v. Shelby, 90 Mo. 302 (1886).* At https://cite.case.law/mo/90/302/.
95 Ibid.
96 Ibid.
97 Ibid.
98 Ibid.
99 Ibid.
100 David Kopel has suggested that the *Lerhr und Wehr Verein* society functioned as a self-defense labor organization for German immigrants. Such organizations formed in response to the use of the police, militias, and sometimes US Army regulars to suppress strikes and labor unrest during the late 1800s. See David Kopel, *Presser v. Illinois* (2018). At https://davekopel.org/2A/Mags/Presser-versus-Illinois.htm.
101 *Presser v. Illinois, 116 U.S. 252 (1886).* At https://supreme.justia.com/cases/federal/us/116/252/.
102 Ibid.
103 Ibid.
104 Ibid.
105 Ibid.
106 Ibid.
107 Ibid.
108 *Miller v. Texas, 153 U.S. 535 (1894).* At https://supreme.justia.com/cases/federal/us/153/535/.
109 Ibid.
110 Ibid.
111 Ibid.

3

The Twentieth Century: *Miller* and the Collective Right Interpretation

> *That the provision in question applies only to the right to bear arms as a member of the state militia ... is also apparent from the second amendment to the federal constitution.*
>
> Justice Adrian Greene, Kansas Supreme Court[1]

Beginning in the twentieth century, the country's generally unquestioned acceptance of firearms began to change. Increasingly, particularly in the cities, newspaper editors, politicians, public officials, and other prominent opinion makers started to question the appropriateness of "civilized" men toting firearms around, even for self-protection. Further, many established Americans, often fearful and suspicious of the growing number of new immigrants from eastern and southern Europe, began to see stringent gun regulations as a possible protection from the "dangerous classes." Then, too, murders and attempted assassinations of prominent individuals—for example, the shooting of William Gaynor, mayor of New York in 1910—gave further support to individuals and organizations wanting to get firearms "off the streets."[2]

At about the same time, the judiciary started to see the right to keep and bear arms in a different light. In place of the arguably more intuitive "individual right" understanding that many state courts took for granted in the previous century, this alternative interpretation of the Second Amendment—as a "collective right"—began to gain favor. Indeed, by the end of the century, the collective view eventually became the favored and predominant interpretation of the Second Amendment on the federal level. It would remain so until early in the twenty-first century, when several Supreme Court opinions laid it to rest.

The sixteen cases highlighted in the chapter illustrate this gradual shift in judicial reasoning. Divided into four time periods, the first period examines four cases spanning the years 1902 to 1921. Three of the cases—*Brickey* in 1902, *Strickland* in 1911, and *Kerner* in 1921—continued in the vein of the prior century, with their opinions reflecting the same "individual right" perspective of that era. The other case—*Blaksley* in 1905—advanced a "collective" view of the Second Amendment, foreshadowing the growing acceptance of that interpretation in the 1930s and the remainder of the century.

Covering the years 1935 to 1942, the second period also examines four cases—*Adams* in 1935, the seminal *Miller* opinion of 1939, *Tot* in 1942, and *Cases*, also in 1942. The Supreme Court's *Miller* adjudication is generally considered the foundational opinion launching the collective rights view, but all four cases were significant in establishing this alternative Second Amendment perspective.

The third period examines five opinions covering the 1970s, after passage of the first major federal gun legislation since the 1934 National Firearms Act (NFA)—the Gun Control Act of 1968. All five cases—*Stevens* in 1971, *Cody* in 1972, *Johnson* in 1974, *Warin* in 1976, and *Oakes* in 1977—are federal court adjudications upholding a collective interpretation of the right to keep and bear arms.

Rounding out the century, the final section presents an additional three opinions from federal circuit courts. These cases cover the years 1982 (*Quilici v. Village of Morton Grove*), 1984 (*Thomas v. Members of City Council of Portland*), and 1996 (*Hickman v. Block*). Arising in three different circuits, these representative adjudications demonstrate the ongoing pervasiveness that *Miller* and the collective right interpretation had on the federal judiciary during this period. As noted, while the collective perspective would dominate courts for much of the twentieth century, this perspective would not survive judicial scrutiny in the twenty-first. Those opinions, and the cases leading up to the re-assertion of the Second Amendment as an individual right, make up the next chapter.

1902–21: Foreshadowing the Collective Right Interpretation

Even prior to the *Miller* opinion in 1939, two state-level, Supreme Court cases offered a "collective right" view of the Second Amendment. As seen in the previous chapter, the earliest case was the 1842 *Buzzard* adjudication, with the Arkansas court noting that the *only* purpose of the amendment was to insure an effective militia—the best security of a free state. In the twentieth century, this notion that the Second Amendment protected only a militia-linked, collective right to arms surfaced again, in the 1905 *Blaksley* case. In that case—a challenge to a ban on carrying firearms within city limits—the Kansas court similarly asserted that the right to keep and bear arms applied only to state militia members. Nonetheless, with this singular exception, court opinions in the early decades of the twentieth century continued the pattern established in the prior century: upholding an individual right to arms with some constitutionally allowable regulation.

This traditional orientation is apparent in both *Brickey*—a 1902 Idaho adjudication dealing with a statutory prohibition on carrying deadly weapons within city and town limits—and in the 1911 *Strickland* case—a Georgia opinion examining the constitutionality of a licensing statute. It is also evident in the 1921 *Kerner* case—a North Carolina opinion dealing with challenges to a concealed-carry statute and a permit requirement. In the 1930s, this "individual" perspective gives way to the "collective" perspective, but the four cases above illuminate the judicial status of the Second Amendment shortly before the transition.

In Re: Brickey (1902): Challenging a Prohibition on Carrying Deadly Weapons

In 1889, the Idaho territorial legislature passed an act prohibiting private persons from carrying firearms and other deadly weapons within any of the territory's cities, towns, or villages. Charged and convicted of violating this statute by carrying a loaded revolver within the city of Lewiston, L. D. Brickey appealed his conviction to the Idaho Supreme Court. In a writ of habeas corpus, he asserted that his imprisonment and confinement in the Nez Perce county jail was unlawful. Chief Justice Ralph Quarles, who would later serve on Hawaii's Supreme Court, authored the short opinion.[3]

Quarles noted that "the only offense charged against the petitioner … is that he carried a deadly weapon within the limits of the city of Lewiston, in contravention of the said act of February 4, 1889."[4] He then quoted the Second Amendment of the federal constitution, as well as the state constitution's Second Amendment analogue: "The people have the right to bear arms for their security and defense, but the legislature shall regulate the exercise of this right by law."[5]

With these guarantees as a basis, Chief Justice Quarles gave his finding: "Under these constitutional provisions, the legislature has no power to prohibit a citizen from bearing arms in any portion of the state of Idaho, whether within or without the corporate limits of cities, towns or villages. The legislature may, as expressly provided in our state constitution, regulate the exercise of this right, but may not prohibit it."[6] He elaborated, "A statute prohibiting the carrying of concealed deadly weapons would be a proper exercise of the police power of the state. But the statute in question does not prohibit the carrying of weapons concealed … but prohibits the carrying of them in any manner …. We are compelled to hold this statute void."[7]

As for Brickey, Quarles concluded, "The statute being void, the said justice's court had no jurisdiction of the subject-matter of the action, and the said judgment of conviction … and the detention of the petitioner … are illegal and void. The said judgment being void, habeas corpus will lie, and the prisoner should be discharged from custody, and it is so ordered."[8] With that, he set Brickey free.

While *Brickey* reflected the then dominant "individual" perspective on the Second Amendment, two years later the *Blaksley* case, in a foreshadowing of judicial rulings to come, presented an alternative "collective" perspective on the amendment.

City of Salina v. Blaksley (1905): Challenging a Ban on Carrying Firearms within City Limits

The issue in *City of Salina v. Blaksley* centered on a state prohibition banning the carrying of firearms and other deadly weapons—whether carried concealed or openly. James Blaksley, a 49-year-old intoxicated stockman, had been arrested and convicted in police court of carrying a revolver within the city under this statute. Pointing to Section 4 of the Kansas Bill of Rights, which affirmed that "the people have the right to bear arms for their defense and security," Blaksley contended that the statute was unconstitutional, and appealed his conviction to the district court. His conviction upheld there, Blaksley then appealed to the Kansas Supreme Court.[9]

In a unanimous opinion, Justice Adrian Greene (a well-regarded Republican Party member prior to his Court appointment) acknowledged that the power of legislatures to regulate or even prohibit the carrying of deadly weapons was controversial. Noting that legal decisions were not uniform and that reasoning varied from court to court, Greene decided to ignore conflicting opinions, and to approach the question "as an original one." He concluded that the provision in Section 4 of the Kansas Bill of Rights

> refers to the people as a collective body. It was the safety and security of society that was being considered when this provision was put into our Constitution. … It deals exclusively with the military. Individual rights are not considered in this section. … That the provision in question applies only to the right to bear arms as a member of the state militia … is also apparent from the second amendment to the federal constitution …. Here, also, the right of the people to keep and bear arms for their security is preserved, and the manner of bearing them for such purpose is clearly indicated to be as a member of a well-regulated militia, or some other military organization as provided for by law.[10]

Justice Greene further supported his argument by citing an 1896 Massachusetts Supreme Court gun case, *Commonwealth v. James A. Murphy*.[11] In this case, despite Massachusetts' similar Bill of Rights (i.e., "the people have a right to keep and bear arms for the common defense"), Greene noted that the defendant James Murphy—not a member of a regularly organized corps of the militia—was convicted of drilling with an inoperable firearm. As the Massachusetts Court explained, inoperable or not, "it is within the police power of the legislature to regulate the bearing of arms" as a matter affecting public security, quiet, and good order. As Greene noted, without a militia connection, Murphy's drilling was not "within the provision of the Bill of Rights and was not protected by its terms." Given that the purpose of Section 4 of the Kansas Bill of Rights also upheld bearing arms only in authorized militia service, Blaksley's personal pistol-bearing behavior was similarly unprotected. The court affirmed his conviction with all justices concurring.[12]

Thus, sixty odd years after the 1842 *Buzzard* opinion, the Supreme Court of Kansas resurrected the idea of a militia-linked Second Amendment that protected only a common and not a private right to arms. But in this ruling, Justice Greene went substantially beyond the ambiguity of *Buzzard*'s militia-linked interpretation of the Second Amendment. The Greene Court plainly asserts that the amendment—as well as Section 4 of the Kansas Bill of Rights—refers not to an individual right to arms but to a collective right, and that the amendment offers protection to bearing arms only as a member of the state militia. The Kansas Supreme Court eventually moderated this position, but many later state and federal opinions endorsed Greene's interpretation of the amendment.

Strickland v. State of Georgia (1911): Challenging a Firearms Licensing Requirement

While Kansas' *Blaksley* opinion anticipated the judicial view of the Second Amendment dominating the latter half of the twentieth century, *Blaksley* remained an adjudication outlier for three decades. For instance, Georgia's Supreme Court in 1911 continued to interpret the right to arms as an individual right, but one open to legitimate and reasonable regulation. In this specific case, Georgia's General Assembly had enacted a new statute in 1910 prohibiting "any person from having or carrying a revolver without first having obtained a license from the ordinary of the county of said state, in which the party resides."[13] Convicted of carrying a pistol without a license, J. L. Strickland appealed the ruling to the state Court of Appeals, asserting that the statute violated both the Second Amendment analogue of the state constitution—"The right of the people to keep and bear arms shall not be infringed, but the General Assembly shall have power to prescribe the manner in which arms shall be borne"—and also the Second Amendment of the federal constitution.[14]

The Court of Appeals requested the state Supreme Court to provide guidance for the proper adjudication of (i.e., "to certify") the two questions raised by Strickland's appeal: Does the statute violate the state's second amendment equivalent, and does the statute violate the federal Second Amendment? Justice Joseph H. Lumpkin II—the son of the chief justice who authored the *Nunn* opinion in 1846—wrote the certifications for the court.

In addressing whether the Georgia statute violated the state constitutional guarantee, Lumpkin noted that most state constitutions contain provisions modeled on the federal constitution's Second Amendment, and that "one of the first questions which was raised under the constitutional provisions on [the right to bear arms] was whether they were violated by laws which prohibited the carrying of concealed weapons."[15] Acknowledging that Kentucky's *Bliss* opinion in 1822 had found a concealed-carry regulation unconstitutional, he observed, "This ruling has not been followed, but severely criticized. The decisions are practically unanimous to the contrary,"[16] citing the opinions of *Aymette*, *Wilforth*, *Reid*, and several others.

Continuing, he wrote,

> In several States, other statutes, regulatory in their nature, or prohibiting the carrying of certain kinds of weapons, or the carrying of weapons under certain circumstances and at certain places, have been upheld. In *Andrews v. State* ... if the weapon designated by the statute was [a soldier's weapon] the absolute prohibition against it was too broad ... but a pocket revolver ...was a weapon the carrying of which the legislature could constitutionally prohibit.[17]

After citing additional cases similarly regulating particular types of firearms, the manner of carrying, and even age requirements, Lumpkin then considered the legal justifications for such prohibitions and regulations.

He observed,

> An examination of the various decisions … will show that two general lines of reasoning have been employed in upholding such statutes: first, that such provisions are to be construed in the light of the origin of the constitutional declarations, of their connection with words declaratory of the necessity for an efficient militia, or for the common defense, or the like … and in view of the general public purpose which such provisions were intended to subserve; and second, that the right to bear arms, like other rights … is to be construed within the police power of the State, and as subject to legitimate regulation thereunder.[18]

Further, Lumpkin noted that state constitutions sometimes expressly recognize this police power, directly containing words indicating the state may regulate the right to arms. But even in the absence of a limiting expression, any judicial

> ruling that the legislature may prohibit the carrying of concealed weapons essentially concedes the police power of regulation to some extent. If this be conceded, the question then becomes one as to whether the particular regulation involved is legitimate and reasonably within the police power, or whether it is arbitrary, and, under the name of regulation, amounts in effect to a deprivation of the constitutional right.[19]

Citing the Georgia Supreme Court's 1846 *Nunn* opinion, Lumpkin drew a parallel between the constitutionality of a statute regulating the manner in which arms may be borne (i.e., "A law which merely inhibits the wearing of weapons in a concealed manner is valid.") and a law requiring a license to carry a revolver. He asserted, "if this argument [i.e., the unconstitutionality of requiring a license] be sound, then practically the whole licensing system would be destroyed on the ground that to require a license is not a regulation, but a prohibition."[20]

Earlier in the opinion, Justice Lumpkin had pointed out (citing *Barron*, *Cruikshank*, *Presser*, and other adjudications) that the federal Second Amendment was a restriction upon the powers of Congress only, making any violation of that amendment moot. Having thus certified the two questions raised by the Court of Appeals, Lumpkin concluded, "We think, upon careful consideration, that the regulatory provisions of the act of 1910 are not so arbitrary or unreasonable as to amount, in effect, to a prohibition of the right to bear arms, or an infringement of that right as protected by the constitution."[21]

Overall, then, Lumpkin's interpretation of the right to arms in *Strickland*—as an individual right subject to limited and reasonable regulation—mirrored the dominant view of the prior century rather than the militia-linked collective view developed in Greene's *Blaksley* opinion. A decade after *Strickland*, Lumpkin's analysis still epitomized judicial thinking on the right to keep and bear arms, as the *Kerner* opinion demonstrates.

State of North Carolina v. Kerner (1921): Challenging a Firearms Permitting Requirement

In 1919, North Carolina's Forsyth County had enacted a three-sectioned statute that regulated the carrying of weapons. Section 1 prohibited the carrying of concealed weapons, Section 2 required a permit to carry a weapon, and Section 3 made carrying a weapon without permit illegal. Specifically, Section 3 stipulated: "If any person, except when on his own premises, shall carry any weapon (named in section 1) without a permit (as provided in section 2) he is guilty of a misdemeanor and punished as provided in section 1 for carrying a concealed weapon."[22]

Accosted on a street in Kernersville by an individual wanting to fight, O. W. Kerner set down the packages he had been carrying, went to his store, and returned to the scene openly carrying a pistol. Kerner was then arrested and indicted on two counts: one for carrying a concealed weapon and the other for carrying a pistol off his premises unconcealed. Convicted, Kerner appealed to the Superior Court of Forsyth Country, arguing that the statute violated both the federal and state constitutions. The court, agreeing that the statute was an unconstitutional infringement on the right to bear arms, directed a verdict of not guilty. The state then appealed to the Supreme Court of North Carolina.[23]

Chief Justice Walter Clark, a former field-grade officer in the Confederate Army first appointed to the court in 1889, authored the Supreme Court's opinion. Clark, citing a number of opinions including *Cruikshank*, dismissed the federal amendment as inapplicable since "the first ten amendments to the United States Constitution are restrictions upon the federal authority and not upon the states."[24] Turning to North Carolina's constitution, he observed that the document's Declaration of Rights asserted "the right of the people to keep and bear arms shall not be infringed [but] nothing herein contained shall justify the practice of carrying concealed weapons or prevent the Legislature from enacting penal statutes against said practice."[25] He then observed, "This exception indicates the extent to which the right of the people to bear arms can be restricted; that is, the Legislature can prohibit the carrying of concealed weapons, but no further."[26]

Arguing that the historical use of pistols as offense and defensive "arms" was beyond controversy, Clark concluded that "the right to bear such arms unconcealed cannot be infringed."[27] Later, in his opinion, he argued,

> The maintenance of the right to bear arms is a most essential one to every free people, and should not be whittled down by technical constructions. It should be construed to include all such "arms" as were in common use, and borne by the people when this provision was adopted. ... The intention was to embrace the "arms," an acquaintance with whose use was necessary for their protection against the usurpation of illegal power—such as rifles, muskets, shotguns, swords, and pistols.[28]

The chief justice further asserted,

> It would also be a reasonable regulation, and not an infringement of the right to bear arms, to prohibit the carrying of deadly weapons when under the influence

> of intoxicating drink, or to a church, polling place, or public assembly, or in a manner calculated to inspire terror, which was forbidden at common law. These from a practical standpoint are mere regulations, and would not infringe upon the object of the constitutional guarantee, which is to preserve to the people the right to acquire and retain a practical knowledge of the use of firearms.[29]

Returning to the facts of the case, Clark declared,

> The statute in this case ... is especially objectionable in that it requires (sec. 2) that in order to carry a pistol off his own premises, even openly, and for a lawful purpose, the citizen must make application to the municipal court .... As a regulation, even, this is void because [it is] an unreasonable regulation, and, besides, it would be void because for all practical purposes it is a prohibition of the constitutional right to bear arms.[30]

Noting that Kerner, acting in self-defense, carried his pistol openly and unconcealed, Clark determined that "the court below most properly adjudged, upon the special verdict, that he was not guilty. No error."[31]

In line with both *Brickey* and *Strickland*, and the predominant interpretation of nineteenth-century courts, Clark's opinion upholding an individual right to arms subject only to limited and reasonable regulation might seem to imply that Greene's *Blaksley* opinion and its collective right interpretation was a judicial oddity. If so, court rulings in the following decades put that implication to rest.

1935–42: *Miller* and the Second Amendment as a Collective Right

The four cases considered in this section—*Adams* in 1935, *Miller* in 1939, *Tot* in 1942, and *Cases* in 1942—provide a set of federal opinions marking the judicial transition from interpreting the right to bear arms as an individual right to a collective right. In the *Adams* case, the defendant challenged a conviction for violating the recently enacted National Firearms Act, arguing that the NFA both usurped state policing power and infringed the Second Amendment. After rejecting Adams's NFA argument, the court advanced a collective interpretation of the Second Amendment, giving short shrift to that aspect of Adams's defense.

In *Miller*, despite its status as the heavy-weight opinion defining the Second Amendment as a militia-linked collective right, the court actually offered a narrower and more ambiguous interpretation of the amendment. Maintaining only that the Second Amendment did not guarantee the defendants' right to keep and bear a weapon that was not part of ordinary militia equipment (such as a short-barreled shotgun), the opinion nonetheless became the cornerstone citation upholding the collective perspective.

The *Tot* and *Cases* adjudications, occurring shortly after *Miller*, demonstrate the judiciary's rapid acceptance—and often elaboration—of the *Miller* opinion. In *Tot*, the Third Circuit denied the defendant's Second Amendment objection to a felon-in-possession conviction, with the court directly quoting from *Miller* and specifically noting that the amendment was not adopted with individual rights in mind. In *Cases*, another felon-in-possession conviction, the First Circuit similarly rejected a Second Amendment defense, also directly quoting *Miller*, and observing that the defendant was neither a member of any military organization nor in training for a military position.

United States v. Adams (1935): Challenging the National Firearms Act of 1934

Charged with several violations of the 1934 NFA's taxing and registration requirements for machine guns and other defined firearms, defendant Adams challenged his indictment, arguing in a demurrer (i.e., a legal plea claiming that, even if all the factual allegations were true, they still would be insufficient to establish a valid cause of action) that the firearms act was unconstitutional. Adams contended that the NFA was not actually a revenue measure but was an attempt by the federal government (using policing power it did not possess) to regulate the sale and use of firearms—solely a state function during this period. He further asserted that the NFA violated the US Constitution's Second Amendment.[32]

Judge Halsted Ritter[33] of the US District Court for Southern Florida authored the opinion. After briefly reviewing and discussing the content of the NFA, Judge Ritter noted:

> The power of United States government to tax is full and complete and includes the power to determine what articles will be taxed. The Harrison Anti-Narcotics Act was held constitutional as a taxing measure .... This act was attacked upon the same grounds as are now asserted against the National Firearms Act. A comparison of the two leads to the conclusion that the latter was formulated upon the former. ... In upholding the Harrison Anti-Narcotic Act ... the court held that the act is a constitutional exercise of the taxing power and said: .... "the fact that other motives may impel the exercise of federal taxing power does not authorize the courts to inquire into that subject. If the legislation enacted has some reasonable relation to the exercise of the taxing authority conferred by the Constitution, it cannot be invalidated because of the supposed motives which induced it. The act may not be declared unconstitutional because its effect may be to accomplish another purpose as well as the raising of revenue."[34]

Judge Ritter then noted, "The National Firearms Act is a revenue measure. Back of it may have been a motive to prevent racketeers, bank robbers, and desperadoes from obtaining sawed-off shotguns and machine guns to run wild in crime but ... the imposition of the tax is the determining feature .... Whatever other motive there may be behind the act is immaterial."[35] Having thus disposed of Adams's first argument in the demurrer, Judge Ritter turned his attention to the Second Amendment contention.

In a short, four-sentence paragraph, Ritter declared that "The second amendment to the constitution … has no application to this act. The Constitution does not grant the privilege to racketeers and desperadoes to carry weapons of the character dealt with in the act. It refers to the militia, a protective force of government; to the collective body and not individual rights."[36] And with those words, Ritter affirmed Adams's conviction and dismissed the Second Amendment's possible role as a protection for a personal right to arms.[37]

Despite the manifest content of his words, Ritter's terse treatment of the Second Amendment allows for some interpretive ambiguity in his analysis. The opinion does not cite *Blaksley*—the clearest prior statement of the collective right interpretation of the Second Amendment—and the two gun cases referenced (*State v. Workman*, West Virginia, 1891; *Hill v. State*, Georgia, 1874) merely upheld statutes imposing specific restrictions on the right to keep and bear arms. Thus, Ritter may only have meant that the amendment is *militia-linked* rather than totally *militia-restricted*. Nonetheless, the opinion furthered a collective interpretation of the amendment, and coincidentally, its outcomes anticipated the results that the Roosevelt Administration apparently desired from *Miller*.[38]

United States v. Miller (1939): Challenging the National Firearms Act of 1934

Background: While crime control has typically been an impetus for gun regulations, such regulation was the purview of the various states—not the federal government—until the twentieth century. The Roaring Twenties and the violence that accompanied Prohibition elevated crime control (and gun regulation) into a national issue, with President Franklin Roosevelt and his attorney general, Homer Cummings, promoting a "New Deal for Crime"—a focus that gave birth to the National Firearms Act of 1934.[39]

The NFA represented the federal government's first involvement in gun control and, constitutionally, it was a controversial act. Among other provisions, the act required firearm dealers, manufacturers, and importers of "NFA-defined" firearms (e.g., machine guns, short-barreled rifles and shotguns, and sound suppressors) to pay a special occupational tax and to register these types of firearms with the government. It further imposed a transfer tax whenever these firearms changed hands and required every retail buyer or transferee to register their possession with the Internal Revenue Service. The act alarmed many in the gun-owning community who questioned its legality. To enhance the act's legitimacy, the Roosevelt Administration desired a Supreme Court precedent confirming the constitutionality of the NFA.[40] The *Miller* case became that precedent.

Convicted of violations of the NFA—the "felonious transport in interstate commerce … [of] a double barrel 12-gauge Stevens shotgun having a barrel less than 18 inches in length … not having registered said firearm … and not having in their possession a stamp-affixed written order for said firearm"[41]—the defendants—Jack

Miller and Frank Layton—appealed their conviction to the US District Court in the Western District of Arkansas.

In District Court: Their appeal's demurrer raised the same legal arguments used in *Adams*: that the NFA was not a revenue measure but an unconstitutional attempt to usurp police powers reserved to the states; and that the act violated the Second Amendment of the Constitution. However, unlike Judge Rittter, Arkansas' district court judge—H. Heartsill Ragon, a prominent state Democrat and gun control advocate appointed to the federal judiciary by President Roosevelt—*sustained* their demurrer and quashed the indictment. This outcome was not entirely unexpected. Ragon's seemingly surprising ruling provided the basis for a government appeal directly to the Supreme Court, where a finding rejecting Second Amendment concerns and supporting the constitutionality of the NFA appeared likely.[42]

At the Supreme Court: Associate Justice James McReynolds—a noted opponent of Roosevelt's New Deal and apparently a bigot who openly snubbed his Jewish colleagues[43]—wrote the short but unanimous opinion reversing Judge Ragon's ruling. Citing a half-dozen prior cases firmly establishing the constitutionality of governmental taxing power regardless of a law's underlying motives, Justice McReynolds quickly rejected the argument that the NFA attempted to appropriate the states' police powers: "the objection that the Act usurps police power reserved to the States is plainly untenable."[44]

Regarding the nature of the Second Amendment and its potential violation, McReynolds' six-page ruling was less straightforward. The government had argued that the amendment protected only a "collective" right to keep and bear arms, and it shielded only weapons commonly used in militia service. Although Miller and Layton were not present (they had disappeared after Judge Ragon had quashed the initial indictment and set them free) and had no representation to counter this interpretation (their court-appointed attorney was unable to find the time or funds to personally present their defense[45]), none of this mattered. McReynolds avoided the collective versus individual right issue, focusing instead on the type of firearm under consideration.

Specifically, he noted,

> In the absence of any evidence tending to show that possession or use of a "shotgun having a barrel of less than eighteen inches in length" at this time has some reasonable relationship to the preservation or efficiency of a well regulated militia, we cannot say that the Second Amendment guarantees the right to keep and bear such an instrument. Certainly it is not within judicial notice that this weapon is any part of the ordinary military equipment, or that its use could contribute to the common defense.[46]

Continuing, McReynolds then examined the Second Amendment relative to the nature and role of the militia. He observed that the amendment's "obvious purpose" was "to assure the continuation and render possible the effectiveness" of militia forces and that the amendment "must be interpreted and applied with that end in view."[47] Reviewing the country's early history and legislation, he noted that

> the Militia comprised all males physically capable of acting in concert for the common defense [who] when called for service ... were expected to appear bearing arms supplied by themselves and of the kind in common use at the time .... [T]he militia system ... implied the general obligation of all adult inhabitants to possess arms .... Clauses intended to insure the possession of arms and ammunition by all who were subject to military service appear in all the important enactments concerning military affairs. Fines were the penalty for delinquency.[48]

He further noted that the General Court of Massachusetts in 1784 directed "that every noncommissioned officer and private soldier of the said militia ... shall equip himself, and be constantly provided with a good firearm."[49] Similarly, the New York Legislature in 1786 directed that "every Citizen ... provide himself, at his own Expense, with a good Musket or Firelock"[50] as did the General Assembly of Virginia, "Every officer and soldier shall ... appear armed, equipped, and accoutered."[51] Ending his analysis, McReynolds acknowledged the existence of varying conclusions among the states regarding the scope of the Second Amendment and the right it protects, "but none of them seems to afford any material support for the challenged ruling of the court below ... We are unable to accept the conclusions of the court below, and the challenged judgment must be reversed."[52] With this judgment on the Second Amendment, and with the dismissal of the police power usurpation argument, McReynolds clearly affirmed the constitutionality of the National Firearms Act.

Less clear were the implications of the court's words for the Second Amendment. On the one hand, the decision certainly linked Second Amendment protections to general militia considerations, for example, to the kinds of weapons involved in militia service and to their potential use in common defense. On the other hand, the decision noted that civilians—the body of the militia—brought their own commonly used arms when engaged in common defense and that civilians were even required by law to possess firearms and ammunition. This implied the amendment contained protections that went beyond simply keeping and bearing arms when collectively engaged in common defense. Indeed, the ambiguity of McReynolds's analysis permitted both gun-control and gun-rights advocates to cite *Miller* as a supporting case. Nonetheless, despite the narrow and inexact nature of the court's opinion, many later federal courts interpreted *Miller* as upholding a "collective right" view of the Second Amendment.

United States v. Tot (1942): Challenging the Federal Firearms Act of 1938

Not long after the *Miller* decision, the *Tot* case again brought Second Amendment challenges to the consideration of the federal judiciary. The case centered on the constitutionality of another newly enacted gun law, the Federal Firearms Act (FFA) of 1938. Among the act's various licensing and other requirements, the FFA prohibited individuals convicted of a violent crime from receiving, transporting, or carrying firearms across state lines. In determining the legality of this prohibition, the court examined the nature of the Second Amendment.

This litigation involved Frank Tot, a petty criminal whom federal officers arrested at his home on a warrant charging theft of cigarettes from an interstate shipment. During the course of the arrest, Tot—who had previously been convicted of a violent crime—acknowledged having a .32-caliber Colt pistol in the pocket of a coat in his wardrobe closet. He was then charged and subsequently convicted as a prohibited person in possession of a firearm, an FFA violation.[53]

Tot appealed his conviction to the Third Circuit Court of Appeals, arguing that the gun's seizure violated Fourth Amendment protections against unreasonable search and seizures. Judge Herbert Goodrich—a University of Pennsylvania law school professor appointed to the federal judiciary by President Roosevelt and writing for the court—found the seizure of the gun without a search warrant to be justified and dismissed Tot's Fourth Amendment complaint. Goodrich then addressed Tot's technical argument that the statute as worded did not include Tot's type of firearm. Goodrich dismissed this contention also, noting that Congressional discussions prior to the FFA's passage plainly showed that Tot's narrow definitional interpretation of the statute was incorrect.[54]

Tot's third argument was that the FFA violated the Second Amendment. Citing *Miller*, Judge Goodrich wrote: "It is abundantly clear ... that this amendment, unlike those providing for protection of free speech and freedom of religion, was not adopted with individual rights in mind, but as a protection for the States in the maintenance of their militia organizations against possible encroachments by the federal power."[55] He continued,

> The contention of the appellant in this case could ... be denied without more under the authority of *United States v. Miller, 1939, 307 U.S. 174.* This was a prosecution under the National Firearms Act of 1934 and the weapon ... was a shotgun of less than 18 inch barrel. The Court said that in the absence of evidence [showing] that possession of such a gun ... has some reasonable relationship to the preservation or efficiency of a well regulated militia, it could not be said that the Second Amendment guarantees the right to keep such an instrument. The appellant here having failed to show such a relationship, the same may be said of the pistol found in his possession.[56]

Judge Goodrich concluded his analysis by noting,

> Weapon bearing was never treated as anything like an absolute right by the common law. It was regulated by statute as to time and place as far back as the Statute of Northampton in 1382 and on many occasions since. The decisions under the State Constitutions show the upholding of regulations prohibiting the carrying of concealed weapons, prohibiting persons from going armed in certain places and other restrictions .... Congress has prohibited the receipt of weapons from interstate transactions by persons who have previously ... been shown to

> be aggressors against society. Such a classification is entirely reasonable and does not infringe upon the preservation of the well regulated militia protected by the Second Amendment.[57]

He subsequently dismissed Tot's appeal and upheld the judgment of the district court.[58]

The *Tot* opinion adhered closely to *Miller* but added a significant inferential claim. Goodrich asserted that the Second Amendment is "unlike those providing for protection of free speech and freedom of religion [and] was not adopted with individual rights in mind." *Miller* neither compared the First and Second Amendments nor examined the individual rights implications of the Second Amendment beyond noting the type of weapons the amendment addressed. Nonetheless, Judge Goodrich's additional assertion not only tied the amendment to militia concerns but also characterized it as distinctly apart from the individual rights protected by the Bill of Rights.

Cases v. United States (1942): Challenging the Federal Firearms Act of 1938

About a month after the *Tot* decision, the federal judiciary again examined the constitutionality of the FFA—and its Second Amendment implications—in a case similar to *Tot*. In this case, the First Circuit Court of Appeals adjudicated the appeal of Jose Cases Velazquez, a prior violent offender convicted in district court of receiving a firearm and ammunition in violation of the FFA.[59]

Velazquez raised a number of arguments in his contention that the FFA was unconstitutional, including that the statute violated the Second Amendment and that it created an unreasonable presumption of guilt—arguments that Tot had also raised. In addition, Velazquez contended that the statute was an ex post facto law, an undue extension of the commerce clause, and a violation of equal protection under the law. Judge Peter Woodbury—a Harvard-trained, New Hampshire Supreme Court Justice elevated to the federal bench by President Roosevelt in 1941—authored the circuit court's opinion. Citing past court rulings, Judge Woodbury rejected all of Velazquez's arguments: "In our view none of these contentions are sound."[60]

In his analysis of the Second Amendment, Woodbury noted that "the right to keep and bear arms is not a right conferred … by the federal constitution. Whatever rights in this respect the people may have depend upon local legislation; the only function of the Second Amendment being to prevent the federal government and the federal government only from infringing that right."[61] After citing two cases in support of this position (*Cruikshank* and *Presser*), he argued that, even at the federal level, the Second Amendment was not unconstrained: "…the Supreme Court in a dictum in *Robertson v. Baldwin* indicated that the limitations imposed upon the federal government by the Second Amendment was not absolute and this dictum received the sanction of the court in the recent case of *United States v. Miller*."[62]

Continuing, Judge Woodbury quoted from *Miller*,

> "In the absence of any evidence tending to show that possession or use of a 'shotgun having a barrel of less than eighteen inches in length' … has some

reasonable relationship to the preservation or efficiency of a well regulated militia, we cannot say that the Second Amendment guarantees the right to keep and bear such an instrument. Certainly it is not within judicial notice that this weapon is any part of the ordinary military equipment or that its use could contribute to the common defense." Apparently, then, under the Second Amendment, the federal government can limit the keeping and bearing of arms by a single individual as well as by a group of individuals, but it cannot prohibit the possession or use of any weapon which has any reasonable relationship to the preservation or efficiency of a well regulated militia.[63]

Judge Woodbury then qualified this interpretation, "However, we do not feel that the Supreme Court in this case was attempting to formulate a general rule applicable to all cases. The rule laid down was adequate to dispose of the [*Miller* case] and that we think was as far as the Supreme Court intended to go."[64] Noting that "some sort of military use seems to have been found for almost any modern lethal weapon,"[65] Judge Woodbury explained that the *Miller* ruling would effectively make the Second Amendment absolute, preventing Congress "from regulating the possession or use by private persons [of] distinctly military arms, such as machine guns, trench mortars, anti-tank or anti-aircraft guns … [an outcome] 'unlikely that the framers of the Amendment intended.' "[66]

Regarding *specific* weapons that the amendment might protect, Woodbury noted, "Considering the many variable factors bearing upon the question, it seems impossible to us to formulate any general test by which to determine the limits imposed by the Second Amendment but that each case … must be decided on its own facts [to determine] what is and what is not a valid federal restriction …."[67]

Returning to the facts of the case, Woodbury observed that Velazquez had received a .38-caliber Colt revolver and ammunition from a comrade, which he used to shoot a patron at a beach club in Puerto Rico. While acknowledging that the revolver might be capable of military use, and that familiarity with it might have some training value, Woodbury dryly concluded,

> Still there is no evidence that the appellant was or ever had been a member of any military organization or that his use of the weapon … was in preparation for a military career. In fact, the only inference possible is that the appellant … was in possession of, transporting, and using the firearm and ammunition purely and simply on a frolic of his own and without any thought or intention of contributing to the efficiency of the well regulated militia which the Second Amendment was designed to foster.[68]

Concluding that the FFA was not in conflict with the Second Amendment, Woodbury subsequently affirmed the judgment of the district court.

Less sweeping than *Tot*—the *Cases* opinion makes no claim that the Second Amendment's protections are unlike the protections provided for speech and religion—the opinion nonetheless contained three significant declarations. First, Woodbury noted that gun rights are not conferred by the Constitution and the Second Amendment but depend upon local legislation (echoing Judge Goodrich's earlier reference to the role of common law in regulating firearms). Second, he asserted that the Second Amendment functions only to constrain the federal government, and even at that level, the amendment's protection is not absolute. Finally, most importantly, he interpreted the *Miller* decision as a narrow, case-specific ruling, but still relied on *Miller* to limit the amendment's protection of arms-keeping to militia weapons and training.

1971–7: The Second Amendment and the Gun Control Act of 1968

For about two decades, from the early 1940s to the early 1960s, the Second World War and post-war prosperity occupied the country's attention. With crime rates at historic lows during much of this period, gun issues and gun regulation receded in national importance. That changed in the 1960s. In this decade, the Decade of Assassinations, the murders of four prominent American leaders—President John F. Kennedy in 1963, Malcolm X in 1965, Dr. Martin Luther King Jr., and Senator Robert Kennedy in 1968—returned gun concerns center stage to American consciousness.

Reacting to these murders, and noting that Kennedy's assassin had used a mail-ordered rifle to slay the president, Senator Thomas Dodd of Connecticut and other legislators called for new federal restrictions on the sale of firearms. Dodd's firearms bill died in committee in 1964, but the three additional assassinations in these years spurred Congress to pass the first major federal gun bill since the NFA and FFA of the 1930s: the Gun Control Act of 1968 (GCA).[69] In addition to new gun control regulations, this act also incorporated the provisions of the two earlier federal statutes.

Violations of the GCA produced multiple defendants that invoked the Second Amendment in an attempt to overturn their convictions. This section examines five such cases from the 1970s: *Stevens* in 1971, *Cody* in 1972, *Johnson* in 1974, *Warin* in 1976, and *Oakes* in 1977. The *Stevens* case is a GCA variation on a felon-in-possession conviction. The *Cody* case involves a conviction for lying on a required federal firearms purchase form, while *Johnson* centers on a prior felon appealing a conviction for transporting a firearm in interstate commerce. The *Warin* case is a Second Amendment challenge to a GCA conviction for possession of an unregistered submachine gun, and the final case in this section, *Oakes*, is a Second Amendment objection to a conviction for the sale of an unregistered machine gun.

Stevens v. United States (1971): Challenging Provisions of the Gun Control Act of 1968

Frank Stevens, convicted in Kentucky of violent felonies in 1958 and 1962, was then charged in 1969 with possession of a 9-mm semiautomatic pistol—a GCA prohibition that barred convicted felons from receiving, possessing, or transporting any firearm "in commerce or affecting commerce."[70] Found guilty in district court, Stevens petitioned the Sixth Circuit Court of Appeals, arguing first that the evidence presented did not establish that the firearm he possessed was "in commerce or affecting commerce" and, second, that the Second Amendment prevents Congress from enacting a statute that prohibits felons from possessing firearms.

For Stevens's first argument regarding the meaning and implications of "in commerce or affecting commerce," Chief Judge Harry Phillips reviewed both the language of the statute and its legislative history and concluded that both upheld the government's position. He then turned to the Second Amendment issue, examining the power of Congress to prohibit the possession of a firearm by a convicted felon. He noted,

> Since the Second Amendment right "to keep and bear arms" applies only to the right of the State to maintain a militia and not to the individual's right to bear arms, there can be no serious claim to any express constitutional right of an individual to possess a firearm. [*Miller* citation.] Stevens asserts, however, that Congress is without constitutional power to deny him this privilege. We hold that Congress has this authority under the commerce clause.[71]

After briefly reviewing the constitutional background of the commerce clause and a number of landmark Supreme Court cases illustrating its implications, Phillips continued,

> We return then to consider the Congressional finding that firearms in the possession of convicted felons pose a threat to interstate commerce. A citation of authorities and statistics ... is unnecessary. All convicted felons have flouted the law at least once. ... There can be no serious doubt that the possession of firearms by convicted felons is a threat to interstate commerce ... firearms are used to highjack airplanes, rob banks ... commit other crimes seriously affecting commerce. ... It is not necessary for Congress to await the total destruction of commerce before it may provide reasonable preventive measures."[72]

With that, Chief Judge Phillips affirmed Stevens' conviction.

From a Second Amendment perspective, the *Stevens* opinion is noteworthy in two respects. First, the opinion quite clearly endorses a "collective right" view of the amendment. Judge Phillips dismissed out of hand that the amendment could protect an individual's right to keep and bear arms. Second, Phillips only cites *Miller* to support this interpretation. Unlike earlier cases, he omitted summarizing or quoting *Miller's* actual findings. Where earlier cases may have contained some ambiguity regarding the amendment's relationship to an individual right, *Stevens* asserted that *Miller* endorses a purely collective interpretation of the Second Amendment.

Cody v. United States (1972): Challenging 18 U.S.C. §922 (a) (6), Federal Firearms Disclosure Form

In this Eighth Circuit adjudication, James Cody challenged his conviction for making false statements to a licensed firearms dealer during his purchase of a .30-caliber carbine. At district trial, Cody had admitted that he signed the federal form required for all firearms purchases but denied having any knowledge of the form's contents. The store owner contradicted Cody's denial, indicating that he had instructed Cody to read the form and that Cody did so. The form in question contained the following statement: "I certify that … I [have not] been convicted of a crime punishable for a term exceeding one year."[73] In fact, Cody had previously been convicted of a felony punishable by five years' imprisonment, which he had stipulated to at trial. Thus, in signing the form, Cody had violated 18 U.S.C. §922 (a) (6), a statute making it unlawful to knowingly submit false statements to a licensed gun dealer when purchasing a firearm. In his appeal, Stevens raised a number of arguments, including the argument that the statute violated the Second Amendment. Judge Myron Bright, a University of Minnesota Law School graduate appointed to the federal judiciary in 1968 by President Lyndon Johnson, authored the court's opinion.

Judge Bright cited *Miller* in rejecting Cody's Second Amendment argument:

> We find no merit in the contention that § 922(a) (6) violates appellant's Second Amendment right to bear arms. Since *United States v. Miller* [Citation provided], it has been settled that the Second Amendment is not an absolute bar to congressional regulation of the use or possession of firearms. The Second Amendment's guarantee extends only to the use or possession which "has some reasonable relationship to the preservation or efficiency of a well regulated militia." … See *United States v. Synnes …*; *Cases v. United States …*, *Cases Velasquez v. United States …*. We find no evidence that the prohibition of § 922(a) (6) obstructs the maintenance of a well regulated militia.[74]

Similarly finding no merit in Cody's other contentions, Bright affirmed Cody's conviction.

While the *Cody* opinion cites *Miller*, it does so ambiguously, merely noting that the Second Amendment has militia-linked implications and is not an "absolute" bar to congressional regulation of firearms. Bright's opinion does not address (like the *Miller* opinion itself) whether the amendment provides any protections for an individual right to arms. Nonetheless, later opinions (e.g., *Warin*, 1976) cited *Cody* as supporting arms-bearing only as a collective right.

United States v. Johnson (1974): Challenging 18 U.S.C. §922 (g), Felon Transporting a Firearm

Major Henry Johnson, previously convicted of forgery in 1970, had purchased a .22-caliber handgun in Virginia in 1973 and then traveled with the pistol to Tennessee. Arrested and charged with violating 18 U.S.C. §922 (g)—"transporting a firearm in interstate commerce by a convicted felon"[75]—Johnson objected that the trial court had improperly instructed the jury about his forgery conviction. He argued that, under Virginia law, the conviction was a misdemeanor, not a felony. And, like Cody, he also challenged the constitutionality of §922 (g) on Second Amendment grounds.

The Fourth Circuit Court of Appeals authored a *per curiam* (i.e., an unsigned and unanimous) opinion.

In his appeal, Johnson noted that Virginia's forgery statute provided that an offender "be confined in the penitentiary not less than two years ... or in the discretion of the [court] ... be confined in jail not less than six months nor more than twelve months."[76] Sentenced only to jail for the forgery, Johnson contended that the decision reduced the character of his offense from a felony to a misdemeanor. Rejecting this argument, this court asserted, "whether forgery is a 'felony' or a "misdemeanor" is determined by the sentence lawfully possible ... and does not depend upon the sentence actually imposed .... Since Johnson was subject to confinement in the penitentiary for a term not to exceed ten years, he was not convicted of a 'misdemeanor,' even though he was given a lenient sentence."[77]

The court then addressed the Second Amendment issue,

> Johnson's argument that section 922(g) is an unconstitutional violation of his Second Amendment right to keep and bear arms is not new. See, e.g., *United States v. Miller (1939).* The courts have consistently held that the Second Amendment only confers a collective right of keeping and bearing arms which must bear a "reasonable relationship to the preservation or efficiency of a well regulated militia." Johnson presents no evidence that section 922(g) in any way affects the maintenance of a well regulated militia. See *Cody v. United States.*[78]

Dispensing with oral arguments, the court affirmed Johnson's conviction.

The court's interpretation of the Second Amendment as conferring only a collective right tied to the preservation of a militia exceeded the more ambiguous collective interpretation provided by Judge Bright in *Cody*, but cited *Cody* in support. While not inappropriate—the *Cody* opinion certainly is *supportive* of the collective right perspective—nuanced differences separating Second Amendment opinions are easily obscured by this citation process, and can suggest a greater judicial consensus around a specific interpretation of the right to arms than is actually present.[79]

United States v. Warin (1976): Challenging Firearms Registration Requirements of the Gun Control Act

Five years after its *Stevens* opinion, the Sixth Circuit Court of Appeals revisited the Second Amendment in *Warin*. As with *Stevens*, the legal issue centered on the constitutionality of certain provisions of the GCA-amended NFA requiring the registration of machine guns (i.e., 26 U.S.C. §§5861 (d) and 5871). Specifically, Francis Warin, a patent-holding engineer and firearms designer, had been convicted of possessing an unregistered 9-mm prototype submachine gun. Judge F. Pierce Lively, appointed to the federal judiciary by President Richard Nixon, authored the court's opinion.

Warin had argued in district court that submachine guns were firearms used by the United States military and had some reasonable relationship to the preservation and efficiency of the military. Further, quoting *Miller*, he contended that the implications of the *Miller* decision meant that ordinary military equipment contributing to the common defense (as opposed to nonmilitary arms such as short-barreled shotguns) *are* protected by the Second Amendment. Thus, as a member of the "sedentary militia," he had a right to possess any weapon having military capability, including a submachine gun, and his conviction violated the amendment.[80]

Judge Lively rejected Warin's argument. He noted,

> In *Miller*, the Supreme Court did not reach the question of the extent to which a weapon which is "part of ordinary military equipment" or whose "use could contribute to the common defense" may be regulated. In holding that the absence of evidence … precluded the trial court from quashing [Miller's] indictment on Second Amendment grounds, the Court did not hold the converse—that the Second Amendment is an absolute prohibition against all regulation of the manufacture, transfer and possession of any instrument capable of being used in military action.[81]

To further support his rejection of Warin's contention, Lively referenced *Cases*, *Tot*, and *Stevens*, as well as *Cody* and *Johnson*. He noted that, in light of these "applicative authoritative decisions, [it] is clear that the Second Amendment guarantees a collective rather than an individual right."[82] Lively then directly quoted the earlier *Stevens* ruling: "Since the Second Amendment right … applies only to the right of the State to maintain a militia and not to the individual's right to bear arms, there can be no serious claim to any express constitutional right of an individual to possess a firearm."[83]

Later in the opinion, he observed,

> Even where the Second Amendment is applicable, it does not constitute an absolute barrier to the congressional regulation of firearms. … *United States v. Tot* [stated that] "weapon bearing was never treated as anything like an absolute right by the common law. It was regulated by statute as to time and place …." There can be no question that an organized society which fails to regulate the importation, manufacture and transfer of the highly sophisticated lethal weapons in existence today does so at its peril. The requirement [to register a submachine gun] is a reasonable regulation for the maintenance of public order. … Furthermore, there is absolutely no evidence that a submachine gun in the hands of an individual "sedentary militia" member would have any, much less a "reasonable relationship to the preservation or efficiency of a well regulated militia." [*Miller* citation]. Thus, we conclude the defendant has no private right to keep and bear arms.[84]

In affirming the district court's judgment, Lively ended by noting that many arguments made by the defendant and by supporting *amicus curiae* briefs "are based on the erroneous supposition that the Second Amendment is concerned with the rights of individuals rather than those of the States or that defendant's automatic membership in the 'sedentary militia' of Ohio brings him within the reach of it guarantees."[85] Thus, Judge Lively dismissed Warin's attempt to frame Miller as partially supporting an "individual right" to arms, choosing only to stress the amendment's role in protecting the state's right to maintain a militia.

This presentation of the Second Amendment exclusively as a "collective right" is notable. Forcefully asserted, the opinion gave little consideration to the ambiguities in *Miller* and in earlier, more nuanced court interpretations. Similarly, limited analysis typified future gun case opinions.

United States v. Oakes (1977): Challenging Firearms Registration Requirements of the Gun Control Act

A year after the *Warin* opinion, the US Court of Appeals for the Tenth Circuit also adjudicated a machine gun violation and also concluded that the Second Amendment was a collective right. Specifically, the defendant, Ted Oakes, had been arrested and convicted of possessing an unregistered machine gun (prohibited under 26 U.S. §5861 (d)) after selling the weapon to a BATFE agent. The agent had posed as a firearms dealer supplying guns to domestic political groups. Oakes had met with the agent on numerous occasions, often inviting the agent into his home where they would discuss guns and politics. Oakes sold the agent firearms on seven different occasions, and one of these sales included the machine gun. Found guilty in district court, Oakes then contested his conviction on two constitutional grounds.[86] Chief Judge David Lewis, appointed to the federal judiciary by President Dwight Eisenhower, wrote the court's opinion.

In his appeal, Oakes argued that, since the agent entered his home seeking evidence of illegally possessed firearms, the agent violated Oakes's fourth amendment right against unlawful search and seizure. The Court rejected this argument, noting that the agent entered Oakes's home by invitation and took nothing that Oakes did not voluntarily give or sell. Citing the prior opinion of a similar drug case, Chief Judge Lewis quoted, "What a person knowingly exposes to the public even in his own home or office, is not a subject of Fourth Amendment protection."[87]

Turning to Oakes's Second Amendment challenge, Judge Lewis acknowledged Oakes's detailed historical analysis of the amendment, but he dismissed Oakes's conclusion—that is, that the analysis showed the amendment established every citizen's absolute right to keep arms. The judge noted,

> This broad conclusion has long been rejected. [*Miller* citation]. [Oakes] contends that, even if the second amendment is construed to guarantee the right to bear arms only to an organized militia, he comes within the scope of the amendment. He points out ... the state militia includes all 'able-bodied male citizens between the ages of twenty-one and forty-five years ...." He further points out that he is a member of "Posse Comitatus, a militia-type organization registered with the state of Kansas."[88]

Lewis continued,

> The purpose of the second amendment as stated by the Supreme Court [in *Miller*] was to preserve the effectiveness and assure the continuation of the state militia. The Court stated that the amendment must be interpreted and applied with that purpose in view. To apply the amendment so as to guarantee appellant's right to keep an unregistered firearm which has not been shown to have any connection to the militia, merely because he is technically a member of the Kansas militia, would be unjustifiable in terms of either logic or policy. This lack of justification is even more apparent when applied to appellant's membership in "Posse Comitatus" an apparently nongovernmental organization. We conclude, therefore, that this prosecution did not violate the second amendment.[89]

In rejecting Oakes's Second Amendment argument, Chief Judge Lewis's reliance on *Miller* alone to dismiss the contention is notable. He obviously saw no need to justify it further with additional citations. Further, taken as a representative group, the *Stevens, Warin, Cody, Johnson, and Oakes* adjudications—opinions mirroring the position of four different federal appeals courts—illustrate the federal judiciary's almost exclusive interpretation of the Second Amendment as a "collective right" four decades after the ambiguous *Miller* opinion.

1982–96: Ending the Century with *Miller*'s Continuing Impact

This pattern of relying on *Miller* to dismiss Second Amendment challenges to perceived infringements on an individual right to arms continued to dominate the judiciary throughout the next two decades. By the end of the 1970s, so prevalent was the collective perspective that even gun cases *not* raising Second Amendment issues sometimes contained references to this judicial conclusion.

For instance, in *United States v. Graves* (a 1977 Third Circuit Appeals Court adjudication), the court included a Second Amendment footnote, observing that "[The defendant] has not attempted to invoke the Second Amendment as a defense in the present prosecution. Even if he had, we would deem controlling the interpretation adopted in *Miller* and the cases following it."[90] Similarly, in a 1980 firearms case not otherwise centered on the Second Amendment (i.e., *Lewis v. United States*), the Supreme Court asserted (also in a footnote) that "these legislative restrictions on the use of firearms are neither based upon constitutionally suspect criteria, nor do they trench upon any constitutionally protected liberties. See *United States v. Miller.*"[91]

The three Second Amendment cases used to highlight this period revolve around gun issues seen earlier. The 1982 *Quilici v. Village of Morton Grove* case centers on a Second Amendment challenge to a municipal ordinance prohibiting handguns within the municipality. The two other cases focus on concealed-carry permit denials.

Thomas v. Members of City Council of Portland is a 1984 First Circuit Court of Appeals adjudication and the second, *Hickman v. Block*, is a 1996 Ninth Circuit opinion.

Quilici v. Village of Morton Grove (1982): Challenging a Handgun Possession Prohibition

In amending Ordinance No. 81–11 regulating firearms and other weapons, the Board of Trustees of Morton Grove, Illinois, prohibited the possession of bludgeons, blackjacks, metal knuckles, switchblade knives, and "any handgun, unless the same has been rendered permanently inoperative"[92] within the village. Victor Quilici objected to the ordinance in state court, but Morton Grove sent the case to the federal district court, where it was consolidated with two similar challenges. There, Quilici and the other plaintiffs argued that the ordinance violated Section 22 of Illinois' state constitution, as well as the Second, Ninth, and Fourteenth Amendments of the federal constitution. Wanting an order declaring the ordinance unconstitutional, the plaintiffs filed for summary judgment (i.e., a judicial decision using already presented statements and evidence to resolve the issue without going to trial).[93]

When the district court denied their motion, and granted summary judgment to Morton Grove instead, the plaintiffs appealed, sending the case to the Seventh Circuit Court of Appeals. There, Judge William Bauer, nominated to the circuit court by President Gerald Ford and later serving as its chief judge, authored the court's opinion. Judge Bauer began his analysis by first reviewing why the district court upheld the handgun ban's constitutionality.

Bauer noted that the district court emphasized three reasons in its assessment. First, the court argued that the ordinance in banning only certain kinds of arms was a valid exercise of Morton Grove's police power, and did not conflict with the state constitution's conditional right to keep and bear arms (i.e., "Subject only to the police power, the right of the individual citizen to keep and bear arms shall not be infringed."[94]). Second, citing *Presser*, the court observed that the right to arms guaranteed by the Second Amendment of the federal constitution was not incorporated by the Fourteenth Amendment and was thus inapplicable to Morton Grove. Finally, the court asserted that the Ninth Amendment does not include the right to possess handguns for self-defense.[95]

Judge Bauer then turned to his own analysis. Having noted the appellants' assertion that the state constitution prohibited a complete ban of any one kind of arm, Bauer remarked,

> Appellants concede that the phrase "subject to the police power" does not prohibit reasonable regulation of arms. … However, they maintain that no authority supports interpreting section 22 to permit a ban on the possession of handguns merely because alternative weapons are not also banned. … In contrast, Morton Grove alleges that "arms" is a general term [and] reads section 22 to guarantee the right to keep only some, but not all, arms …. It argues that the Ordinance

> passes constitutional muster because standard rifles and shotguns are [available] and Ordinance No. 81-11 does not ban these weapons.[96]

To resolve this issue, Bauer examined the original constitutional debates around Section 22. While the debates showed that handguns were within the class of arms protected, they also showed that Section 22 recognized only a narrow individual right to arms subject to substantial legislative control. Quoting the district court, Bauer observed, "[t]o the extent that one looks to the convention debate for assistance in reconciling the conflict between the right to arms and the exercise of police power, the debate clearly supports a narrow construction of the individual right."[97] Asserting that Section 22's plain language grants only the right to keep and bear arms—not handguns specifically—Bauer concluded, "We agree with the district court that the right to keep and bear arms in Illinois is so limited by the police power that a ban on handguns does not violate that right."[98]

Judge Bauer then considered whether the ordinance violated the Second Amendment of the federal constitution. The appellants had argued that the amendment protected a fundamental right to keep and bear arms which the state could not regulate, and to bolster this claim, they asserted that the *Presser* opinion in fact supported this position. They argued that the right to arms under *Presser* was an attribute of national citizenship and thus not subject to state restriction. Bauer disagreed, and quoted *Presser*: "[t]he Second Amendment declares that it shall not be infringed, but this ... means no more than it shall not be infringed by Congress. This is one of the amendments that has no other effect than to restrict the powers of the National government."[99]

Having anticipated just such an objection, the appellants had also argued that the Fourteenth Amendment had "implicitly incorporated" the entire Bill of Rights to apply to the states. Bauer dismissed this argument also, noting "their theory of implicit incorporation is wholly unsupported. The Supreme Court has specifically rejected the proposition that the entire Bill of Rights applies to the states through the fourteenth amendment. [Citations given]. Since we hold that the second amendment does not apply to the states, we need not consider the scope of its guarantee of the right to bear arms."[100]

Nonetheless, Judge Bauer proceeded to offer some analysis of the amendment's scope:

> Construing this language [of the amendment] according to its plain meaning, it seems clear that the right to bear arms is inextricably connected to the preservation of a militia. This is precisely the manner in which the Supreme Court interpreted the second amendment in *United States v. Miller* [Citation given], the only Supreme Court case specifically addressing that amendment's scope. There the Court held that the right to keep and bear arms extends only to those arms which are necessary to maintain a well regulated militia. In an attempt to avoid the *Miller* holding that the right to keep and bear arms exists only as it relates to protecting the public security, appellants argue that "[t]he fact that the right to keep and bear

> arms is joined with language expressing one of its purposes in no way permits a construction which limits or confines that right." [Citation given]. They offer no explanation for how they arrived at this conclusion.[101]

Continuing, Bauer observed, "Alternatively, they argue that handguns are military weapons. [Citation and footnote given]. Our reading of *Miller* convinces us that it does not support either of these theories. ... Under the controlling authority of *Miller*, we conclude that the right to keep and bear handguns is not guaranteed by the second amendment."[102] In a footnote, Judge Bauer noted, "A similar conclusion has been reached by numerous other courts. *United States v. Oakes ... United States v. Warin ... Cody v. United States ... Stevens v. United States*."[103]

Having concluded that the ordinance did not violate the Second Amendment, Bauer then considered whether it violated the Ninth Amendment (i.e., that the Constitution's listing of certain rights cannot be interpreted to deny other, unlisted rights retained by the people). Bauer observed,

> Appellants argue that, although the right to use commonly-owned arms for self-defense is not explicitly listed in the Bill of Rights, it is a fundamental right protected by the ninth amendment. Citing no authority ... they rely on the debates in the First Congress ... to establish that ... firearms for self-defense is an absolute and inalienable right .... Since appellants do not cite, and our research has not revealed, any Supreme Court case holding that any specific right is protected by the ninth amendment, appellants' argument has no legal significance. ... the fact remains that the Supreme Court has never embraced this theory.[104]

Concluding that the ordinance did not violate the state constitution or any of the federal amendments, Judge Bauer held that the ordinance was a "proper exercise of Morton Grove's police power" and affirmed the decision of the district court.[105]

The *Quilici* opinion is notable in illustrating the federal judiciary's continued view of the Second Amendment as a collective right. Despite indicating that the amendment did not apply to the states and thus did not warrant further consideration, Judge Bauer nevertheless *does* consider it further. In analyzing *Miller*, he made clear that the amendment did not protect a personal right to keep and bear a handgun and by extension (in citing *Oakes*, *Warin*, *Cody*, and *Stevens*) implicitly suggested the amendment may not protect a personal right to firearms at all.

Thomas v. City Council of Portland (1984): Challenging a Concealed-Carry Permit Denial

Peter Thomas had applied to the city of Portland, Maine, for a concealed-carry handgun permit, which the city denied. Arguing in district court, Thomas asserted that the disapproval infringed his Second Amendment rights, but the district court upheld the city's denial. Thomas then brought his case to the First Circuit Court of Appeals.[106]

In a short, one-page *per curiam* opinion, that court asserted,

> Established case law makes clear that the federal Constitution grants appellant no right to carry a concealed handgun. See, e.g., *United States v. Miller* [citation given] (second amendment applies only to weapons that have a "reasonable relationship to the preservation or efficiency of a well regulated militia."); *United States v. Oakes* … *United States v. Johnson* … *Presser v. Illinois* [Citations given] (second amendment confers rights as against activity by the "federal government only") … *Quilici v. Village of Morton Grove* … *Cases v. United States* … *United States v. Warin* [Citations given] (second amendment grants right to the state not the individual) … *Stevens v. United States.*[107]

After listing several more supporting citations, the court concluded, "The judgment of the district court, dismissing appellant's case, is *affirmed*."[108]

As with the *Quilici* opinion, the significance of *Thomas* from a Second Amendment perspective is the federal court's heavy reliance on (but only cursory discussion and analysis of) *Miller* and prior gun cases. In evaluating Thomas's claim to an individual right to arms, the First Circuit merely provided three one-sentence parenthetical remarks before dismissing his argument.

Hickman v. Block (1996): Challenging a "May-Issue" Permitting Policy

In a 1996 adjudication, the Ninth Circuit Appeals Court also invoked *Miller* when it let stand a concealed-carry permit denial. Douglas Hickman, a federally licensed firearms dealer and owner of a security alarm company, had applied for and been denied a concealed weapons permit by both the County of Los Angeles and the City of San Fernando. California at that time had a "may-issue" gun licensing approach, and in such jurisdictions the licensing authority (e.g., the county sheriff) is not obligated to issue a firearms permit, even if an individual meets all statutory requirements. The licensing authority typically has leeway in determining whether to grant a permit, and the authority may deny a permit if the applicant cannot show a "special need"—notably distinguishable from the general community—for one.

In Hickman's case, both jurisdictions had this "good cause" provision in their issuing policy, requiring an individual to show substantial evidence of an obvious and current life-threatening danger—one that law enforcement resources could not handle. The policy noted that no job classification in itself constituted "good cause" for the issuance of a license. Both jurisdictions determined that Hickman did not meet this standard and declined to issue a permit.

Hickman challenged the US District Court's summary dismissal of his case, and appealed to the US Circuit Court on Second Amendment grounds. He argued that the amendment obliges the states to regulate firearm possession and use in a "reasonable" manner. Judge Cynthia Hall, a Ronald Reagan nominee to the federal bench, authored the court's opinion.[109]

After reviewing the background of the case and the multiple avenues Hickman pursued to obtain a permit, Judge Hall summarized Hickman's appeal as a question of whether the Second Amendment "confers upon individual citizens standing to enforce the right to keep and bear arms."[110] She answered the question this way: "We follow our sister circuits in holding that the Second Amendment is a right held by the states, and does not protect the possession of a weapon by a private citizen. We conclude that Hickman can show no legal injury, and therefore lacks standing to bring this action."[111]

Hall continued,

> This case turns on ... whether Hickman has shown injury to an interest protected by the Second Amendment. We note at the outset that no individual has ever succeeded in demonstrating such injury in federal court. The seminal authority in this area continues to be *United States v. Miller* [Citation given]. ... The Court rejected [Miller's] hypothesis that the Second Amendment protected his possession of that weapon [i.e., a sawed-off shotgun]. Consulting the text and history of the amendment, the Court found that the right to keep and bear arms is meant solely to protect the right of the states to keep and maintain militia. ... Thus, it is only in furtherance of state security that 'the right of the people to keep and bear arms' is finally proclaimed.[112]

Hall next quoted from the *Warin* opinion, "[i]t is clear that the Second Amendment guarantees a collective rather than an individual right [Citation given]."[113] Then, after citing several other supporting cases (including the *Thomas* opinion), she concluded,

> Because the Second Amendment guarantees the right of the states to maintain armed militia, the states alone stand in the position to show legal injury when this right is infringed. ... Because Hickman has not sued to defend the state's right to keep an armed militia, he has failed to show "injury" as required by constitutional standing doctrine. Accordingly, we have no jurisdiction to hear his appeal.[114]

She affirmed the judgment of the district court.

Thus, by the end of the century and as *Hickman* illustrates, the notion of the Second Amendment as a *collective* right was firmly established in the federal judiciary. Relying first on the ambiguously reasoned *Miller* opinion, and then on follow-up opinions that cited *Miller* but overlooked its ambiguity, federal courts for over six decades interpreted the Second Amendment as protecting only a state's right to an efficient and effective militia. Nonetheless, despite the federal courts' interpretation, the amendment's nineteenth-century interpretation prevalent in state counts—as an individual right to arms with certain limits—did not simply disappear. As the next chapter shows, one federal court in the new century would return to this interpretation, as would the US Supreme Court.

Some Observations

The cases examined in this chapter sharply illustrate the changing judicial understanding of the Second Amendment. In these opinions, twentieth-century courts discard the interpretative strategy taken by nineteenth-century courts. Where these earlier courts acknowledge a private right to arms—but uphold limited restrictions on that right to insure community safety and security—twentieth-century courts, relying on *Miller*, simply dismiss the Second Amendment as not securing a private right at all.

The federal judiciary's substantial reliance on the *Miller* case is difficult to fathom. Although a Supreme Court opinion, the ruling itself is short, ambiguous, and poorly written. Its consideration of the Second Amendment is undeveloped and narrowly focused, and it never directly addresses the nature of the amendment, as either an individual or collective right. So how did such a deficient decision become so judicially pivotal?

As suggested in this chapter and Chapter 1, when the Supreme Court decided *Miller*, President Roosevelt—probably responding to the violence and mob shootings of that era—supported limiting firearms. His administration actively championed gun regulations, using the federal government's commercial and taxing powers to do so—for example, the NFA and the FFA. This entrance of the federal government into a regulatory arena previously the exclusive domain of the states was not lost on a presumably amenable Supreme Court, or on the federal judiciary as a whole. The cursory examinations given *Miller* in later federal gun cases—justified now by precedent—insured that the arguable "collective right" interpretation of the Second Amendment became (for a time) the accepted, "settled" interpretation.

The cases in the chapter also suggest how *Miller* and lack of incorporation helped reduce the Second Amendment to "second class citizenship" relative to the other protections safeguarded by the Bill of Rights. As a collective right merely supporting the states' ability to arm and train an organized militia, its legal—and practical—influence on the lives of individual citizens was minimal. Individuals would have no reason to ever challenge a state's right to arm a militia, and the amendment's collective right construal effectively invalidated any other type of Second Amendment claim.

Finally, some irony exists in Judge Bauer's *Quilici* assessment that the Second Amendment "clearly preserved" only a militia-based, collective right. In that case, the appellants argued that the prefatory clause of the Second Amendment—regarding the need for a well-regulated militia—expressed only *one* of the Amendment's purposes. They urged the court to recognize that "language expressing one of its purposes in no way permits a construction that limits or confines" the right to arms. Dismissing this assertion, the judge observed, "They offer no explanation for how they arrived at this conclusion." But in *Heller*, Justice Scalia would make (and support) precisely the same argument about the prefatory clause in rejecting the collective right interpretation of the amendment.

Notes

1 *Salina v. Blaksley, 72 Kan. 230, 83 P. 619, 3 L.R.A. (N.S.) 168, 115 Am. St. Rep. 196, 7 Am. & Eng. Ann. Cas. 925 (1905).* At https://guncite.com/court/state/83p619.html.

2 Donald Campbell, *America's Gun Wars: A Cultural History of Gun Control in the United States* (Santa Barbara, CA: Praeger, 2019), pp. 31–43. Also, Lee Kennett and

James Anderson, *The Gun in America* (Westport, CT: Greenwood Press, 1975), pp. 165–86.

3 *Re: Brickey, Idaho Supreme Court, 1902.* At https:// handgunlaw.us/documents/agopinions/IDSupremeCtBrickeyRulingOnOpenCarry1902.pdf.

4 Ibid.

5 Ibid.

6 Ibid.

7 Ibid.

8 Ibid.

9 *Salina v. Blaksley, 72 Kan. 230, 83 P. 619, 3 L.R.A. (N.S.) 168, 115 Am. St. Rep. 196, 7 Am. & Eng. Ann. Cas. 925 (1905).* At https://guncite.com/court/state/83p619.html.

10 Ibid.

11 *Commonwealth v. Murphy (Mass.) [166Mass. 171,] 44 N.E. 138, 32, L.R.A. 606 (1896).* At https://guncite.com/court/state/166ma171.html.

12 *Salina v. Blaksley.*

13 *Strickland v. State, 137 Ga. 1, 72 S. E. 260 (1911).* At https://cite.case.law/ga/137/1/.

14 Ibid.

15 Ibid.

16 Ibid.

17 Ibid.

18 Ibid.

19 Ibid.

20 Ibid.

21 Ibid.

22 *State v. Kerner, 181 N.C. 574, 107 S.E. 222 (1921).* At https://guncite.com/court/state/107se222.html.

23 Ibid.

24 Ibid.

25 Ibid.

26 Ibid.

27 Ibid.

28 Ibid.

29 Ibid.

30 Ibid.

31 Ibid.

32 *United States v. Adams, 11 F. Supp. 216 (S.D. Fla. 1935).* At https://law.justia.com/cases/federal/district-courts/FSupp/11/216/1975956/.

33 Soon after this case, Ritter would achieve some notoriety for questionable financial dealings. He would be impeached and removed from office in 1936, "for bringing the judiciary into disrepute." See https://www.govinfo.gov/content/pkg/GPO-HPREC-DESCHLERS-V3/pdf/GPO-HPREC-DESCHLERS-V3-5-5-5.pdf.

34 Ibid.

35 Ibid.

36 Ibid.

37 Ibid.

38 See Brian Frye, "The Peculiar Story of United States v. Miller," *NYU Journal of Law & Liberty*, 3:48 (2008): pp. 61–5. At http://www.law.nyu.edu/sites/default/files/ECM_PRO_060964.pdf.

39 Adam Winkler, "Franklin Roosevelt: The Father Of Gun Control," *New Republic*, December 18, 2012. At https://newrepublic.com/article/111266/franklin-roosevelt-father-gun-control.
40 Frye, "The Peculiar Story of United States v. Miller."
41 *United States v. Miller, 307, U.S. 174 (1939*). At https://www.law.cornell.edu/supremecourt/text/307/174.
42 Frye, "The Peculiar Story of United States v. Miller."
43 See James Clark McReynolds, CQ Press, Supreme Court Collection (n.d.). At https://library.cqpress.com/scc/document.php?id=bioenc-427-18168-979398&v=939eb8666c2b1160.
44 *United States v. Miller, 307, U.S. 174 (1939*).
45 Frye, "The Peculiar Story of United States v. Miller," p. 67.
46 *United States v. Miller, 307, U.S. 174 (1939*).
47 Ibid.
48 Ibid.
49 Ibid.
50 Ibid.
51 Ibid.
52 Ibid.
53 *United States v. Tot, 131 F. 2d 261—Circuit Court of Appeals, 3rd Circuit 1942.* At https://scholar.google.com/scholar_case?case=9144907181119218157&q=U.S.+v+Tot&hl=en&as_sdt=4003.
54 Ibid.
55 Ibid.
56 Ibid.
57 Ibid.
58 Tot's appeal also presented a fourth contention. He claimed to have had possession of the firearm long before the FFA's enactment, making that statute's presumption of his receiving the gun in violation of the FFA unsupportable, and thus warranting a directed dismissal of the indictment. Judge Goodrich, noting that the district court rejected this argument, also rejected it. Tot then appealed his conviction to the US Supreme Court in 1943. This court ruled that the government's presumption that Tot obtained the gun after passage of the FFA—based solely on the fact that he possessed it—was unsustainable and a violation of the due process clauses of the Fifth and Fourteenth Amendments. On this basis, the court reversed Tot's conviction.
59 *Cases v. United States, 131 F.2d 916 (1st Cir. 1942)*. At https://law.justia.com/cases/federal/appellate-courts/F2/131/916/1511728/.
60 Ibid.
61 Ibid.
62 Ibid.
63 Ibid.
64 Ibid.
65 Ibid.
66 Ibid.
67 Ibid.
68 Ibid.
69 Donald Campbell, *America's Gun Wars: A Cultural History of Gun Control in the United States* (Santa Barbara, CA: Praeger, 2019), pp. 54–6 and 75.

70 *Stevens v. United States 440 F.2d 144 (1971)*. At https://casetext.com/case/stevens-v-united-states-12.
71 Ibid.
72 Ibid.
73 *Cody v. United States 460 F.2d 34 (8th Cir. 1972)*. At https://casetext.com/case/cody-v-united-states-2.
74 Ibid.
75 *United States v. Johnson 497 F.2d 548 (4th Cir. 1974)*. At https://casetext.com/case/united-states-v-johnson-167.
76 Ibid.
77 Ibid.
78 Ibid.
79 Justice Scalia, in *Heller*, was perhaps indirectly alluding to this loss of nuance when he referred to the "hundreds of judges" who over-read *Miller*.
80 *U.S. v. Warin, 530 F.2d 103 (6th Cir.), cert. denied, 426 U.S. 948 (1976)*. At https://guncite.com/court/fed/530f2d103.html.
81 Ibid.
82 Ibid.
83 Ibid.
84 Ibid.
85 Ibid.
86 *U.S. v. Oakes, 564 F.2d 384 (1977)*. At https://casetext.com/case/united-states-v-oakes-3.
87 Ibid.
88 Ibid.
89 Ibid.
90 *United States v. Graves, 554 F.2d 65 (1977)*. At https://cite.case.law/f2d/554/65/.
91 *Lewis v. United States, 445 U.S. 55 (1980)*. At https://supreme.justia.com/cases/federal/us/445/55/.
92 *Quilici v. Village of Morton Grove (1982) 695 F.2d 261*. At https://casetext.com/case/quilici-v-village-of-morton-grove.
93 Ibid.
94 Ibid.
95 Ibid.
96 Ibid.
97 Ibid.
98 Ibid.
99 Ibid.
100 Ibid.
101 Ibid.
102 Ibid.
103 Ibid.
104 Ibid.
105 Ibid.
106 *Thomas v. Members of the City Council of Portland, 730 F.2d 41 (1984)*. At https://cite.case.law/f2d/730/41/.
107 Ibid.
108 Ibid.

109 *Hickman v. Block 81 F.3d 98 (9th Cir. 1996).* At https://casetext.com/case/hickman-v-block.

110 Ibid.

111 Ibid.

112 Ibid.

113 Ibid.

114 Ibid. In a final footnote, Hall added, "Moreover, even if we determined that Hickman had standing to sue for violation of the Second Amendment, his suit would nevertheless fail because the Second Amendment is not incorporated into the Bill of Rights."

4

The Twenty-First Century: The *Heller* Resolution

The real purpose of Second Amendment was to insure that state armies—the militia—would be maintained for the defense of the state.

Attributed to Chief Justice Warren Burger[1]

As for the "hundreds of judges" who have relied on … Miller: If so, they over-read Miller. And their erroneous reliance upon an uncontested and unreasoned case cannot nullify … the true meaning of the right to keep and bear arms.

Associate Justice Antonin Scalia[2]

Coming into the twenty-first century, the idea that the Second Amendment protected only a collective, militia-based right to arms dominated gun adjudications in the federal districts. Without further explicit direction from the US Supreme Court, and with the murky 1939 *Miller* decision as a foundational basis, federal courts simply followed the accumulated precedents that had arisen in their districts over the intervening sixty years. The nineteenth-century interpretation of the amendment—as an individual right to keep and bear arms, subject to reasonable regulations for public safety—received scant judicial endorsement or support. But in 2001, this earlier view of the Second Amendment as a guarantee of an individual right reemerged in a Fifth Circuit case, *United States v. Emerson*. After examining *Miller* in detail, and analyzing the text and history of the amendment in depth, this court rejected the collective right view in favor of the individual right interpretation.

Despite *Emerson's* meticulous arguments, the federal judiciary nonetheless regarded the opinion as a judicial outlier, reflecting a flawed reading of the amendment. About a year later, in 2002, the Ninth Circuit specifically rebuffed *Emerson's* "individual right" interpretation, and provided in *Silveira v. Lockyear* a counter-point analysis that strongly upheld the correctness of the collective right perspective. Not surprisingly, the federal judiciary chose to follow *Silveira* rather than *Emerson* in their adjudications and continued to interpret the amendment as a collective right, as demonstrated by two representative Sixth Circuit opinions, in 2003 (i.e., *United States v. Bournes*) and in 2006 (i.e., a second *United States v. Warin*).

However, in 2007, the US Court of Appeals for the District of Columbia adjudicated a case (*Parker v. District of Columbia*) that, like *Emerson*, also concluded that the Second Amendment protected an individual right to arms.

On appeal, the US Supreme Court reviewed the *Parker* case—now as *District of Columbia v. Heller*—and established (as *Emerson* and *Parker* had argued) that the amendment's appropriate interpretation was as an individual right subject to reasonable regulation. While this landmark decision confirmed that the amendment protected an individual right, *Heller* entrusted the determination of "reasonable regulation" to future adjudications.

Further, given the amendment's lack of incorporation, the opinion left open its degree of applicability to state-imposed gun restrictions. Thus, despite broadly resolving the individual-versus-collective right issue, the opinion declined to address the amendment's boundaries and limitations. Lower courts—using different levels of scrutiny in assessing gun statutes and regulations—arrived at varying conclusions regarding the constitutionality of potential infringements, and these differing opinions continued to require Supreme Court clarification. The first of these post-*Heller* clarifications came in 2010, with a second landmark adjudication—*McDonald v. City of Chicago*. With this opinion, the court incorporated the Second Amendment, making it applicable to the states. Thus, by the end of the new century's first decade, the country's foremost gun issues that had beleaguered the American judiciary for more than a half-century were—at least in broad outline—finally resolved.

The chapter divides the examination of the seven cases noted above into three sections. The first section reviews *Emerson* and *Silveira*, the cases that initially set the stage for the later *Heller* decision. The second section also contains two cases—*Bournes* and *Warin II*—reflecting the continuing impact of the collective right interpretation in federal courts. The last section examines *Parker* (the case that became *Heller*), *Heller* (the case establishing the Second Amendment as reflecting an individual right), and *McDonald* (the case that incorporated the Second Amendment as applicable to the states). As pivotal adjudications, the *Heller* and *McDonald* opinions both receive extended examination.

2001–2: The Split in Circuit Courts

At the start of the new century, two federal courts came to starkly different conclusions about the nature of the Second Amendment. In 2001, the Fifth Circuit Court of Appeals in *Emerson* reviewed a district court ruling that had adopted an "individual right" interpretation of the Second Amendment and had dismissed the defendant's indictment for gun possession while under a temporary restraining order. The circuit court upheld the state's appeal but, going against precedent, concluded that the lower court's assessment of the amendment as guaranteeing an individual right to arms was, in fact, correct. However, a year later, the Ninth Circuit Court of Appeals, in *Silveira*, rejected a challenge to California's 1989 Assault Weapons Control Act (AWCA) on the grounds that the Second Amendment was a collective right, and thus the plaintiff had no standing to sue. The Supreme Court refused a request to review this case, but with two circuit courts holding two opposed views of the amendment, it was clear that the court would eventually have to resolve the conflict.

United States v. Emerson (2001): Challenging Unlawful Possession of a Pistol

Dr. Timothy Emerson, under a temporary restraining order during his divorce proceedings, had been indicted for unlawfully possessing a Beretta pistol while subject to the restraining order. Such possession violated 18 U.S.C. §922 (g) (8) (C) (ii). This statute made it unlawful "for any person who is subject to a court order that includes a finding that such person represents a credible threat to the physical safety of such intimate partner or child ... to ship or transport ... or possess ...any firearm or ammunition ... which has been shipped or transported in interstate or foreign commerce."[3]

In district court, Emerson moved to dismiss the indictment, arguing that the statute violated the Second Amendment and the Due Process Clause of the Fifth Amendment. He also contended that the statute was an improper exertion of federal power under the Commerce Clause, and unconstitutionally usurped powers reserved to the states by the Tenth Amendment. District Judge Sam Cummings rejected these last two contentions, but accepted Emerson's Second and Fifth Amendments arguments. Regarding the Second Amendment specifically, the district judge noted (after conducting a textual and historical analysis of the amendment),

> It is absurd that a boilerplate state court order can collaterally and automatically extinguish a law-abiding citizen's Second Amendment rights .... That such a routine civil order has such extensive consequences totally attenuated from divorce proceedings makes the statute unconstitutional. There must be a limit to government regulation on lawful firearm possession. This statute exceeds that limit, and therefore it is unconstitutional.[4]

The judge dismissed the indictment, and the government then appealed the dismissal.

Judge William Garwood—appointed to the US Court of Appeals, Fifth Circuit by President Ronald Reagan—received the state's appeal and wrote the court's opinion. After dismissing Emerson's preliminary contentions that the language of 922(g)(8)(C)(ii) was problematic and ambiguous, Judge Garwood turned to the district court's analysis of Emerson's Fifth Amendment Due Process argument. The district court had noted that (1) Emerson did not know his possession of a firearm while subject to the restraining order was a crime, (2) had no reason to suspect that the order would criminalize otherwise lawful behavior, (3) as a defendant representing himself (i.e., "*pro se*"), Emerson would have had difficulty discovering the specific provisions of the statute; and (4) possessing a firearm is not inherently evil. Based on these considerations, the district court had concluded that Emerson's due process rights were in fact violated.[5]

Garwood disagreed. Citing various federal court precedents indicating that "ignorance of the law is no excuse," and observing that Emerson had signed BATF Form 4473 in purchasing the Beretta pistol—a form indicating it is illegal for individuals under restraining orders to possess firearms—he determined that the district court had erred in granting Emerson's motion to dismiss on due process grounds. Regarding Emerson's Commerce Clause argument, citing relevant precedents, Garwood decided that the district court had correctly rejected this argument to dismiss. Finally, since the circuit court brief contained no claim that Emerson's Tenth Amendment rights were violated, Garwood considered that argument abandoned.[6]

Judge Garwood then undertook an analysis of Emerson's Second Amendment argument. He noted that "the district court held that the Second Amendment recognizes the right of individual citizens to own and possess firearms … [but] [t]he government opines that *stare decisis* requires us to reverse the district's court embrace of the individual rights model."[7] Garwood observed that

> courts and commentators have offered … three different interpretations of the Second Amendment. The first is that the Second Amendment does not apply to individuals; rather it merely recognizes the right of a state to arm its militia …. Proponents of the next model admit that the Second Amendment recognizes some limited species of individual right. However, this supposedly 'individual' right to bear arms can only be exercised by members of a functioning, organized state militia …. The third model is simply that the Second Amendment recognizes the right of individuals to keep and bear arms. This is the view advanced by Emerson and adopted by the district court.[8]

To answer the question of whether the district court erred in adopting the individual rights model, Garwood first examined the *Miller* precedent. He noted, "The government steadfastly maintains that the Supreme Court's decision in *United States v. Miller… (1939)* mandated acceptance of the collective rights or sophisticated collective rights model, and rejection of the individual rights or standard model …. We disagree."[9] After analyzing the details of the *Miller* opinion, Garwood declared,

> We conclude that *Miller* does not support the government's collective rights or sophisticated collective rights approach to the Second Amendment. Indeed, to the extent that *Miller* sheds light on the matter it cuts against the government's position. … However, we do not proceed on the assumption that *Miller* actually accepted an individual rights … interpretation of the Second Amendment. Thus, *Miller* itself does not resolve the issue. We turn, therefore, to an analysis of history and wording of the Second Amendment for guidance.[10]

Before continuing, Garwood noted that most other circuit courts had rejected the "individual rights" interpretation, but that "it respectfully appears to us that all or almost all of these opinions have done so on the erroneous assumption that *Miller* resolved the issue or without sufficient articulated examination of the history and text of the Second Amendment."[11] After conducting his own examination of the amendment's text—the meaning and implications of "people," "bear arms," and "keep arms" in the amendment's substantive guarantee—he concluded that "Taken as a whole, the text of the Second Amendment's substantive guarantee is not suggestive of a collective rights or sophisticated collective rights interpretation."[12]

Similarly, in examining the amendment's preamble—referencing a well-regulated militia and its connection to the security of a free state—he concluded that

> the preamble implies that the substantive guarantee is one which tends to enable, promote or further the existence, continuation or effectiveness of that "well-regulated Militia" which is "necessary to the security of a free State." Accordingly, the preamble does not support an interpretation of the amendment's substantive guarantee in accordance with the collective rights or sophisticated collective rights model, as such an interpretation is contrary to the plain meaning of the text of the guarantee, its placement within the Bill of Rights and the wording of the other articles thereof and of the original Constitution as a whole.[13]

Closing his textual analysis, Garwood observed,

> Perhaps the most accurate conclusion one can reach with any confidence is that the core meaning of the Second Amendment is a populist/republican/federalism one: Its central object is to arm "We the People" so that ordinary citizens can participate in the collective defense .... But it does so not through directly protecting a right on the part of the states ... to arm the populace as they see fit. Rather, the amendment achieves its central purpose by assuring that the federal government may not disarm individual citizens without some unusually strong justification .... That assurance in turn is provided through recognizing a right (admittedly of uncertain scope) on the part of individuals to possess and use firearms in defense of themselves and their homes.[14]

Turning to a historical analysis of the amendment, Judge Garwood then provided an account of the Federal Convention of 1787, including why the Anti-Federalists wanted the US Constitution to include a bill of rights, and why the Federalists believed such a bill unnecessary and redundant. Moving on to the Constitution's ratification, Garwood noted how numerous states proposed constitutional amendments—including the right to keep and bear arms—and refused to ratify the Constitution unless these amendments were included. Reviewing delegate debates and popular exchanges among prominent Americans regarding a bill of rights and keeping arms, Garwood pointed out that "Extreme Anti-Federalists ... would not be placated by mere recognition ... of the right of the people to keep and bear arms. ... [They] simply rejected the Federalists repeated arguments that there was no need to worry ... as long as individuals were armed."[15]

Finally, Judge Garwood considered the writings of noted nineteenth-century constitutional scholars—St. George Tucker, William Rawle, Justice Joseph Story, and Thomas Cooley—and noted that they all "recognized that the Second Amendment guarantees the right of individual Americans to possess and carry firearms."[16] Ending his analysis, Garwood asserted, "The history we have recounted largely speaks for itself. ...[W]e find nothing inconsistent with the conclusion that as ultimately proposed by

Congress and ratified by the states [the Second Amendment] was understood and intended in accordance with the individual rights model."[17]

For Timothy Emerson, Garwood's analysis—agreeing with the district court that the Second Amendment protected an individual right to privately keep and bear their own firearms—was a hollow victory.[18] Garwood also concluded that the temporary restraining order was sufficient—if only minimally so—to justify the deprivation of Emerson's Second Amendment rights. Thus, the circuit court reversed the district court's dismissal and upheld Emerson's original indictment. Nonetheless, Emerson's case established—albeit only for states in the Fifth Circuit—that the Second Amendment protected an *individual* right. One year later, *Silveira v. Lockyer* disputed this view.

Silveira v. Lockyer (2002): Challenging California's "Assault Weapons" Ban

In this case, Sean Silveira contested California's Roberti-Roos Assault Weapons Control Act (AWCA). Passed in 1989 after an elementary school shooting in Stockton, California, killed six and wounded twenty-nine, the AWCA was the nation's first legislative prohibition limiting certain assault-styled rifles, and it became the model for a similar federal ban on such firearms about five years later. The statute made it a felony to possess, sell, transfer, make, or import into California any of the identified semiautomatic firearms without a permit.[19]

While the statute contained a grandfather clause allowing individuals already owning such firearms to keep them, owners were required to register the rifles with the state's Department of Justice and had to abide by significant restrictions on their use. The legislature justified the ban—initially involving about forty firearms models—noting that the guns' high firing rate and high cartridge capacity posed a danger to ordinary citizens that significantly outweighed their use in legitimate sport or recreational shooting.[20]

In a 1999 amendment to the AWCA, California increased the number of banned guns but allowed both active and retired law enforcement officers to own and use such firearms. At that point, Silveira and eight other individuals sued the state, arguing that the AWCA requirements violated their Second Amendment rights, and that the active and retired law officer exemptions violated the Fourteenth Amendment's Equal Protection Clause of the plaintiffs who were not active or retired police officers.[21]

Judge Stephen Reinhardt, elevated to the federal judiciary by President Carter and known as the "liberal lion" of the Ninth Circuit,[22] authored the court's opinion. Given that he regarded the Second Amendment as a "relatively obscure constitutional provision [that has] attracted little judicial or scholarly attention,"[23] Judge Reinhardt's opinion is noteworthy both for its detailed analysis of the amendment's scope and for its systematic consideration of the historical factors and legal precedents making the amendment controversial.

Reinhardt's analysis, paralleling Judge Garwood's approach in *Emerson*, noted that

> three principal schools of thought [have formed] the basis for the [controversy]. The first ... the "traditional individual rights" model, holds that the Second

> Amendment guarantees to individual private citizens a fundamental right to possess and use firearms for any purpose at all, subject only to limited government regulation. ... The second view ... the "limited individual rights" model [holds that] individuals maintain a constitutional right to possess firearms insofar as such possession bears a reasonable relationship to militia service. The third, a wholly contrary view, commonly called the "collective rights" model, asserts that the Second Amendment right to "bear arms" guarantees the right of the people to maintain effective state militias, but does not provide any type of individual right to own or possess weapons. Under this [model], the federal and state governments have the full authority to enact prohibitions and restrictions on the use and possession of firearms, subject only to generally applicable constitutional constraints, such as due process, equal protection and the like.[24]

Reinhardt further noted,

> Long the dominant view of the Second Amendment, and widely accepted by the federal courts, the collective rights model has recently come under strong criticism from individual rights advocates. After conducting a full analysis of the amendment, its history, and its purpose, we affirm our conclusion in *Hickman v. Block* that it is the collective rights model which provides the best interpretation of the Second Amendment.[25]

In buttressing this conclusion, Reinhardt referenced an array of additional opinions, including the *Miller* and *Lewis* Supreme Court decisions. He characterized the *Miller* opinion thusly,

> The Supreme Court's most extensive treatment of the amendment is a somewhat cryptic discussion in *United States v. Miller*. ... As a result of its [negative] phrasing ... the Miller Court's opinion stands only for the proposition that the possession of certain weapons is not protected, and offers little guidance as to what rights the Second Amendment does protect. ... What *Miller* does strongly imply, however, is that the Supreme Court rejects the traditional individual rights view.[26]

Similarly, in discussing a footnote referencing *Miller* in *Lewis* (an opinion that rejected a Fifth Amendment defense against a felon-in-possession conviction), Reinhardt again concluded that, despite the negative phrasing of its statements (indicating what the amendment does not protect), "*Lewis* does, however, reinforce the strong implication in *Miller* that the Court rejects the traditional individual rights model."[27] Reinhardt further noted,

> Our court, like [almost] every other court of appeals ... has interpreted *Miller* as rejecting the traditional individual rights view. [But] Like the other courts, we reached our conclusion ... on the basis of the rather cursory discussion in *Miller* ... [and] Appellants contend that we misread *Miller* in *Hickman*. They point out

> that … *Miller* … fails to provide much reasoning in support of its conclusion. We agree that our determination in *Hickman* that *Miller* endorsed the collective rights position is open to serious debate. We also agree that the entire subject of the meaning of the Second Amendment deserves more consideration than we, or the Supreme Court, have thus far been able (or willing) to give it.[28]

Judge Reinhardt then acknowledged that, since publication of the *Hickman* opinion, the Fifth Circuit Court of Appeals had rendered a contrary decision, concluding in *United States v. Emerson* that the Second Amendment confirms an *individual* right to keep and bear arms. Reinhardt further noted that the position of the government, as conveyed by the Solicitor General to the Supreme Court, reflected a traditional "individual right" interpretation: "the current position of the United States is that the Second Amendment more broadly protects the rights of individuals … to possess and bear their own firearms, subject to reasonable restrictions."[29]

The *Emerson* court had based its reasoning on a textual analysis of the amendment itself and on pertinent scholarly, historical, and legal materials. Adopting a similar approach, Reinhardt also investigated the amendment's text and structure, and the historical context surrounding it. But contrary to *Emerson*, and contrary to the plaintiffs' contention that the court had misread *Miller* in *Hickman*, Reinhardt's extended analysis determined that

> the conclusion we reached in *Hickman* was correct. Appellants contend that the California Assault Weapons Control Act and its 1999 revisions violate their Second Amendment rights. We unequivocally reject this contention. We conclude that although the text and structure of the amendment, standing alone, do not conclusively resolve the question of its meaning, when we give the text its most plausible reading and consider the amendment in light of the historical context … we are compelled to reaffirm the collective rights view we adopted in *Hickman*: The amendment protects the people's right to maintain an effective state militia, and does not establish an individual right to own or possess firearms for personal or other use.[30]

Reinhardt continued,

> What renders the language and structure of the amendment particularly striking is the existence of a prefatory clause, a syntactical device that is absent from all other provisions of the Constitution, including the nine other provisions of the Bill of Rights. Our analysis thus must address not only the meaning of each of the two clauses … but the unique relationship that exists between them. The first or prefatory clause … sets forth the amendment's purpose and intent. An important aspect of ascertaining that purpose … is determining the import of the term "militia." … [T]he Fifth Circuit [has] taken the position that the term "militia" was meant to refer to all citizens, and, therefore, that the first clause simply restates the second in more specific terms. … Relying on their definition of "militia," they

> conclude the prefatory clause was intended to simply reinforce the grant of an individual right that they assert is made by the second clause. … If militia refers, as the Fifth Circuit suggests, to all persons in a state, rather than to the state military entity, the first clause would have one meaning—a meaning that would support the concept of traditional individual rights. If the term refers … to the entity ordinarily identified by that designation, the state-created and -organized military force, it would likely be necessary to attribute a considerably different meaning to the first clause … and to the amendment as a whole.[31]

After reviewing linguistic and other evidence supporting the argument that the term "militia" refers to a state military force, Judge Reinhardt concluded that the prefatory clause

> declares the importance of state militias to the security of the various free states within the confines of their newly structured constitutional relationship. … [W]e now turn to the meaning of the second clause …. We consider it highly significant … that the second clause does not purport to protect the right to "possess" or "own" arms, but rather to "keep and bear" arms. This choice of words is important because the phrase "bear arms" is a phrase that customarily relates to a military function.[32]

Citing historical evidence that the term "bear arms" generally referred to the carrying of arms in military service and not to the private use of arms for personal purposes, Reinhardt asserted, "Thus the use of the phrase 'bear arms' … strongly suggests that the right that the Second Amendment seeks to protect is the right to carry arms in connection with military service."[33]

Reinhardt continued,

> When the second clause is read in light of the first … we believe the most plausible construction of the Second Amendment is that it seeks to ensure the existence of effective state militias in which the people may exercise their right to bear arms, and forbids the federal government to interfere with such exercise. … In the end, however,… we would be reluctant to say that the text and structure alone establish with certainty which of the various views is correct. Fortunately, we have available … other important sources … includ[ing] records that reflect the historical context in which the amendment was adopted … significant portions of the contemporary debates relating to the adoption.[34]

Reinhardt then reviewed the colonies' distrust of the Crown's standing army; the debates within the Constitutional Convention regarding the proper balance between state and federal control over military matters; and the concerns among Anti-Federalists that if the federal Congress organized, armed, and disciplined the militia, "Congress would also have the implied power to disarm the state militias—and thus the people as well."[35]

Judge Reinhardt ended his analysis of the Second Amendment by asserting that text, history, and precedent all sustained the collective rights view of the amendment:

> We affirm our earlier adherence to the collective rights interpretation of the Second Amendment .... The historical record makes it equally plain that the amendment was not adopted in order to afford rights to individuals with respect to private gun ownership or possession. ... Thus, we hold that the Second Amendment imposes no limitation on California's ability to enact legislation regulating or prohibiting the possession or use of firearms, including dangerous weapons such as assault weapons. Plaintiffs lack standing to assert a Second Amendment claim, and their challenge to the Assault Weapons Control Act fails.[36]

Judge Reinhardt's analysis of the Second Amendment provided the federal judiciary its most robust justification for a "collective right" interpretation of the amendment; this offered a counter-point to the equally detailed "individual right" interpretation presented in *Emerson*. These two incompatible views coexisted in the country's legal system for several years and, during this period, federal courts continued to see the amendment as guaranteeing a collective right.

2002–6: The Collective Right Interpretation Continues

The *Emerson* opinion did not establish a precedent that federal courts outside the Fifth region had to follow. Nonetheless, the opinion offered the judiciary an alternative to the "collective right" interpretation of the Second Amendment that had dominated the courts since *Miller*. However, as two representative opinions (*United States v. Bournes* in 2003 and *United States v. Warin* in 2006) show, *Emerson*'s actual judicial impact was limited. Both cases deal with Second Amendment objections to particular registration requirements of the National Firearms Act, and in each, the court adopted a collective right view of the amendment in rejecting the defendant's argument.

United States v. Bournes (2003): Challenging Unregistered Machine Gun Violations

After the federal district court denied his motion to dismiss his unregistered firearms violation, Robert Bournes appealed his indictment contending that the statute (26 U.S.C. §5861 (d)) violated his right to bear arms under the Second Amendment and that his conviction violated his right to due process because he could not comply with its terms.[37] Judge Martha Daughtrey, nominated to the Sixth Circuit Court of Appeals by President Bill Clinton, authored the court's opinion.

Involved with certain militant groups in Michigan, Bournes had purchased parts and built a Sten-type 9-mm machine gun, as well as a .30-caliber belt-fed, bipod-mounted machine gun. In January of 1998, a confidential informant working for the Bureau of Alcohol, Tobacco, and Firearms brought an undercover ATF agent to Bournes's residence, where Bournes showed off the two machine guns and later let the agent fire the fully automatic weapons. In March, ATF agents executed a search warrant and confiscated the machine guns. In May, Bournes made some efforts to register the weapons, but lacking the appropriate license for manufacturing automatic firearms, was unable to do so.[38]

A year later, in May of 1999, a federal grand jury indicted Bournes for possession of unregistered firearms in violation of 26 U.S.C. §5861 (d). After the indictment, Bournes again attempted to register the machine guns. When this failed, he moved to dismiss the indictment on several grounds. He argued, first, that there was no grounds for federal involvement, since his possession of the machine guns was not related to interstate commerce. Second, as a member of the Michigan Militia Corps Wolverines, he had a Second Amendment right to possess the firearms. Third, the federal government prevented him from registering the guns, and thus could not prosecute him for failing to do so; and finally, 26 U.S.C. §5861 (d) and 18 U.S.C. §922 (o)—provisions prohibiting the transfer or possession of machine guns—violate the Second Amendment by banning all machine guns. The district court denied his motion to dismiss the indictment, leading to his appeal.[39]

Bournes limited his appeal to just two contentions: that the statutes violated his Second Amendment right to bear arms; and that his conviction violated his right to due process because he could not comply with the statutes' terms. First addressing Bournes's Second Amendment argument, Judge Daughtrey cited *United States v. Warin* (Sixth Circuit, 1976). She observed,

> In reviewing [a Second Amendment] claim, we have held … that "the Second Amendment guarantees a collective rather than an individual right." Accordingly, "there can be no serious claim to any express constitutional right of an individual to possess a firearm." *Stevens v. United States* [Citation provided]. [Further], we have reaffirmed *Warin* on at least two occasions in the interim. See *United States v. Baker* [citation provided]; *United States v. Napier* [Citation provided]. Without a subsequent *en banc* ruling to the contrary, we are therefore bound to apply *Warin* in this case.[40]

Regarding Bournes's contention that the government violated his due process rights—the terms of the two acts making it impossible for him to register his machine guns—Daughtrey asserted: "We hold that compliance with the relevant provisions of both [acts] is easily achieved: Bournes could have complied by electing not to possess the machine guns at issue in this case. … It follows that the defendant's conviction was not fundamentally unfair or otherwise a violation of due process."[41] Sustaining the district court's denial to dismiss the indictment, Judge Daughtrey affirmed Bournes conviction and sentence in all respects.

From a Second Amendment perspective, perhaps the most notable aspect of the *Bournes* opinion is the brief treatment—less than a half-page—that the court devotes to the defendant's "right to arms" argument. Relying on earlier Sixth Circuit precedents (e.g., *Warin*), Judge Daughtrey merely asserts that the Second Amendment guarantees a collective right. The individual right alternative developed in *Emerson* warranted not even a passing comment. Three years later, in the second *Warin* (2006) case, *Emerson's* impact is more evident, showing the increased willingness of the judiciary to address—even if ultimately to reject—the amendment's possible "individual right" implications.

United States v. Warin (2006): Challenging National Firearms Act/Gun Control Act Provisions

Argued in the Sixth Circuit Court of Appeals, this case once again pitted Francis J. Warin against the government. As discussed in Chapter 3, Warin in 1976 had challenged certain provisions of the GCA, arguing that a correct reading of *Miller* supported his right to personally possess any firearm having military application. Asserting that the Second Amendment only guaranteed a collective right, the circuit court dismissed Warin's appeal, and a further appeal to the Supreme Court ended when that body declined to hear the case.[42] Thirty years later, after deliberately provoking new charges, Warin returned to the Sixth Circuit Appeals Court, having been found guilty in district court of once again violating federal firearms statutes.

In 1999, Assistant US Attorney Lawrence Kiroff had confiscated twenty-two guns from Warin in a civil forfeiture; soon after that, Warin arrived at the attorney's office demanding to be arrested for firearms possession. When Kiroff declined to do so, Warin eventually forced his hand by sending Kiroff a package containing a homemade .22-caliber gun and a silencer. Charged and convicted of having an unregistered NFA item (a "silencer") and felon-in-possession violations, Warin challenged these newest convictions with the same arguments he advanced in 1976: "that the Second Amendment protects an individual's right to possess arms, and Congress' efforts to regulate and register firearms possession were unconstitutional."[43]

Judge David Lawson, nominated to the federal judiciary by President Bill Clinton in 1999, wrote the court's opinion. Noting that Warin had advanced the identical defense in 1976, Lawson observed,

> As the court did twenty-nine years ago, we likewise today reject that argument and affirm Warin's federal firearms convictions. … [T]he defendant and the government … both believe that the Second Amendment must be construed to confer individual—not collective—rights, a viewpoint espoused by the Fifth Circuit alone. *See United States v. Emerson* [Citation provided]. However, this court has had several opportunities to reassess its position since *United States v. Warin* was decided in 1976 and has continued to hold to its view that the Second Amendment confers only collective rights. *See United States v. Bournes* [Citation provided]; *United States v. Napier* [Citation provided] …. We subscribe to that interpretation as well.[44]

Lawson continued,

> Moreover … even under the individual rights model articulated in *Emerson*, the firearms statutes under which Warin was convicted would be upheld as they were in that case as "limited, narrowly tailored specific exceptions … that are reasonable

> and not inconsistent with the right of Americans generally to individually keep and bear their private arms as historically understood in this country. … [I]t is clear that felons … may be prohibited from possessing firearms." *Emerson* [Citation provided]. Warin makes no argument that the statutes he violated are somehow unreasonable. … we AFFIRM the defendant's conviction.[45]

Despite the surface appearances that *Warin (2006)* is simply another federal opinions in an extended line of federal opinions upholding a collective view of the Second Amendment, this opinion was qualitatively different from prior rulings. Judge Lawson recognized that the "individual" perspective now required some consideration. Unlike the assertion made thirty-five years earlier in *Stevens v. United States* (discussed in Chapter 3)—"there can be no serious claim to any express constitutional right of an individual to possess a firearm"[46]—the assertion in *Warin (2006)* is noticeably more muted.

2007–10: The Second Amendment—An Individual Right

Regardless of the isolated acknowledgments that an "individual right" interpretation of the Second Amendment existed, the collective right view remained firmly ensconced in the federal judiciary. Laurence Silberman, Senior Circuit Judge on the District of Columbia Court of Appeals, noted that either the collective right interpretation or the sophisticated collective right view was upheld at one time or another in at least eleven of the thirteen US Circuit Courts. He similarly observed that these interpretations were also commonly advanced in state appellate court opinions, with at least ten such appellate courts adopting the collective right position.[47]

Nonetheless, the idea that the Second Amendment preserved an individual right to arms was not as odd—nor as anomalous—as these appellate court opinions might suggest. Scores of gun cases, particularly in nineteenth- and twentieth-century state courts, either directly or indirectly recognized a personal right to own and possess firearms. This "individual right" interpretation reemerged in the three cases examined in this section.

In the first case (*Parker v. District of Columbia*), the petitioners appealed the district court's dismissal of their challenge to the District of Columbia's handgun registration requirements. When the circuit court agreed that the requirements violated the Second Amendment and found for the petitioners, the District of Columbia appealed the case to the Supreme Court. In this adjudication—known as *District of Columbia v. Heller* because of standing issues with some of the original petitioners—the Supreme Court affirmed the circuit court's judgment, asserting that the correct interpretation of the Second Amendment is that it guarantees an *individual* right to arms. The last case in the section (*McDonald v. City of Chicago*) reaffirmed the conclusions reached in *Heller* and extended Second Amendment limitations to state legislation as well.

Parker v. District of Columbia (2007): Challenging the District's Registering/Licensing Requirements

After the district court had dismissed their challenge to provisions of three DC gun statutes, Shelly Parker and five other residents of the district (including Dick Heller) appealed the dismissal to the circuit court. They complained that the DC provisions violated their Second amendment rights. The provisions in question were DC Code §7–2502.02 (a) (4), which barred the registration of handguns, with an exception for retired DC police officers; DC Code §22–4504, which prohibited the carrying of a pistol without a license (insofar as that provision stopped a registrant from moving a residence-kept firearm from one room to another); and DC Code §7–2507.02, which required that all lawfully owned firearms be kept unloaded and disassembled, or bound by a trigger lock.[48]

The Court of Appeals noted that the residents simply claimed a right to possess a functional firearm, one that would be readily accessible and effective for home self-defense. They did not assert a right to carry a firearm outside the home, or challenge the district's authority to require the registration of firearms. In dismissing the case, the district court asserted that the Second Amendment (at most) only protected an individual's right to bear arms for service in the "militia," defined as an organized military body such as the National Guard. Senior Circuit Judge Laurence Silberman, a former deputy attorney general nominated to the US Court of Appeals by President Ronald Reagan, authored the court's opinion.[49]

Before offering an analysis of the Second Amendment, the circuit court addressed the question of the appellants' standing to bring the case. In a similar 2005 challenge to DC's gun registration and licensing provisions—*Seegars v. Gonzales*[50]—the circuit court had held that those plaintiffs advanced a "pre-enforcement challenge" to the district's firearms provisions. Since they had not actually violated the district's provisions, and since prosecution was not imminent, the plaintiffs had not suffered an injury-in-fact, and thus lacked constitutional standing to challenge the provisions.[51]

In the present case, Silberman noted that at least one of the defendants—Dick Heller, a DC special police officer—had actually applied for and been denied a registration certificate to own a handgun. He had in fact suffered an injury independent of the district's prospective enforcement of its gun laws. Silberman concluded that Heller had standing to pursue the license denial and that gave him standing to subsume and pursue the other claims as well.[52]

After quoting the Second Amendment's prefatory and operative clauses, Judge Silberman observed,

> Appellants' argument is focused on their reading of the Second Amendment's operative clause. According to appellants, the Amendment's language flat out guarantees an individual right "to keep and bear arms." Appellants [contend] that the prefatory clause … may inform the meaning of an ambiguous term like "Arms," [but it] does not qualify the right guaranteed by the operative portion of the amendment.[53]

Silberman continued,

> The District of Columbia argues that the prefatory clause declares the Amendment's only purpose—to shield the state militias from federal encroachment—and that the operative clause, even when read in isolation, speaks only to military affairs and guarantees a civic, rather than an individual right. ... both clauses share an explicitly civic character. The District claims that the Second Amendment "protects private possession of weapons only in connection with the performance of civic duties as part of a well-regulated citizens militia organized for the security of a free state." ... But because the District reads "a well-regulated Militia" to signify only the organized militias of the founding era—institutions that ... are no longer in existence today—invocation of the Second Amendment right is conditioned upon service in a defunct institution. ... In short, we take the District's position to be that the Second Amendment is a dead letter.[54]

Silberman further noted,

> We are told by the District ... the Amendment should be understood to check federal power to regulate firearms only when federal legislation was directed at the abolition of state militias, because the Amendment's exclusive concern was the preservation of those entities. At first blush, it seems passing strange that ... the First Congress (including James Madison) would have expressed a sole concern for state militias with the language of the Second Amendment. Surely there was a more direct locution, such as "Congress will make no law disarming the state militias" or "States have a right to a well-regulated militia."[55]

Acknowledging, however, that the district's argument was not an isolated one, Silberman then reviewed the implications of the three interpretations of the amendment, that is, as a collective right, as an individual right, and as a "sophisticated collective right." Dismissing the last as a "distinction without a difference," he observed that past courts have disagreed on whether the amendment protects an individual or a collective right. Noting that no direct precedent provided "a square holding on the question," Silberman then undertook his own analysis of the amendment, starting with a consideration of the amendment's operative clause.[56]

Analyzing "the right of the people," he noted that "the people" is a term found in the First, Second, Fourth, Ninth, and Tenth Amendments, and observed,

> the authors of the Bill of Rights were perfectly capable of distinguishing between "the people" on the one hand, and "the states" on the other. The natural reading of "the right of the people" in the Second Amendment would accord with usage elsewhere in the Bill of Rights. The District's ... strained interpretations of "the people" simply cannot be squared with the uniform construction of our other Bill of Rights provisions. ... When we look at the Bill of Rights as a whole, the setting of the Second Amendment reinforces its individual nature. The Bill of Rights was

> almost entirely a declaration of individual rights and the Second Amendment's inclusion therein strongly indicates that it, too, was intended to protect personal liberty.[57]

Regarding "keep and bear arms," Silberman noted that the district insisted the phrase "should be read as purely military language, and thus indicative of a civic, rather than private, guarantee." He disagreed,

> But it is not accurate to construe it exclusively so. First, the word "bear" in this context is simply a more formal synonym for "carry," i.e., "Beware of Greeks bearing gifts." ... Just as it is clear that the phrase "to bear arms" was in common use as a byword for soldiering in the founding era ... it is equally evident from a survey of late eighteenth- and early nineteenth-century state constitutional provisions that the public understanding of "bear Arms" also encompassed the carrying of arms for private purposes of self-defense.[58]

Continuing, Silberman observed that, unlike "bear," the District offered only a cursory analysis of "keep." He questioned this dismissive treatment,

> We think "keep" is a straightforward term that implies ownership or possession of a functioning weapon by an individual for private use. The term "bear arms," when viewed in isolation, might be thought ambiguous; it could have a military cast. But since "the people" and "keep" have obvious and individual meanings, we think those words resolve any supposed ambiguity in the term "bear arms."[59]

In analyzing the prefatory clause, Judge Silberman noted that both the appellants and the district agreed the clause had a civic purpose—insuring the continuance of the militia system—but disagreed on whether that purpose was exclusive. He observed,

> Appellants argue that the militia referenced in the Second Amendment's prefatory clause was "practically synonymous" with the "people" referenced in the operative clause. The District advances a much more limited definition. According to the District, the militia was a body of adult men regulated and organized by state law as a civilian fighting force. The crucial distinction ... goes to the nature of the militia: Appellants claim no organization was required, whereas the District claims a militia did not exist unless it was subject to state discipline and leadership.[60]

Referencing *Miller* and Convention debates, Silberman noted, that at the founding,

> the Militia comprised of all males physically capable of acting in concert for the common defense. "A body of citizens enrolled for military discipline" [who] were expected to appear bearing arms supplied by themselves and of the kind in use at the time. ... The crucial point is that the existence of the militia preceded its organization by Congress and it preceded the implementation of Congress's

> organizing plan by the states. The District's definition of the militia is just too narrow. The militia was a large segment of the population—not quite synonymous with the "people" as the appellants contend—but certainly not the organized "divisions, brigades, regiments, battalions, and companies" mentioned in the second Militia Act [of 1792].[61]

> Silberman further noted that

> even after the foundering-era militia became "well-regulated," it did not lose its popular character. The militia still included the majority of adult men ... [it] was not an elite or select body. ... The important point ... is that the popular nature of the militia is consistent with an individual right to keep and bear arms: Preserving an individual right was the best way to insure that the militia could serve when called.[62]

After his analysis, Silberman then reviewed and critiqued a selection of court cases—*Miller*, *Emerson*, *Silveira*, *Aymette*, and others—that also addressed the nature of the Second Amendment. Based on his analysis and review, he summarized,

> we conclude that the Second Amendment protects an individual right to keep and bear arms. That right existed prior to the formation of the new government ... and was premised on the private use of arms .... [T]he activities it protects are not limited to militia service, nor is an individual's enjoyment of the right contingent upon his or her continued or intermittent enrollment in the militia.[63]

Silberman also addressed two other arguments raised by the district. The first—that as a purely federal entity and not a state, the District of Columbia was not subject to Second Amendment constraints—he dismissed, asserting that the district "mistakenly reads 'a free State' to mean an actual political unit of the United States, such as New York, etc., rather than a hypothetical polity."[64] The second argument—that even if the amendment applied to the district, it did not bar the district's prohibition of handgun ownership because modern handguns were not covered by the amendment—he analyzed using the arms test advanced in *Miller*. Maintaining that "Pistols certainly bear 'some reasonable relationship to the preservation or efficiency of a well regulated militia' [and that] they are also in 'common use' today,"[65] Silberman rejected this argument also.

Silberman continued his analysis by observing that the government was not absolutely barred from regulating the use and ownership of pistols. He noted that Second Amendment protections were subject to the same reasonable restrictions on time, place and manner that limited other rights, such as those protected by the First Amendment. Even so, he concluded that the district's firearms provisions amounted to "a complete prohibition on the lawful use of handguns for self-defense," and were an "unreasonable restriction of a constitutional right."[66] Thus, reversing the judgment of the district court, he ordered that court to grant summary judgment to Heller.

With the *Parker* decision, two federal appellate courts had now endorsed the "individual right" interpretation of the Second Amendment, in conflict with the opinions of numerous prior appellate rulings. The need for a US Supreme Court opinion to resolve the conflict was glaringly evident, and the district's decision to appeal *Parker* (now *Heller*) provided that court with the necessary opportunity to do so.

District of Columbia v. Heller (2008): Defending DC's Handgun Prohibition Provisions

The US Supreme Court opened this opinion stating, "We consider whether a District of Columbia prohibition on the possession of usable handguns in the home violates the Second Amendment to the Constitution."[67] Noting that it was a crime to carry an unregistered handgun in the district, and that the district also prohibited the registration of handguns, the court briefly summarized the underlying facts of the district's appeal.

Specifically, respondent Dick Heller had applied for a handgun registration certificate to keep a firearm at home, and when he was denied a certificate, he filed a lawsuit in district court on Second Amendment grounds. The court dismissed his complaint, but on appeal, the circuit court found that the district's total ban on handguns (and its requirement that firearms in the home be kept non-functional) violated Heller's right to possess firearms. The district's appeal of that opinion brought the case to the US Supreme Court.[68]

Associate Justice Antonin Scalia, nominated to the Supreme Court by President Ronald Reagan and the first Italian-American to serve on that court, authored the opinion for the court. He began by first examining the meaning of the Second Amendment. He prefaced his examination stating, "In interpreting this text, we are guided by the principle that '[t]he Constitution was written to be understood by the voters; its words and phrases were used in their normal and ordinary as distinguished from technical meaning.' *United States v. Sprague … (1931);* see also *Gibbons v. Ogden … (1824)*."[69]

He continued,

> The two sides in this case have set out very different interpretations of the Amendment. Petitioners and today's dissenting Justices believe that it protects only the right to possess and carry a firearm in connection with militia service. … Respondent argues that it protects an individual right to possess a firearm unconnected with military service, and to use that arm for traditionally lawful purposes, such as self-defense within the home.[70]

Noting that the amendment is divided into a prefatory and operative clause, Scalia then cited legal authorities and an *amicus* brief by linguists, maintaining that the prefatory clause did not limit the operative clause grammatically, but only announced a purpose: "But apart from that clarifying function, a prefatory clause does not limit or expand the scope of the operative clause."[71]

Scalia then began his textual analysis with the operative clause's "right of the people" phrase. He noted that the phrase also occurred in the First Amendment's Assembly-and-Petition Clause, and in the Fourth Amendment's Search-and-Seizure Clause. Further, noting that the Ninth Amendment contained a highly similarly construction—"rights … retained by the people"—Scalia asserted, "All three of these instances unambiguously refer to individual rights, not 'collective' rights, or rights that may be exercised only through participation in some corporate body."[72]

He then argued, "Reading the Second Amendment as protecting only the right 'to keep and bear Arms' in an organized militia therefore fits poorly with the operative clause's description of the holder of that right as 'the people.' We start therefore with the strong presumption that the Second Amendment right is exercised individually and belongs to all Americans."[73]

Analyzing the phrase, "keep and bear arms," Scalia noted that dictionaries contemporaneous with the Second Amendment's enactment defined "arms" as "weapons of offence or armour of defence"; and as "any thing that a man wears for his defence, or takes into his hands, or uses in wrath to cast at or strike another."[74] Citing both judicial decisions and legal dictionaries construing the meaning of "arms," Scalia further argued,

> The term was applied, then as now, to weapons that were not specifically designed for military use and were not employed in a military capacity. [Further] Some have made the argument … that only those arms in existence in the 18th century are protected by the Second Amendment. We do not interpret constitutional rights that way. Just as the First Amendment protects modern forms of communication … the Second Amendment extends, prima facie, to all instruments that constitute bearable arms, even those that were not in existence at the time of the founding.[75]

Regarding the phrases "keep arms" and "bear arms," Scalia observed,

> No party has apprised us of an idiomatic meaning of "keep Arms." Thus, the most natural reading of "keep Arms" in the Second Amendment is to "have weapons." … Petitioners point to militia laws that required militia members to "keep" arms in connection with militia service, and they conclude from this that the phrase "keep Arms" has a militia-related connotation. [Instead] "Keep arms" was simply a common way of referring to possessing arms, for militiamen *and everyone else*.[76]

Again citing past court decisions and dictionaries, Scalia continued,

> At the time of the founding, as now, to "bear" meant to "carry." … When used with "arms," however, the term has a meaning that refers to carrying for a particular purpose—confrontation. In *Muscarello v. United States* [Citation provided] … the meaning of "carries a firearm" [was] "being armed and ready for offensive or defensive action in case of conflict …." We think [this view] accurately captured the natural meaning of "bear arms." Although the phrase implies that the carrying

> of a weapon is for the purpose of "offensive or defensive action," it in no way connotes participation in a structured military organization.[77]

> Scalia further noted,

> From our review of founding-era sources, we conclude that this natural meaning was also the meaning that "bear arms" had in the 18th century. In numerous instances, "bear arms" was unambiguously used to refer to the carrying of weapons outside of an organized militia. The most prominent examples are ... state constitutional provisions ... which enshrined a right of citizens to "bear arms in defense of themselves and the state" .... It is clear from these formulations that "bear arms" did not refer only to carrying a weapon in an organized military unit.[78]

Scalia then inferred the meaning of the operative clause, "Putting all these textual elements together, we find that they guarantee the individual right to possess and carry weapons in case of confrontation. This meaning is strongly confirmed by the historical background of the Second Amendment."[79]

After briefly reviewing English history and legal commentary relevant to the amendment, as well as noting *Cruikshank's* assertion that the amendment codified a *preexisting* right, Scalia drew the following conclusion,

> There seems no doubt, on the basis of both text and history, that the Second Amendment conferred an individual right to keep and bear arms. Of course, the right was not unlimited, just as the First Amendment's right of free speech was not .... Thus, we do not read the Second Amendment to protect the right of citizens to carry arms for *any sort* of confrontation.[80]

He then analyzed the prefatory clause, starting with "a well regulated militia." He contrasted the understanding of that phrase found in *Miller*—"the Militia comprised all males physically capable of acting in concert for the common defense"—with the view put forth by the district—"militias are the state- and congressionally-regulated military forces described in the Militia Clauses (art. I, §8, cls. 15–16)."[81] He agreed with the district that "militia" meant the same thing in Article I and in the amendment, but he asserted that the district

> identified the wrong [militia], namely the organized militia. Unlike armies and navies, which Congress is given the power to create ... the militia is assumed by Article I already to be *in existence*. Congress is given the power to "provide for calling forth the militia," ... and the power not to create, but to "organiz[e]" it—and not to organize 'a' militia ... but to organize "the" militia, connoting a body already in existence .... Finally, the adjective "well-regulated" implies nothing more than the imposition of proper discipline and training.[82]

Scalia next turned to the phrase, "security of a free state." Citing the writings of Justice Joseph Story and others, Scalia noted that the phrase meant

> "security of a free polity," not security of each of the several States as the dissent [contends] .... [T]he phrase ... and close variations seem to have been terms of art in 18th-century political discourse, meaning a "free country" .... [and] ... many reasons [explain] why the militia was thought to be "necessary to the security of a free state." First ... it is useful in repelling invasions and suppressing insurrections. Second, it renders standing armies unnecessary .... Third, when the able-bodied men ... are trained in arms and organized, they are better able to resist tyranny. We reach the question, then: Does the preface fit with the operative clause that creates an individual right to keep and bear arms? It fits perfectly, once we know the history that the founding generation knew.[83]

He further observed, "if petitioners are correct, the Second Amendment protects citizens' right to use a gun in an organization from which Congress has plenary authority to exclude them. It guarantees a select militia of the sort the Stuart kings found useful, but not the people's militia that was the concern of the founding generation."[84] Scalia buttressed his interpretation of the amendment by reviewing individually oriented, arms-bearing provisions in various state constitutions adopted before and after the Second Amendment. He noted, "The historical narrative that [the District] must endorse would thus treat the Federal Second Amendment as an odd outlier, protecting a right unknown in state constitutions or at English common law, based on little more than an overreading of the prefatory clause."[85]

Justice Scalia then turned to the historical writings of three highly respected Founding-Era legal scholars—St. George Tucker, William Rawle, and Joseph Story. He asserted that "all three understood [the Second Amendment] to protect an individual right unconnected with military service. ... Tucker elaborated: 'This [amendment] may be considered the true palladium of liberty .... The right to self-defense is the first law of nature: in most governments it has been the study of rulers to confine the right within the narrowest limits possible.' "[86]

Quoting from Rawle's analysis of the amendment, Scalia extracted, "The prohibition is general. No clause in the constitution could by any rule of construction be conceived to give congress a power to disarm the people. Such a flagitious attempt could only be made under some general pretense by a state legislature. But if ... either should attempt it, this amendment may be appealed to as a restraint on both."[87] Quoting from Story's writing, "One of the ordinary modes, by which tyrants accomplish their purpose without resistance, is, by disarming the people and making it an offense to keep arms."[88]

Considering pre-Civil War case law, Scalia argued,

> The 19th-century cases that interpreted the Second Amendment universally support an individual right unconnected to militia service. ... In *Nunn v. State*

> [Citation given] the Georgia Supreme Court construed the Second Amendment as protecting the "*natural* right of self-defense" and therefore struck down a ban on carrying pistols openly. … Likewise in *State v. Chandler* [Citation given] the Louisiana Supreme Court held that citizens had a right to carry arms openly: "This is the right guaranteed by the Constitution of the United States."[89]

Scalia also commented on the Tennessee Supreme Court's 1840 decision in *Aymette v. State.* Claiming that advocates of a militia-centered interpretation of the Second Amendment cite the case approvingly, he emphasized that *Aymette* did not support that proposition. Rather, the opinion simply held that the state constitutional guarantee of the right to "bear" arms permitted the banning of concealed weapons. Scalia further observed that the Tennessee Supreme Court had in both *Simpson* and *Andrews* endorsed the right of Tennesseans to keep and bear arms for their defense and other ordinary purposes.[90]

Scalia next turned to post-Civil War legislation. He quoted from the Freedmen's Bureau Act of 1866, "The right … including the constitutional right to bear arms, shall be secured to and enjoyed by all the citizens." From a congressional discussion of the Civil Rights Act of 1871, he quoted a Representative, "Section eight is intended to enforce the well-known constitutional … right of the citizen 'to keep and bear arms.'" Regarding the proposed Fourteenth Amendment, he referenced a senator, who termed a man's "right to bear arms for the defense of himself and family and his homestead" as an "indispensable" safeguard of liberty.[91]

Justice Scalia then considered the evidence provided by post-Civil War commentators. He argued,

> Every late-19th-century legal scholar … interpreted the Second Amendment to secure an individual right unconnected with militia service. The most famous was the judge and professor Thomas Cooley who wrote … "The alternative to a standing army is a 'well-regulated militia,' but this cannot exist unless the people are trained to bearing arms." … Cooley understood the right not as connected to militia service, but as securing the militia by ensuring a populace familiar with arms.[92]

Scalia provided additional comments from individuals covering other decades, noting that they all concurred with Cooley.

Justice Scalia then addressed the impact of past court decisions on his analysis. Examining *Cruikshank*, he noted the court simply held that the Second Amendment applied only to the federal government. He concluded,

> The limited discussion of the Second Amendment in *Cruikshank* supports, if anything, the individual rights interpretation. There was no claim … that the victims had been deprived of their rights to carry arms in a militia …. [The Court held] "the people [must] look for their protection against any violation by their fellow citizens of the rights it recognizes" to the State's police power.[93]

Regarding *Presser*, which upheld Illinois' right to prohibit armed bodies of men from parading or drilling in public, Scalia contended, "This does not refute the individual-rights interpretation of the Amendment; no one supporting that interpretation has contended that States may not ban such groups. ... *Presser* said nothing about the Second Amendment's meaning or scope, beyond the fact that it does not prevent the prohibition of private paramilitary organizations."[94]

Addressing *Miller*, Justice Scalia observed that Justice Stevens placed heavy reliance on that opinion:

> "Hundreds of judges," we are told, "have relied on the view of the amendment we endorsed there," and "[e]ven if the textual and historical arguments ... were evenly balanced, respect for the well-settled views of all our predecessors on this Court, and for the rule of law itself ... would prevent most jurists from endorsing such a dramatic upheaval in the law."[95]

Rejecting this argument, Scalia asserted,

> It is entirely clear that the [*Miller*] Court's basis for saying the Second Amendment did not apply was *not* that the defendants were [bearing arms for nonmilitary use] .... Rather, it was that the *type of weapon at issue* was not eligible for Second Amendment protection: "In the absence of any evidence [showing that a short-barreled shotgun] ... has some reasonable relationship to the preservation or efficiency of a well regulated militia, we cannot say that the Second Amendment guarantees the right to keep and bear *such an instrument.*" (emphasis added). ... Beyond that the opinion provided no explanation of the content of the right.[96]

Scalia continued,

> This holding is not only consistent with, but positively suggests, that the Second Amendment confers an individual right to keep and bear arms (though only arms that "have some reasonable relationship to the preservation or efficiency of a well regulated militia"). Had the Court believed that the Second Amendment protects only those serving in the militia, it would have been odd to examine the character of the weapon rather than simply note that the two crooks were not militiamen. ... *Miller* stands only for the proposition that the Second Amendment right, whatever its nature, extends only to certain types of weapons.[97]

He further observed,

> The respondent made no appearance in the case, neither filing a brief nor appearing at oral argument; the Court heard from no one but the Government .... The Government's *Miller* brief [also] provided scant discussion of the history of the Second Amendment—and the Court was presented with no counterdiscussion.

> As for the text of the Court's opinion itself, that discusses *none* of the history of the Second Amendment. It … reviews some historical materials dealing with the nature of the militia, and in particular with the nature of the arms their members were expected to possess …. Not a word (*not a word*) about the history of the Second Amendment. This is the mighty rock upon which the dissent rests its case.[98]

Returning to the types of weapons permitted, Scalia quoted *Miller*—"men were expected to appear bearing arms supplied by themselves and of the kind in common use at the time"[99]—and *Kessler* —"'In the colonial and revolutionary war era, [small arms] weapons used by militiamen and weapons used in defense of person and home were one and the same.' … We therefore read *Miller* to say only that the Second Amendment does not protect those weapons not typically possessed by law-abiding citizens for lawful purposes."[100]

Concluding that "nothing in our precedents forecloses our adoption of the original understanding of the Second Amendment,"[101] Justice Scalia then examined limitations on the right to keep and bear arms. He noted that the majority of nineteenth-century courts upheld prohibitions on carrying concealed weapons; and he asserted, "nothing in our opinion should be taken to cast doubt on longstanding prohibitions on the possession of firearms by felons and the mentally ill, or laws forbidding the carrying of firearms in sensitive places … or laws imposing conditions and qualifications on the commercial sale of arms."[102]

Scalia further observed,

> We also recognize another important limitation …. *Miller* said … that the sorts of weapons protected were those "in common use at the time." … [Yet] the historical tradition of prohibiting the carrying of "dangerous and unusual weapons" [also exists]. It may be objected that if weapons that are most useful in military service—M-16 rifles and the like—may be banned, then the Second Amendment right is completely detached from the prefatory clause. … It may well be true today that a militia … would require sophisticated arms that are highly unusual in society at large. … But the fact that modern developments have limited the degree of fit between the prefatory clause and the protected right cannot change our interpretation of the right.[103]

Focusing finally on the law at issue, Scalia noted that the central issue was the inherent right of self-defense. He argued,

> The handgun ban amounts to a prohibition of an entire class of "arms" that is overwhelmingly chosen by American society for that lawful purpose. The prohibition extends, moreover, to the home, where the need for defense of self, family, and property is most acute. Under any of the standards of scrutiny … banning from the home "the most preferred firearm in the nation …" would fail constitutional muster.[104]

Emphasizing the severity of the District's handgun ban, Scalia pointed out state courts had struck down less harsh restrictions in *Nunn*, *Andrews*, and *Reid*. He rejected the district's argument that the allowance of other firearms (e.g., rifles) made the ban on handguns permissible. He asserted, "the American people have considered the handgun to be the quintessential self-defense weapon … and a complete prohibition of their use is invalid."[105] Similarly, addressing the district's requirement that firearms in the home be kept inoperable, he concluded, "This makes it impossible for citizens to use them for the core lawful purpose of self-defense and is hence unconstitutional."[106]

Scalia then considered Justice Breyer's contention that, even if the Second Amendment guaranteed a personal right to arms, the district's handgun ban remained valid. Citing various colonial laws restricting firearms, Justice Breyer contended that the district's law "imposes a burden … proportionately no greater than restrictions in existence at the time the Second Amendment was adopted."[107] Asserting that the cited laws were not equivalent to the district's handgun ban, Scalia dismissed them. He argued, "Those laws provide no support for the severe restrictions in the present case. … The District law … far from imposing a minor fine, threatens citizens with a year in prison (five years for a second violation) for even obtaining a gun in the first place."[108]

Justice Breyer also criticized the majority opinion for not adopting an "interest-balancing" approach that would ask "whether the statute burdens a protected interest in a way or to an extent that is out of proportion to the statute's salutary effects upon other important governmental interests."[109] Scalia rejected this argument also, observing, "We know of no other enumerated constitutional right whose core protection has been subjected to a freestanding 'interest-balancing' approach. … A constitutional guarantee subject to future judges' assessment of its usefulness is no constitutional guarantee at all."[110]

Concluding the court's opinion, Justice Scalia ended, "In sum, we hold that the District's ban on handgun possession in the home violates the Second Amendment, as does it prohibition against rendering any lawful firearm in the home operable for the purpose of immediate self-defense. … the District must permit [Heller] to register his handgun and must issue him a license to carry it in the home. … We affirm the judgment of the Court of Appeals."[111]

With *Heller*, the US Supreme Court judicially resolved the "collective vs. individual right" debate, and firmly established the individual nature of the Second Amendment. Nonetheless, as Justice Breyer complained and as the court acknowledged, the opinion left many questions about the right to keep and bear arms in doubt. Two years later, in *McDonald v. City of Chicago*, the process of addressing unanswered questions began.

McDonald v. City of Chicago (2010): Challenging a Municipal Handgun Ban

In a case sharing similarities to *Heller*, the US Supreme Court again examined the constitutionality of an ordinance restricting an individual's possession of handguns. Enacted by the city of Chicago and the village of Oak Park prior to the *Heller* decision, the court noted that "A City ordinance provides that '[n]o person shall … possess … any firearm unless such person is the holder of a valid registration certificate for such firearm.' Chicago, Ill., Municipal Code §8-20-040 (a) (2009). The code then prohibits registration of most handguns, thus effectively banning handgun possession by almost all private citizens who reside in the City."[112] Oak Park—a suburb of Chicago—had an equivalent ordinance. Otis McDonald and three other Chicago residents—feeling vulnerable to criminals, and wanting to keep handguns in their homes for self-protection—challenged the Chicago ordinance.

Despite *Heller*, the district court ruled against the plaintiffs, noting that the Seventh Circuit had upheld the constitutionality of a handgun ban a quarter of a century earlier (citing *Quilici v. Morton Grove*). The district court noted that the *Heller* opinion did not address the incorporation issue—whether the Second Amendment applied to the states—and thus the court had to follow Seventh Circuit precedents "even though the logic of more recent caselaw may point in a different direction."[113] When the Seventh Circuit Court of Appeals also upheld the handgun ban—citing *United States* v. *Cruikshank*, *Presser v. Illinois*, and *Miller v. Texas* as determining precedents—McDonald appealed to the Supreme Court. Justice Samuel Alito, nominated to the court by President George H. Bush, authored the court's opinion.[114]

Alito noted the two reasons the petitioners claimed that the municipal ordinance was unconstitutional: Primarily, the "right [to keep and bear arms] is among the 'privileges or immunities of citizens of the United States' and ... [secondarily], the Fourteen Amendment's Due Process Clause 'incorporates' the Second Amendment right."[115] He then noted Chicago's counter-argument:

> A right set out in the Bill of Rights applies to the States only if that right is an indispensable attribute of any "civilized" legal system. [Citation provided]. If it is possible to imagine a civilized country that does not recognize the right ... then that right is not protected by due process. And since there are civilized countries that ban or strictly regulate the private possession of handguns ... due process does not preclude such measures.[116]

To resolve these differing positions, Alito began by reviewing the Supreme Court's past analysis of the relationship of the Bill of Rights to the states.

Citing the 1833 *Barron* opinion of Chief Justice John Marshall, Alito pointed out that the court had rejected the proposition that the first eight amendments limited the states: "It is now settled that those amendments [in the Bill of Rights] do not extend to the states,"[117] and that they apply only to the federal government. Further, observing that the amendments adopted after the Civil War significantly altered the federal system, Alito specifically examined the implications of the Fourteenth Amendment. He noted that the amendment provides that "a State may not abridge 'the privileges or immunities of citizens of the United States' or deprive 'any person of life, liberty, or property without due process of law.'"[118] Referencing the Supreme Court's 1873 *Slaughter-House Cases*[119] opinion, Alito allowed that the court interpreted the "privileges or immunities" phrase narrowly—the "Clause protects only those rights 'which owe their existence to the Federal Government, its National character, its Constitution, or its laws' ... other fundamental rights ... were not protected by the Clause."[120]

However, Alito also observed, "Four Justices dissented .... Today, many legal scholars dispute the correctness of the narrow *Slaughter-House* interpretation. ... 'Virtually no serious modern scholar ... thinks that this [interpretation] is a plausible reading of the Amendment'; ... 'an overwhelming consensus among leading constitutional scholars' that the opinion is 'egregiously wrong' [Citations provided]."[121] Justice Alito then turned to three nineteenth-century cases the Seventh Circuit Court cited in upholding the handgun ban: *Cruikshank*, *Presser*, and *Miller*.

In *Cruikshank*, he observed that the court reversed all the convictions stemming from the infamous Colfax Massacre, "including those relating to the deprivation of the victims' right to bear arms .... 'The second amendment,' the Court [wrote], 'declares that it shall not be infringed; but this ... means no more than it shall not be infringed by Congress.'"[122] Alito similarly observed, "Our later decisions in *Presser v. Illinois* ... and *Miller v. Texas* ... reaffirmed that the Second Amendment applies only to the Federal Government."[123] Noting that the Seventh Circuit relied on these decisions to reject McDonald's claims, Alito acknowledged that, nevertheless, "In the petitioners' view, the Privileges or Immunities Clause protects all the rights set out in the Bill of Rights ... but petitioners are unable to identify the Clause's full scope ... [n]or is there any consensus on that question among the scholars who agree that the *Slaughter-House Cases'* interpretation is flawed."[124]

Rather than reconsider the *Slaughter-House Cases'* narrow interpretation of the Fourteenth Amendment's Privileges or Immunities Clause, Alito proposed to analyze McDonald's claims under the amendment's Due Process Clause. He argued, "*Cruikshank*, *Presser*, and *Miller* all preceded the era in which the Court began the process of 'selective incorporation' under the Due Process Clause, and we have never previously addressed the question whether the right to keep and bear arms applies to the States under that theory."[125] After discussing the legal history, characteristics, and requirements of due-process, Alito declared,

> We now turn directly to the question whether the Second Amendment right to keep and bear arms is incorporated in the concept of due process. In answering that question ... we must decide whether the right ... is fundamental to *our* scheme of ordered liberty [Citation provided] or ... whether this right is "deeply rooted in this Nation's history and tradition," [Citation provided].[126]

To address these issues, Justice Alito referenced *Heller*,

> Our decision in *Heller* points unmistakably to the answer. Self-defense is a basic right, recognized by many legal systems ... and in *Heller* we held that individual self-defense is "the *central component*" of the Second Amendment right. ... [W]e found that this right applies to handguns because they are "the most preferred firearm in the nation to 'keep' and use for protection of one's home and family," .... Thus, we concluded, citizens must be permitted "to use [handguns] for the core lawful purpose of self-defense." *Heller* makes it clear that this right is "deeply rooted in this Nation's history and traditions."[127]

To buttress this assertion, Alito provided a brief summary of *Heller*'s discussion of the right to keep arms for self-defense. He argued,

> *Heller* explored the right's origins, noting that the 1689 English Bill of Rights explicitly protected a right to keep arms for self-defense … and that in 1765 Blackstone was able to assert that the right … was "one of the fundamental rights of Englishmen" …. The right … was considered no less fundamental by those who drafted and ratified the Bill of Rights. … Antifederalists and Federalists alike agreed that the right to bear arms was fundamental to the newly formed system of government. … But those who were fearful that the new Federal Government would infringe traditional rights such as the right to keep and bear arms insisted on the adoption of the Bill of Rights as a condition for ratification of the Constitution. … This is surely powerful evidence that the right was regarded as fundamental in the sense relevant here.[128]

Alito also referenced *Heller*'s discussion of states that had adopted analogues similar to the Second Amendment before and after its ratification and the emphasis that Founding-Era legal commentators—Tucker, Rawle, and Story—placed on the importance of the right to keep and bear arms. Moving into the 1800s, Alito pointed to the abolitionist authors who supported the right to arms and the Republican Party's 1856 political platform protesting that, "in Kansas … 'the right of the people to keep and bear arms' had been infringed."[129] He also alluded to the opinion's discussion of post-Civil War developments, noting that "the laws of some States formally prohibited African Americans from possessing firearms. … Throughout the South, armed parties, often consisting of ex-Confederate soldiers serving in state militias, forcibly took firearms from newly freed slaves."[130]

Acknowledging that Union Army commanders had tried to protect the right of arms for all citizens, Justice Alito noted that, nevertheless,

> the 39th Congress concluded that legislative action was necessary. Its efforts to safeguard the right … demonstrate that the right was still recognized as fundamental. The most explicit evidence [is] the Freedmen's Bureau Act of 1866 …. Section 14 … explicitly guaranteed that "all the citizens," black and white, would have "the constitutional right to bear arms." The Civil Rights Act of 1866 … similarly sought to protect the right …. [This] Act, like the Freedmen's Bureau Act, aimed to protect "the constitutional right to bear arms" and not simply to prohibit discrimination.[131]

Continuing, Alito argued that Congress ultimately saw these legislative remedies as insufficient:

> Southern resistance, Presidential vetoes, and this Court's pre-Civil War precedent persuaded Congress that a constitutional amendment was necessary to provide full protection … it is generally accepted that the Fourteenth Amendment was

> ... a constitutional basis for protecting the rights set out in the Civil Rights Act of 1866. ... Evidence from the period immediately following the ratification of the Fourteenth Amendment ... confirms that the right to keep and bear arms was considered fundamental. ... And in debating the Civil Rights Act of 1871, Congress routinely referred to the right to keep and bear arms and decried the continued disarmament of blacks in the South. ... In sum, it is clear that the Framers and ratifiers of the Fourteenth Amendment counted the right to keep and bear arms among those fundamental rights necessary to our system of ordered liberty.[132]

Alito then turned to the arguments of the City of Chicago. He began,

> Despite all this evidence, municipal respondents contend that Congress ... merely sought to outlaw "discriminatory measures taken against freedmen, which it addressed by adopting a non-discrimination principle" and that even an outright ban on the possession of firearms was regarded as acceptable, "so long as it was done in a non-discriminatory manner." They argue that ... Congress overwhelmingly viewed §1 of the Fourteenth Amendment "as an antidiscrimination rule" ... outlaw[ing] discriminatory measures. This argument is implausible.[133]

Acknowledging that §1 of the Fourteenth Amendment contains an "antidiscrimination rule"—the amendment's Equal Protection Clause—Alito argued,

> Respondents can hardly mean that §1 does no more than prohibit discrimination. If that were so, then the First Amendment, as applied to the States, would not prohibit nondiscriminatory abridgements of ... freedom of speech or ... of religion; the Fourth Amendment ... would not prohibit all unreasonable searches and seizures but only discriminatory searches and seizures .... We assume that this is not municipal respondents' view, so what they must mean is that the Second Amendment should be singled out for special—and specially unfavorable—treatment. We reject this view.[134]

He also pointed out the city's contention

> ignores the clear terms of the Freedmen's Bureau Act of 1866, which acknowledged the existence of the right to bear arms. ... §14 speaks of, and protects, "the constitutional right to bear arms," an unmistakable reference to the right protected by the Second Amendment. ... [Further] if the 39th Congress had outlawed only those laws that discriminate on the basis of race or previous condition of servitude, African Americans in the South would likely have remained vulnerable to attack by many of their worst abusers: the state militia and state peace officers. ... a law banning the possession of guns by all private citizens ... would have permitted the possession of guns by those acting under the authority of the State .... [Also] [the City's] purely antidiscrimination theory ... disregards the plight of whites in the

> South who opposed the Black Codes. ... [they] would have been left without the means of self-defense—as had abolitionists in Kansas in the 1850's.[135]

Alito marshalled a final objection to the city's antidiscrimination interpretation of the Fourteenth Amendment. Pointing to contemporary proposals to disband and disarm the Southern militias, he noted,

> Despite recognizing and deploring the abuses of these militias, the 39th Congress balked at [disarming] them. Disarmament, it was argued, would violate the members' right to bear arms, and it was ultimately decided to disband the militias but not to disarm their members [Citations provided]. It cannot be doubted that the right to bear arms was regarded as a substantive guarantee, not a prohibition that could be ignored so long as the States legislated in an evenhanded manner.[136]

Asserting that the city's remaining arguments conflicted with the court's central holding in *Heller*—that the Second Amendment protects a personal right to arms for self-defense within the home—Justice Alito complained that the city wants the court

> to treat the right recognized in *Heller* as a second-class right, subject to an entirely different body of rules than the other Bill of Rights guarantees that we have held to be incorporated into the Due Process Clause. ... Municipal respondents submit that the Due Process Clause protects only those rights "recognized by all temperate and civilized governments, from a deep and universal sense of [their] justice." ... if it is possible to imagine *any* civilized legal system that does not recognize a particular right, then the Due Process Clause does not make that right binding on the States.[137]

Alito rejected this argument, asserting that it was

> inconsistent with the long-established standard we apply in incorporation cases [Citations given]. ... For example, many of the rights that our Bill of Rights provides for ... are virtually unique to this country. If *our* understanding of a right to a jury trial, the right against self-incrimination, and the right to counsel were necessary attributes of *any* civilized country, it would follow that the United States is the only civilized Nation in the world.[138]

Continuing, Alito noted,

> Municipal respondents [also] maintain that the Second Amendment differs from all the other provisions of the Bill of Rights because it concerns the right to possess a deadly instrument and thus has implications for public safety. ... The right to keep and bear arms is not the only constitutional right that has controversial public safety implications. All of the constitutional provisions that impose restrictions on law enforcement and on the prosecution of crime fall into the same category. ...

> Municipal respondents cite no case in which we have refrained from holding a provision of the Bill of Rights [as] binding on the states [because] the right at issue has disputed public safety implications.[139]

While acknowledging that different jurisdictions have divergent views on gun control, Justice Alito also rejected the city's contention that making the Second Amendment binding on the States would stifle experimentation and was inconsistent with the principles of federalism. He asserted,

> Municipal respondents … urge us to allow state and local governments to enact any gun control law they deem to be reasonable, including a complete ban on the possession of handguns in the home for self-defense. There is nothing new in the argument that, in order to respect federalism … a federal constitutional right should not be fully binding on the States. This argument was made repeatedly and eloquently by Members of this Court who rejected the concept of incorporation …. [Citations provided]. Time and again, however, those pleas failed. Unless we turn back the clock or adopt a special incorporation test applicable only to the Second Amendment, municipal respondents' argument must be rejected.[140]

Because the city also argued that state courts have used "interest-balancing" to sustain a variety of restrictions on firearm rights, Alito addressed that issue. Citing *Heller*, he declared,

> We expressly rejected the argument that the scope of the Second Amendment right should be determined by judicial interest balancing …. As evidence that the Fourteenth Amendment has not historically been understood to restrict the authority of the States to regulate firearms, municipal respondents … cite a variety of state and local firearms laws that courts have upheld. But what is most striking … is the paucity of precedent sustaining bans comparable to those at issue here and in *Heller*. …It is important to keep in mind that *Heller* … recognized that the right to keep and bear arms is not "a right to keep and carry any weapon whatsoever in any manner whatsoever …." We made it clear in *Heller* that our holding did not cast doubt on longstanding regulatory measures …. Despite municipal respondents' doomsday proclamations, incorporation does not imperil every law regulating firearms.[141]

The city's final argument was that the Second Amendment right was unlike other amendments in the Bill of Rights. Those rights were "valued for their own sake" while the Second Amendment right had only instrumental value: to use firearms for self-defense. As an instrumental right, the right was not "implicit in the concept of ordered liberty." Alito also rejected this argument, "we have never previously suggested that incorporation of a right turns on whether it has intrinsic as opposed to instrumental value, and quite a few of the rights previously held to be incorporated … are clearly instrumental by any measure."[142] He then commented on the two dissenting opinions, one written by Justice Stevens and the other by Justice Breyer.

Justice Stevens had argued, "the rights protected against state infringement by the Fourteenth Amendment's Due Process Clause need not be identical in shape or scope to the rights protected against Federal Government infringement."[143] Citing an earlier opinion by Justice Brennan, Alito dismissed this contention, observing that "the Court, for the past half-century, has moved away from the two-track approach. … The relationship between the Bill of Rights' guarantees and the States must be governed by a single, neutral principle."[144]

Regarding Justice Breyer's dissent, Alito noted that Breyer asserted the Fourteenth Amendment does not incorporate the Second for four primary reasons: (1) there is no popular consensus that the right is fundamental; (2) the right does not protect minorities or persons neglected by those holding political power; (3) incorporation would amount to a significant incursion on a traditional and important area of state concern; and (4) determining the scope of the Second Amendment right will require judges to answer difficult empirical questions outside their area of expertise.[145]

Justice Alito dismissed (1), asserting "we have never held that a provision of the Bill of Rights applies to the States only if there is a 'popular consensus' that the right is fundamental." He dismissed (2), noting that "petitioners and many others who live in high crime areas dispute the proposition that the Second Amendment does not protect minorities and those lacking political clout." He dismissed (3), observing that incorporation "will to some extent limit the legislative freedom of the States, but this is always true when a Bill of Rights provision is incorporated. Incorporation always restricts experimentation … but this has not stopped the Court from incorporating virtually every other provision of the Bill of Rights."[146]

Regarding (4), Alito asserted,

> Finally, Justice Breyer is incorrect that incorporation will require judges to assess the costs and benefits of firearms restrictions and thus to make difficult empirical judgments …. [*Heller*] specifically rejected that suggestion. "The very enumeration of the right takes out of the hands of government—even the Third Branch—the power to decide on a case-by-case basis whether the right is *really worth* insisting upon."[147]

Justice Alito concluded the court's opinion, asserting, "[A] provision of the Bill of Rights that protects a right that is fundamental from an American perspective applies equally to the Federal Government and the States [Citation given]. We therefore hold that the Due Process Clause of the Fourteenth Amendment incorporates the Second Amendment right recognized in *Heller*. The judgment of the Court of Appeals is reversed."[148]

The *McDonald* decision, together with *Heller*, resolved the two great gun debates that long swirled around the Second Amendment. By affirming that the amendment protected a personal right to own and carry firearms, and that this protection limited the states as well as the federal government, the court endorsed and reinforced the original historical understanding of the provision's twenty-seven words. Nonetheless, while these two decisions broadly answered—*defined*—the amendment's "meaning," both made clear that *some* limitations on the right were allowed. Because judgments about the permissibility of specific gun rules and regulations have differed, refining the scope and practical implications of the amendment have required additional judicial attention. The following topical chapters explore these refinements, beginning with contentions over the licensing and registration of firearms.

Some Observations

For individuals interested in judging for themselves whether *Heller* "got it right" or "upended settled law" in defining the Second Amendment, two cases in this chapter—*Emerson* and *Silveira*—are especially valuable. Unlike the terse, hazy treatment of the amendment in *Miller*, the well-thought-out analyses in these two dueling cases are detailed, comprehensive, and clear. Both cases approach the amendment similarly and consider much the same material. They both concede that the evidence is not so straightforward as to support one interpretation as completely, self-evidently correct. Rather, as is usual with complex judicial analyses, they both agree it is the overall "weight of the evidence" that governs whether the amendment protects an individual or a collective right. In their gauging of the evidence, the two judges come to totally opposed conclusions. After considering the two contrasting analyses, individuals can determine for themselves the interpretation favored by the "weight of the evidence."

Judge Garwood, in *Emerson*, conducts a textual, historical, and scholarly analysis of the amendment. In his textual analysis of the specific words and phrases contained in the amendment's operative clause (e.g., "people," "bear arms," keep arms," etc.), Garwood concludes that the phrasing does not support a collective right interpretation. Similarly, in considering the amendment's prefatory clause, he asserts that this preamble simply promotes the continuation of a needed, well-regulated militia, but certainly not a collective right. He bases this supposition on the amendment's placement within the Bill of Rights, the individually focused other amendments, and the wording of the Constitution generally.

He further argues that the most accurate conclusion about the amendment's central purpose is that it is to arm "the people"—permitting ordinary individuals to engage in collective defense. But this objective is accomplished not by protecting the *states'* right to arm the people as they see fit in a militia; but rather by preventing individuals' disarmament by the *federal* government. Recognizing an individual's right to own and use firearms for home and self-protection assures such prevention.

Judge Reinhardt, in *Silveira*, also examines the amendment's text and structure, its historical context, and its treatment in prior court adjudications. He asserts that the amendment's prefatory clause—a syntactical device missing in the other nine amendments—is especially important because it establishes the amendment's intent. Arguing that linguistic analysis and other evidence suggest that the term "militia" denotes a state military force, he asserts that this interpretation is further reflected in the militaristic wording of the substantive clause: "keep and bear arms" rather than "possess" and "own" arms. Putting both clauses together, he concludes that the amendment's most plausible interpretation is that it seeks to insure effective state militias, where people exercise their right to arms in connection with military service. However, Reinhardt acknowledges that textual analysis alone is not sufficient to establish the meaning of the amendment. Thus, he turns to historical context to buttress his interpretation.

He notes that contemporary debates and debates within the Constitutional Convention often centered on military matters, particularly on the proper balance of state versus federal control of military affairs. He emphasizes the Anti-Federalist concern that, if the federal government controlled the militia, that government could also disarm it. Thus, after his review of text, history, and past precedents, Reinhardt affirms the collective right interpretation of the amendment.

Judge Garwood's historical analysis covers similar ground but with a different emphasis. He stresses the Anti-Federalists' demands that the Constitution include a bill of individual rights. He notes that many states demanded amendments that included the right to arms and refused to ratify the Constitution otherwise. Moving on to eminent constitutional scholars of the period, Garwood points out they all treated the amendment as a right of the individual to own and use firearms. He concludes that past history is clear in showing that the amendment protects an individual right.

Many of the arguments and historical analyses in *Emerson* and *Silveira* are examined again in the *Heller* decision. In that opinion, the Supreme Court also looks at the weight of the textual and historical evidence and concludes that it supports a personal right. Individuals familiar with these opinions are free to determine for themselves what the overall evidence supports.

Notes

1 Appearing on many internet sites (e.g., https://www.google.com/search?client=firefox-b-1-d&q=warren+burger+2nd+amendment+meme) and attributed either to a January 14, 1990 *Parade Magazine* article (https://guncite.com/burger.html) or a December 16, 1990 MacNeil/Lehrer News Hour Report (https://www.youtube.com/watch?v=Eya_k4P-iEo), the quote captures the overall implications of Burger's remarks, but neither source actually contains this specific comment.

2 *District of Columbia v. Heller, Supreme Court of the United States, No. 07–290 (2008).* At https://www.supremecourt.gov/opinions/07pdf/07-290.pdf.

3 *United States v. Emerson, 270 F.3d 203 (2001).* At https://casetext.com/case/us-v-emerson-16.

4 *United States v. Emerson, 46 F. Supp. 2d 598 (N.D. Tex. 1999).* At https://law.justia.com/cases/federal/district-courts/FSupp2/46/598/2488037/.

5 *United States v. Emerson, 270 F.3d 203 (2001).* At https://casetext.com/case/us-v-emerson-16.

6 Ibid.

7 Ibid.

8 Ibid.

9 Ibid.

10 Ibid.
11 Ibid.
12 Ibid.
13 Ibid.
14 Ibid.
15 Ibid.
16 Ibid.
17 Ibid.
18 Emerson's loss in this case began a tragic downward spiral, including suspension of his medical license, continued problems with law enforcement, and homelessness. See *The Emerson Case*. At http://www.ejfi.org/emerson.htm.
19 *Silveira v. Lockyer 312 F.3d 1052 (9th Cir.* 2002*)*. At https://casetext.com/case/silveira-v-lockyer-2.
20 Ibid.
21 Ibid.
22 Maura Dolan, "Did the 'Liberal Lion' of the 9th Circuit Bully and Mistreat His Clerks?," *SLS News and Media*, February 20, 2020. At https://law.stanford.edu/press/did-the-liberal-lion-of-the-9th-circuit-bully-and-mistreat-his-clerks/.
23 *Silveira v. Lockyer 312 F.3d 1052 (9th Cir.* 2002).
24 Ibid.
25 Ibid.
26 Ibid.
27 Ibid.
28 Ibid.
29 Ibid.
30 Ibid.
31 Ibid.
32 Ibid.
33 Ibid.
34 Ibid.
35 Ibid.
36 Ibid. The opinion also sustained the plaintiffs' Fourteenth Amendment challenge to the AWCA's exemption for retired police officers, but it rejected the challenged exemption for off-duty police officers.
37 *U.S. v. Bournes 339 F.3d 396 (6th Cir. 2003).* At https://casetext.com/case/us-v-bournes.
38 Ibid.
39 Ibid.
40 Ibid.
41 Ibid.
42 Ibid.
43 *United States of America v. Francis J. Warin, No. 04-3431 (6th Cir. 2006).* At https://law.justia.com/cases/federal/appellate-courts/ca6/04-3431/06a0071n-06-2011-02-25.html.
44 Ibid.
45 Ibid.
46 Ibid. Warin had also raised a due-process claim that the NFA was an improper application of the government's taxation powers. Citing applicable precedents, the

court concluded that no due process violation occurred. The court did conclude that Warin's sentence was more severe than warranted and remanded for resentencing.

47 *Stevens v. United States 440 F.2d 144 (6th Cir. 1971*). At https://casetext.com/case/stevens-v-united-states-12.

48 See *Parker v. District of Columbia, 478 F.3d 370 (2007)* Notes 3, 4, and 6. At https://scholar.google.com/scholar_case?case=11156910755936011541&hl=en&as_sdt=6&as_vis=1&oi=scholar.r

49 *Parker v. District of Columbia, 478 F.3d 370 (2007).* At https://scholar.google.com/scholar_case?case=11156910755936011541&hl=en&as_sdt=6&as_vis=1&oi=scholarr.

50 *Seegars v. Gonzales, 396 F.3d 1248 (D.C.Cir.2005).* At https://caselaw.findlaw.com/us-dc-circuit/1050823.html.

51 *Parker v. District of Columbia, 478 F.3d 370 (2007).*

52 Ibid.

53 Ibid.

54 Ibid.

55 Ibid.

56 Ibid.

57 Ibid.

58 Ibid.

59 Ibid.

60 Ibid.

61 Ibid.

62 Ibid.

63 Ibid.

64 Ibid.

65 Ibid.

66 Ibid.

67 *District of Columbia v. Heller, 554 U.S. 570 (2008).* At https://supreme.justia.com/cases/federal/us/554/570/.

68 Ibid.

69 Ibid.

70 Ibid.

71 Ibid.

72 Ibid.

73 Ibid.

74 Ibid.

75 Ibid.

76 Ibid.

77 Ibid.

78 Ibid.

79 Ibid.

80 Ibid.

81 Ibid.

82 Ibid.

83 Ibid.

84 Ibid.

85 Ibid.

86 Ibid.
87 Ibid.
88 Ibid.
89 Ibid.
90 Ibid.
91 Ibid.
92 Ibid.
93 Ibid.
94 Ibid.
95 Ibid.
96 Ibid.
97 Ibid.
98 Ibid.
99 Ibid.
100 Ibid.
101 Ibid.
102 Ibid.
103 Ibid.
104 Ibid.
105 Ibid.
106 Ibid.
107 Ibid.
108 Ibid.
109 Ibid.
110 Ibid.
111 Ibid.
112 *McDonald v. City of Chicago, 561 U.S. 742 (2010).* At https://supreme.justia.com/cases/federal/us/561/742/.
113 Ibid.
114 Ibid.
115 Ibid.
116 Ibid.
117 Ibid.
118 Ibid.
119 The *Slaughter-House Cases* involved challenges to a Louisiana law regulating butchering animals in New Orleans. The court ruled that the Privileges or Immunities Clause protected only rights associated with national citizenship, not rights associated with state citizenship.
120 *McDonald v. City of Chicago, 561 U.S. 742 (2010).*
121 Ibid.
122 Ibid.
123 Ibid.
124 Ibid.
125 Ibid.
126 Ibid.
127 Ibid.
128 Ibid.
129 Ibid.

130 Ibid.
131 Ibid.
132 Ibid.
133 Ibid.
134 Ibid.
135 Ibid.
136 Ibid.
137 Ibid.
138 Ibid.
139 Ibid.
140 Ibid.
141 Ibid.
142 Ibid.
143 Ibid.
144 Ibid.
145 Ibid.
146 Ibid.
147 Ibid.
148 Ibid.

5

Permits, Licenses, and the *Bruen* Decision

> *We know of no other constitutional right that an individual may exercise only after demonstrating to government officials some special need.*
>
> Associate Justice Clarence Thomas[1]

As *Heller* and *McDonald* emphasized, the Second Amendment's guarantee of an individual right to arms is not unlimited. Both opinions noted that the amendment's protections are subject to "reasonable regulation." However, the court left the boundaries of such regulation mostly unexamined, for future courts to construct. Unsurprisingly, given the significance of such constructions in defining the amendment, clarifying potential limits became the focus of gun cases in the following decades. The first clarifications focused on licensing approaches, specifically "may-issue"/"proper-cause" licensing schemes. Under this approach, an administrative official—typically a judge or law-enforcement officer—uses subjective evaluative criteria (e.g., a "special need" to carry a firearm) to determine which applicants qualify for such permits.

Between 2012 and 2017, five different federal courts of appeal wrestled with the implications of this type of licensing. The Second Circuit first considered the licensing's constitutionality in *Kalchalsky v. County of Westchester* in 2012. In 2013, both the Third Circuit in *Drake v. Filko* and the Fourth Circuit in *Woollard v. Gallagher* addressed the issue. In 2014, the Ninth Circuit covered the same question in *Peruta v. County of San Diego*, arriving at a different conclusion than its sister circuits. Then, in 2016, the Ninth Circuit revisited *Peruta* and reversed *(en banc)*. Finally, in 2017, the DC Circuit also addressed the "may issue/proper reason" question in *Wrenn v. District of Columbia.*[2] Because of conflicting conclusions and the use of "intermediate scrutiny" in the adjudications, the US Supreme Court itself ultimately addressed "may issue / proper cause" licensing in its *New York Rifle and Pistol Association v. Bruen* opinion in 2022.

"Proper cause" licensing did not arise in a legal vacuum. The approach fits into the judicial history of permitting schemes more generally. Typically, courts upheld permitting schemes when the scheme simply "regulated" the use of firearms, but overturned schemes that "prohibited" the use of arms. For instance, in the 1911 *Strickland* case (see Chapter 3), Justice Joseph Lumpkin II upheld a Georgia licensing requirement for carrying a revolver. He argued that the requirement was "not so arbitrary or unreasonable as to amount, in effect, to a prohibition of the right to bear arms, or an infringement of that right as protected by the constitution,"[3] but he did stress that a restriction that *did* result in a prohibition would be unacceptable.

In *Kerner*,[4] Chief Justice Walter Clark went further. In 1921, he found a North Carolina statute requiring a permit to carry a pistol off personal premises unreasonable and a violation of the constitutional right to bear arms (see Chapter 3). More recently, Judge Cynthia Hall in 1996 let stand a "may issue" licensing approach in *Hickman v. Block*,[5] but she did so on the grounds that Hickman had no standing to challenge the California statute (see Chapter 3). This chapter includes several additional cases focused on licensing and permitting to also put the twenty-first century "proper cause" challenges into context.

The chapter divides the dozen cases examined into four time periods. Four cases illustrate the judiciary's treatment of permitting early in the twentieth century. Three adjudications—*State of Vermont v. Rosenthal* in 1903, *Darling v. Warden of the City Prison* in 1913, and *People v. Zerillo* in 1922—examined the police power of the state to regulate firearms for the public's peace and safety, but they reached different conclusions regarding how far that regulation could extend. The fourth case, *Matter of Moore v. Gallup* in 1943, jumps to mid-century and illustrates judicial developments in New York's Sullivan Laws thirty years after *Darling*.

Moving into the 1980s and 1990s, the second period contains three cases. The first—*Shubert v. DeBard (1980)*—is an Indiana's Court of Appeals adjudication testing self-defense as a "proper reason" for a handgun permit. Then, continuing with judicial thinking in New York prior to *Bruen*, the next adjudications (*Matter of Klenosky v. New York City Police Department* in 1980 and *Matter of O'Connor v. Scarpino* in 1994) are short cases delving into the meaning of "proper cause" for handgun permits. The third period contains four circuit court cases from the twenty-first century (*Kalchalsky*, *Drake*, *Woollard*, and *Peruta*); while the last period examines the 2022 *Bruen* decision.

1903–22: Permitting at the Start of the Twentieth Century

As earlier chapters have shown, courts frequently have had to balance an individual's right to arms with society's right to a safe and secure community. In the nineteenth century, the judiciary supported the state's police power to regulate an individual's way of carrying firearms, typically by upholding prohibitions against concealed carry if open carry was allowed. Similarly, in the twentieth century, the judiciary usually viewed gun carry permits and licensing regulations as reasonable exercises of the state's police power, if the acquisition of a permit or license did not unduly burden the Second Amendment.

The cases below—*Rosenthal* from Vermont, *Darling* from New York, and *Zerillo* from Michigan—illustrate how different states handled the individual/societal tension created by these regulations early in the century. The mid-century New York case, *Moore*, confirms that the precedent established by *Darling* continued to guide that state's licensing approach.

State of Vermont v. Rosenthal (1903): Challenging a Firearms Licensing Requirement

The city of Rutland had enacted an ordinance that prohibited the carrying of brass knuckles, stilettos, pistols, and similar weapons within the city and had made the carrying of any concealed weapon without the written permission of the mayor or chief of police illegal.[6] Andrew Rosenthal was charged and convicted of carrying a loaded and concealed pistol without permission.

Rosenthal, on demurrer, had contended that the Rutland ordinance violated the state constitution's Second Amendment analogue: "The people of the State have a right to bear arms for the defense of themselves and the State."[7] The Municipal Court overruled the demurrer and Rosenthal appealed to the state's Supreme Court. Associate Justice John Watson, who would later become the court's chief justice, wrote the court's opinion.

After acknowledging that the state constitution gave people a right to bear arms for self-defense, the state attorney general defended the ordinance by noting that "This by-law does not prevent one from carrying a pistol in defense, only it must not be concealed. Nor is the by-law inconsistent with the laws of the state. It supersedes the general law on the subject."[8] In considering this argument, Justice Watson noted that Rutland's charter only gave the city council power to

> "make and establish … rules and ordinances which they deem necessary for the well-being of said city and not repugnant to the Constitution or laws of the State." Power to make the ordinance in question was not expressly given to the council and they had no power to make it, beyond what is given under the general clause above quoted.[9]

He then noted,

> But by V. S. [Vermont Statute] 4922, a person is prohibited from carrying a dangerous weapon or deadly weapon, openly or concealed, with the intent or avowed purpose of injuring a fellow man; … But section 4926 provides that [statute 4922] shall not apply where firearms are used in self-defense, or in the discharge of official duty, or in the case of justifiable homicide. Under the general laws, therefore, a person … may carry a dangerous or deadly weapon, openly or concealed, unless he does it with the intent or avowed purpose of injuring another….[10]

Watson further observed,

> By the ordinance in question, no person can carry such weapon concealed on his person within the city of Rutland in any circumstances, nor for any purpose, without permission of the mayor or chief of police in writing. Therein neither the intent nor purpose of carrying them enters into the essential element of the

> offense. Simply to carry them concealed without such permission constitutes a violation of the ordinance. But if permission is procured from either of those officials, there is no violation … even though the carrying of the weapon be with the intent or avowed purpose of injuring another person; … Consequently, unless special permission is granted by the mayor or chief of police, a person is prevented from carrying such weapons in circumstances where the same is lawful by the Constitution and the general laws of the State; and there is nothing in the ordinance to prevent the granting of such permission, notwithstanding it be in circumstances to constitute a crime under the general laws.[11]

Watson concluded,

> The result is that Ordinance No. 10 so far as it relates to the carrying of a pistol, is inconsistent with, and repugnant to, the Constitution and the laws of the State, and it is therefore, to that extent, void. Whether this renders the whole ordinance illegal, or whether it contains any other invalid provisions, are questions not now before the court.[12]

With that, Watson sustained Rosenthal's demurrer, set aside his sentence, and ordered him discharged without delay.

Based on Vermont's Second Amendment analogue and the state's general laws, Justice Watson's *Rosenthal* opinion is only indirectly relevant to the federal amendment. Nonetheless, his analysis not only demonstrated the same judicial assumption prevalent in court adjudications of the nineteenth century—that bearing arms was an individual right subject only to some limited regulation for public safety—it actually went further in noting that a person might carry a *concealed* firearm if the individual harbored no intention of harming another.

Regarding the constitutionality of the statute's "written permission" requirement for concealed carry, his opinion was ambiguous. While implicitly indicating that this requirement might also raise constitutional issues—that is, "whether it contains other invalid provisions"—Watson limited his determination to the statute's absolute prohibition of concealed carry generally. The permit requirement was not a question "now before the court." A decade later in New York City, that question *did* come directly before the court, in a test of the constitutionality of the city's recently enacted "Sullivan Law."[13]

Darling v. Warden of City Prison (1913): Challenging a Permit Requirement for a Home-Kept Pistol

In 1911, New York amended Section 1897 of its Penal Law, adding a provision which stated, "Any person over the age of sixteen years who shall have in his possession … any pistol … of a size which may be concealed upon the person, without a written license therefor, … shall be guilty of a misdemeanor."[14] Joseph Darling, a New York City political figure and libertarian, deliberately violated the statute by notifying the police that he kept a pistol in his house without a permit. Arrested for breaching §1897 and brought before a city magistrate, Darling was held for trial at Special Sessions Court, where he was discharged.[15]

The court asserted that "possession" in the statute meant physical possession, not a constructive possession:

> The act in question is a penal statute, and under well-settled principles is to be strictly construed. To hold that every possible kind of constructive possession is made a crime would be to give to the language a very broad significance. By limiting it to physical possession, the necessary requirements of the language are met, and … I do not think it proper to extend its meaning beyond the actual requirements of the language used.[16]

New York City disagreed, and appealed Darling's discharge, with Justice John Clarke writing the opinion for New York's Appellate Division. Clarke, a Yale graduate and a classmate of William Howard Taft, would later serve as Presiding Justice of the Appellate Division.

In the appeal, Darling chose to defend the dismissal of his conviction on Second Amendment grounds rather than on the interpretation of "constructive possession," as developed by the Special Sessions Court. Nonetheless, despite his repudiation of this defense, the appellate court addressed both arguments in its opinion, examining the Special Sessions' argument first.

Clarke began his analysis by reviewing the 1910 provisions of §1897. In addition to prohibiting the carrying or possession of various dangerous weapons (e.g., billy clubs, brass knuckles, dirks, etc.), this section of the penal code also noted: "Any person … who shall have or carry concealed upon his person … any pistol, revolver or other firearm without a written license … shall be guilty of a misdemeanor."[17] He then observed that the legislature later amended §1897, increasing the list of prohibited weapons, and raising offenses from misdemeanors to felonies. The amendment also inserted additional material into the section: "Any person … who shall have in his possession … any pistol, revolver, or other firearm of a size which may be concealed upon the person, without a written license … shall be guilty of a misdemeanor."[18]

From this, Clarke concluded,

> Evidently, the Legislature intended to define, and provide punishment for, a different offense from any that had been theretofore covered by this section. [… individuals] who shall have carried concealed upon his person a pistol without a license should be guilty of a felony; … [but an individual] "who shall have in his possession … any pistol … of a size which may be concealed upon the person, without a written license therefor, … shall be guilty of a misdemeanor."[19]

Elaborating, Clarke continued,

> The learned court at Special Term has limited the language of the paragraph added to the section by, in effect, writing into the language thereof words which the

legislature left out …. [That court's] construction would make the offense a felony or a misdemeanor, depending on whether the pistol [was carried] concealed, or not; and the sole effect of the act, which was passed … in an attempt to limit crimes of violence, would be to provide against the open carrying of pistols which were of a size to be concealed—an utterly unreasonable conclusion …. The language itself … indicated that the Legislature intended exactly what it said, to prohibit a person at any time, and in any place, within a city, village or town, to have such a pistol in his possession without the permit required.[20]

Clarke then noted that Darling repudiated the Special Sessions Court's construction of the statute. In his appeal brief, Darling wrote, "It seems fair to believe that the Legislature did mean to prohibit constructive possession in the home of the unlicensed home revolver. The only question that realtor [i.e., Darling] submits on this appeal is the constitutionality of the law for licensing the possession of the home revolver."[21] Asserting that Darling's defense now stood upon "the inherent and inalienable right to keep and bear arms … alluded to in the second amendment to the Constitution of the United States,"[22] Clarke further observed,

It is settled by a long line of authorities that the first ten amendments to the Constitution of the United States are not operatives on the states. *Barron v. Baltimore* …; *Spies v. Illinois* …; *Brown v. New Jersey* …. And it has been specifically held that the second amendment, here relied upon, has no other effect than to restrict the powers of the national government, as said by the Chief Justice in *United States v. Cruikshank* …. See, also, *Presser v. Illinois* …; *Miller v. Texas* …; *Andrews v. State*.[23]

Continuing, Justice Clarke pointed out,

The legislatures of nearly all the states have enacted statutes making it an indictable offense to carry concealed weapons. The general rule is …: "The provisions of the state statutes prohibiting the carrying of concealed weapons do not infringe any constitutional right … but are merely police regulations forbidding the carrying [of] weapons in a particular manner which is found dangerous to the safety and peace of the citizen." …the Legislature has passed a regulative, not a prohibitory act. Legislation which [promotes] public welfare and safety falls within the scope of police power and must be submitted to …. The rights of the individual are subordinate to the welfare of the state. The only question … is whether the means employed are appropriate and reasonably necessary … and are not unduly oppressive.[24]

After citing a half-dozen prior adjudications supporting his assertion, Clarke observed,

No court … has ever declared such a law [i.e., prohibiting concealed carry] in violation of the Constitution or the Bill of Rights. …the Legislature has now

> picked out one particular kind of arm ... the favorite weapon of the turbulent criminal class, and has said that ... where the public peace is protected by the officers of organized government, the citizens may not have that particular kind of weapon without a permit, as it had already said that he might not carry it on his person without a permit. If he has it in his possession, he can readily stick it in his pocket when he goes abroad. ... [This act] is an attempt to keep away temptation, opportunity. ... I am unable to persuade myself that such an act, regulating a right that is not denied, is not a legitimate exercise of the police power of the state. ... I think it must be sustained by the courts.[25]

With that, Justice Clarke reversed the findings of the Special Sessions Court, and ordered Darling remanded.

As Justice Clarke observed, requiring a permit for concealed carry was not unusual, with several other states having enacted such statutes in the past. The distinctive aspect of the statute Darling challenged was requiring a permit for simply keeping a handgun at home. This restriction, together with the procedures mandated for obtaining a permit (i.e., an application fee, a police interview, fingerprints, photographs, and having a "good reason" for needing a handgun) made New York's firearm law the most stringent gun control statute in America during that time.[26] While Darling's case did not specifically involve the "good-reason" clause of the permitting process, later court adjudications would test that aspect of the statute.

In the next case, contrasting with the priority Justice Clarke placed on the state's police power, Michigan's Supreme Court stressed the individual's Second Amendment rights when examining a handgun permitting requirement. This court concluded that the state had no power to criminalize the possession of a revolver kept for legitimate self-defense—even for non-citizens.

People of Michigan v. Zerillo (1922): Challenging a Conviction for Pistol Possession without Permit

James Zerillo, an unnaturalized foreign-born resident of Michigan, had been arrested and convicted of violating *Act No. 14, Public Acts 1921*. This Michigan game law made it illegal for an unnaturalized foreign-born resident to possess a firearm without a permit from the county sheriff. Zerillo, in Detroit, had been seated at the wheel of a touring car at five o'clock in the morning, with several other men in the car holding shotguns. While Zerillo had no shotgun, his door pocket contained a .38-caliber revolver, and the presence of this firearm led to his arrest and conviction.[27] Zerillo appealed, and the case came before Michigan's Supreme Court, with Justice Howard Wiest (who neither graduated high school nor attended law school, but who would go on to become the court's chief justice) authoring the court's opinion.

Justice Wiest observed that

> The complaint was laid under the game law, but did not charge the defendant with hunting ... or intending to do so. Does the game law make it unlawful for

> an unnaturalized foreign-born resident of the state to possess a revolver? The act mentioned makes it a misdemeanor for an unnaturalized foreign-born resident to hunt for or capture or kill any wild birds or animals … excepting in defense of his person or property, "and to that end," such a person shall not own or be possessed of a shotgun or a rifle of any make or a pistol or firearms of any kind. The act provides that, on the recommendation of two citizens, the sheriff of the county, upon a showing of necessity, may issue a permit to an unnaturalized foreign-born resident to possess firearms.[28]

Wiest then noted,

> Defendant insists that the act, so far as it deprives him of the right to possess a revolver, for a legitimate purpose, is in conflict with the provisions of the Constitution of the state, and therefore void. The *Constitution of this state (article 2, section 5)* provides: "Every person has a right to bear arms for the defense of himself and the state." … Firearms serve the people of this country a useful purpose wholly aside from hunting, and under a constitution like ours, granting to aliens who are bona fide residents … the same rights … as native-born citizens, and to *every person* the right to bear arms for the defense of himself and the state, while the Legislature has power … to regulate the carrying and use of firearms, that body has no power to constitute it a crime for a person, alien or citizen, to possess a revolver for the legitimate defense of himself and his property.[29]

Continuing, Wiest asserted,

> The provision in the Constitution granting the right to all persons to bear arms is a limitation upon the powers of the Legislature to enact any law to the contrary. The exercise of a right guaranteed by the Constitution cannot be made subject to the will of the sheriff. The part of the act under which the prosecution was planted is not one of regulation but is one of prohibition and confiscation. It is not regulation to make it a crime … to possess a revolver, unless permitted to have one by the sheriff …. Game being property of the state the Legislature may enact laws for its protection, but under the guise of protection of game may not disarm any class … of the right to bear arms in defense of themselves.[30]

Wiest next pointed out some absurdities that would arise if the People's construction of the act was accepted:

> Must an alien owner of a farm sit with folded arms and watch henhawks steal his chickens? No, the act permits him to kill noxious birds and animals, when necessary, in defense of his person or property. But what is he going to use for that purpose? Until the occasion arises … it is a crime for him to possess a firearm, and he therefore cannot be prepared to exercise the leave granted without committing a crime. Woodchucks could burrow in his yard and meadows with impunity, owls

> rob his henroost, rats run about his feet ... wolves could sit on his very doorstep .... Must he request the burglar to come unarmed because he has been unarmed by the law?[31]

Citing another, later game act passed by the Michigan legislature, Wiest noted another problem with the People's position. This act later provided that "No person, while in an automobile shall carry a gun or other firearm, except a pistol or revolver, unless the same be unloaded."[32] The Justice then asked, "Shall unnaturalized owners of automobiles be held guilty under one game law for exercising a right under another game law? It would be absurd to so hold."[33]

Wiest concluded the opinion:

> The part of the act making it a crime for an unnaturalized foreign-born resident to possess a revolver, unless so permitted by the sheriff, contravenes the guaranty of such right in the Constitution of the state, and is void. The statute ... [in] so far as it makes it a crime for unnaturalized residents to possess a revolver for the legitimate defense of their persons and property it is void. ... [T]he defendant should have been adjudged not guilty. The conviction is set aside and the defendant is discharged.[34]

Several factors may account for the totally different treatment of gun-permitting statutes in the courts of Justices Clarke and Wiest. Socioculturally, general attitudes toward firearms differed between the urban East Coast and the more rural Midwest.[35] Not only were New York City's gun problems less pressing in the heart of the nation, but Michigan's constitution contained a Second Amendment analogue not found in the New York State constitution. New York's protection of individual rights were embodied in statutes (i.e., the *Civil Rights Law of 1909*)[36]—a less stringent form of protection. Finally, the New York permitting statute was merely "regulatory," while the Michigan statute, by demanding a permit for *any* firearm, was "prohibitive."

The next case, a war-time adjudication, shows the ongoing influence of New York's Sullivan Law thirty years after its passage. As noted, *Darling* only challenged the statute's requirement of a police permit for mere possession of a concealable firearm. The statute also created a stringent set of rules for obtaining a permit,[37] including a "good cause" requirement. The *Moore* case tested this requirement.

Matter of Moore v. Gallup (1943): Challenging a Permit Renewal Denial

In January, 1939, LeRoy Moore, an honorably discharged war veteran, had applied to the county judge of Albany County, New York, for a concealed-carry pistol permit. Trained in firearms during his military service, he had possessed a permit since 1937. On the permit application, Moore indicated only that he wanted the license to engage in target practice. With the application, he attached the two required testimonials attesting to his good character. Following the procedures established by New York's Penal Law, the county judge then forwarded the application packet to the Chief of Police of Albany for investigation.[38]

Without in any way questioning Moore's good moral character, the police chief recommended that the judge disapprove Moore's application. In an attempt to determine if "proper cause" existed to issue the license, the judge afforded Moore two personal hearings to present additional information. Remaining unconvinced that proper cause existed, the judge denied the license. He believed that "a dangerous and unwise precedent would be established if all citizens of good moral character were to be licensed to carry pistols upon a simple showing of a desire on their part to engage in unregulated and unsupervised target practice which would not constitute the 'proper cause' prescribed by the legislature in enacting the statute in question."[39]

Moore appealed the denial, and at Special Sessions Court, the official referee reviewed the matter and, after a trial, rendered a report containing five "findings of fact" and two "conclusions of law." The referee noted in the report's "fact" section that Moore was a person of good moral character, had for many years legally owned pistols, had been licensed to carry them, and was experienced and skillful in their use. He also noted that Moore only listed "target shooting" in his application for a permit; and his only purpose and reason for shooting at a target "is his personal amusement or entertainment, and he desires to transport the pistols to some place or places away from his residence to thus amuse or entertain himself."[40]

In the report's "law" section, the referee concluded,

> First: The target shooting as practiced and intended to be practiced by petitioner bears no relation to the safety or protection of the life or property of any person. Second: The use to be made of the pistols, as described above, does not constitute "proper cause" such as to require the issuance of a license "to have and carry concealed a pistol" under the provision of subdivision 9 of Section 1897 of the Penal Law.[41]

The referee directed a dismissal of the proceeding, noting that Moore could apply for a license to possess pistols on his premises, that is, under Subdivision 8 of Section 1987 of the Penal Law. Moore filed exceptions to these conclusions, sending the case to New York's Appellate Division. This court's opinion was authored by Justice Gilbert Schenck.

While Moore's appeal petition invoked Second Amendment guarantees, Justice Schenck observed,

> Obviously, petitioner cannot rest his case upon the Second Amendment which is a limitation upon the exertion of the power of Congress and the national government, but not upon that of the State. (*United States v. Cruikshank …; Presser v. Illinois….*) Moreover, the Second Amendment created no right to bear arms, a right which long ante-dated the adoption of the Federal Constitution …. Again, the Supreme Court of the United States has held that the right to keep and bear arms is not infringed by laws prohibiting the carrying of concealed weapons (*Robertson v. Baldwin ….*).[42]

Having thus established that concealed-carry permits do not violate the Second Amendment generally, Schenck then turned to the "may-issue" aspects of the permitting process.

Justice Schenck noted,

> Petitioner's assertion of a vested right acquired by him through the granting of earlier licenses is untenable in the light of this utterance by the Court of Appeals: "A power to grant a privilege to one is inconsistent with the possession on the part of another of an absolute right to exercise such privilege. The requirement that a person must secure leave from someone … to exercise a right, carries with it, by natural implication, a discretion on the part of the other to refuse to grant it, if, in his judgment, it is improper or unwise to give the required consent." (*People ex rel. Schwab v. Grant …*).[43]

Schenck continued,

> Petitioner insists that a mandatory meaning is to be ascribed to the provision of subdivision 9 of section 1897 of the Penal Law that "it shall be lawful" for the Magistrate, upon compliance with the conditions prescribed in the statute, to issue a license to have and carry concealed a pistol or revolver. While the language of a statute permissive in terms may be accorded a mandatory meaning … it is hard to believe … the permissive words "it shall be lawful" … is open to any interpretation except that the latter phrase was designed by the Legislature to be permissive only. Writing for this court, Justice HENRY T. KELLOGG … said: "The instances are numerous in which administrative officers [are] *empowered* but not expressly *required* by statute to grant licenses and certificates … [and] have been held to possess an absolute discretion not to grant or make them." (*Matter of Barresi v. Biggs …*).[44]

Pointing out that the statute required an investigation to verify all statements made in the application packet, Schenck asserted,

> Thus is manifested a legislative intent that the local authorities, having in view considerations of public safety and the maintenance of law and order in their communities, shall ascertain whether "proper cause exists for the issuance" of the desired license. Necessarily, the solution of that question involves the exercise of discretion on the part of the local officials [who have] the responsibility of making the determination. It is to be presumed that the refusal of the County Judge to grant petitioner a license was actuated by a desire to guard the public safety and conserve the general welfare. …With the conclusions fairly reached by the County Judge, fortified by the recommendation by the chief of police, the courts should not interfere.[45]

After a discussion of several other non-firearms adjudications supporting "may-issue" licensing, Justice Schenck affirmed the report of the Official Referee.

The *Moore* opinion, by firmly upholding the constitutionality of the statute's "proper cause" requirement, significantly strengthened the state's police power in controlling civilian possession of handguns. At least as applied in New York City, regardless of the reason the applicant might offer for wanting a handgun—even for self-defense and personal safety—the permit was almost always denied.[46]

1980–94: "Proper Cause" Four Decades Later

By 1980, the "may-issue" approach to handgun permitting had spread to other states, but the determination of "proper cause" in these states was not always as stringent as in New York. The Indiana Court of Appeals, for instance, determined in *Schubert v. DeBard* that "self-defense" fulfilled the proper cause requirement for a handgun permit. In contrast, the New York's judiciary continued to construe "proper cause" quite narrowly and to severely restrict concealed-carry permits, as *Matter of Klenosky v. N.Y. City Police Department* and *Matter of O'Connor v. Scarpino* demonstrate.

Schubert v. DeBard (1980): Challenging a Firearms Licensing Denial

Concluding that Joseph Schubert did not have a "proper reason" for carrying a handgun, the superintendent of the Indiana State Police rejected Schubert's permit request; and at trial, the county court sustained the superintendent's decision. Schubert then proceeded to the Indiana Court of Appeals, where Presiding Judge William Garrard, a former prosecuting attorney, authored the court's opinion.[47]

Garrard noted that Schubert wanted a permit to carry a handgun for self-protection and that he had held carry permits in the past, when he was engaged in part-time security work. The judge also noted that Schubert had held a special police commission from the City of Fort Wayne and a Deputy Sheriff's commission from St. Joseph's County, but that both had been revoked prior to his permit application.[48]

As evidence of his need for self-protection, Schubert provided two mailed threats, which he suspected his brother had sent. Additionally, he testified that his brother at one point had also fired a rifle at a van in which he was riding. Despite notifying the prosecutor's office about the shooting, no charges were brought. Based on these incidents, Schubert claimed he feared for his life and needed to carry a handgun for protection.[49]

Judge Garrard then referenced a 1971 background investigation report undertaken when Schubert applied for a private detective's license. Garrard observed,

> That report concluded that appellant was a "chronic liar" suffering from a "gigantic police complex." The report, as well as testimony of a police officer at the hearing, indicated that on occasion, when he had been licensed to carry a gun, appellant had carried and displayed his pistol at inappropriate times which did not require the use of a gun for personal safety or to expedite the duties of his employment. … Several of those interviewed … including former employers and the sheriff

who both created and revoked his deputy sheriff's commission, felt appellant had "mental problems."[50]

Turning to Indiana's licensing statute, Garrard reviewed the statute, which provided,

> The officer to whom the application is made shall conduct an investigation … and verify thereby the applicant's character and reputation … and shall forward this information together with his recommendation for approval or disapproval …. *If it appears to the superintendent that the applicant has a proper reason for carrying a handgun and is of good character and reputation and a proper person to be so licensed*, he shall issue to the applicant either a qualified or an unlimited license to carry any handgun or handguns lawfully possessed. (emphasis added)[51]

Asserting that this licensing procedure was "not violative of the right to bear arms as guaranteed by the Second Amendment or Art. 1, Sec. 32 of the Indiana Constitution," Garrard noted that "Schubert contends, however, that the Indiana Constitution affords him the right to bear arms for own defense. Thus, he urges where self-defense is properly asserted as the reason for desiring a firearms license, and the applicant is otherwise qualified, the license cannot be withheld upon an administrative official's subjective determination of whether the applicant needs defending."[52]

Continuing, Garrard pointed out that Indiana's Second Amendment analogue is worded differently than the Second Amendment, simply stating, "The people will have a right to bear arms, for the defense of themselves and the State."[53] After reviewing some historical background regarding the framers' intent in enacting the analogue, Judge Garrard asserted, "We think it is clear that our constitution provides our citizenry the right to bear arms for their self-defense. Furthermore, in *Matthews v. State* … our Supreme Court held that if it is determined … that the applicant has met the conditions of the statute, the superintendent has no discretion to withhold the license."[54]

Garrard further stated,

> In Schubert's case it is clear from the record that the superintendent decided the application on the basis that the statutory reference to "a proper reason" vested in him the power and duty to subjectively evaluate an assignment of "self-defense" as a reason for desiring a license and the ability to grant or deny the license upon the basis of whether the applicant "needed" to defend himself. Such an approach contravenes the essential nature of the constitutional guarantee. It would supplant a right with a mere administrative privilege …. We therefore hold that Schubert's assigned reason which stood unrefuted was constitutionally a "proper reason" within the meaning of [the statute.][55]

The judge recognized that other evidence questioned Schubert's suitability for a firearms license, but noted that the original determination did not attempt to resolve those issues. Thus, he concluded, "We therefore reverse the determination and direct that the matter be remanded for a new hearing … and for further proceedings consistent herewith. Reversed and remanded."[56]

Despite the "character and reputational" issues left unresolved by the case, the *Schubert* opinion clearly established that—at least in Indiana—a simple desire for self-protection qualified as meeting the "proper cause" requirement for obtaining a firearms license. Indeed, the Indiana Court of Appeals reiterated this finding a year later in *Shettle v. Shearer*,[57] a similar case involving a firearms licensing denial. But in New York City, as the next adjudication shows, a simple desire for self-protection remained insufficient for fulfilling "proper cause" requirements.

Matter of Klenosky v. New York City Police Dept. (1980): Reversing a Handgun Carry-Permit Grant

In a short, unsigned opinion, the Appellate Division of the Supreme Court of New York unanimously reversed the county court's decision granting petitioner Klenosky a pistol carrying permit. The appellate court asserted, "it is clear that the administrative determination denying petitioner's application for a pistol carrying permit (as distinct from an on-premises license) on the basis of failure to demonstrate 'proper cause … for the issuance thereof' is supported by substantial evidence and is not arbitrary or capricious."[58]

The opinion noted,

> Petitioner, a 52-year-old attorney engaged in matrimonial and criminal law practice, did not sufficiently demonstrate a special need for self-protection distinguishable from that of the general community or of persons engaged in the same profession. The receipt of cash and checks (not in unusually high amounts) … and threats from dissatisfied clients involved with the criminal law or threats related to the matrimonial practice, are not uncommon occurrences sufficient to distinguish petitioner from other attorneys engaged in similar practice.[59]

The opinion continued,

> Further, petitioner's disability (an artificial right leg which necessitates walking with a limp) does not, of itself, amount to such an unusual circumstance as to warrant issuance of a permit to carry a concealed pistol. Finally, petitioner's professed fear of burglary in his home and office would be satisfied by issuance of an "on-premises" license, which type of license was, in fact, offered to petitioner, but refused.[60]

With that, the court denied Klenosky's permit application and dismissed the petition.

As *Klenosky* indicated (and as *Schubert* intimated), some states have issued handgun permits with various restrictions. Reflecting the "proper cause" approach to permitting, restricted licenses allow individuals to possess firearms, but limit their use to specific activities (e.g., hunting or target practice) or to possession in specific places (e.g., one's home or business). These restrictions reduce the gun's self-protection value, and individuals have challenged them trying to obtain an unqualified carry permit. The next case, adjudicated by New York State's highest court (confusingly called the Court of Appeals) dealt with such a challenge. The case also highlights the impact of the Sullivan Law eight decades after its passage.

Matter of O'Connor v. Scarpino (1994): Challenging Denial of a Firearms Carry License

In an unsigned memorandum, New York's highest court reviewed restricted firearms licensing appeals from two different Appellate Divisions. Petitioner Eddy's appeal—objecting to a "hunting, fishing, target practice" restriction on her firearms license—originated in the Appellate Division's Second Judicial Department. Petitioner O'Connor's appeal—objecting to a "target shooting, hunting only" restriction—originated in the Appellate Division's Fourth Judicial Department.[61]

The court observed that both petitioners objected to the restrictions, arguing that the statute did not expressly empower licensing officers to impose conditions. The justices disagreed, noting that

> the licensing officers' power to determine the existence of "proper cause" for the issuance for a license necessarily and inherently includes the power to restrict the use to the purposes that justified the issuance. Without such a power to condition, the licensing officer's authority to allow possession of a handgun would be rendered meaningless and the obvious regulatory purpose of the statute would be frustrated.[62]

The justices further noted that the statute made provision for varying types of permits:

> The other licenses allowed by the statute are narrowly circumscribed to the circumstances justifying their issuance .... Were we to read the carry license ... to allow possession of firearms generally once good cause was shown, there would be no reason for applicants to seek the more restrictive licenses ... when they could just as easily qualify for the broader carry license.[63]

In each case, the court affirmed the judgment of the appellate divisions.

While *O'Connor* and the other cases above all upheld the constitutionality of a "proper cause" requirement for firearms licenses, the variability and latitude in determining a given reason's acceptability as proper cause is notable. Unsurprisingly, as the next section shows, permit seekers' dissatisfaction with seemingly arbitrary "proper cause" denials continued to spark judicial tests of these judgments into the twenty-first century.

2012–14: Leading to *Bruen*

The second decade of the new century produced a flurry of new legal challenges to "may-issue," "proper-cause" licensing. With the *Heller* decision in 2008 and *McDonald* in 2010—both emphasizing an individual's general right to keep and bear firearms—the timing of these cases was not coincidental. *Heller* and *McDonald*, together with a Supreme Court sympathetic to gun rights, gave twenty-first-century petitioners reason to anticipate more favorable judicial outcomes than in past permitting cases. Consequently, challenges to this type of licensing originated in New York (*Kachalsky*, 2012), Maryland (*Woollard*, 2013), New Jersey (*Drake*, 2013), California (*Peruta*, 2014/2016), and the District of Columbia (*Wrenn*, 2017).

Kachalsky v. County of Westchester (2012): Challenging New York's Proper Cause Requirement

Alan Kachalsky, as well as four other plaintiffs, wanted to carry handguns outside the home for self-protection. They each had sought a full-carry concealed handgun license, but New York licensing authorities had rejected their applications, for failing to establish "proper cause" as required. With the support of the Second Amendment Foundation (a gun rights advocacy organization), the plaintiffs then challenged the denials in federal district court, arguing that the proper cause provision violated the Second Amendment as interpreted in *Heller*.[64]

The district court granted the County of Westchester summary judgment, holding that the Second Amendment Foundation lacked standing to sue on behalf of its members or itself. The court also asserted that carrying concealed handguns in public exceeded *Heller*'s core Second Amendment concern—that of self-defense in the home. Further, the court held that, even if the proper cause provision posed a Second Amendment concern, the requirement would still pass constitutional scrutiny. Disputing the ruling, the plaintiffs brought their case to the Court of Appeals for the Second Circuit.[65] Judge Richard Wesley, appointed to the federal bench by President Bush in 2003, wrote the court's opinion.

Wesley summarized the case issue in a single sentence: "Does New York's handgun licensing scheme violate the Second Amendment by requiring an applicant to demonstrate 'proper cause' to obtain a concealed handgun in public?"[66] Noting that New York had a long history in regulating the possession and use of firearms, Wesley emphasized the circumstances resulting in New York's Sullivan Law, and that this regulatory law had survived the constitutional attack posed by the early *Darling* case. The law in 1913 required an applicant for a firearms permit to demonstrate good moral character and proper cause to obtain a license, and the judge observed that those requirements remained a central feature of New York's statutory scheme a hundred years later.[67]

Wesley acknowledged that

> "proper cause" is not defined by the Penal Law, but New York State courts have defined the term to include carrying a handgun for target practice, hunting, or

self-defense. When an applicant demonstrates proper cause to carry a handgun for target practice or hunting, the licensing offer may restrict a carry license "to the purposes that justified the issuance." *O'Connor, 83, N.Y.2d* .... To establish proper cause to obtain a license without any restrictions ... an applicant must "demonstrate a special need for self-protection distinguishable from that of the general community ...." *Klenosky v. N.Y. City Police Dept.* .... There is a substantial body of law instructing licensing officials on the application of this standard.[68]

Continuing, Wesley asserted,

Unlike a license for target shooting or hunting, "[a] generalized desire to carry a concealed weapon to protect one's person and property does not constitute 'proper cause.'" [Citations provided]. Good moral character plus a simple desire to carry a weapon is not enough. [Citations provided]. Nor is living or being employed in a "high crime area []." [Citations provided]. The application process for a license is 'rigorous'.... Every application triggers a local investigation by police into the applicant's mental health history, criminal history, moral character, and, in the case of a carry license, representations of proper cause. ...Licensing officers ... are 'vested with considerable discretion' in deciding ... whether proper cause exists.... [Citations provided]. ... A licensing officer's decision will be upheld unless it is arbitrary and capricious. [Citation provided]."[69]

He further noted,

Four of the five Plaintiffs made no effort to comply with New York's requirements for a full-carry license, that is, they did not claim a special need for self-protection distinguishable from that of the general community .... Plaintiff Kachalsky asserted that the Second Amendment "entitles him to an unrestricted permit without further establishing 'proper cause.'" ... Plaintiffs Nance and Marcucci-Nance asserted that they demonstrated proper cause because they were citizens in "good standing" in their community and were gainfully employed. ... Plaintiff Detmer asserted that he demonstrated proper cause because he was a federal law enforcement officer with the U.S. Coast Guard. ... Plaintiff Nikolov attempted to show a special need for self-protection by asserting that as a transgender female, she is more likely to be the victim of violence. ... she also asserted that being a law-abiding citizen in itself entitled her to a full-carry license.[70]

Before addressing the plaintiffs' Second Amendment argument, Judge Wesley finished his overview of the case, observing, "Plaintiffs' applications were all denied for the same reason: Failure to show any facts demonstrating a need for self-protection distinguishable from that of the general public. ... Nikolov's contention that her status as a transgender female put her at risk of violence was rejected because she did not 'report ... any type of threat to her own safety anywhere.'"[71]

Turning then to the Second Amendment question, Wesley observed,

> Defendants [argue] that the proper cause requirement does not burden conduct protected by the Second Amendment. They share the district court's view that … *Heller* limits the right to bear arms for self-defense to the home. *Heller* provides no categorical answer to this case. … Because the Second Amendment was directly at odds with a complete ban on handguns in the home … the [Supreme] Court simply noted that the handgun ban would be unconstitutional "[u]nder any of the standards of scrutiny that we have applied to enumerated constitutional rights." … *Heller* was never meant "to clarify the entire field of Second Amendment jurisprudence. …In *McDonald*, the Court struck down a Chicago law that banned handguns in the home. But it also reaffirmed *Heller's* assurances that Second Amendment rights are far from absolute and that many longstanding handgun regulations are 'presumptively lawful.' "[72]

After asserting that Second Amendment guarantees are clearly strongest within the home, Wesley acknowledged that "the amendment must have *some* application in the very different context of the public possession of firearms."[73] He noted that the plaintiffs argue "history and tradition demonstrate that there is a 'fundamental right' to carry handguns in public, and though a state may regulate open or concealed carrying of handguns, it cannot ban *both*. … Thus, according to plaintiffs, 'access to [New York's] only available carry license can[not] be qualified by 'proper cause.' "[74]

Wesley acknowledged that "some nineteenth-century state courts offered interpretations of the Second Amendment … that are similar to Plaintiffs' position,"[75] specifically referencing *State v. Reid*, *Nunn v. Georgia*, and *State v. Chandler*. However, he also noted that these interpretations were not universal, with at least four states—Arkansas, Wyoming, Tennessee, and Texas—having once banned both the concealed and open carrying of pistols and other weapons in public. Additionally, citing *Fife v. State*, *Andrews v. State*, and *English v. State*, he observed that—given the judiciary's understanding of the Second Amendment at that time—the Arkansas, Tennessee, and Texas bans withstood constitutional challenges.[76] Asserting that "History and tradition do not speak with one voice here,"[77] Judge Wesley further argued that, even if they did, the cited sources failed to address the specific issue of whether New York can limit handgun licenses "to those demonstrating a special need for self-protection."[78]

He asserted that "the question becomes how closely to scrutinize New York's statute,"[79] observing that *Heller* expressly avoided deciding the standard of review for a law burdening the Second Amendment. While conceding that the Second Circuit applied a heightened form of review for restrictions that heavily limit an individual's ability to possess a firearm for self-defense, the judge contended that heightened scrutiny did not always involve "strict scrutiny." He asserted, "we believe that applying less than strict scrutiny when the regulation does not burden the 'core' protection of self-defense in the home makes eminent sense in this context and is in line with the approach taken by our sister circuits. It is also consistent with jurisprudential experience analyzing other enumerated rights."[80]

Wesley continued,

> The proper cause requirement falls outside the core Second Amendment protections identified in *Heller*. New York's licensing scheme affects the ability to carry handguns *in public*, while the District of Columbia ban applied *in the home* .... This is a critical difference. The state's ability to regulate firearms and ... conduct is qualitatively different in public than in the home. ...while the state's ability to regulate firearms is circumscribed in the home, "outside the home, firearm rights have always been more limited, because public safety interests often outweigh individual interests in self-defense." *Masciandaro*, 638, F.3d.[81]

After a detailed review of various states regulating the possession and use of firearms in public because of community safety concerns, Wesley reiterated that, in the 1800s, many states completely banned the carrying of concealed weapons. He argued that these bans were similar to New York's law in that only an extremely few states included a self-defense exception in the ban. Then, taking all the reviewed material into consideration, Judge Wesley asserted, "Because our tradition so clearly indicates a substantial role for state regulation of the carrying of firearms in public, we conclude that intermediate scrutiny is appropriate in this case. The proper cause requirement passes constitutional muster if it is substantially related to the achievement of an important governmental interest."[82]

After noting all parties agreed that New York had a substantial governmental interest in public safety and crime prevention, the judge asserted, "The only question then is whether the proper cause requirement is substantially related to these interests. We concluded that it is."[83] In making this determination, Wesley noted that the judgment of the legislature warranted substantial deference, in that the legislature was better equipped than the judiciary to make policy judgments concerning the dangers of carrying firearms. He argued that the court's role was only to assure that, in formulating its judgments, New York had drawn reasonable inferences based on substantial evidence. He asserted, "Unlike strict scrutiny, we are not required to ensure that the legislature's chosen means is 'narrowly tailored' or the least restrictive available means .... To survive intermediate scrutiny, the fit between the challenged regulation need only be substantial, 'not perfect.' "[84]

Explaining that the 1913 legislative decision to regulate handgun possession was designed to increase safety and decrease crime, Wesley noted that

> [New York chose] not to ban handgun possession but to limit it to those individuals who have an actual reason ("proper cause") to carry the weapon. In this vein, licensing is oriented to the Second Amendment's protections. ... And proper cause is met ... when a person has an actual and articulable—rather than merely speculative or merely specious—need for self-defense. ... Restricting handgun possession in public to those who have a reason ... is substantially related to New York's interest in public safety .... It is not, as Plaintiffs contend, an arbitrary

> licensing regime ....New York's law need only be substantially related to the state's important public safety interest. A perfect fit ... is not required.[85]

Addressing the plaintiffs' contention that the desire for self-defense is all the "proper cause" required—that the exercise of a right cannot be made dependent on a *need* to exercise that right—the judge argued,

> State regulation under the Second Amendment has always been more robust than of other enumerated rights. ... In light of the state's considerable authority—enshrined within the Second Amendment—to regulate firearms possession in public, requiring a showing that there is an objective threat to a person's safety—a "special need for self-protection"—before granting a carry license is entirely consistent with the right to bear arms.[86]

Concluding the court's opinion, Judge Wesley asserted,

> Our review of the history and tradition of firearm regulation does not "clearly demonstrate []" that limiting handgun possession in public to those who show a special need for self-protection is inconsistent with the Second Amendment. Accordingly, we decline Plaintiff's invitation to strike down New York's one-hundred-year-old law .... For the foregoing reasons the judgment of the district court is AFFIRMED.[87]

In upholding the constitutionality of New York's "proper cause" requirement, the *Kachalsky* opinion emphasized three deciding considerations. First, the regulation of concealed carry in public had a long-standing legal pedigree; second, the regulation—focused on bearing a firearm outside the home—did not involve a core Second Amendment concern; and, third, even if the requirement *did* raise core concerns, the requirement would certainly pass constitutional muster using intermediate-level scrutiny. Less than four months later, the US Court of Appeals for the Fourth Circuit applied similar reasoning in *Woollard v. Gallagher*, overturning a district's court contrary finding and upholding Maryland's "good-and-substantial-reason" standard in issuing handgun permits.

Woollard v. Gallagher (2013): Challenging Maryland's Good-and-Substantial-Reason Requirement

In 2002, Raymond Woollard, residing on a remote rural farm in Baltimore County, suffered a home invasion. Kris Abbott, his son-in-law high on drugs, had shattered a window and entered the house in search of car keys for a drug run into Baltimore. Woollard initially restrained Abbott by training a shotgun on him, but Abbott wrested the shotgun away. Woollard's son then intervened with a second gun, holding Abbott until the police arrived, more than two hours later. After the incident, Woollard applied for and obtained a handgun permit. The permit was renewed in 2006, shortly after Abbott was released from prison, but in 2009 the Permit Review Board denied a second renewal, indicating that Woollard no longer satisfied Maryland's good-and-substantial reason requirement.[88]

The Board noted that Woollard offered only the 2002 incident in support of the second renewal, despite acknowledging that he had had no contact with Abbott since then. The Board further noted that Woollard did not document any threats occurring beyond his residence, where he already could legally carry a handgun. Concluding that Woollard had "not demonstrated a good and substantial reason to wear, carry, or transport a handgun as a reasonable precaution against apprehended danger," the Board denied the second renewal; rather than appeal the Board's decision, Woollard (together with the Second Amendment Foundation) elected to challenge the constitutionality of the good-and-substantial reason requirement in federal court. There, the district court, citing *Heller*, asserted that the right to possess and carry firearms extended beyond the home, and that the good-and-substantial reason requirement violated the Second Amendment. The State then appealed this court's "trailblazing" opinion.[89]

Judge Robert King, nominated to the federal bench in 1998 by President Bill Clinton, wrote the opinion for the circuit court. After discussing exceptions to Maryland's permitting scheme—for example, permits are not required for having handguns in the home—King turned to the "good-and-substantial reason" requirement, and its associated notion of "apprehended danger." He observed that a determination of "apprehended danger" is an objective inquiry and cannot be established by vague threats or a general fear of living in a dangerous society. The inquiry weighs multiple factors—for example, whether the threat can be verified and whether it is particular to the applicant—but treats those factors as non-exhaustive, and "takes the applicant's entire situation into account when considering whether a 'good-and-substantial reason' exists."[90]

King then noted that the district court, purporting to use intermediate scrutiny,

> recognized that the good-and-substantial reason requirement is undergirded by a substantial government interest in protecting public safety and preventing crime, but determined that "[t]he Maryland statute's failure lies in the overly broad means by which it seeks to advance this undoubtedly legitimate end. ... [the statute] is insufficiently tailored to the State's interest in public safety ... [and] impermissibly infringes on the right to keep and bear arms."[91]

After observing that *Heller* was principally concerned with the possession and use of arms in the home, and noting per *Kachalsky* that the degree of permissible government gun regulation outside the home was still undetermined, King determined to follow—"like several of our sister circuits"[92]—a two-part approach in considering the challenged requirement. Under this approach, the first part would determine whether a challenged law imposes a burden on Second Amendment guarantees; if so, the second part would determine if the burden is acceptable under an appropriate level of means-end scrutiny. King then pointed out that many appeal courts handling post-*Heller* gun challenges avoided definitive rulings on the first step and, instead, resolved the challenge by just examining the second step.[93]

Citing *Masciandaro*, a Fourth Circuit opinion that used this approach and concluded that intermediate scrutiny was appropriate when examining firearm rights outside the home, Judge King proceeded to examine whether a substantial governmental interest undergirded the state's enactment of its handgun permitting scheme. Referencing violent crime statistics involving the use of handguns, and noting that the district court itself recognized that the prevention of crime was a compelling government interest, King concluded that such a government interest did exist.[94]

He then examined whether the state had demonstrated a "reasonable fit" between the good-and-substantial reason requirement and the state's objective of protecting public safety. He observed, "Importantly, the State must show a fit that is 'reasonable, not perfect.' ... There is no necessity either that the good-and-substantial reason requirement 'be the least intrusive means ... or that there be no burden whatsoever on' Woollard's Second Amendment right."[95]

King concluded,

> The State has clearly demonstrated that the good-and-substantial-reason requirement advances the objectives of protecting public safety and preventing crime because it reduces the number of handguns carried in public. That is, limiting the public carrying of handguns ... inhibits crime by ... decreasing the availability of handguns to criminals via theft .... Lessening "the likelihood that basic confrontations between individuals would turn deadly," ... Curtailing the presence of handguns during police-citizen encounters, ... Facilitating the identification of those persons carrying handguns who pose a menace .... We are convinced by the State's evidence that there is a reasonable fit between the good-and-substantial-reason requirement and Maryland's objective in protecting public safety and preventing crime.[96]

After asserting that the district court "improperly conducted a review more reminiscent of strict scrutiny than intermediate scrutiny," King summarized, "although we assume Appellee Woollard's Second Amendment right is burdened by the good-and-substantial-reason requirement, we further conclude that such burden is constitutionally permissible. ... Pursuant to the foregoing, we reverse the judgment of the district court. REVERSED."[97]

In reversing the judgment of the district court, the Fourth Circuit Court implied that the constitutionality of Maryland's permit requirement hinged on the level of scrutiny used in making the determination. Strict scrutiny would find the requirement unconstitutional, as suggested by the district court's decision, but, as Judge King argued, intermediate scrutiny would not. A few months later, the Third Circuit Court of Appeals, in *Drake v. Filko*, would also adopt intermediate scrutiny in a permit-challenge case, and would reach the same conclusion.

***Drake v. Filko (2013)*: Challenging New Jersey's Justifiable Need Handgun Permit Standard**

Four New Jersey citizens—a reserve sheriff's deputy, a civilian FBI employee, an owner of an ATM cash restocking business, and a victim of an interstate kidnapping—applied for handgun carry permits but were denied for want of justifiable need. They appealed their denials in federal district court, arguing that the statute's justifiable need requirement violated the Second Amendment. In rejecting their challenge, the district court asserted that the Second Amendment does not protect a general right to carry a firearm outside the home, and even if the law "implicated" some narrow right to carry a gun outside the home, as a long-standing regulation, the law is presumptively constitutional. Finally, the court also asserted that, regardless of all the above, the statute would survive intermediate scrutiny in any event.[98] Unhappy with the court's ruling, the appellants brought their case to the circuit court. There, Judge Leonard Stark, nominated to the federal bench by President Barack Obama, authored the court's opinion.

After noting that handgun permits are "the most closely regulated aspect"[99] of New Jersey's gun control laws, and listing the process and requirements for obtaining a permit, Judge Stark focused on the meaning of "justifiable need." Quoting the definition found in the New Jersey Administrative Code—"the urgent necessity for self-protection, as evidenced by specific threats or previous attacks which demonstrate a special danger to the applicant's life that cannot be avoided by means other than by issuance of a permit to carry a handgun"[100]—he observed that the appellants had failed to satisfy a police official or court judge that they had a justifiable need for a carry permit. In reviewing the case, he determined to use the two-step approach the Third Circuit had followed in previous gun adjudications.

In the first step, Stark noted, "we ask whether the challenged law imposes a burden on conduct falling within the scope of the Second Amendment's guarantee. If it does not, our inquiry is complete. If it does, we evaluate the law under some form of means-end scrutiny. If the law passes muster under that standard, it is constitutional. If it fails, it is invalid."[101] After discussing the Second Amendment implications of several earlier cases (i.e., *Heller*, *Kachalsky*, *Masciandaro*, and others), Stark concluded, "we decline to definitively declare that the individual right to bear arms … extends beyond the home … [but we] do, however, recognize that the Second Amendment's individual right to bear arms may have some application beyond the home. … we refrain from answering this question definitively because it is not necessary to our conclusion."[102]

Judge Stark elaborated,

> Here, we agree with the District Court that even if some protected right to carry arms outside the home exists, the challenged requirement that applicants demonstrate a "justifiable need" … qualifies as a "longstanding," "presumptively lawful" regulation. … this Court has stated that "presumptively lawful" regulatory measures are "exceptions to the Second Amendment guarantee." … The "justifiable need" standard Appellants challenge has existed in New Jersey in some form for

> nearly 90 years. … [Further] New Jersey's longstanding handgun permitting schema is not an anomaly. … A close analogue … can be found in New York's permit schema which has required a showing of need, or "proper cause," for a century.[103]

Stark then observed,

> Even assuming that the "justifiable need" standard is not a longstanding regulation enjoying presumptive constitutionality … it withstands the appropriate intermediate level of scrutiny, and accordingly we would uphold the continued use of the standard on this basis as well. … [The appellants] contend that only strict scrutiny could possibly apply to the case at bar because the burden imposed by the "justifiable need" standard "is substantial, implicating the core rights of responsible, law-abiding citizens to engage in an activity whose protection is literally enumerated." We disagree. … the core of the right conferred … by the Second Amendment is the right to possess usable handguns in the home for self-defense. … We agree with the District Court, therefore, that strict scrutiny should not apply here …. Accordingly, we will apply intermediate scrutiny here.[104]

After observing that intermediate scrutiny requires the State to show a "reasonable" fit between a significant governmental interest and laws regulating that interest, Stark noted that New Jersey clearly had a significant interest in protecting citizens' safety. Additionally, he argued,

> It is New Jersey's judgment that when an individual carries a handgun in public for his or her own defense, he or she necessarily exposes members of the community to a somewhat heightened risk that they will be injured by that handgun. New Jersey has decided this somewhat heightened risk to the public may be outweighed by the potential safety benefit to an individual with a "justifiable need" to carry a handgun. Furthermore, New Jersey has decided that it can best determine when the individual benefit outweighs the increased risk to the community through careful case-by-case scrutiny of each applicant by the police and a court.[105]

After asserting that the "justifiable need" standard did not impose more of a burden than reasonably necessary, Judge Stark concluded, "the District Court correctly determined that the requirement that applicants demonstrate "justifiable need' to publicly carry a handgun for self-defense … does not burden conduct within the scope of the Second Amendment's guarantee …. [It also] withstands intermediate scrutiny and is therefore constitutional. Accordingly, we will affirm the judgment of the District Court."[106]

With Judge Stark's opinion, by the summer of 2013, three different circuit courts had upheld some type of "may issue/proper cause" approach to issuing gun permits for public carry. Nonetheless, indicators existed suggesting that the issue was not as fully settled as it appeared. Notably, Maryland's "trailblazing" district court, though subsequently overturned, had ruled against such a scheme, and, further, all three circuit courts had used intermediate scrutiny—a lower standard of review—in forming their opinions. California's *Peruta* gun case in 2014 highlighted this uncertainty.

Peruta v. County of San Diego (2014/16): Challenging California's "Good Cause" Requirement

Edward Peruta, a San Diego County resident, had applied for and been denied a concealed-carry license in 2009, on the grounds that he could not meet the "good cause" requirement for such a license. He (and several other residents) then sued the county, arguing that the "good cause" requirement infringed his right to bear arms under the Second Amendment. Using intermediate scrutiny, the district court upheld the requirement, reasoning that California's substantial interest in public safety trumped the applicants' Second Amendment interest. The applicants then appealed to the circuit court, where Judge Diarmuid O'Scannlain, nominated to the federal bench by President Ronald Reagan, wrote the majority opinion.[107]

After noting the California requirements for obtaining a concealed-carry license—for example, having good moral character, completing a training course, and establishing good cause—O'Scannlain observed that *Heller* established self-defense as a central component of the Second Amendment, but that neither *Heller* nor *McDonald* addressed "the scope of the Second Amendment right outside the home or to what it takes to 'infringe' it. … The first question [raised] … Does the restricted activity—here, a restriction on a responsible, law-abiding citizen's ability to carry a gun outside the home for self-defense—fall within the Second Amendment right to keep and bear arms for the purposes of self-defense?"[108] To answer this question and "arrive at the original understanding of the right," O'Scannlain consulted "both text and history."[109] He emphasized that the scope of the right "is determined by historical analysis and not interest balancing."[110]

After reviewing relevant historical and judicial passages regarding the meaning of "bearing arms" (e.g., *Muscarello*, *Moore v. Madigan*, *Masciandaro*), O'Scannlain argued, "These passages alone, though short of dispositive, strongly suggest that the Second Amendment secures a right to carry a firearm in some fashion outside the home."[111] He then turned to nineteenth-century case adjudications. He further observed, "Many of the same cases that the *Heller* majority invoked as proof that the Second Amendment secures an individual right [i.e., *Bliss*, *Simpson*, *Huntly*, *Andrews*, *Aymette*, *Reid*, *Nunn*] may just as easily be cited for the proposition [of a] general right to carry a common weapon outside the home for self-defense."[112]

Similarly, after examining post-Civil War legislative and political history, he summarized,

> Just as it was "plainly the understanding in the post-Civil War Congress that the Second Amendment protected an individual right for self-defense" … it appears that the right was also understood to encompass carrying weapons in public in

> case of confrontation. … The weight of authority suggests that the right to bear arms, as understood in the post-Civil War legal commentary, included the right to carry weapons outside the home for self-defense, which … is consistent with … nineteenth century court opinions.[113]

Citing *Drake*, *Woollard*, and *Kachalsky*, O'Scannlain then noted that these circuit courts have also acknowledged that the right to bear arms includes the right to carry a firearm outside the home for self-defense. He further observed,

> We … disagree with those courts—including the district court in this case—that have taken the view that it is not necessary … to decide whether carrying a gun in public for the lawful purposes of self-defense is a constitutionally protected activity. … Understanding the scope of the right is not just necessary, it is key to our analysis. For if self-defense outside the home is part of the core right to "bear arms" and the California regulatory scheme prohibits the exercise of that right, no amount of interest-balancing under a heightened form of means-ends scrutiny can justify San Diego County's policy.[114]

Continuing, O'Scannlain stated, "Our first task, therefore, is to assess the nature of the infringement … does it burden the right or, like in *Heller*, does it destroy the right altogether?"[115] He noted that, under California law, open carry is prohibited and illegal; while concealed carry is severely restricted. He noted,

> In California, the only way the typical … citizen can carry a weapon in public for the lawful purpose of self-defense is with a concealed carry permit. And, in San Diego County, that option has been taken off the table. The San Diego County policy specifies that concern for "one's personal safety alone" does not satisfy the "good cause" requirement for issuance of a permit. … Given this requirement, the "typical" responsible, law-abiding citizen in San Diego County cannot bear arms in public for self-defense.[116]

Before concluding his analysis, O'Scannlain elaborated on why his opinion differed from the other circuit courts. He argued,

> By evading an in-depth analysis of history and tradition, the Second, Third, and Fourth Circuits missed a crucial piece of the Second Amendment analysis. They failed to comprehend that carrying weapons in public for the lawful purpose of self-defense is a central component of the right to bear arms. … And further, they failed to comprehend that regulations on the right, although permissible to an extent, could not go so far as to enjoin completely a … citizen's right to carry in public for self-defense. … Because the Second, Third, and Fourth Circuits eschewed history and tradition in their analysis of the constitutionality of these regulations … we find their approaches unpersuasive.[117]

He additionally questioned the use of intermediate scrutiny in these earlier adjudications. Noting that his analysis did not adopt this approach (making a discussion of its potential application not "particularly instructive"), he argued,

> Nonetheless, to the extent those opinions suggest that the type of regulation at issue here can withstand some form of heightened scrutiny, it is worth noting our disagreement with their reasoning. … First, the analysis … is near identical to the freestanding "interest-balancing inquiry" that Justice Breyer proposed—and the majority explicitly rejected—in *Heller*. … [and second] In light of the states' failure to demonstrate sufficient narrow tailoring in *Drake*, *Woollard*, and *Kachalsky*, the gun regulations at issue in those cases should have been struck down even under intermediate scrutiny.[118]

With that, O'Scannlain noted that the district court erred in rejecting the applicant's motion for summary judgment, finding that the "good cause" requirement impermissibly infringed on the Second Amendment. He reversed and remanded.

Ninth Circuit *En Banc* Reversal (2016)

However, Judge O'Scannlain did not have the final word on the matter. On appeal, the Ninth Circuit *en banc* court reviewed and reversed O'Scannlain's three-member panel opinion two years later. Judge William Fletcher, nominated to the federal bench by President Bill Clinton, wrote the opinion for the court. He opened the opinion by stating, "We hold that the Second Amendment does not preserve or protect a right of a member of the general public to carry concealed firearms in public,"[119] and then proceeded to explain the court's reasoning.

After noting that the plaintiffs do not contend that the Second Amendment protects a free-standing right to carry concealed firearms—that they seek relief only against the "good cause" requirement—Fletcher observed,

> We do not reach the question whether the Second Amendment protects some ability to carry firearms in public …. we reach only the question whether the Second Amendment protects, in any degree, the ability to carry concealed firearms in public. Based on the overwhelming consensus of historical sources, we conclude that the protection of the Second Amendment—whatever the scope of that protection may be—simply does not extend to the carrying of concealed firearms in public by members of the general public.[120]

Turning to the historical record, the judge continued,

> In determining whether the Second Amendment protects the right to carry a concealed weapon in public, we engage in the same historical inquiry as *Heller* and *McDonald*. As will be seen, the history relevant to both the Second Amendment and

> its incorporation by the Fourteenth Amendment leads to the same conclusion: The right of a member of the general public to carry a concealed firearm in public is not, and never has been, protected by the Second Amendment.[121]

After an extended historical discussion of the right to bear arms in England from the 1290s through the 1780s, Fletcher summarized his findings: "Thus, by the end of the eighteenth century, when our Second Amendment was adopted, English law had for centuries consistently prohibited carrying concealed (and occasionally the even broader category of concealable) arms in public."[122] He then reviewed the right to bear arms in colonial America, noting, "We have found nothing in the historical record suggesting that the law in the American colonies with respect to concealed weapons differed significantly from the law in Enland."[123]

In considering the historical record after the country's independence, Fletcher cited *Bliss*, *Reid*, *Aymette*, *Buzzard*, *Nunn*, and several others. He pointed out, "with the exception of *Bliss*, those pre-Civil War state courts ... all upheld prohibitions against concealed weapons. ... Moreover, the two-to-one *Bliss* decision did not last."[124] Continuing, he then turned to the post-Civil War constitutions of a number of states and territories, and noted, "In the decades immediately after the adoption of the Fourteenth Amendment, all of the state courts that addressed the question upheld the ability of their state legislatures to prohibit concealed weapons."[125]

In summarizing his historical analysis, Fletcher stated,

> We therefore conclude that the Second Amendment right to keep and bear arms does not include, in any degree, the right of a member of the general public to carry concealed firearms in public. ... Our holding ... fully answers the question before us. ... any prohibition or restriction a state may choose to impose on concealed carry—including a requirement of 'good cause' however defined—is necessarily allowed by the Amendment.[126]

Then, addressing O'Scannlain's panel ruling, Fletcher noted, "A key premise of the opinion was that the Second Amendment required the states to 'permit *some form* of carry for self-defense outside the home.'"[127] Observing that the California statute allows "many residents, in many contexts, to carry a firearm outside the home," Fletcher continued, "it does not permit law-abiding citizens ... to do so without a particular interest in self-defense."[128]

Fletcher next addressed a dissenting argument. Since California restricted both open and concealed carry, the restrictions considered together were virtually a complete ban on bearing arms outside the home, and therefore violated the Constitution. The judge dismissed this reasoning as a logical fallacy. He argued,

> The Second Amendment may or may not protect to some degree a right of a member of the general public to carry a firearm in public. If there is such a right, it is only a right to carry a firearm openly. But Plaintiffs do not challenge California's restriction on open carry; they challenge only restrictions on concealed carry. ... if

> that right [of open carry] is violated, the cure is to apply the Second Amendment to protect that right. The cure is not to apply the Second Amendment to protect a right that does not exist under the Amendment.[129]

Given the narrow focus of the court's *en banc* analysis, the reversal of O'Scannlain's panel opinion was not surprising, in that the two courts framed the underlying Second Amendment issue differently. As a question of whether the amendment permitted restrictions on concealed carry, the historical evidence and long tradition answered affirmatively. As a question of whether the amendment permitted a virtual ban on public carrying, evidence and tradition provided a different, negative response. The *en banc* court specifically chose to limit its analysis to the permissibility of a concealed-carry restriction, while the panel court considered the impact of this restriction more broadly, in light of California's additional ban on open carry.

After the *en banc* ruling, Peruta petitioned for a writ of certiorari to the Supreme Court, but that court denied the petition in 2017. However, that same year in *Wrenn v. District of Columbia*, the US Court of Appeals for DC wrestled with the constitutionality of the district's similar "good-reason" permit requirement. Directly citing Judge O'Scannlain's assertion that prior circuits "failed to comprehend that carrying weapons in public for the lawful purpose of self-defense is a central component of the right to bear arms," Judge Thomas Griffith, writing for the DC court, struck down the requirement.[130] The court noted, "In fact, the Amendment's core at a minimum shields the typically situated citizen's ability to carry common arms generally. The District's good-reason law is necessarily a total ban on exercises of that constitutional right .... That's enough to sink this law under *Heller I*."[131]

When the Supreme Court denied Peruta's writ of certiorari, Justices Thomas and Gorsuch dissented. After questioning the *en banc* court's limited Second Amendment analysis, these justices noted the multiple court opinions on both sides of the public carry question, asserting "the time has come for the [Supreme] Court to answer this important question definitively."[132] Five years later, the court provided that definitive answer with its *Bruen* adjudication.

2022: The *Bruen* Decision

As the *Peruta* certiorari dissent implied, some justices of the Supreme Court had thought for some time that the federal judiciary's general treatment of the Second Amendment was problematical. Varying judicial interpretations of *Heller* and *McDonald* had contributed to conflicting court opinions (as exemplified by the disagreements surrounding the "proper cause" issue), and confusion regarding the proper standard of review for evaluating Second Amendment questions also existed. Despite *Heller*'s rejection of the "interest balancing" evaluative approach inherent in "intermediate scrutiny," federal courts continued to apply this method in their adjudications. The *Bruen* case allowed the court to address these issues.

New York State Rifle & Pistol Association v. Bruen (2022): Challenging "Proper Cause"

Brandon Koch and Robert Nash, residents of New York State and members of the New York State Rifle & Pistol Association (a Second Amendment advocacy organization), had both applied for and been denied an unrestricted handgun license. In Nash's case, the licensing officer in 2015 granted him a restricted license for hunting and target shooting, but when Nash asked to have the restrictions removed in 2016 (after a series of robberies in his neighborhood), the officer denied the request. Similarly, between 2008 and 2017, Koch also had a restricted license—he faced no special dangers—but wanted to carry a handgun for general self-defense. In 2017, citing his lengthy safe experience with firearms, he also applied to have the restrictions removed, but was likewise denied.[133]

Claiming that the denial of an unrestricted license for lack of "proper cause" violated their Second and Fourteen Amendment rights, the petitioners sued in federal court. The district court dismissed the complaint, and the Court of Appeals affirmed the dismissal, with both courts citing the 2012 *Kalchasky* opinion. Appealed to the Supreme Court, that court granted certiorari in 2021. Justice Clarence Thomas, nominated to the Supreme Court in 1991 by President George H. W. Bush, authored the opinion for the majority.[134]

Thomas began his analysis by noting as follows:

> In the years since [*Heller* and *McDonald*], the Courts of Appeals have coalesced around a "two-step" framework for analyzing Second Amendment challenges that combine history with means-end scrutiny. Today, we decline to adopt that two-part approach. In keeping with *Heller*, we hold that when the Second Amendment's plain text covers an individual's conduct, the Constitution presumptively protects that conduct. To justify its regulation, the government may not simply posit that the regulation promotes an important interest. Rather, the government must demonstrate that the regulation is consistent with this Nation's historical tradition of firearm regulation. Only if a firearm regulation is consistent with this Nation's historical tradition may a court conclude that the individual's conduct falls outside the Second Amendment's "unqualified command."[135]

The justice then described the questionable two-step approach the courts of appeal had been using:

> At the first step, the government may justify its regulation by "establish[ing] that the challenged law regulates activity falling outside the scope of the right as originally understood." … If the government can prove that the regulated conduct falls beyond the Amendment's original scope, "then the analysis can stop there; the regulated activity is categorically unprotected." [Citation provided]. But if the historical evidence at this step is "inconclusive or suggests that the regulated

activity is *not* categorically unprotected," the courts generally proceed to step two. [Citation provided].[136]

At the second step, courts often analyze "how close the law comes to the core of the Second Amendment right and the severity of the law's burden on that right." ... If a "core" Second Amendment right is burdened, courts apply "strict scrutiny" and ask whether the government can prove that the law is "narrowly tailored to achieve a compelling governmental interest." [Citation provided]. Otherwise, they apply intermediate scrutiny and consider whether the Government can show that the regulation is "substantially related to the achievement of an important governmental interest." [Citation provided].[137]

Continuing, Thomas asserted,

Despite the popularity of this two-step approach, it is one step too many. Step one ... is broadly consistent with *Heller*, which demands a test rooted in the Second Amendment's text, as informed by history. But *Heller* and *McDonald* do not support applying means-end scrutiny in the Second Amendment context. Instead, the government must affirmatively prove that its firearms regulation is part of the historical tradition that delimits the outer bounds of the right to keep and bear arms.[138]

The justice elaborated on why the two-step approach violated *Heller*. He noted that *Heller* accepted the widely held notion that the Second Amendment codified a *preexisting* right, and that an examination of legal and other relevant texts contemporaneous with the amendment's enactment was necessary to determine the public understanding of that preexisting right. Thus, the court studied various sources for establishing the meaning of the amendment and used historical analysis to "demark" possible limits on the amendment's protections. Thomas observed that the court "assessed the lawfulness of that [District of Columbia] handgun ban by scrutinizing whether it comported with history and tradition. ... [W]e did not engage in means-end scrutiny when resolving the constitutional question. Instead, we focused on the historically unprecedented nature of the District's ban."[139]

Thomas further emphasized the court's problem with the two-step approach,

Heller's methodology centered on constitutional text and history. ... It did not invoke any means-end test such as strict or intermediate scrutiny. Moreover, *Heller* and *McDonald* expressly rejected the application of any "judge-empowering 'interest-balancing inquiry' that 'asks whether the statute burdens a protected interest in a way or to an extent that is out of proportion to the statute's salutary effects on other important governmental interests.'" ... In sum, the Courts of Appeals' second step is inconsistent with *Heller*'s historical approach and its rejection of means-end scrutiny.[140]

Thomas acknowledged the difficulties involved in conducting historical analysis to determine constitutional questions but argued that

> reliance on history to inform the meaning of constitutional text—especially text meant to codify a *pre-existing* right—is, in our view, more legitimate, and more administrable, than asking judges to "make difficult empirical judgments" about "the costs and benefits of firearms restrictions," especially given their "lack [of] expertise" in the field. [Citation provided]. ... federal courts tasked with making such difficult empirical judgments regarding firearm regulations under the banner of "intermediate scrutiny" often defer to the determinations of legislatures. But while [such deference] is understandable ... it is not deference that the Constitution demands here.[141]

He then discussed considerations that courts should bear in mind when conducting an assessment of modern firearms regulations. He argued,

> when a challenged regulation addresses a general societal problem that has persisted since the 18th century, the lack of a distinctly similar historical regulation ... is relevant evidence that the challenged regulation is inconsistent with the Second Amendment. Likewise, if earlier generations addressed the societal problem, but did so through materially different means, that could also be evidence that a modern regulation is unconstitutional. And if some jurisdictions actually attempted to enact analogous regulations during this timeframe, but those proposals were rejected on constitutional grounds, that rejection surely would provide some probative evidence of unconstitutionality.[142]

Turning to New York's "proper-cause" requirement, Thomas asserted that the requirement addressed the same concern raised in *Heller*—handgun violence in an urban area. Following the *Heller* approach of searching for historical precedents from before, during, and even after the founding, Thomas indicated, "And as we explain below, we find no such [comparable tradition of regulation] in the historical materials."[143] However, before presenting that explanation, the justice conceded that firearms cases dealing with unique societal concerns or new technological changes may require a more nuanced approach than *Bruen*.

Noting that modern regulatory challenges do not always parallel those in 1791 or in 1868, Thomas argued,

> Although [the amendment's] meaning is fixed according to the understandings of those who ratified it, the Constitution can, and must, apply to circumstances beyond those the Founders specifically anticipated. ... We have already recognized in *Heller* ... one way in which the Second Amendment's historically fixed meaning applies to new circumstances: Its reference to "arms" does not apply "only [to] those arms in existence in the 18th century." [Citation provided]. "Just as the First Amendment protects modern forms of communication, and the Fourth Amendment applies to modern forms of search, the Second Amendment extends, prima facie, to all instruments that constitute bearable arms, even those that were not in existence at the time of the founding."[144]

Continuing, Thomas added,

> Much like we use history to determine which modern "arms" are protected … so too does history guide our consideration of modern regulations that were unimaginable at the founding. … [T]his historical inquiry … will often involve reasoning by analogy—a commonplace task for any lawyer or judge. … [D]etermining whether a historical regulation is a proper analogue for a distinctly modern firearm regulation requires a determination whether the two regulations are "relevantly similar." … While we do not now provide an exhaustive survey of the features that render regulations relevantly similar … we do think *Heller* and *McDonald* point toward at least two metrics: how and why the regulations burden a law-abiding citizen's right to armed self-defense. … [W]hether modern and historical regulations impose a comparable burden on the right of armed self-defense and whether that burden is comparably justified are "'central'" considerations when engaging in analogical inquiry."[145]

After noting that a constitutionally acceptable modern analogue need not be a "twin" of a historical regulation, Thomas cited as an example early laws prohibiting firearms in "sensitive places" such as schools, legislative assemblies, and courthouses. He asserted, "courts can use analogies … to determine that modern regulations prohibiting the carrying of firearms in *new* and analogous sensitive places are constitutionally permissible."[146] Thomas then observed,

> We do think respondents err in their attempt to characterize New York's proper-cause requirement as a "sensitive-place law." In their view, "sensitive places" … include all "places where people typically congregate and where law-enforcement and other public-safety professionals are presumptively available." … But expanding the category of "sensitive places" simply to all places of public congregation … defines the category of "sensitive places" far too broadly. Respondents' argument would exempt cities from the Second Amendment and would eviscerate the general right to publicly carry arms for self-defense.[147]

Having clarified the constitutional standard endorsed in *Heller*, the justice applied that standard to New Yok's "proper-cause" requirement. Asking whether the plain text of the Second Amendment protected Koch's and Nash's proposed conduct of publicly carrying handguns for self-defense, he answered, "We have little difficulty concluding that it does. … Nothing in the Second Amendment's text draws a home/public distinction with respect to the right to keep and bear arms."[148]

Citing *Heller* and *Muscarello*, Thomas observed that the amendment's "bear arms" textual element

> naturally encompasses public carry. Most gun owners do not wear a holstered pistol … in their bedroom or … at the dinner table. … To confine the right to "bear" arms to the home would nullify half of the Second Amendment's operative

> protections. Moreover, confining the right to "bear" arms to the home would make little sense given that self-defense is "the *central component* of the [Second Amendment] right itself."[149]

Concluding that the amendment's plain text "thus presumptively guarantees petitioners Koch and Nash a right to 'bear' arms in public for self-defense," Thomas examined whether the State could show that the proper-cause restriction was "consistent with this Nation's historical tradition of firearm regulation."[150] He noted that the state presented evidence from five different historical periods—1200s to the early 1900s—to show such consistency. Emphasizing the importance of the categorization periods, Thomas argued, "when it comes to interpreting the Constitution, not all history is created equal. 'Constitutional rights are enshrined with the scope they were understood to have *when the people adopted them*.' [Citation provided]. The Second Amendment was adopted in 1791; the Fourteenth in 1868. Historical evidence that long predates either date may not illuminate."[151]

Regarding early English practices, the Justice argued that "it [is] better not to go too far back into antiquity"[152] for interpreting the Constitution.

> Similarly, we must also guard against giving post-enactment history more weight than it can rightly bear. … "where a governmental practice has been open, widespread, and unchallenged since the early days of the Republic, the practice should guide our interpretation …." But to the extent later history contradicts what the text says, the text controls. … Thus, "post-ratification adoption or acceptance of laws that are inconsistent with the original meaning of the constitutional text obviously cannot overcome or alter that text" [Citations provided].[153]

Thomas further stated that post-Civil War discussions of the right to arms, taking place seventy-five years after the amendment's ratification, also provided only limited insight into its original meaning.

Thomas acknowledged that the government traditionally subjected public arms-bearing "to well-defined restrictions governing the intent for which one could carry arms, the manner of carry, or the exceptional circumstances under which one could not carry arms."[154] But he also asserted that the state's historical evidence

> does not demonstrate a tradition of broadly prohibiting the public carry of commonly used firearms for self-defense. Nor is there any such historical tradition limiting public carry only to those law-abiding citizens who demonstrate a special need for self-defense. We conclude that respondents have failed to meet their burden … justifying New York's proper-cause requirement. Under *Heller*'s text and history standard, the proper-cause requirement is therefore unconstitutional.[155]

Justice Thomas supported the court's conclusion with a detailed examination of the historical evidence contained in each of the state's five time periods. Ending his review of the first period, Thomas argued, "we cannot conclude from this historical record that, by the time of the founding, English law would have justified restricting the right to publicly bear arms … only to those who demonstrate some special need for self-protection."[156] For the colonial/early Republic period, Thomas noted, "there is no historical basis for concluding that the pre-existing right enshrined in the Second Amendment permitted broad prohibitions on all forms of public carry."[157]

For period three, ante-bellum America, Thomas observed,

> Only after the ratification of the Second Amendment in 1791 did public carry restrictions proliferate. Respondents rely heavily on these restrictions … common-law offenses, statutory prohibitions, and "surety" statutes. None of these restrictions impose a substantial burden on public carry analogous to the burden created by New York's restrictive licensing regime. … The historical evidence … does demonstrate that *the manner* of public carry was subject to reasonable regulation. … [But] none operated to prevent law-abiding citizens with ordinary self-defense needs from carrying arms in public for that purpose.[158]

In examining the Reconstruction period, Thomas asserted,

> Evidence from around the adoption of the Fourteenth Amendment also fails to support respondents' position. … Respondents … direct our attention primarily to two late-19th-century cases in Texas. … [W]hile we recognize the support that postbellum Texas provides for respondents' views, we will not give disproportionate weight to a single state statute and a pair of state-court decisions. As in *Heller*, we will not "stake our interpretation of the Second Amendment upon a single law, in effect in a single [State], that contradicts the overwhelming weight of other evidence regarding the right to keep and bear arms for defense" in public.[159]

For the final period covering late-nineteenth-century and early-twentieth-century developments, Thomas dismissed the State's twentieth-century evidence in a footnote, noting that "the 20th century evidence presented … does not provide insight … when it contradicts earlier evidence."[160] He addressed the state's nineteenth-century material—gun regulations principally originating in the Western Territories—but noted that the State's reliance on these regulations had additional "serious flaws even beyond their temporal distance from the founding."[161] After briefly discussing the regulations, Thomas asserted, "These territorial restrictions fail to justify New York's proper-cause requirement."[162]

Justice Thomas ended "this long journey through the Anglo-American history of public carry" by concluding, "respondents have not met their burden to identify an American tradition justifying the State's proper-cause requirement. … [The requirement] … prevents law-abiding citizens with ordinary self-defense needs from exercising their right to keep and bear arms. We therefore reverse the judgment of the Court of appeals and remand the case for further processing consistent with this opinion."[163]

Some Observations

The cases in this chapter illustrate the tension around gun issues that exists between a conservatively oriented Supreme Court and a more liberal federal judiciary. Despite *Heller*'s 2008 explicit rejection of an "interest-balancing" approach in deciding Second Amendment questions, many federal courts—as Judge O'Scannlain implied in his *Peruta* decision—simply used "intermediate scrutiny" for over a decade to achieve the same socially salutary but constitutionally questionable ends. The Ninth Circuit's argument reversing O'Scannlain's ruling also reflects this tension. The court's deliberately narrow focus on the permissibility of concealed-carry prohibitions—despite acknowledging that it effectively resulted in a complete gun-carrying ban given California's prohibition on open carry—contains the type of judicial animosity toward the Second Amendment that *Heller* and *McDonald* attempted to alter.

This federal-level hostility toward gun rights is also arguably evident in the willingness of strict gun-control states to pass constitutionally questionable firearms legislation, presumably in the hope that gun-opposed federal magistrates might adjudicate and deny the inevitable challenges. For example, in the *Bruen* opinion, the Supreme Court expressly characterized New York's attempt to enlarge the category of gun-prohibited "sensitive places" to virtually all areas where people gather as far too broad. Shortly thereafter, New York responded by passing the Concealed Carry Improvement Act.

This Act prohibited firearms in an extensive array of public locations—health centers, churches, parks, and zoos; bars and restaurants; theaters; banquet halls; conference centers; and so forth. The act was found unconstitutional in district court, but the appeal to the Second Circuit upheld most of the law's provisions. Other gun-strict states—for example, California, Maryland, New Jersey—have likewise passed equally broad gun-free zone laws, notwithstanding *Bruen*'s guidance that such broad designations are constitutionally suspect.

Similarly, judicial support for legislative bans on assault-style weapons and large-capacity magazines—despite *Heller*'s indications that firearms in common use are constitutionally protected—also hints that many on the federal bench continue to oppose the Supreme Court's interpretation of the amendment. Chapter 9 contains an extended discussion of the specific cases alluded to. As noted in that chapter, even with *Bruen*'s seeming clarity on determining Second Amendment protections and boundaries, federal court gun disagreements appear poised to keep the Supreme Court busy.

Notes

1 *New York State Rifle & Pistol Assn., INC. v. Bruen* 597 U. S. *(2022)*. At https://www.supremecourt.gov/opinions/21pdf/20-843_7j80.pdf.

2 Since the *Wrenn* opinion is consistent with the US Supreme Court's later *Bruen* decision, it is only briefly examined in passing.

3 *Strickland v. State, 137 Ga. 1, 72 S. E. 260 (1911).* At https://cite.case.law/ga/137/1/.
4 *State v. Kerner, 181 N.C. 574, 107 S.E. 222 (1921).* At https://guncite.com/court/state/107se222.html.
5 *Hickman v. Block 81 F.3d 98 (9th Cir. 1996).* At https://casetext.com/case/hickman-v-block.
6 *State v. Rosenthal, 75 Vt. 295, 55 A. 610 (1903).* At https://guncite.com/court/state/55a610.html.
7 Ibid.
8 Ibid.
9 Ibid.
10 Ibid.
11 Ibid.
12 Ibid.
13 See Donald Campbell, *America's Gun Wars: A Cultural History of Gun Control in the United States* (Santa Barbara, CA: Praeger, 2019), pp. 31–3 for a discussion of the law's cultural significance.
14 *People ex Rel. Darling v. Warden of City Prison, 154 App. Div. 413 (N.Y. App. Div. 1913) 139 N.Y.S. 277.* At https://casetext.com/case/people-ex-rel-darling-v-warden-of-city-prison/.
15 Ibid.
16 Ibid.
17 Ibid.
18 Ibid.
19 Ibid.
20 Ibid.
21 Ibid.
22 Ibid.
23 Ibid.
24 Ibid.
25 Ibid.
26 See J. Brabner-Smith, "Firearm Regulation," *Law & Contemporary Problems*, 1 (1933): 400–14. Cited in Briggs Depew and Isaac Swensen, "The Effects of Concealed Carry and Handgun Restrictions on Gun-Related Deaths: Evidence from the Sullivan Act of 1911," August 2019. At https://www.montana.edu/swensen/documents/DS_SullivanAct.pdf.
27 *People v. Zerillo, 219 Mich. 635, 189 N.W. 927 (1922).* At https://constitution.org/1-Constitution/2ll/2ndcourt/state/2st.htm.
28 Ibid.
29 Ibid.
30 Ibid.
31 Ibid.
32 Ibid.
33 Ibid.
34 Ibid.
35 See Campbell, *America's Gun Wars: A Cultural History of Gun Control in the United States.*
36 See *People ex Rel. Darling v. Warden of City Prison.*

37 Briggs Depew and Isaac Swensen, "The Effects of Concealed Carry and Handgun Restrictions on Gun-Related Deaths.": Evidence from the Sullivan Act of 1911
38 *Matter of Moore v. Gallup, 267 A.D. 64 (N.Y. App. Div. 1943) 45 N.Y.S.2d 63.* At https://casetext.com/case/matter-of-moore-v-gallup-3.
39 Ibid.
40 Ibid.
41 Ibid.
42 Ibid.
43 Ibid.
44 Ibid.
45 Ibid.
46 David Kopel, "Background Checks for Firearm Sales and Loans: Law, History, and Policy," *Harvard Journal on Legislation*, 53:1 (2016): pp. 303–67, 347. At https://harvardjol.com/archive/volume-53-number-1/.
47 *Schubert v. DeBard, 398 NE 2d 1339 (Ind: Court of Appeals, 3rd Dist. 1980).* At https://law.justia.com/cases/indiana/court-of-appeals/1980/3-177a10-6.html.
48 Ibid.
49 Ibid.
50 Ibid.
51 Ibid.
52 Ibid.
53 Ibid.
54 Ibid.
55 Ibid.
56 Ibid.
57 *Shettle v. Shearer, 425 N.E.2d 739 (Ind. Ct. App. 1981).* At https://casetext.com/case/shettle-v-shearer.
58 *Matter of Klenosky v. N.Y. City Police Dept, 75 A.D.2d 793 (N.Y. App. Div. 1980).* At https://casetext.com/case/matter-of-klenosky-v-ny-city-police-dept.
59 Ibid.
60 Ibid.
61 *Matter of O'Connor v. Scarpino, 83 N.Y.2d 919 (1994) 615 N.Y.S.2d 305 638 N.E.2d 950.* At https://law.justia.com/cases/new-york/court-of-appeals/1994/83-n-y-2d-919-0.html.
62 Ibid.
63 Ibid.
64 *Kachalsky v. County of Westchester, 701 F.3d 81 (2d Cir. 2012).* At https://casetext.com/case/kachalsky-v-cnty-of-westchester.
65 Ibid.
66 Ibid.
67 Ibid.
68 Ibid.
69 Ibid.
70 Ibid.
71 Ibid.
72 Ibid.
73 Ibid.
74 Ibid.

75 Ibid.
76 In a footnote, Judge Wesley acknowledged that "These cases were decided on the basis of an interpretation of the Second Amendment—that pistols and similar weapons are not 'arms' within the meaning of the Second Amendment … [a view] that conflicts with the Supreme Court's present reading of the Amendment."
77 *Kachalsky v. County of Westchester.*
78 Ibid.
79 Ibid.
80 Ibid.
81 Ibid.
82 Ibid.
83 Ibid.
84 Ibid.
85 Ibid.
86 Ibid.
87 Ibid.
88 *Woollard v. Gallagher, 12-1437 (4th Cir. 2013).* At https://caselaw.findlaw.com/us-4th-circuit/1625675.html.
89 Ibid.
90 Ibid.
91 Ibid.
92 Ibid.
93 Ibid.
94 Ibid.
95 Ibid.
96 Ibid.
97 Ibid.
98 *Drake v. Filko, 12–1150 (3rd Cir. 2013).* At https://caselaw.findlaw.com/us-3rd-circuit/1640513.html.
99 Ibid.
100 Ibid.
101 Ibid.
102 Ibid.
103 Ibid.
104 Ibid.
105 Ibid.
106 Ibid.
107 *Peruta v. County of San Diego, 742 F.3d 1144 10-56971 (*9th *Cir. 2014).* At https://www.leagle.com/decision/infco20140213124.
108 Ibid.
109 Ibid.
110 Ibid.
111 Ibid.
112 Ibid.
113 Ibid.
114 Ibid.
115 Ibid.
116 Ibid.

117 Ibid.
118 Ibid.
119 *Peruta v. County of San Diego, 11-16255 (9th Cir. 2016).* At https://law.justia.com/cases/federal/appellate-courts/ca9/10-56971/10-56971-2016-06-09.html.
120 Ibid.
121 Ibid.
122 Ibid.
123 Ibid.
124 Ibid.
125 Ibid.
126 Ibid.
127 Ibid.
128 Ibid.
129 Ibid.
130 *Wrenn v. Dist. of Columbia, No. 16-7025.* (DC Cir. 2017). At https://law.justia.com/cases/federal/appellate-courts/cadc/16-7025/16-7025-2017-07-25.html.
131 Ibid.
132 *Peruta v. California, on petition for writ of certiorari to the U.S. Court of Appeals for the Ninth Circuit. 582 U.S. ___ (2017).* At https://www.supremecourt.gov/opinions/16pdf/16-894_p86b.pdf.
133 *New York State Rifle & Pistol Assn., INC. v. Bruen 597 U. S. (2022).*
134 Ibid.
135 Ibid.
136 Ibid.
137 Ibid.
138 Ibid.
139 Ibid.
140 Ibid.
141 Ibid.
142 Ibid.
143 Ibid.
144 Ibid.
145 Ibid.
146 Ibid.
147 Ibid.
148 Ibid.
149 Ibid.
150 Ibid.
151 Ibid.
152 Ibid.
153 Ibid.
154 Ibid.
155 Ibid.
156 Ibid.
157 Ibid.

158 Ibid.
159 Ibid.
160 Ibid.
161 Ibid.
162 Ibid.
163 Ibid.

6

Dangerous Weapons: Lethal, Hazardous, and Crime-Friendly Firearms

This case is not about extraordinary weapons ... bazookas, howitzers, or machine guns. This is an average case about average guns used in average ways for average purposes.

US District Judge Roger T. Benitez[1]

For any noncombatant in America's gun–culture war, the notion of categorizing just selected firearms as "dangerous" may at first appear somewhat confusing and ironic. All firearms are potentially lethal, and weighing the degree of a specific gun's lethality would seem a particularly academic concern. But on reflection, substantive justifications for examining and perhaps limiting a firearm's lethality emerge. In terms of destructive firepower, a modern sporting rifle is certainly far more lethal than the standard eighteenth-century battle rifle of England's Royal Army, and contemporary fully automatic rifles and pistols certainly seem far more deadly than their semiautomatic equivalents.

Nonetheless, while differences in the potential "dangerousness" of various firearms are real, this recognition raises difficult questions about the Second Amendment's arms guarantees. The amendment itself does not limit its protections based on lethality considerations. Indeed, at the time of its enactment, civilian arms (those used by the militia) and "military" arms were virtually interchangeable, and differences in lethality nonexistent. Modern military firearms have ended this uniformity, and civilian adaptations of these guns are frequently debated as perhaps too dangerous for private citizens. With the amendment itself silent on the matter, state legislatures—and Congress—have sometimes waded into this debate. At different times, these bodies have concluded that particular types of firearms—because of some unique quality or characteristic—are inappropriate and too dangerous for civilian use. Challenges to these legislative bans and restrictions have frequently required the judiciary to determine the constitutionality of the law or regulation that placed a selected weapon outside Second Amendment protections.

These judicial determinations have often revolved around the court's (and presumably the larger society's) beliefs regarding specific qualities that separate some weapons from others. Historically, the nature of these especially threatening or inappropriate characteristics has been fluid, varying from era to era. For most of the nineteenth century, courts typically considered the size and easy concealability of a weapon as qualities that heightened dangerousness. Judges typically believed such concealability made small firearms the weapons of choice for thieves and thugs, and others "up to no good." Thus, the judiciary often upheld legislation banning the carrying of small, concealable pocket pistols, while still recognizing an individual's right to bear or wear much larger, military "horse pistols." As the century unfolded, legislatures and courts came to view concealed firearms—regardless of size—as especially troublesome and dangerous, and often banned such carry.

Later in the twentieth century, the small size and concealability of a revolver or pistol continued to garner legislative attention, but not especially because the criminal class preferred these firearms. After all, many law-abiding citizens also valued the convenience and carrying ease of a smaller gun, and the introduction of concealed-gun permitting made accommodating the needs of these citizens easily achievable. Instead, American society in this period saw a problem in the proliferation of a small subset of easily concealable, inexpensive pistols, popularly known as "Saturday Night Specials" (SNSs). Cheap materials and indifferent manufacturing made these guns particularly hazardous. Appealing to individuals unable to afford the major gun brands' more costly pistols, the unreliability and poor quality of SNSs presented unexpected perils to both shooters and bystanders, and resulted in legislative restrictions that made them the subject of much gun litigation.

Later in the century, influenced by a spate of mass shootings, Congress reacted to widespread perceptions that the semi-automatic AR-15 rifle and its various clones were "assault rifles" identical to the military's M-16 automatic rifle—a machine gun. Thus regarded as particularly lethal and especially dangerous, the AR-15 rifle was deemed by many a war weapon, and Congress passed legislation curtailing its manufacture and sale to civilians. The legislation—popularly known as the Assault Weapons Ban—expired in 2004 after ten years. The ban apparently had little impact on mass shootings or crime reduction overall,[2] but many in society continued to call for a prohibition on these "assault-style" weapons. When the federal ban expired, a number of states imposed their own restrictions and bans on such guns, and courts have had to determine whether and to what degree the Second Amendment protects these firearms.

Following this historical pattern, the chapter divides the cases examined into the same three periods. Since Chapter 2 discusses at length a number of nineteenth-century concealed pocket pistol cases, this chapter's first period considers only two similar cases. These cases—*Wilson v. State of Arkansas* and *Dabbs v. Arkansas*—reflect typical nineteenth-century judicial attitudes toward small pistols and their special dangers. In a third case—*People of New York v. Perce*—the court considered whether an individual's carrying intentions perhaps mitigated a weapon's dangerousness.

The second period examines a representative set of three twentieth-century cases focused on the dangers of SNSs. While these adjudications frequently revolved around defective guns, the often novel liability theories developed in these cases implied that even well-designed, quality firearms might be considered unreasonably dangerous under certain circumstances. Indeed, to address this potential threat, the gun industry eventually lobbied Congress for legislative protection.

The chapter's final section looks at judicial developments in the twenty-first century, examining five cases that explore and clarify the meaning of "especially dangerous and unusual," as that phrase applies to firearms and other weapons potentially lying outside the scope of Second Amendment protection.

1878–1912: Concealed Pistols, Criminals, and Public Safety

Courts have wrestled with the constitutionality of regulating concealed weapons almost since the founding of the country. While an 1822 Kentucky court[3] voided a statute prohibiting concealment of a weapon as "incompatible" with the right to bear arms, less than twenty years later a Tennessee court rejected this conclusion. This court noted that the state legislature had the right to prohibit the wearing of arms typically used only in private broils, or by criminals or murderers—arms dangerous to citizens' peace and safety, and not usually employed in "civilized warfare."[4] A few years later, in 1846, a Georgia court suggested that the size of a pistol was less important than whether the firearm was carried "secretly"—in a concealed manner—and dismissed a defendant's indictment because his pocket pistol was not carried secretly.[5]

Similarly, in 1872, after noting the Georgia court's finding that state regulation of concealed carry was constitutionally permitted, a Texas court also concluded that the state could regulate deadly weapons—pistols, dirks, sword canes, and other unusual or non-militia arms—for community safety and the prevention of crime.[6] In 1876, an Arkansas court followed suit, upholding the conviction of a defendant arrested for carrying a pocket pistol. The court observed that the legislature had the authority to outlaw "weapons dangerous to the peace and safety of the citizens" and which were unusual "in civilized warfare."[7] A decade later, a Missouri court upheld a defendant's conviction for carrying a concealed pistol, observing that prohibitions on the concealed carry of a dangerous or deadly weapon were designed to enhance citizen security and to limit lawless behavior.[8]

Three additional cases further detail the judiciary's view of concealed carry and dangerous weapons. The state of Arkansas offers two more examples from around the turn of the nineteenth century: *Wilson v. State of Arkansas* and *Dabbs v. State of Arkansas*. These cases reaffirm the important distinction contemporary courts made between pocket pistols and military-sized pistols. The third case, a 1912 New York adjudication, elaborates on the nature of dangerous weapons and the characteristics that make them dangerous.

Wilson v. State of Arkansas (1878): Challenging a Concealed-Carry Statute

Chancy Wilson had been charged and convicted in the circuit court of Arkansas of "unlawfully carrying a pistol as a weapon, contrary to the statute … and against the peace and dignity of the State."[9] In an appeal to the Arkansas Supreme Court, Chief Justice Elbert English noted that Wilson had borrowed from an acquaintance

> a large army size six shooter, a revolving pistol, 44 caliber, eight inches in the barrel, such as is commonly used in warfare, ... The appellant, among other instructions, [had] asked the [circuit] court to charge the jury that if they believed from the evidence, that the pistol carried by him was an army size pistol, such as are commonly used in warfare, they should acquit; which was refused by the court.[10]

The Chief Justice then observed that the Arkansas Supreme Court had earlier ruled that "the Legislature might constitutionally prohibit the carrying of such pistols and other arms easily concealed about the person, as are used in quarrels, brawls and fights between maddened individuals, but that the Constitution guaranteed to the citizens the right to keep and bear arms for defense, etc."[11] Continuing, he wrote,

> The Legislature might, in the exercise of the police power of the State, regulate the mode of wearing war arms, and no doubt the occasions of wearing such arms may be to some extent regulated. Thus, it has been made an offense to wear a pistol, etc. concealed (*Gantt's Dig., sec.1517*) and this may well apply to the character of the pistol used as a war arm. So hunting with a gun ... or shooting for amusement, on the Sabbath, are made offenses. *Gantt's Dig., sec. 162.* No doubt in time of peace, persons might be prohibited from wearing war arms to places of public worship, or elections, etc.[12]

The court then concluded,

> But to prohibit the citizen from [generally] wearing or carrying a war arm ... is an unwarranted restriction upon his constitutional right to keep and bear arms. If cowardly and dishonorable men sometimes shoot unarmed men with army pistols or guns, the evil must be prevented by the penitentiary and gallows, and not by a general deprivation of a constitutional right. The judgment is reversed.[13]

The court's analysis clearly implies that the easy concealability of a small pistol made that type of firearm especially dangerous and thus its prohibition constitutionally permitted. In contrast, the court indicated that the legislature could only regulate a war arm. It could not ban the wearing or carrying of that firearm despite its identical capacity for lethal use by evil and dishonorable individuals. The judicial arguments in this case mirrored the general position of many state courts during the period. The next case highlights this orientation even as it extended to the sale of pocket pistols.

Dabbs v. State of Arkansas (1882): Challenging a Pocket Pistol Sales Prohibition

In 1881, Arkansas enacted a pistol regulation that, among other restrictions, made it a misdemeanor "for any person to sell a dirk or bowie knife, a sword or spear in a cane, brass or metal knucks, or any pistol except such as are used in the army or navy of the United States and known as the navy pistol."[14] The expressed purpose of the act was captured in the act's title: "to preserve the public peace and prevent crime."[15] Caught selling a pocket pistol, Dabbs was indicted, convicted, and fined for violating the regulation. He appealed his conviction to the Arkansas Supreme Court, arguing that the act violated Arkansas' Constitution and also the Commerce Clause and the Fourteenth Amendment of the Constitution of the United States.

Justice William Smith, newly elected to the court, dismissed Dabbs's Commerce and Fourteenth Amendment arguments. He noted that

> the exclusive power vested in Congress to regulate commerce with foreign nations and among the several States, has been uniformly construed not to extend to commerce, which is strictly internal and carried on entirely within the limits of a State. [Citations provided.] Thus it has been held competent for the Legislature of a State to regulate, and even suppress, the traffic in intoxicating liquors within its borders. [Citations provided.] And the scope and purpose of the fourteenth amendment were to secure to negroes all the civil rights that white citizens enjoy.[16]

Continuing, Smith stated,

> Nor does it conflict with *sec. 2 of art. 4 of the Constitution of the United States*, which provides that the citizens of each State shall be entitled to all privileges and immunities of citizens of the several States .... The citizen of Tennessee can not sell the forbidden articles upon the territory of Arkansas any more than one of our own citizens. ... The act certainly does not attempt to deprive any man of his property... time was allowed to the dealers in such articles to dispose of their stock in trade. And after [that], they might ship such goods out of state and there sell them.[17]

The court acknowledged that citizens have the right to acquire, hold, and dispose of property but that

> the Government may justly prescribe for the general good. In the exercise of its police power, the State may, and does, regulate and control .... It is difficult to assign bounds to the police power of the State. It extends to the protection of the lives, health, comfort and quiet of all persons and the protection of all property within the State. [Citation given]. The law was enacted as a measure of precaution for the prevention of crimes and calamities. It is leveled at the pernicious habit of wearing such dangerous or deadly weapons as are easily concealed about the person. It does not abridge the constitutional right of citizens to keep and bear arms for the common defense; for it in no wise restrains the use or sale of such arms as are useful in warfare. [Citation given.][18]

With that, Justice Smith affirmed Dabbs' conviction.

Going beyond simply prohibiting the concealed carrying of small pistols, this opinion implies that such pistols are so inherently dangerous as to warrant banning even their sale. The court does not elaborate on why a prohibition on concealed carry alone was not sufficient to protect the lives and peace of the community.

People of New York v. Perce (1912): Challenging a Possession of a Deadly Weapon Conviction

The defendant in this New York Court of Appeals[19] adjudication argued that an "intention to use" a dangerous, prohibited weapon was a required statutory factor for upholding a weapons-possession conviction. While *Wilson* and *Dabbs* both emphasized that certain firearms posed increased danger simply because of their small, concealable nature, the *Perce* case raised criminal or evil "intentions" as a basis for determining a weapon's dangerousness.

Appellant Perce was indicted and convicted of possessing and carrying

> "a certain instrument and weapon of the kind commonly known as a slungshot." … At the time in question section 1897 of the Penal Law provided: "A person who attempts to use against another, or who carries, or possesses any instrument or weapon of the kind commonly known as a slungshot, billy, sand club, or metal knuckles, or who with intent to use the same against another, carries or possesses a dagger, dirk, or dangerous knife is guilty of a felony."[20]

Justice Frank Hiscock, who would later become chief justice, wrote the court's opinion. He noted that the trial judge charged,

> "If this defendant … carried or possessed, knowingly possessed of course, any instrument or weapon known as a slungshot he is guilty of a felony. That is all there is to the case." And he refused to charge several propositions presented by the appellant which made intent to use the weapon against another an essential element to be found by the jury before they could convict him.[21]

Hiscock asserted,

> The court correctly refused to hold, as requested, that proof was necessary of intent to use the slungshot. … The appellant argues that … an intent to thus use must be found in the case of each weapon before a violation is made out. This is an erroneous view. … [That section of the statute] is not to be construed as requiring intent to use where the crime as defined by the preceding section is made out without proof of any such intent as in the case of a slungshot. The ambiguity … is due to an amendment of the first section. … When this change was made [the section in question] was not correspondingly amended as would have been quite appropriate, although in our judgment not essential.[22]

Continuing, he observed,

> The legislature has the undoubted power to declare that various acts … shall be criminal without proof of other intent …. If we give to the statute under consideration a rational interpretation it becomes clear that the carrying or possession of a slungshot even without proof of specific ulterior criminal intent are within the character of acts which the legislature may thus condemn. … Given to the statute thus a reasonable interpretation, and its enactment readily and clearly comes within the police power. The evidence and the well-understood character of slungshots, billies, sandbags and brass knuckles make it evident that the legislature were entirely justified in regarding them as dangerous and foul weapons seldom used for justifiable purposes but ordinarily the effective and illegitimate implements of thugs and brutes in carrying out their unlawful purposes.[23]

Justice Hiscock concluded,

> It is obvious that one of the proper and efficient methods by which to prevent the commission of crime … was to make their possession of itself criminal without delaying until opportunity had bred and perhaps permitted the accomplishment of some particular evil design. This is what has been done and there is no infringement of the Constitution in this aspect of the legislation. [Citation given.] Neither is there any constitutional provision securing the right to bear arms which prohibits legislation with reference to such weapons that are specifically before us … the act in question relates to instruments which are ordinarily used for criminal and improper purposes and which are not among those ordinary and legitimate weapons of defense and protection which are contemplated by the Constitution and the Bill of Rights.[24]

The court thus affirmed Perce's conviction.

As these three illustrative cases imply, in the nineteenth and early twentieth century, two general qualities placed specific firearms and certain weapons outside Second Amendment guarantees. Smallness and easy concealability typically invalidated a firearm's claim to constitutional shielding, and, similarly, weapons having a strong appeal to "thugs and brutes" and the criminal class were also beyond constitutional protection. Both these qualities suggest that an arm's increased "dangerousness" centered on the weapon's likelihood of involvement in illegal assaults or violent disturbances of community peace and safety. Cases in the next section continue to focus on the special dangers associated with "criminal-friendly firearms" but also examine the heightened perils created by poorly designed and manufactured guns.

1985–7: The Danger of Saturday Night Specials

The introduction of police-issued discretionary firearms permits—a strategy first initiated by New York City near the turn of the century—assumedly reduced the criminal use of small pocket pistols and the increased dangers created by them. Nonetheless, defendants continued to invoke Second Amendment protection when arrested and convicted of possessing other prohibited and potentially dangerous weapons. Edward Harris in 1967, for instance, was initially arrested on a shoplifting violation, but an ensuing search showed that he also carried a tear gas pen—a violation of a 1955 Nevada weapons statute.[25]

Convicted of possessing such a weapon, Harris challenged the statute, arguing it was an infringement of the Second Amendment of the US Constitution. After observing that the right to bear arms was not an individual right,[26] Nevada's Supreme Court affirmed Harris's conviction. The court noted that state regulation of tear gas weapons was a proper exercise of the state's police powers.

Similarly, a 1983 Oregon Court of Appeals adjudication revolved around pistol ammunition and its contribution to a firearm's increased dangerousness. Arrested for carrying a *loaded* .32-caliber firearm in his car (violating a Portland City ordinance), Michael Boyce contested his conviction on constitutional grounds. He argued that the ordinance making it unlawful for a person to carry a firearm in a public place, or have it in a vehicle, unless all ammunition had been removed from the gun's cylinder or magazine, violated the state's Second Amendment analogue. The court disagreed.[27]

Noting that firearms are "extraordinarily dangerous" and that the "danger is particularly severe when the firearms are in public places and loaded," the court ruled that the city's need to protect its citizens "from the hazards that are created when people are permitted to roam free with loaded guns at their sides" justified a restrained exercise of the state's police power. Asserting that the ordinance was constitutional in that it did not proscribe the possession of either firearms or ammunition, the court observed that an individual could still possess both—even in a public place—so long as the firearm was unloaded.[28]

Moving to the federal level, the National Firearms Act (NFA) and its periodic amendments have attempted to identify firearms and other weapons considered especially dangerous and presumably outside Second Amendment protections. Challenges to the Act can also offer insight into the nature of especially dangerous arms. A 1971 US Supreme Court adjudication[29] centered on the possession of hand grenades—weapons requiring federal registration under the Act—is an example.

Acknowledging that the Act does not require a possessor to have specific knowledge that unregistered hand grenades are a violation, the court emphasized that the Act was "a regulatory measure in the interest of public safety [and a person] would hardly be surprised to learn that possession of hand grenades is not an innocent act. They are highly dangerous offensive weapons."[30] Concurring with the court's judgment, one justice observed,

> The firearms covered by the Act are major weapons such as machineguns and sawed off shotguns; deceptive weapons such as flashlight guns and fountain pen guns; and major destructive devices such as bombs, mines, rockets, and large caliber weapons, including mortars, antitank guns, and bazookas. Without exception, the

likelihood of government regulation of the distribution of such weapons is so great that anyone must be presumed to be aware of it.[31]

In addition to the types of weapons and circumstances discussed above, the judiciary during this period also wrestled with a separate class of firearms many individuals considered especially dangerous and warranting prohibition: the "SNS." Often employing novel interpretations of liability statutes (to avoid potential Second Amendment complications), plaintiffs sought to hold the manufacturers, distributors, and sellers of small, cheaply made handguns responsible for the heightened dangers presumably posed by these firearms. This section examines several of these cases, beginning with a 1985 Maryland adjudication examining a gun manufacturer's liability for producing an "abnormally dangerous" handgun.

Kelley v. R.G. Industries, Inc. (1985): Adjudicating a Firearm Liability Dispute

Shot in the chest during an armed robbery of the grocery store where he worked, Olen Kelley filed a tort action against Rolm Gesellschaft and R.G. Industries. Kelley argued that Rolm Gesellschaft and R.G. Industries were liable for his injuries because the weapon used in the shooting—a Rohm RG-38S revolver—was "abnormally dangerous."[32] He also contended that the gun was "defective in its 'marketing, promotion, distribution and design,' rendering it 'unreasonably dangerous.' "[33]

As a subsidiary of Rolm Gesellschaft (the West German corporation that had designed and marketed the revolver), R.G. Industries moved for summary judgment in US District Court, noting that it was not involved in the revolver's marketing or distribution. The court granted this stipulation, dismissing R.G. Industries from the case. Rolm Gesellschaft then moved to dismiss, "for failure to state a claim … [arguing] that 'the plaintiff's contentions [must] fail because the handgun performed as it was supposed to perform and because Rolm Gesellschaft is not responsible for the criminal and tortious acts of Mr. Kelley's assailant.' "[34]

The US District Court, after finding no controlling precedents governing the liability issues, certified several questions to the Court of Appeals of Maryland.

> Question 1: Is a handgun, which inflicts injury as the norm, rather than the exception, a defective or unreasonably dangerous product? If the answer to Question 1 is "No" then—Question 2: Is a Rohm Revolver Handgun Model RG38S, which inflicts injury as the norm, rather than the exception, a defective or unreasonably dangerous product? Question 3: Is the marketing of handguns an abnormally dangerous activity? … If the answer to Question 3 is "No," then Question 4: Is the marketing of Rohm Revolver Handgun Model RG38S an abnormally dangerous activity?[35]

The Court of Appeals decided to rephrase the questions in the following way:

> 1) Is the manufacturer or marketer of a handgun, in general, liable under any strict liability theory to a person injured as a result of the criminal use of the product? 2) Is the manufacturer or marketer of a particular category of small, cheap handguns, sometimes referred to as "Saturday Night Specials," and regularly used in criminal activity, strictly liable to a person injured by such handgun during the course of a crime? 3) Does the Rohm Revolver Handgun Model RG38S … fall within the category referred to in question 2?[36]

Judge John Eldridge authored the opinion for the appeals court. Regarding the issue of whether the manufacturing or marketing of handguns is an "abnormally dangerous activity," Eldridge noted,

> Maryland law would not permit liability to be imposed on a handgun manufacturer or marketer under this theory … the abnormally dangerous activity doctrine does not apply to the manufacture or marketing of handguns. Other jurisdictions which have addressed the issue are in accord. [Citations provided.] ("… the injuries of which the plaintiffs complain were not caused by the marketing itself, but rather resulted only when there was substandard conduct on the part of third parties.").[37]

Eldridge provided additional case support for this conclusion: "'ultrahazardous activity doctrine applies only to the use of a product, not to its manufacture or sale;' [Citation provided.] … 'We have found no decision other than *Richman* that has held that the lawful sale of a non-defective product can be an ultrahazardous activity.' [Citation provided.]"[38]

The judge then considered the question of whether a handgun is an abnormally dangerous product. Noting that Maryland's law requires such a product to be "in a defective condition at the time that it left the possession or control of the seller, (2) that it was unreasonably dangerous to the user or consumer, (3) that the defect was the cause of the injuries"[39] Eldridge emphasized that the law

> expressly requires that the product be defective when sold. … Contrary to Kelley's argument, a handgun is not defective merely because it is capable of being used during criminal activity to inflict harm. … Kelley confuses a product's normal function, which may very well be dangerous, with a defect in a product's design or construction. … a handgun is dangerous because its normal function is to propel bullets with deadly force. That alone is not sufficient for a manufacturer to incur liability.[40]

Having established that handgun manufacturers or marketers generally would not be liable for injuries resulting from the criminal use of a firearm, Eldridge then continued,

> There is, however, a limited category of handguns which clearly is not sanctioned as [being consistent with] public policy. To impose strict liability upon the

> manufacturers and marketers of these handguns, in instances of gunshot wounds caused by criminal use, would not be contrary to the policy embodied in the enactments of the General Assembly. This type of handgun, commonly known as a "Saturday Night Special," presents particular problems for law enforcement officials.[41]

Elaborating, Eldridge observed that these guns "are generally characterized by short barrels, light weight, easy concealability, low cost, use of cheap quality materials, poor manufacture, inaccuracy and unreliability. These characteristics render the SNS particularly attractive for criminal use and virtually useless for the legitimate purposes of law enforcement, sport, and protection."[42] Further, quoting various authorities in footnotes, the court noted,

> "because of their poor construction and low quality, [SNS] are extremely dangerous weapons, not only to intended targets and bystanders, but also to the user himself. They misfire, fire accidently, and backfire with some degree of regularity. They are notoriously inaccurate at even short distances."[43] Quoting a New York City police commissioner, "there is absolutely no legitimate reason to permit … the sale of these weapons … They are sought only by people who have illicit motives but who may have some difficulty securing a better gun."[44]

Based on these findings and other congressional reports, Eldridge asserted, "The legislative policies of both the United States Congress and the Maryland General Assembly reflect the view that 'Saturday Night Specials' comprise a distinct category of handguns that, because of their characteristics, should be treated differently than other handguns."[45] Reiterating that this category of firearms had no legitimate purpose in society, and that the manufacturer or marketer ought to know the gun is principally used in criminal activity, Eldridge stated that "it is entirely consistent with public policy to hold the manufacturers and marketers of Saturday Night Special handguns strictly liable to innocent persons who suffer gunshot injuries from the criminal use of their product. Furthermore … the imposition of such liability is warranted by today's circumstances."[46]

After acknowledging that no clear-cut definition of an SNS existed, and that some high-quality, small, short-barreled handguns had legitimate uses in law enforcement, Eldridge addressed the question of whether the Rohm revolver at issue qualified as an SNS. Noting that some firearms commentators considered R.G. Industries the nation's major producer of SNSs; that some Rohms were described as "junk guns" in Senate hearings; and that the Bureau of Alcohol, Tobacco and Firearms considered and classified Rohms as being of the poorest quality and least expensive of all seized handguns, the judge ruled that the firearm was indeed a SNS and found in favor of Olen Kelley.[47]

With this decision, Judge Eldridge recognized that the court's ruling was unusual, in that it did not follow from any of the existing theories of strict liability discussed in the case. Arguing that "common law adapts to fit the needs of society,"[48] the court chose to recognize a new, limited area of strict liability for the manufacturers and marketers of SNSs. But two years later, a federal district court adjudicating a similar New Mexico filing rejected Eldridge's novel liability theory.

Armijo v. Ex Cam, Inc. (1987): Adjudicating a Firearm Liability Dispute

In April 1983, after lethally shooting his brother-in-law, Steven Armijo assaulted his sister (Dolores Armijo, the plaintiff) and her young daughter, both of whom had witnessed the shooting. He attempted to shoot them also, but the gun failed to go off. Dolores eventually brought suit against Ex Cam, Inc., the importer and distributor of the firearm, alleging that the gun used in the murder was known as a "Saturday Night Special." US District Judge Juan Guerrero Burciaga presided over the case.[49]

Judge Burciaga noted that the plaintiff's argument supporting her claim involved four theories: "strict products liability, liability under an 'ultra-hazardous activity' theory, negligence liability, and a narrow form of strict products liability for 'Saturday Night Specials' articulated by the Supreme Court of Maryland in *Kelley v. R.G. Industries, Inc.*"[50] After reviewing the various elements that plaintiffs must meet to establish liability under New Mexico law, Burciaga stated, "The Court does not believe that the New Mexico Courts would adopt any of these theories to recognize a cause of action in this case."[51] He then evaluated each of the four theories in turn.

He observed,

> Plaintiff's argument for strict liability fails on the first of these elements, that the product must be "defective." Plaintiff does not allege … that the gun in question misfired or otherwise worked improperly. Plaintiff does not allege that the gun performed otherwise than exactly as intended. Rather Plaintiff argues that the *risk* of intentional criminal misuse of such a firearm … is so great as to outweigh any potential benefit of the product, thus rendering it defective. No New Mexico case law supports this novel theory. … [A] product which has inherent and obvious dangers, which the average consumer would certainly recognize, is not "defective," merely because it was placed on the marketplace with such obviously dangerous propensities. … The mere fact that a product is capable of being misused to criminal ends does not render the product defective.[52]

Turning to the second theory, Burciaga stated, "Plaintiff argues … that marketing of handguns should be classed as an 'ultrahazardous activity' subject to strict liability. Such a theory with respect to handgun manufacturers is not supported by New Mexico case law. … New Mexico courts [have tended] to confine 'ultrahazardous activity' liability to a specific setting: activities carried out on real property."[53]

Regarding the third theory, the court noted,

> Plaintiff additionally seeks to impose liability … under a negligence standard. Plaintiff argues that Defendants breached a duty of reasonable care in marketing a product which carried some degree of risk that it might be used in a criminal

> enterprise. However, this Court is not persuaded that the New Mexico courts would be inclined to impose such a duty. … In the area of firearm manufacture and sale, the New Mexico legislature, while imposing certain restrictions, has not seen fit to make such distribution *per se* unlawful. In the absence of any legislative action … this Court will not impose a "duty" upon manufacturers of firearms not to sell their products, merely because such products have the potential to be misused for purposes of criminal activity.[54]

For the last theory, Judge Burciaga briefly reviewed the findings of the *Kelley* case regarding SNSs, noting that the Maryland court "allowed liability to be imposed upon the manufacturers of these specific types of guns."[55] However, he then stated, "This Court finds it unnecessary to engage in any lengthy discussion of the *Kelley* doctrine. To recognize such a cause of action in New Mexico would require an abrogation of the common law in a way bordering on judicial legislation."[56]

Continuing, he argued,

> Furthermore, creation of such a doctrine is extremely problematic insofar as *which* manufacturers would be held liable. All firearms are capable of being used for criminal activity. Merely to impose liability upon the manufacturers of the cheapest type of handguns will not avoid that basic fact. … persons shot with cheap guns will be able to recover [damages], while those shot with expensive guns, admitted by the Kelley court to be more accurate and therefore deadlier, would [get] nothing. This Court does not believe New Mexico courts would adopt such a doctrine.[57]

Judge Burciaga then granted the defendant's motion to dismiss the case.

The disparate rulings in the *Kelley* and *Armijo* cases serve to highlight the difficulties associated in determining whether SNSs are especially dangerous firearms, and whether the additional risks they pose warrant manufacturer and seller liability. Ten years later, a US Court of Appeals opinion in a Missouri SNS gun case examined circumstances where manufacturer liability appeared merited.

Bryco Arms v. Chronister (1997): Adjudicating a Firearm Liability Dispute

In 1994, Joseph Chronister purchased a "Bryco 59" 9-mm pistol for personal protection. At target practice, the first time he and several friends fired the weapon, the gun misfed and jammed several times. On Chronister's final shooting attempt, the cartridge detonated while the chamber was open. Chronister testified that "he staggered back and fell, got some soot and shrapnel in his face, was temporarily blinded, and lost his hearing in his right ear for several hours and in his left ear for a shorter period."[58] He was not wearing any hearing protection during the shooting session, despite warnings on both the gun and ammunition boxes that such protection was required.[59]

Chronister then brought suit against Bryco, under theories of strict liability and negligence. He asserted that the firearm had design defects, as evidenced by its excessive number of misfeeds, and also by its use of the gun's firing pin to eject each spent cartridge after firing. Chronister stated that his gun exploded "when a live cartridge jammed while feeding into the open chamber and while the firing pin was still exposed."[60] To support this assertion, Chronister called an expert witness who had test-fired five Bryco 59 pistols purchased at various places around the country.

The expert testified that every one of the five firearms misfired between 20 and 50 percent of the time. Further, on at least three occasions, a gun misfed and jammed while the firing pin was exposed to the cartridge and the chamber was open. The expert suggested that Chronister's accident was likely the result of such a misfeed, "with the extra misfortune that the firing pin happened to strike the primer, rather than some other part of the cartridge."[61] The jury was shown a videotape of the tests.

The federal district court permitted the jury to return a separate verdict for each of Chronister's two claims, strict liability (on the basis of design defect) and negligence (on the basis of failure to warn about hearing loss). The jury found for Chronister on both claims. Bryco then moved for a judgment as a matter of law—a motion asserting that, given the presented evidence, no reasonable jury could find for the other side and asking the judge to render a judgment. When the court denied this motion, Byrco moved for a new trial—also denied. [62]

Appealed to the circuit court, Byrco alleged that the lower court erred in three ways: (1) denying the motion for a judgment as a matter of law (JAML), (2) instructing the jury on strict liability failure to warn, and (3) denying the motion for a new trial based on alleged evidentiary and trial errors. Judge Arlen Beam authored the opinion for the circuit court. The judge first dealt with the JAML motion, noting that a motion seeking to set aside a jury verdict requires that the court "view the 'evidence in the light most favorable to the prevailing party.'"[63]

He further noted Missouri law in a strict liability case requires the plaintiff to establish that "the product was then in a defective condition unreasonably dangerous when put to a reasonably anticipated use."[64] He then considered Bryco's two arguments for why the company was not liable for Chronister's ear injuries: (1) Byrco could not reasonably foresee someone using its handguns without hearing protection and (2) using a product contrary to that product's warnings is not a reasonably anticipated use. Rejecting both arguments, Beam asserted,

> a manufacturer cannot escape strict liability for a defective product that has been misused by the plaintiff if that misuse is reasonably foreseeable. [Citation provided.] ... This is the rule in Missouri .... "The concept of reasonably anticipated use includes misuse and abnormal use which is objectively foreseeable." ... Bryco could have foreseen that some target shooters might choose not to wear hearing protection.[65]

The judge concluded that Bryco was not entitled to judgment as a matter of law on this issue.

Bryco had also argued that Chronister's liability claim for "failure to warn" should not have been submitted to the jury because the company had included adequate warnings of the hearing danger and because "its product did not cause Chronister's injury because no warning would have altered his behavior."[66] In turn, Chronister argued that the provided warnings were insufficient, noting that they neglected to indicate the Bryco 59 was prone to misfeeding, with the potential result of a disastrous cartridge mishap. The general warning to use hearing protection failed to advise of the gun's specific risks, and "only clearly encompassed routine discharge of the weapon, not a sudden, catastrophic explosion of the cartridge in the open chamber."[67]

While acknowledging that precedents existed for requiring a plaintiff to show that a warning would have altered his behavior, Judge Beam concluded that

> we find no error in allowing the jury to consider whether Bryco's cautionary language adequately warned of the particular risks of using its products. ... The jury could reasonably have concluded that, had an adequate warning of the Bryco 59's particular risks been present, Chronister would have altered his behavior. The district court did not err in submitting the failure to warn theory to the jury.[68]

After considering and dismissing the several secondary issues Bryco raised in moving for a mistrial—finding them to be "without merit"[69]—Beam affirmed the ruling of the district court.

Courts continued to wrestle with SNSs and the peculiar dangers they presumably create in the new century. Often alleging foreseeable design risks and unnecessary peril, plaintiffs continued to use novel theories and interpretations of liability statutes to bring suits against gun manufacturers and distributers. For instance, four years after *Chronister*, Bryco Arms was again in court. In this New Mexico case (*Smith v. Bryco Arms*, 2001), plaintiffs alleged that Bycro's failure to incorporate certain safety features into a Bryco pistol contributed to the accidental shooting of a minor.[70]

The trial court, noting that Bryco had no legal duty to incorporate the safety features in question (i.e., a magazine-out safety and a loaded chamber indicator), ruled that the firearm was not unreasonably dangerous, did not present an unreasonable risk of injury, and granted Bryco summary judgment. However, on appeal, that court interpreted New Mexico's products liability and negligence laws differently, and remanded that case for trial.[71]

In yet another dangerous gun design case involving Bryco (*Maxfield v. Bryco Arms*, 2005),[72] California's Court of Appeal affirmed a trial court's judgment in favor of the plaintiff. Accidentally shot at age seven and rendered a quadriplegic, Brandon Maxfield argued that the pistol's poor design—requiring the shooter to unload the gun by first setting the gun's safety to the "fire" position—created a substantial and unnecessary hazard known to the defendant. Bryco countered by arguing that the trial court made numerous procedural errors (such as allowing the pistol to be described as a "Saturday Night Special"); and that the evidence itself was insufficient to support the verdict.[73]

After examining and rejecting Bryco's procedural arguments (noting, for example, that Bryco itself used the term "Saturday Night Special" in the description and marketing of the gun), the appeals court also examined and rejected Bryco's substantive argument. The court ruled that the evidence was indeed sufficient for the jury to reach the conclusion it did.[74]

Responding to the legal uncertainties inherent in the new liability theories now often advanced in gun cases, firearm manufacturers sought legislative relief from Congress, and in late 2005, Congress passed the Protection of Lawful Commerce in Arms Act (PLCAA). This Act granted immunity to firearms manufacturers and dealers from any lawsuit alleging harm and asking damages for actions resulting from the criminal or unlawful misuse of a firearm by a person or a third party.

Glock and several other gun manufacturers swiftly benefited from the act, in a California case alleging wrongful death, negligence, and public nuisance claims. In this case (*Ileto v. Glock*, 2006),[75] a convicted felon (prohibited from possessing any firearm) had used a Glock handgun and other firearms to carry out a mass shooting. The plaintiffs brought suit, arguing (among other issues) that the manufacturers had used reckless marketing strategies and had intentionally oversaturated the legitimate gun market, knowing that illegal purchasers would acquire the surplus guns. Glock and the other defendants moved to dismiss the case, citing the provisions of PLCAA.[76]

After considering the arguments, US District Judge Audrey Collins granted the motion to dismiss. She quoted the purpose of the act, noting that it was to "prohibit causes of action against manufacturers, distributors, dealers, and importers of firearms or ammunition products … for the harm solely caused by the criminal or unlawful misuse of [these] products by others when the product functioned as designed and tested."[77]

PLCAA did not shield the firearms industry from product liability suits centered on poorly designed or clearly flawed guns, and plaintiffs could still bring suit against manufacturers and distributors of truly defective and dangerous SNSs. But the act ended firearm cases based primarily on creative interpretations of liability statutes.

While substantially relieved from dealing with SNS cases, twenty-first-century courts have encountered another category of controversial arms that many individuals consider especially dangerous: "assault" weapons. Because of the weapons' perceived greater lethality, gun control proponents in particular have lobbied to have these firearms prohibited or severely restricted. But unlike the SNS product liability adjudications that avoided Second Amendment constitutional entanglements, the attempts to ban or severely regulate assault-style semiautomatic firearms have faced significant Second Amendment obstacles.

2001–21: Assault-Style Weapons and Their Lethality

Prior to the late 1980s, few Americans would have described any of the commonly sold semiautomatic rifles and pistols as assault weapons. But in 1988, Josh Sugarmann, a prominent gun control proponent, published an influential advocacy report—*Assault Weapons and Accessories in America.*[78] In the report, he argued that the military appearance of certain semiautomatic rifles (e.g., AR-15s and AK-47s), and the public's confusion over semiautomatic and automatic firing, created an opportunity to garner public support for gun restrictions simply by labeling the rifles "assault weapons." Shortly after publication, in January 1989, a horrific school shooting involving a semiautomatic AK-47 occurred in Stockton, California, and the media quickly adopted the term, and gave it widespread use in the years following. Even before 1989 ended, California enacted the Assault Weapons Control Act (AWCA), banning dozens of semiautomatic rifles and pistols.[79]

Proponents of the California ban—and a similar federal ban enacted in 1994—argued that, semiautomatic or not, the prohibited firearms had rates of fire and cartridge capacities that made them more lethal than standard hunting rifles, and were too dangerous for unrestricted civilian possession. While the federal ban on assault-style firearms ended in 2004—as noted, the evidence examining its effectiveness was mixed and inconclusive—California and other states opted to keep such bans in place, contending that the guns posed dangerous health and safety threats to the lives of peaceable Americans. Gun rights proponents, pointing to the functional equivalence of the banned guns to legally acceptable semiautomatic firearms, disagreed, and they challenged the bans as unacceptable Second Amendment infringements.[80]

Of the five cases examined in this section, two cases—*United States v. Marzzarella* (2010) and *Caetano v. Massachusetts* (2016)—are not assault weapon adjudications. Each is certainly important in its own right, but they are included here primarily for their consideration of the term "dangerous and unusual," a notion highly relevant to the three assault weapons cases—*Merrill v. Navegar, Inc.* (2001), *Heller v. District of Columbia* (2011), and *Miller v. Bonta* (2021). Thus, instead of examining the five adjudications chronologically, *Marzzarella* and *Caetano* are discussed first.

United States v. Marzzarella (2010): Possession of a Serially Defaced Handgun

After selling stolen handguns with partially defaced serial numbers to an undercover agent, Michael Marzzarella was indicted for possession of a firearm with an obliterated serial number. He moved to dismiss the indictment, arguing that the law on which it was based (i.e., §922 (k)) "violated his Second Amendment right to keep and bear arms, as recognized by the Supreme Court in *District of Columbia v. Heller*."[81]

The district court denied his motion, holding that §922 (k) did not meaningfully burden the "core" right recognized in *Heller*—the right to possess firearms for self-defense. The court noted that the law was "analogous to several longstanding limitations on the right to bear arms identified as presumptively valid in *Heller* [and] even if Marzzarella's possession of the Titan pistol was protected by the Second Amendment, § 922(k) would pass muster under intermediate scrutiny as a constitutionally permissible regulation."[82] Sentenced to nine months imprisonment, Marzzarella appealed to the Third Circuit Court of Appeals, where Judge Anthony Scirica, appointed to the federal bench by President Ronald Reagan, authored the court's opinion.

Scirica first analyzed whether possession of a defaced firearm in the home was protected by the right to bear arms. He observed that Second Amendment protection extended only to weapons commonly owned by law-abiding citizens. It was not unlimited and did not extend to the carrying of "dangerous and unusual weapons."[83]

But Scirica acknowledged that §922 (k)'s prohibition on the possession of firearms with removed or obliterated serial numbers was not directly considered in *Heller*, and that unmarked firearms were functionally no different than marked firearms: "with or without a serial number, a pistol is still a pistol."[84]

Nevertheless, he observed, "It is arguably possible to extend the exception for dangerous and unusual weapons to cover unmarked firearms … there would appear no compelling reason why a law-abiding citizen would prefer an unmarked firearm. These weapons would have value primarily for persons seeking to use them for illicit purposes."[85] On the other hand, he noted that an unmarked handgun seemed distinct from other weapons typically considered unusual and dangerous, such as "sawed-off shotguns … bazookas, mortars, pipe bombs, and machine guns. An unmarked firearm is no more damaging than a marked firearm."[86]

Scirica eventually concluded, "We cannot be certain that the possession of unmarked firearms in the home is excluded from the right to bear arms."[87] However, he additionally noted that §922 (k) is narrowly tailored and serves a compelling government interest—preventing crime. He asserted, "Accordingly, § 922(k) passes muster under intermediate scrutiny [and] even if strict scrutiny were to apply to § 922(k), the statute still would pass muster. … Marzzarella's conviction must stand."[88]

Two aspects of the *Marzzarella* opinion are especially noteworthy. First is the court's acknowledgment of the ambiguity that sometimes resides in *Heller*'s "dangerous and unusual" weapons exception to the right to bear arms. Despite the functional equivalence of marked and unmarked guns, the opinion concedes that a defaced firearms might qualify as a "dangerous and unusual" weapon. Scirica's comment implies that a weapon's functional equivalence to a "normal" firearm may not guarantee Second Amendment protection for that weapon.

The second noteworthy feature is the court's use of means-ends analysis—intermediate and strict scrutiny—to determine the case outcome. That approach, typical in gun adjudications during the first two decades of the twenty-first century, was repudiated by the Supreme Court, first in *Heller* in 2008 and again in *Bruen* in 2022. It is unclear how Marzzarella would have fared had Scirica applied the current "text, history and tradition" standard now in use.

As the next case shows, the US Supreme Court in 2016 attempted to clarify the meaning of a "dangerous and unusual" weapon in an opinion centered on a stun gun. In a sharp rebuke to the Supreme Court of Massachusetts, which held that stun guns were dangerous and unusual, the court rejected such reasoning as not merely wrong but "bordering on the frivolous."[89] In examining the problems contained in the Massachusetts opinion, the court also examined the implications of "dangerous and unusual" for Second Amendment adjudications.

Caetano v. Massachusetts (2016): Appealing a Stun Gun Possession Conviction

In an abusive relationship with a boyfriend, Jaime Caetano obtained a stun gun for self-protection after multiple restraining orders proved ineffective. One evening, the ex-boyfriend—almost a foot taller and 100 pounds heavier—confronted Caetano after work, screaming she should be home with their children. She displayed the stun gun, warned him she would use it, and told him to leave her alone. Alarmed, the ex-boyfriend left.[90]

A state statute made the mere possession of a stun gun illegal, and when the police later discovered the weapon, Caetano was arrested, tried, and convicted. Appealed to the Massachusetts Supreme Court, that court affirmed the conviction, holding that a stun gun "is not the type of weapon that is eligible for Second Amendment protection" because it was "not in common use at the time of [the Second Amendment's] enactment."[91] Appealed to the US Supreme Court, that court vacated the Massachusetts ruling.

The Supreme Court noted that the Massachusetts court provided three arguments in asserting that the Second Amendment did not apply to stun guns. The first was that such guns were not in common use in the late eighteenth century; the second was that the weapon was dangerous and unusual; and the third was that stun guns were not readily adaptable to military use. The Supreme Court considered each argument and, citing the 2008 *Heller* decision, rejected all three. Regarding Massachusetts's first argument, the court observed, "This is inconsistent with *Heller's* clear statement that the Second Amendment 'extends … to … arms … that were not in existence at the time of the founding.' "[92]

The court rejected Massachusetts's second contention that stun guns were dangerous and unusual weapons simply because they were "a thoroughly modern invention."[93] The court observed, "By equating 'unusual' with 'in common use at the time of the Second Amendment's enactment,' the [Massachusetts] court's second explanation is the same as the first; [and] it is inconsistent with *Heller* for the same reason."[94] Concerning Massachusetts's final argument, the court pointed out, "*Heller* rejected the proposition 'that only those weapons useful in warfare are protected.' "[95] The court concluded, "For these three reasons, the explanation the Massachusetts court offered for upholding the law contradicts this Court's precedent. Consequently … the judgment … is vacated, and the case is remanded for further proceedings not inconsistent with this opinion."[96]

Justice Alito (joined by Justice Thomas) wrote a concurring opinion that elaborated on the court's reasoning. Commenting on "dangerous and unusual weapons," Alito noted,

> This is a conjunctive test: A weapon may not be banned unless it is *both* dangerous and unusual. … As to "dangerous," … the relative dangerousness of a weapon is irrelevant when the weapon belongs to a class of arms commonly used for lawful purposes. See *Heller* [Citation given]. … If *Heller* tells us anything, it is that firearms cannot be categorically prohibited because they are dangerous. [Citation given.] *A fortiori*, stun guns … cannot be banned on that basis.[97]

Alito then turned to "unusual." He emphasized that "unusualness" did not depend on—as the Massachusetts court held—whether a weapon was useful to the militia. He pointed out that *Heller*

> actually said it would be a "startling reading" of *Miller* to conclude that "only weapons useful in warfare are protected." [Citation given]. Instead, *Miller* and *Heller* recognized that militia members traditionally reported for duty carrying "the sorts of lawful weapons that they possessed at home," and that the Second Amendment therefore protects such weapons as a class, regardless of any particular weapon's suitability for military use.[98]

Both cases underscore the complicated judicial considerations involved in determining the characteristics that make a weapon dangerous and unusual, and consequently place it outside Second Amendment protection. In the following case, the court adjudicated a California product-liability dispute occurring prior to the passage of PLCAA. The dispute centers on an infamous "assault-style" firearm and the features that presumably make it especially treacherous and unfit for civilian ownership.

Merrill v. Navegar, Inc. (2001): Defending against Design/Negligence Claims

In 1993, a deranged individual used a semiautomatic assault pistol—a TEC-9/DC9 firearm manufactured by Navegar, Inc.—to kill eight people and wound six others in a San Francisco office building. Survivors and victim representatives sued Navegar, alleging that " 'making the [TEC-9/DC9] available for sale to the general public' was 'an abnormally dangerous activity.' "[99] Their suit asserted that Navegar's decision "to make available for sale to the general public guns … which [it] knew or should have known have 'no legitimate sporting or self-defense purpose' and which are 'particularly well-adapted to a military-style assault on large numbers of people' [Citation]."[100] was negligent.

The plaintiffs further claimed that Navegar—knowing that the "TEC-9/DC9 was particularly attractive to criminals and particularly suited to mass killings"[101]—breached a legal duty of care by offering the gun to civilians. They asserted that Navegar's advertising underscored the foreseeability of the criminal use of the firearm in circumstances such as the San Francisco massacre. Pointing to a typical advertisement touting the design features of the TEC9/DC9, the plaintiffs noted the emphasis on "32 rounds of firepower," that the gun "stands out among high capacity 9mm assault-type pistols," and that it "deliver[s] more gutsy performance and reliability than ANY gun on the market."[102]

In other Navegar material, the plaintiffs pointed to the company's stress on the gun's finish, which claimed that the finish provided "natural lubicity [*sic*] to increase bullet velocities, [and] excellent resistance to finger prints."[103] Further, the gun's accompanying manual asserted that the gun was " 'a radically new type of semi-automatic pistol … designed to deliver a high volume of firepower' and 'thanks to its dimensions and designs' could 'be used in modes of fire impossible with most handguns' … including 'hipfire at shortest range.' "[104]

Navegar responded that the plaintiffs' case was based on the "benefit–risk" theory of negligence—that TEC-9/DC9s "are used disproportionately to commit crimes and have no sporting or self-defense utility."[105] Citing Section 1714.4 of the Civil Code, the company argued that California law barred this type of action: "no firearm or ammunition shall be deemed defective on the basis that the benefits of the product do not outweigh the risk of injury posed by its potential to cause serious injury, damage or death when discharged."[106] The trial court did not accept this argument (noting that the plaintiffs were not asserting a products-liability theory) but did grant Navegar's motion to dismiss.[107]

The court asserted that the plaintiffs' negligence claim was "based on Navegar's decision to make available for sale … assault-type guns which it knew or reasonably should have known have 'no legitimate sporting or self-defense purpose' and which are 'particularly well-adapted to a military-style assault on large numbers of people.' "[108] But the court then noted that the guns were legally manufactured and sold, and that California common law did not impose on Navegar a duty "not to manufacture or sell assault weapons."[109]

Elaborating, the court observed, "in case after case … courts have refused to impose a duty on manufacturers of firearms not to sell their products merely because of the potential of misuse of the product by a third party."[110] Regarding the plaintiffs' ultrahazardous activity argument, the court found that "as a matter of law, the manufacture and distribution of a firearm, even an assault weapon, is not inherently dangerous."[111]

On appeal, that court affirmed the trial court's ultrahazardous activity decision, but reversed its negligence finding. The court argued, "the manufacturer and distributor of a legal and nondefective firearm may not be found negligent merely because it manufactured and/or distributed the weapon [but Navegar had] a legal duty not to manufacture, market and distribute this weapon in a manner that increases the risk of harm inherent in the presence of handguns in society."[112] Continuing, the court justified the imposition of this legal duty on "the strength of the evidence that the harm appellants suffered was or should have been foreseeable, the equally strong evidence Navegar's marketing increased the risk of such harm, and the evidence that there is no legitimate civilian use for the TEC-DC9."[113]

Navegar petitioned California's Supreme Court to review the findings regarding the negligence claim. Justice Ming Chin authored the opinion for the Supreme Court, and he began by noting that the plaintiffs, to prevail on the negligence claim,

> must show that Navegar owed them a legal duty, that it breached that duty, and that the breach was a proximate or legal cause of their injuries. … Navegar argues that this statute [1714.4], by establishing a state policy of exempting manufacturers of legal, nondefective firearms "from liability for their criminal use," bars plaintiffs' negligence claim. Plaintiffs respond that … they "seek to hold Navegar liable for its negligent conduct, not for making a defective product" … or, as plaintiffs alternatively state, because Navegar "negligently designed, distributed, and marketed" the weapon.[114]

To resolve the conflicting positions, Justice Chin reviewed tort law principles. He concluded that, under such principles,

> to recover from a manufacturer, a plaintiff must prove a defect caused injury. … Under these principles, we reject the plaintiffs' arguments that section 1714.4 is inapplicable …. [I]n asserting that the TEC-9/DC9 had a "negligent design" and that Navegar "negligently designed" it, plaintiffs have in fact alleged that the TEC-9/DC9 is, in the words of section 1714.4, subdivision (a), "defective in design."[115]

Further, Chin asserted,

> Moreover … the record demonstrates that plaintiffs do, in fact, seek to hold Navegar liable precisely because, as the trial court stated, the TEC-9/DC9's "potential for harm substantially outweighs any possible benefit to be derived from [it]." In their brief, plaintiffs assert that Navegar is liable because it "designed and widely distributed a weapon uniquely suited for mass killing and lacking legitimate civilian uses." … the plaintiffs argue, "[t]he Legislature has restricted the [TEC-9] based upon a finding that it has such a high rate of fire and capacity for firepower that its function as a sports or recreational firearm is outweighed by the danger that it can be used to kill or injure human beings." … these allegations squarely fit within the risk/utility test for defective design.[116]

Continuing, the Justice observed,

> Thus … this is a products liability action … which asserts that the TEC-9/DC9 was defective in design because the risks of making it available to the general public outweighed the benefits …. Plaintiffs may not avoid this conclusion, or the legislative policy section 1714.4 reflects, simply by declining to use the word "defect" or "defective." …We therefore reject the view … that plaintiffs' claim … falls outside of section 1714.4's scope. … Because the Legislature, in section 1714.4, has precluded the weighing of the risks and benefits of selling a firearm to the general public in determining whether the firearm is defective, we conclude that neither a court nor a jury may undertake this same task.[117]

The Justice then considered the findings of the Court of Appeal. He noted that the appeal court "effectively read the AWCA [i.e., California's Assault Weapons Control Act] policy statements as an implied repeal of section 1714.4 as it applies to any of the firearms the AWCA specifies"[118] [such as the TEC9]. But Chin observed,

> The AWCA contains no express declaration of legislative intent to repeal section 1714.4 or to affect it in any way. Nor does anything in AWCA's legislative history suggest that one of its purposes was to establish an exception to section 1714.4 for the listed weapons. … Unlike the Court of Appeal, we find that AWCA does not render section 1714.4 inapplicable. … Accordingly, we conclude the trial court properly granted Navegar summary judgment. … The judgment of Court of Appeal is reversed with directions to affirm summary judgment for defendant.[119]

While the *Navegar* case effectively highlighted certain characteristics that make a firearm especially dangerous, the adjudication's primary focus was on product liability. And since California law specifically barred liability suits using the theory advanced by the plaintiffs—that the societal costs of such a weapon outweighed any benefits—the Second Amendment question of whether that firearm (and "assault" firearms like it) were outside the amendment's protection and could be prohibited, never arose. In the next case, sometimes referred to as *"Heller II,"* the US Court of Appeals for the District of Columbia directly examined this possibility.

Heller v. District of Columbia (2011): Challenging Registration Requirements and Bans

In 2008, the US Supreme Court ruled that DC's law restricting possession of firearms in the home was an unconstitutional violation of the Second Amendment. That same year, responding to that ruling, the district adopted the Firearms Registration Amendment Act (FRA). Among other requirements, the FRA mandated the registration of all firearms, prohibited the registration of "assault weapons," and banned the possession of magazines holding more than ten rounds of ammunition. Dick Heller, the plaintiff in the original challenge to the district's restrictive gun law (i.e., *Heller I*), also objected to the district's FRA provisions. He filed suit, and argued that the FRA provisions were not within the district's congressionally legislative authority or, if they were, they violated the Second Amendment.[120]

After the district court granted summary judgment for the district, Heller and the other plaintiffs appealed. Judge Ruth Bader Ginsburg—later a justice on the Supreme Court—wrote the opinion for the US Court of Appeals (which also included Judge Brett Kavanaugh, himself a future Supreme Court justice).[121]

Judge Ginsburg noted that the plaintiffs objected to multiple requirements of the FRA. These requirements—mandatory every time a person applied for a Metropolitan Police Department registration certificate—included appearing in person with the unregistered firearm, disclosing self-identifying information, submitting the pistol for ballistic identification testing, registering no more than one pistol in a thirty-day period, and renewing each registration certificate every three years.[122]

Additionally, the applicant had to submit to being fingerprinted and photographed, demonstrate knowledge of the district's firearms laws, attend a firearms training or safety course consisting of at least one hour of live-fire training and four hours of classroom instruction, and undergo a background check every six years. The applicant also had to have vision qualifying the individual for a driver's license.[123]

Ginsburg further noted that the plaintiffs similarly objected to the FRA's prohibition of "assault weapons" and magazines holding more than ten rounds. She observed that, in district court, the plaintiffs had argued that all DC gun laws—by statute—had to be "usual and reasonable," and that the FRA's requirements were neither. Or, if they were, they violated the plaintiffs' Second Amendment rights. In reply, the district court had asserted that the FRA's requirements were usual and reasonable police regulations and, as such, did not exceed the district's authority under local law. Further, while acknowledging that the registration requirements involved Second Amendment considerations, the district court held that all the FRA provisions would survive intermediate scrutiny and, consequently, granted summary judgment for the district.[124]

In adjudicating the plaintiffs' challenges, the Court of Appeals turned first to the district's statutory authority to enact the FRA. The appeals court agreed with the district court that the DC Home Rule Act (HRA) of 1973 gave the district the authority over "all rightful subjects of legislation"[125] and that this included the power to enact the FRA. Judge Ginsburg summarized,

> We agree with the District that it was authorized to enact the challenged gun laws. The HRA granted the District broad legislative power, subject to a few exceptions, none of which is relevant here. … Accordingly, we need not decide whether the laws at issue are "usual and reasonable" because we hold the district has authority under the HRA to enact laws regulating firearms.[126]

The court then addressed whether the Second Amendment permitted the challenged laws. Noting that the Supreme Court had asserted the Second Amendment allowed some exceptions to the right to keep and bear arms, Ginsburg observed that "the historical tradition of prohibiting the carrying of dangerous and unusual weapons"[127] was an example of one such exception. Continuing, she wrote, "We accordingly adopt, as have other circuits, a two-step approach to determining the constitutionality of the District's gun laws. [Citations provided.] We ask first whether a particular provision impinges upon a right protected by the Second Amendment; if it does, then we go to determine whether the provision passes muster under the appropriate level of constitutional scrutiny."[128]

In applying this framework, the court considered whether the challenged registration requirements impinged on the Second Amendment. For basic registration requirements, Ginsburg observed,

> We uphold the requirement of mere registration because it is longstanding, hence "presumptively lawful" and the presumption stands unrebutted. … The record supports the view that basic registration of handguns is deeply enough rooted in our history to support the presumption that a registration requirement is constitutional. …[T]he basic requirement to register a handgun is longstanding in American law, accepted for a century in diverse states and cities and now applicable to more than one fourth of the nation by population. Therefore, we presume the District's basic registration requirement … does not impinge upon the right protected by the Amendment."[129]

After noting that the basic registration provisions were constitutional for handguns but—given no historical precedents—not necessarily for rifles, the court considered the district's multiple other new registration demands. The court observed that these provisions (i.e., the ballistics-identification requirement, the one-pistol-per-30-day rule, re-registration of each firearm every three years, demonstration of knowledge about firearms, etc.) were also not "longstanding" and that they "make it considerably more difficult for a person lawfully to acquire and keep a firearm"[130] for the core purpose of the Second Amendment: self-defense in the home. Concluding that these provisions impinged upon the amendment, the court determined that they required constitutional evaluation.

To do that, Judge Ginsburg asserted that the court

> must first determine the degree of scrutiny to which they are appropriately subject. The plaintiffs argue that strict scrutiny is the appropriate standard of review .... The District responds that strict scrutiny would be inappropriate because ... the right to keep and carry arms has always been heavily regulated. ... As with the First Amendment, the level of scrutiny applicable under the Second Amendment surely "depends on the nature of the conduct being regulated and the degree to which the challenged law burdens that right." [Citations given]. ... That is, a regulation that imposes a substantial burden upon the core right of self-defense ... must have a strong justification, whereas a regulation that imposes a less substantial burden should be proportionally easier to justify.[131]

Noting that strict scrutiny does not apply to fundamental rights when infringement is only incidental, the court asserted,

> between strict and intermediate scrutiny, we conclude the latter is the more appropriate standard for review of gun registration laws. As the Third Circuit reasoned in *Marzzarella* ... registration requirements "do not severely limit the possession of firearms." [Citation given]. Indeed, none of the District's registration requirements prevent an individual from possessing a firearm in his home or elsewhere, whether for self-defense, or hunting, or any other lawful purpose.[132]

To survive intermediate scrutiny, the court observed that the new requirements must substantially connect to an important governmental objective. Ginsburg wrote,

> We think the District has advanced ... two important governmental interests ... *viz.*, to protect police officers and to aid in crime control. ... We cannot conclude, however, that the novel registration requirements ... survive intermediate scrutiny based upon the record as it stands because the District has not demonstrated a close fit between those requirements and its governmental interests. ...the District fails to present any data or other evidence to substantiate its claim that these requirements can reasonably be expected to promote either of the important governmental interests it has invoked .... Therefore, the District needs to present some meaningful evidence, not mere assertions, to justify its predictive judgments. ...we conclude the District has not supplied evidence adequate to show a substantial relationship between any of the novel registration requirements and an important governmental interest.[133]

After remanding the novel registration requirements (and *all* registration requirements as applied to long guns) to the district court for further evidentiary proceedings, the court then turned to the ban on specific semiautomatic rifles and large-capacity magazines (LCMs). Judge Ginsburg noted,

> The plaintiffs contend semi-automatic rifles, in particular the AR variants, are commonly possessed for self-protection in the home as well as for sport. They also argue magazines holding more than ten rounds are commonly possessed for self-defense and other lawful purposes .... The District, by contrast, argues that neither assault weapons nor weapons with large capacity magazines are among the "Arms" protected by the Second Amendment because they are both "dangerous and unusual," [*Heller* citation] and because prohibiting them minimally burdens the plaintiffs; hence, the District maintains the bans are constitutional.[134]

While the court agreed with the plaintiffs that the evidence showed semiautomatic rifles and LCMs were in common use, Ginsburg asserted,

> Nevertheless, based upon the record as it stands, we cannot be certain whether these weapons are commonly used or are useful specifically for self-defense or hunting and therefore whether the prohibitions ... meaningfully affect the right to keep and bear arms. ... Unlike the law held unconstitutional in *Heller*, the laws at issue here do not prohibit the possession of "the quintessential self-defense weapon," to wit, the handgun.[135]

Continuing, she argued,

> We are reasonably certain the prohibitions do not impose a substantial burden upon that right [to keep and bear arms]. ... Accordingly, we believe intermediate rather than strict scrutiny is the appropriate standard of review. In this we agree with the reasoning in the Third Circuit in *Marzzarella*. The court there applied intermediate scrutiny to the prohibition of unmarked firearms ... because the prohibition left a person "free to possess any otherwise lawful firearm" .... Here, too, the prohibition of semi-automatic rifles and large capacity magazines does not effectively disarm individuals or substantially affect their ability to defend themselves.[136]

After noting that intermediate scrutiny requires the government to show a reasonable fit between the prohibitions and its interest in protecting police and controlling crime, the court asserted,

> The record evidence substantiates that the District's prohibition is substantially related to those ends. The Committee on Public Safety relied upon a report by the ATF, which described assault weapons as creating "mass produced mayhem." ... [Another] source also suggests assault weapons are preferred by criminals,

> and place law enforcement officers "at particular risk ... because of their high firepower" .... *Heller* suggests "M-16 rifles and the like" may be banned because they are "dangerous and unusual" [citation provided]. The Court had previously described the "AR-15" as "the civilian version of the military's M-16 rifle." Although semi-automatic firearms ... fire "only one shot with each pull of the trigger," [they] still fire almost as rapidly as automatics. [Citation provided].[137]

Further, the court observed,

> Indeed, it is difficult to draw meaningful distinctions between the AR-15 and the M-16. *See Staples* [citation provided.] ("Many M-16 parts are interchangeable with those in the AR-15, and can be used to convert the AR-15 into an automatic weapon"); ... In short, the evidence demonstrates a ban on assault weapons is likely to promote the Government's interest in crime control in the densely populated urban area that is the District of Columbia. ... The record also supports the limitation on magazine capacity to ten rounds. The Committee [noted] that "[t]he threat posed by military-style assault weapons is significantly increased if they can be equipped with high-capacity ammunition magazines" because "[b]y permitting a shooter to fire more than ten rounds without reloading, they greatly increase the firepower of mass shooters."[138]

The court also noted that the evidence presented

> supports the District's claim that high capacity magazines are dangerous in self-defense situations because "the tendency is for defenders to keep firing until all bullets have been expended, which poses grave risks to others in the household, passersby, and bystanders." ...Overall, the evidence demonstrates that large-capacity magazines tend to pose a danger to innocent people and particularly to police officers, which supports the District's claim .... We conclude the District has carried its burden .... Accordingly, the bans do not violate the plaintiffs' constitutional right to keep and bear arms.[139]

In upholding the district's prohibition on AR-15 rifles and LCMs, the circuit court made it clear that these weapons were especially dangerous, and outside Second Amendment protections. But in an extensive dissent, Judge Kavanaugh argued that the court's reliance on intermediate scrutiny in upholding the district's prohibitions was inappropriate. As an "interest-balancing" standard, he claimed *Heller* explicitly rejected such an approach, noting that "the idea *Heller* precludes heightened scrutiny has eluded every circuit to have addressed [a Second Amendment] question since *Heller* was issued."[140]

A decade later, a US District Court in California, also examining an AR-15 ban, went a step further. The court found that, even using intermediate scrutiny, an AR-15 ban infringed on plaintiffs' Second Amendment rights.

Miller v. Bonta (2021): Challenging the Roberti-Roos Assault Weapons Control Act

James Miller, a California gun owners' association member and other plaintiffs, contested the constitutionality of a set of interlocking statutes that imposed criminal restrictions on the possession of firearms defined by California as "assault weapons." US District Judge Roger Benitez, nominated to the federal bench by President George W. Bush, adjudicated the case. He introduced his analysis by noting that the firearms deemed "assault weapons" by the AWCA were fairly ordinary, popular, modern rifles—not machine guns or bazookas. He noted that FBI murder statistics showed that murder by knife occurred seven times more often than murder by rifle—any type—in California.[141]

Benitez further observed that, in 1989, when California enacted the AWCA, the Act

> was a policy choice unencumbered by constitutional considerations. The California Legislature weighted only the firearm's value for sports and recreation against the relative dangerousness of the weapon and the danger of it being misused by criminals. It was a different time in legal history. In 1989, most judicial thinking about the Second Amendment was incorrect. … the California legislature was not concerned with maintaining room for a citizen's constitutional right to have a common firearm of one's choosing to defend hearth and home. … In the pre-*Heller* jurisprudential milieu, the pure policy choice made sense.[142]

After noting that California in 2000 began to define "assault weapons" by using a "prohibited features" approach, Judge Benitez asserted,

> The Attorney General has not identified any relevant legislative history or legislative findings about the societal dangers of pistol grips, flash hiders, telescoping stocks, flare launchers, or barrel shrouds. …there are no studies of criminal gun use recounted. There are no assault weapon experiences of other states or cities recited. … As an aside, the "assault weapon" epithet is a bit of a misnomer. These prohibited guns, like all guns, are dangerous weapons. However, these prohibited guns, like all guns, can be used for ill or for good. They could just as well be called "home defense rifles" or "anti-crime guns."[143]

The judge observed that, according to the plaintiffs, the AWCA's prohibited design features actually help a person under pressure to shoot more accurately—and a more accurate gun is better for everyone. But according to the attorney general, "better accuracy makes [the gun] a more dangerous weapon. …'assault weapons enable a shooter to fire more rounds rapidly in a given period, increasing the likelihood that more individuals will be shot and suffer more numerous injuries.'"[144] Benitez acknowledged the state's goal of reducing the number of innocent victims in a possible mass shooting event, but suggested,

> it is not at all clear that a less accurate rifle would reduce the number of victims. A less accurate rifle ... may very well result in different victims, but not necessarily less victims. On the other hand, in the self-defense context, which seems to be more common, taking accurate shots at attackers is vitally important for the innocent victim.[145]

To conclude his introductory comments, Judge Benitez focused on the criminal sanctions associated with the AWCA, and quoted a law review paper,

> [m]ere possession of an object that is commonplace and perfectly legal under federal law and in forty-four states will land you in prison, [will] result in the loss of your rights including likely the right to vote, and probably [will] cause you irreparable monetary and reputational damage, as well as your personal liberty. All of this despite the absence of even a single victim.[146]

In a footnote, the judge also added the forfeiture of the firearm itself to the list.

Benitez then began his analysis, pointing out the Supreme Court in *Caetano* made clear that the Second Amendment extends to common modern arms useful for home self-defense, and that its protection "includes both common arms and weapons that may also be useful in warfare."[147] With these principles in mind, he proposed to test the constitutionality of the AWCA, first applying the *Heller* test and then the Ninth Circuit's two-step levels of scrutiny test. Benitez asserted, "*Heller* draws a distinction between firearms commonly owned for lawful purposes and unusual arms adapted to unlawful uses .... As applied to AWCA, the *Heller* test asks: is a modern rifle commonly owned by law-abiding citizens for a lawful purpose? For the AR-15 type rifle the answer is 'yes.'"[148]

He elaborated,

> The overwhelming majority of citizens who own and keep the popular AR-15 rifle and its many variants do so for lawful purposes, including self-defense at home. Under *Heller*, that is all that is needed. Using the easy to understand *Heller* test, it is obvious that the California assault weapon ban is unconstitutional. Under the *Heller* test, judicial review can end right here.[149]

He then supported this assertion with evidence documenting the popularity of the rifle both in California and nationally.

Benitez concluded,

> Yet, California has banned, and continues to ban these popular rifles. Perhaps the State has a long-range plan of taking incremental steps toward more and more gun control. But it should be obvious that barring total extinction of the Second Amendment, no amount of "common sense" gun control laws will prevent criminals from misusing guns. Whatever the reason, these laws are still on the books. ... [But] Under no level of heightened scrutiny can the law survive.[150]

The judge then analyzed the Ninth Circuit's two-step framework.

In this approach, the first step examines whether the law is one of the "presumptively lawful" regulatory measures discussed in *Heller*; or whether persuasive evidence exists showing that similar regulations were historically approved. If either condition applies, the inquiry ends and the regulation at issue is presumed lawful. Benitez noted that the California ban meets neither condition. He argued,

> First, a complete ban on modern rifles is not one of the presumptively lawful measures identified in *Heller*. Second, a ban on modern rifles has no historical pedigree. Prior to the 1990's, there was no national history of banning weapons because they were equipped with furniture like pistol grips, collapsible stocks, flash hiders, flare launches, or barrel shrouds. In fact, prior to California's 1989 ban, so-called assault weapons were lawfully manufactured, acquired, and possessed throughout the United States.[151]

Dismissing the attorney general's claims that the AWCA was analogous to one early District of Columbia law, Benitez quoted from *Heller*,

> "We would not stake our interpretation of the Second Amendment upon a single law, in effect in a single city, that contradicts the overwhelming weight of other evidence regarding the right to keep and bear arms for defense of the home." Yet, this is what the Attorney General is proposing. In view of *Heller's* caution, this Court finds that the District of Columbia regulation is insufficient .... AWCA's ban has no historical pedigree.[152]

Benitez then noted that the second step of the Ninth Circuit's two-step approach involves determining the appropriate level of scrutiny to apply to a challenged regulation. The court weighs how closely the challenged law comes to the "core" of the Second Amendment right and how severely the law burdens that right. Benitez held that California's ban—interfering with the right of self-defense in the home—struck at the core of the Second Amendment. He observed, "When it comes to self-defense in the home, AWCA hits the bull's eye—a direct burden on the core right. The California statutes not only directly burden the core, but impose the *severest* burden—a complete ban."[153] He declared further, "When a severe restriction on the core right of self-defense amounts to a destruction of the Second Amendment right, it is unconstitutional under any level of scrutiny. [Citation provided]. Once again, judicial review could end right here."[154]

After noting that AWCA would fail "strict scrutiny" (as suggested above), the judge asserted that AWCA would also fail "intermediate scrutiny." This standard requires that the government's regulatory goal must be important and that the "fit" of the law to that goal must be reasonable. Benitez acknowledged that reducing gun crime is an important governmental objective—meeting the first requirement—but asserted that the "fit" between this objective and the current law was not reasonable. He noted that, while intermediate scrutiny does not require the government to use the *least* restrictive means of furthering its objective, a law still cannot "burden" a protected activity substantially more than is necessary to further the government's interest. He concluded, "AWCA fails the intermediate fit test."[155]

In supporting his conclusion, Benitez declared, "Moving through the trial record here, it becomes clear that AWCA's assault weapons ban-by-prohibited features was not designed to address a real harm, and even if it did, does not alleviate the harm in a material way."[156] He dismissed the attorney general's argument that the plaintiffs bear the burden of proof in showing the law is unconstitutional, asserting, "this is exactly wrong. The constitutional imperative is on the government to not infringe. The correct starting orientation is that no arm may be prohibited. If a plaintiff challenges the government's prohibition, it is on the government first to prove the banned arm is dangerous and unusual."[157]

The judge next addressed the attorney general's argument that the AWCA did not destroy the fundamental right of self-defense of the home because other guns remained lawful to keep in the home. Benitez rejected the attorney general's notion that the Second Amendment right was only moderately burdened because of these available alternatives. He noted, "The problem is that the alternatives-remain argument has no limiting principle and would justify incremental bans until there is only a single-shot derringer remaining for lawful self-defense. The same argument … was rejected in *Heller* and is rejected here."[158]

Regarding legislative history—a potentially relevant consideration for an intermediate scrutiny review—Benitez observed,

> While there are legislative findings for the enactment of AWCA, there are none for the prohibited-features amendments … [and] no consideration by the California Legislature was given to the ban's burden on home defense or militia use. … In 1989, California's Legislature predicted an assault weapons ban would eliminate or reduce mass shootings [but] even the State's evidence demonstrates that mass shootings with assault weapons continue to occur at the same average rate as before the ban. If Congress is correct, the national assault weapon ban also did not work. … No case has held that intermediate scrutiny permits a state to impinge on the Second Amendment right by continuing to employ a known failed experiment. … As for the legislative history of [this law], it tells only of prosaic interest balancing undertaken without regard for the constitutional rights of individuals.[159]

In reviewing the evidence relevant to the gun's dangerousness and involvement in violent crime, Benitez observed,

> The Attorney General does not take offense at the fragility of his evidence. Instead, the Attorney General argues that the law excuses it. He reminds us that under intermediate scrutiny, the government may "rely on any evidence 'reasonably believed to be relevant' to substantiate its interest." [Citation given]. He says that his evidence need not be particularly robust or persuasive. On the contrary, he

> says the "evidence need only 'fairly support' the government's conclusions." … The Attorney General's lack of direct evidence is noted.[160]

The judge observed that about 14,000 pages of evidence and testimony were submitted and reviewed by the court. Asserting that "firearm possession for the defense of home, self, and family is at the core of the Second Amendment right,"[161] Benitez determined, "Without question, there is clear evidence that AR-15 rifles are and have been used for self-defense."[162] After describing several such cases, he suggested that the prohibited features of the rifle were actually one reason the rifle was such a good home-defense weapon.

He elaborated,

> The evidence shows that … [t]he AR-15, in particular, is an easy firearm to shoot accurately and is generally easier to fire accurately than a handgun. When burglars break and enter, a homeowner with a modern rifle has thirty rounds at the ready …. The adjustable stock can be quickly set for one's arm length. The pistol grip gives a homeowner a secure hold …. A flash suppressor prevents the nighttime home defender from being blinded …. A barrel shroud serves as a way to attach a flashlight or laser pointer …. The straight-line design [reduces] muzzle rise. The gas piston design reduces recoil.[163]

Benitez also questioned the inherent logic of some of the AWCA's prohibitions. Noting that an adjustable telescoping stock allows a single rifle to fit and be used by multiple family members, he asked, "If the total length of the rifle is 30 inches as required, what difference would it make if the telescoping stock would lengthen the rifle to 31, 32, or 34 inches?"[164] Similarly, he questioned AWCA's prohibition on folding stocks, observing, "A folding stock, though it makes the firearm more portable, does not turn a semi-automatic rifle into a common instrument of crime, since it does not make a rifle easily concealable for most criminal activities."[165]

Turning to California's reasons for banning these arms, Benitez noted,

> "the State here is concerned about … particular arms that have proven to be the most lethal in mass shooting situations" [and] is concerned with rapidly firing accurate rifles. … The Attorney General views rapid-fire accuracy as a danger to be outlawed. … The State wants rifles that are less accurate during rapid fire because rapid firing, it is claimed, correlates with criminal use. And there is no need for rapid fire for self-defense, according to the Attorney General.[166]

Questioning this argument, Benitez asserted, "it [i.e., accurate rapid fire] actually enhances a firearm's constitutional protection for militia readiness. … For home defense, accuracy is always important, not only for hitting an attacker, but also for hitting *only* an attacker."[167]

After viewing a video comparison of two AR-15 rifles—one with all the prohibited features and one "featureless"—Benitez observed,

> The results were remarkably similar. Each rifle fired at approximately the same speed and accuracy. Any difference was hardly noticeable. … The State says that a modern rifle without the prohibited features works just fine. Since the features are just cosmetic, then there is no burden on Second Amendment rights. The Plaintiffs say that if a modern rifle without the prohibited features is just as lethal, the State's ban of rifles with the features is pointless … if what the state labels "combat-oriented features" have no effect, then they are not really combat-oriented features. The ban fails to achieve its purpose of prohibiting a "more lethal" firearm. … In the end, the Court finds that the prohibited features do not change an AR-15 rifle from a benign weapon into an "incredibly effective killing machine."[168]

Continuing, the judge addressed the potential criminal use of the AR-15. He noted,

> The Attorney General stresses the notion that modern rifles are disproportionally used in crime … but [this] is not supported by the evidence … handguns [are] disproportionately used in crime. … By comparison, modern rifles are not used in crime nearly as often as handguns. … if modern rifles are misused in crime (even disproportionately), the government must deal with those wrongful acts directly; it may not deal with the problem by suppressing the rights of law-abiding citizens to have modern rifles for lawful uses. Thus, disproportionality is not a valid constitutional concern. Common ownership by law abiding citizens for lawful purposes is the test.[169]

Rejecting the statistical evidence the attorney general marshalled to support disproportionality—a single citation to a decades-old Congressional report—Benitez asserted,

> evidence at the time of the federal ban [indicated] that assault weapons were rarely used as crime guns. Even today, most national estimates suggest assault weapons are used in crimes less than 7% of the time. … In [one] landmark 2004 report … "the estimates consistently show that AWs [assault weapons] are used in a small fraction of gun crimes," and "most survey evidence on the actual use of AWs suggests that offenders rarely use AWs in crime."[170]

The judge next considered the presence of the AR-15 rifle in mass shooting events. He noted that one expert concluded that the "evidence suggests LCM [large capacity magazines] restrictions reduce mass shootings and are more potent than AW-only restrictions [but] the evidence is not yet sufficient to draw definitive conclusions."[171] Further, Benitez questioned the credibility of past estimates of the frequency of such events. He asserted, "The problem is a disagreement over the definition of a 'mass shooting' combined with the lack of a reliable database maintained by a disinterested organization or governmental entity. Instead, these unreliable collections of shooting stories are generally not based on police reports but [on] after-the-fact, sometimes sensationalized, news reporting."[172]

Discussing California, Benitez emphasized that,

> Contrary to public misinformation, mass shooting events are rare events. … According to [one analysis], the total number of persons, killed *or* injured, during *all* mass shooting events *with an assault weapon* during the years of 2003 to 2007 was 38. … In contrast, during the same five years, 7,700 women may not have been raped and 266,560 homeowners may not have suffered a violent victimization during the burglary of their home had they been armed with an assault weapon. … [A]n assault weapon ban that trenches on the rights of 266,560 citizens to protect themselves from violent assault … balanced against possibly reducing the shooting risk to 38 people, is lopsided.[173]

After reviewing the evidence showing that—contrary to the claims of the Attorney General—wounds from assault rifles are actually *less* severe than wounds from traditional hunting rifles, the court considered the argument that bullets from an AR-15 fired in self-defense might penetrate a wall and strike a bystander. Benitez remarked, "The Court is unaware of any evidence that such an event has ever been reported. One thing is clear, there is no evidence that home defenders using AR-15s hitting bystanders with stray bullets through walls is a common problem."[174]

At this point, Judge Benitez referenced the attorney general's position that assault weapons are uncommon and unusually dangerous, that other guns are available for self-defense, and that every other federal circuit court has upheld assault weapon restrictions under intermediate scrutiny. Asking rhetorically, "How can one argue with every other federal circuit court," Benitez answered,

> In the past, Second Amendment cases were wrongly decided by following a majority of circuit courts down the wrong path. That is what happened in 1996 when the Ninth Circuit erroneously decided that the Second Amendment does not confer on private citizens a right to possess a firearm …. It also happened the last time the Ninth Circuit upheld AWCA. *See Silveira v. Lockyer* …. Before *Heller*, hundreds of judges erroneously overread *Miller*, as *Heller* itself points out.[175]

After critiquing a half-dozen federal cases cited by the Attorney General from different circuits, Benitez summed up,

> None of [these] out-of-circuit decisions comfortably fit this case. None of the cases went to trial. None of the cases had substantial evidence that AR-15 type rifles are useful and used by law-abiding citizens …. None of the cases considered an AR-15's militia use. None of the cases scrutinized a statute like California's [AWCA] …. Perhaps intermediate scrutiny is still required under our Ninth Circuit precedents, but not because the out-of-circuit decisions are similar to this case.[176]

Before moving on to examine the potential militia uses of the AR-15, Benitez observed that federal courts have long considered machine guns "dangerous and

unusual weapons" beyond Second Amendment protection. He emphasized, however, that *Heller* and *McDonald* did not deny such protection to semiautomatic pistols, which also fire at a rapid rate. The judge asserted,

> Most of what the Attorney General says are dangerous features on a prohibited modern rifle are also features on a Second Amendment-protected semi-automatic pistol. ... At bottom, guns are dangerous. ... The prohibited rifles shoot further than pistols, but not as far as other permissible rifles. Beyond that, the prohibited firearms share most of the same dangerous characteristics as permissible pistols like the 1911 and the Glock 17.[177]

The court concluded its analysis by asserting that AWCA failed intermediate scrutiny because it imposes a burden on the Second Amendment right to own a firearm that is ideal for militia use. Noting that the evidence overwhelmingly shows that the AR-15 rifles are particularly useful in both citizens' and state-organized militias—given the rifle's standardization, reliability, low cost, and light weight—Benitez argued, "It is therefore categorically protected by the Second Amendment."[178] Continuing, he asserted,

> Government is not free to impose its own new policy choices on American citizens where constitutional rights are concerned. ... California may certainly conceive of a policy that a modern rifle is dangerous in the hands of a criminal, and that therefore it is good policy to keep modern rifles out of the hands of every citizen. The Second Amendment stands as a shield from government imposition of that policy.[179]

Benitez entered judgment in favor of the plaintiffs, declaring AWCA unconstitutional.

Some Observations

Two aspects of the opinions covered in this chapter are particularly noteworthy. First, as a group, the cases illustrate the difficulty in specifying the precise characteristics that make an inherently lethal weapon—a firearm—especially dangerous and unusual. With the exception of the nineteenth-century adjudications focused on the size and concealability of a pistol, more modern efforts to pin down "especially dangerous and unusual" have encountered logical and practical hurdles. Certainly exploding, poorly designed or manufactured handguns are especially dangerous, but product liability statutes typically short-circuit any Second Amendment concerns.

Further, as Judge Benitez illustrated in *Bonta*, the use of various firearm features—flash suppressors, pistol grips, and so forth—are questionable for determining if a gun is especially dangerous. As Benitez noted, the proscribed characteristics likely make the firearm more accurate, but not more dangerous—unless increased accuracy is considered dangerous. Even focusing on a firearm's capability to fire multiple rounds rapidly does not help: virtually all modern firearms—both rifles and handguns—have this capability.

The second noteworthy aspect of these cases is the contrasting analytical treatments found in *Heller II* and *Bonta.* Using intermediate scrutiny in *Heller II*, Judge Ginsburg upholds the District's ban on semi-automatic "assault-type" rifles and LCMs. While acknowledging that these rifles and magazines are in common use, she questions whether these weapons are commonly used for self-defense or hunting. Asserting that the ban does not impose a substantial burden on the right to arms, she concludes that a reasonable fit exists between the ban and the state's goal of controlling crime and protecting the police and public.

In *Bonta*, Benitez shreds the use of *any* type of heightened scrutiny to evaluate California's similar rifle and magazine ban. He asserts that *Heller I* distinguishes between commonly owned firearms used for legitimate purposes, and unusual arms used for criminal activities. Under this *Heller* test, he notes that the California ban on widely owned firearms is obviously unconstitutional. But he further notes that the ban—completely prohibiting the rifles—is a direct, *severe* burden on a core constitutional right, and fails both intermediate and strict scrutiny. Somewhat ironically, one of the judges in *Heller II*—Brett Kavanaugh—also questioned (in a dissent) the appropriateness of relying on intermediate scrutiny to resolve the district case.

In adjudicating *Bonta*, Judge Benitez conducted his analysis before the US Supreme Court had issued its 2022 ruling in the landmark *Bruen* case. That case emphasized "text, history and tradition" as the correct standard for evaluating Second Amendment-based gun law challenges. California appealed Benitez's opinion (see Chapter 9 for details), but it appears likely that a review using text, history, and tradition will confirm his analysis and uphold his ruling.

In the next chapter, court opinions continue to look at the relationship between "dangerousness" and limitations on Second Amendment protections—but the focus is on dangerous people rather than dangerous weapons. The cases examine whether an individual's particular personal characteristics or past behaviors—long-term or temporary in nature—make that person so dangerous as to justify restricting the person's Second Amendment rights.

Notes

1 *James Miller, et al. v. Rob Bonta, No. 19-cv-1537-BEN-JLB, (2021) U.S. District Court, Southern District of California, 2021.* At https://casetext.com/case/miller-v-bonta.
2 Donald Campbell, *Guns in America: Examining the Facts* (Santa Barbara, CA: ABC-CLIO, 2021), pp. 32–8.
3 *Bliss v. Commonwealth.* At https://press-pubs.uchicago.edu/founders/documents/amendIIs8.html.
4 *Aymette v. The State, 21 Tenn. (2Hump.)154 (1840).* At https://casetext.com/case/aymette-v-state.
5 *Nunn v. State, 1 Ga. 243 (1846).* At https://cite.case.law/ga/1/243/.

6 *English v. State, 35 Tex. 473, 14 Am. Rep. 374 (1872).* At https://guncite.com/court/state/35tx473.html.
7 *Fife v. State, 31 Ark. 455 (1876).* At https://cite.case.law/ark/31/455/.
8 *State v. Shelby, 90 Mo. 302 (1886).* At https://cite.case.law/mo/90/302/.
9 *Wilson v. State, 33 Ark. 557 (1878)..* At https://cite.case.law/ark/33/557/.
10 Ibid.
11 Ibid.
12 Ibid.
13 Ibid.
14 *Dabbs v. State, 39 Ark. 353 (1882).* At https://guncite.com/court/state/39ar353.html.
15 Ibid.
16 Ibid.
17 Ibid.
18 Ibid.
19 New York State's Supreme Court is confusingly called the Court of Appeals.
20 *People v. Perce, 204 NY 397 (1912).* At https://casetext.com/case/people-v-persce-1.
21 Ibid.
22 Ibid.
23 Ibid.
24 Ibid.
25 *Harris v. State of Nevada, 432 P.2d 929 (1967).* At https://law.justia.com/cases/nevada/supreme-court/1967/5303-1.html.
26 *Harris* was decided prior to the landmark 2008 *Heller* ruling that rejected this view.
27 *State of Oregon v. Boyce, 658 P.2d 577 (Or. Ct. App. 1983).* At https://casetext.com/case/state-v-boyce-26.
28 Ibid.
29 *United States v. Freed, 401 U.S. 601 (1971).* At https://supreme.justia.com/cases/federal/us/401/601/.
30 Ibid.
31 Ibid.
32 *Kelley v. R.G. Industries, Inc.304 Md. 124 (Md. 1985). 497 A.2d 1143.* At https://casetext.com/case/kelley-v-rg-industries-inc.
33 Ibid.
34 Ibid.
35 Ibid.
36 Ibid.
37 Ibid.
38 Ibid.
39 Ibid.
40 Ibid.
41 Ibid.
42 Ibid.
43 Ibid.
44 Ibid.
45 Ibid.
46 Ibid.
47 Ibid.
48 Ibid.

49 *Armijo v. Ex Cam, Inc., 656 F. Supp. 771 (D.N.M. 1987).* At https://law.justia.com/cases/federal/district-courts/FSupp/656/771/1394630/.
50 Ibid.
51 Ibid.
52 Ibid.
53 Ibid.
54 Ibid.
55 Ibid.
56 Ibid.
57 Ibid.
58 *Bryco Arms v. << Chronister, No. 96-355 (1997).* At https://caselaw.findlaw.com/court/us-8th-circuit/1096698.html.
59 Ibid.
60 Ibid.
61 Ibid.
62 Bryco also alleged a fourth error, in not allowing the jury to apportion fault to the ammunition manufacturer. The circuit court dismissed this argument, noting that "there was no evidence at trial that the cartridge was defective or in any way partly responsible for the accident."
63 Ibid.
64 Ibid.
65 Ibid.
66 Ibid.
67 Ibid.
68 Ibid.
69 Ibid.
70 *Smith v. Bryco Arms, 131 N.M. 87 (N.M. Ct. App. 2001).* At https://casetext.com/case/smith-v-arms.
71 Ibid.
72 *Maxfield v. Bryco Arms, CA1/4 (Alameda County Super. Ct. No. 841636-4 2005).* At http://www.brandonsarms.org/inthenews/releases/affirmed.pdf.
73 Ibid.
74 Ibid.
75 See *Ileto v. Glock, Case No.: CV 01-9762 ABC (RNBx) (C.D. Cal. Mar. 20, 2006).* At https://casetext.com/case/ileto-v-glock.
76 Ibid.
77 Ibid.
78 JoshSugarmann, "Assault Weapons and Accessories in America," *Violence Policy Center*, 1988. At https://www.vpc.org/studies/awacont.htm.
79 Donald Campbell, *America's Gun Wars: A Cultural History of Gun Control in the United States* (Santa Barbara, CA: Prager), pp. 92–3.
80 Ibid., pp. 102–3.
81 *United States v. Marzzarella, 614 F.3d 85 (2010).* At https://caselaw.findlaw.com/court/us-3rd-circuit/1533305.html.
82 Ibid.
83 Ibid.
84 Ibid.

85 Ibid.
86 Ibid.
87 Ibid.
88 Ibid.
89 *Caetano v. Massachusetts, 577 U.S. ___ (2016).* At https://supreme.justia.com/cases/federal/us/577/14-10078/.
90 Ibid.
91 Ibid.
92 Ibid.
93 Ibid.
94 Ibid.
95 Ibid.
96 Ibid.
97 Ibid.
98 Ibid.
99 *Merrill v. Navegar, Inc. 26 Cal. 4th 465 (2001).* At https://law.justia.com/cases/california/supreme-court/4th/26/465.html.
100 Ibid.
101 Ibid.
102 Ibid.
103 Ibid.
104 Ibid.
105 Ibid.
106 Ibid.
107 Ibid.
108 Ibid.
109 Ibid.
110 Ibid.
111 Ibid.
112 Ibid.
113 Ibid.
114 Ibid.
115 Ibid.
116 Ibid.
117 Ibid.
118 Ibid.
119 Ibid.
120 *Heller v. District of Columbia, 670 F.3d 1244 (D.C. Cir. 2011).* At https://casetext.com/case/heller-v-district-of-columbia-10-7036-dc-cir-10-4-2011.
121 Ibid.
122 Ibid.
123 Ibid.
124 Ibid.
125 Ibid.
126 Ibid.
127 Ibid.
128 Ibid.

129 Ibid.
130 Ibid.
131 Ibid.
132 Ibid.
133 Ibid.
134 Ibid.
135 Ibid.
136 Ibid.
137 Ibid.
138 Ibid.
139 Ibid.
140 Ibid.
141 *Miller v. Bonta, 542 F. Supp. 3d 1009 (S.D. Cal. 2021)*. At https://casetext.com/case/miller-v-bonta.
142 Ibid.
143 Ibid.
144 Ibid.
145 Ibid.
146 Ibid.
147 Ibid.
148 Ibid.
149 Ibid.
150 Ibid.
151 Ibid.
152 Ibid.
153 Ibid.
154 Ibid.
155 Ibid.
156 Ibid.
157 Ibid.
158 Ibid.
159 Ibid.
160 Ibid.
161 Ibid.
162 Ibid.
163 Ibid.
164 Ibid.
165 Ibid.
166 Ibid.
167 Ibid.
168 Ibid.
169 Ibid.
170 Ibid.
171 Ibid.
172 Ibid.
173 Ibid.

174 Ibid.
175 Ibid.
176 Ibid.
177 Ibid.
178 Ibid.
179 Ibid.

7

Dangerous People: The Felons

The very structure of the Gun Control Act demonstrates that Congress ... sought broadly to keep firearms away from the persons Congress classified as potentially irresponsible and dangerous ... to keep firearms out of the hands of those not legally able to possess them because of age, criminal background, or incompetency.

Associate Justice Harry Blackmun, US Supreme Court[1]

When the US Supreme Court in the 2008 *Heller* decision affirmed an individual's right to keep and bear arms, it specifically noted that the right (like all rights) was not unlimited. The court suggested that Second Amendment protections did not extend to dangerous and untrustworthy individuals—people who may have traditionally been debarred from the possession or use of arms. However, aside from noting a few specific examples, *Heller* left for future litigation the task of clarifying precisely who might be considered dangerous and untrustworthy, and left unspecified Second Amendment curtailments potentially appropriate for such individuals.

These legal ambiguities are more complex than they may at first appear. For instance, currently, convicted felons—individuals found guilty of a crime resulting in a sentence greater than one year—lose their right to keep and bear arms. Most Americans likely endorse the notion that felons having a propensity for *violence* (perhaps demonstrated by a conviction for assault or worse) should surely have their rights to own and carry a firearm restricted. But what of felons convicted and sentenced to more than a year in prison for a *non-violent* (e.g., white-collar) crime? Are these dangerous and untrustworthy individuals who should also lose their Second Amendment rights? More generally, is the *lifelong* abrogation of an individual's self-defense rights—rights residing at the heart of the Second Amendment—for felonious crimes or behaviors constitutional?

The implications of the court decisions in this chapter for understanding the Second Amendment are substantial and extend beyond the specific details of the cases. If Second Amendment protections are unavailable to some categories of "dangerous" individuals, legislative or governmental actions establishing other categories of dangerous and untrustworthy people (e.g., those who refuse to adhere to emergency health guidelines) presumably might result in a significant proportion of citizens excluded from the right to keep and bear arms—a concern explicitly raised in several of the cases considered below.

Categories of Dangerous Individuals

While "dangerous" and "untrustworthy" are often subjective evaluations, involving various personal and situation factors, in a practical sense, the criteria for determining who is too questionable to have access to firearms is quite objective. ATF Form 4473 (the Firearms Transaction Record) is a document required for purchasing a firearm from federally licensed dealers. The form lists multiple categories of prohibited buyers who are ineligible to receive, possess, or purchase a gun. Among these categories are illegal aliens, persons who have renounced their United States citizenship, and persons dishonorably discharged from the armed forces.

Five categories are especially significant from a Second Amendment perspective. Two classifications include (1) anyone convicted (or under indictment) for a felony and (2) anyone convicted of misdemeanor domestic violence or subject to an intimate partner restraining order. Three other prohibited buyer classes include (1) anyone adjudicated as a mental defective or previously committed to a mental institution; (2) unlawful users of controlled substances and drugs; and (3) individuals under the age of twenty-one (for handguns; eighteen for rifles).[2] This chapter focuses on convicted felon adjudications and domestic violence gun cases. The next chapter examines age restriction challenges, drug and narcotic use challenges, and mental incompetency cases.

1974–2023: Convicted Felons as Dangerous Individuals

Violent individuals possessing guns have always concerned the judiciary. Tennessee in 1833, for example, charged and convicted William Simpson of creating an "affray"—he "with force of arms [and] being arrayed in a war-like manner ... unlawfully, and to the great terror and disturbance of divers good citizens ... an affray did make, in contempt of the laws of the land ... and against the peace and dignity of the state."[3] While Simpson apparently did not actually assault anyone, the state proceeded against him on the basis that, "in some cases, there may be an affray where there is no actual violence, as where a man arms himself with dangerous and unusual weapons, in such a manner as will naturally cause terror to the people."[4] Despite later being overturned on appeal, Simpson's initial conviction highlights long-standing societal fears about firearms and potentially violent people.

Nonetheless, the modern solution for easing these fears—the imposition of a lifetime ban on gun possession and ownership for serious (i.e., felonious) crime—is a relatively recent development. Prior to the twentieth century, state courts typically separated violent or dangerous individuals from their arms simply by incarcerating the law-breaker or by confiscating the weapons. Even then, individuals usually were free to reacquire arms after resolving their legal troubles.[5] With the passage of the Federal Firearms Act (FFA) in 1938, and the Gun Control Act (GCA) thirty years later, the country's approach to guns and potentially dangerous people changed. By establishing classes of "prohibited individuals" and imposing severe gun penalties on such individuals, these federal gun control laws raised constitutional issues centered on the Second Amendment. Not surprisingly, they also led to many court challenges.

The challenges broadly involved two types of felons. The first type were individuals previously convicted of violent felonious crimes, and who were later apprehended in possession of a firearm. These individuals typically argued on Second Amendment grounds that the statute making such possession a crime was "on its face" (i.e., overall) unconstitutional. The second type were individuals previously convicted of a nonviolent felonious crime, and who argued that the statute—at least as it applied to them as *nonviolent* felons—was unconstitutional. The following section examines both types of cases, beginning with a 1974 US Supreme Court adjudication that underscores the complexity of the issues involved.

Huddleston v. United States (1974): Violating 18 U.S.C. 922 (a) (6) of the 1968 Gun Control Act

Previously convicted in California for writing checks without sufficient funds—a crime punishable with a maximum fourteen-year sentence—William Huddleston later pawned several of his wife's firearms in an Oxnard pawnshop. Later, when he went to redeem the weapons, the shop owner (a federally licensed firearms dealer) had Huddleston complete and sign ATF Form 4473, the Firearms Transaction Record for each firearm redeemed. A question on those forms requires respondents to indicate whether they have ever been convicted of a crime punishable by imprisonment for a term exceeding one year. The question also notes that the actual sentence imposed does not matter. A "yes" is required even if the imposed sentence is less than a year.[6]

Huddleston answered "no" to this question, affixing

> his signature to each certification that the answers were true and correct, and that he understood that a person who answers any of the questions in the affirmative is prohibited by federal law from "purchasing and/or possessing a firearm," and that he also understood that the making of any false statement with respect to the transaction is a crime punishable as a felony.[7]

Huddleston was subsequently charged with violating 18 U.S.C. 922 (a) 6 and 924 (a). He challenged his indictment, arguing that 922 (a) 6 was not intended to apply to an individual's redemption of pawned weapons. The court denied this motion, and Huddleston then pleaded not guilty and waived a jury trial.[8]

The government's case consisted of the signed ATF 4473 forms, evidence of Huddleston's prior felony conviction, and the shop owner's federal gun license. Additionally, a government agent testified that, after being advised of his rights, Huddleston admitted that he had knowingly lied when he answered in the negative on the ATF forms. Testifying in his own defense, Huddleston claimed that "he did not knowingly make a false statement; that he did not read the form and simply answered 'no' upon prompting from the pawnbroker; and that he was unaware that his California conviction was punishable by a term exceeding one year."[9]

The district judge found Huddleston guilty on all counts, and the US Court of Appeals in a divided vote affirmed the conviction. The dissenting judge agreed that the statute was constitutional, but concluded that Huddleston merely "reacquired" the firearms and that "reacquire" was not necessarily covered by the statute's term "acquire." To resolve a conflict among the circuit courts regarding whether the statute covered the redemption of firearms from a pawnshop, the Supreme Court agreed to take Huddleston's case. Associate Justice Harry Blackmun authored the court's opinion.[10]

Justice Blackmun succinctly summarized the issue at hand: "whether 18 U.S.C. 922 (a) 6 … covers the redemption of a firearm from a pawnshop."[11] He noted that Huddleston's argument consisted of two points. The first was that the statute's language and its legislative history indicated Congress did not intend for pawnshop redemption to be covered by the statute. The second was that, even if Congress so intended, the law's ambiguity was so great that the legal maxim of resolving ambiguity in a criminal statute in favor of the defendant applied.[12]

Blackmun elaborated on Huddleston's first point, observing that Huddleston

> attaches great significance to the word "acquisition." He urges that it suggests only a sales-like transaction. … [S]ince a pawn transaction is only a temporary bailment of personal property, … [the] transaction is no more than an interruption in the pawnor's possession. The pawnor simply repossesses his own property …. At most, he "reacquires" the object, and reacquisition … is not necessarily included in the statutory term "acquisition." On its face, this argument might be said to have some force. A careful look at the statutory language and at complementary provisions of the Act, however, convince us that the asserted ambiguity is contrived.[13]

The court then presented linguistic and prior case evidence to support its assertion that the ambiguity was contrived. It rejected Huddleston's argument by noting,

> In sum, the word "acquisition" as used in 922 (a) 6 is not ambiguous, but clearly includes any person, by definition, who "come[s] into possession, control, or power of disposal" of a firearm. As noted above, "acquisition" and "sale or other disposition" are correlatives. … And because Congress explicitly included pawnbrokers in the Act … we are not at liberty to tamper with the obvious reach of the statute in proscribing the conduct in which the petitioner engaged.[14]

Before turning to Huddleston's second argument, the court reviewed the legislative history of the Act. It asserted that the review also supported its reading of the statute:

> When Congress enacted the provisions under which petitioner was convicted, it was concerned with the widespread traffic in firearms and with their general availability to those whose possession thereof was contrary to the public interest. [References given]. Congress determined that the ease with which firearms could be obtained contributed significantly to the prevalence of lawlessness and violent crime in the United States. … Section 922 (a) 6 … was enacted as a means of

> providing adequate and truthful information about firearms transactions. Information drawn from these records … was a prime guarantee of the Act's effectiveness in keeping "these lethal weapons out of the hands of … persons whose possession of them is too high a price in danger to us all to allow."[15]

Regarding Huddleston's second argument—that the statute should be narrowly construed in his favor because of its pawnshop ambiguity—Blackmun wrote, "We perceive no grievous ambiguity or uncertainty in the language or structure of the Act. The statute in question clearly proscribes petitioner's conduct …. The question he answered untruthfully was preceded by a warning in boldface type that 'an untruthful answer may subject you to criminal prosecution.' The question itself was forthright and direct."[16] After dismissing some secondary issues as having no import, the court affirmed the judgment of the Court of Appeals.

The Supreme Court's treatment of the *Huddleston* case is noteworthy for two reasons. First, the case revolves around interpretation of an important section of the GCA of 1968. This Act and the Omnibus Crime Control Act of the same year were the federal government's most potent tools for keeping firearms from dangerous individuals. Thus, the court's analysis established how lower courts approached future challenges to the GCA. Second, because Huddleston never raised any Second Amendment challenges to the GCA, the court never addressed any Second Amendment issues. Considering the nonviolent nature of Huddleston's prior felony conviction (the basis for his prohibited status), this omission is somewhat peculiar. Later twenty-first-century cases will raise this issue.

The next case—a "felon in possession" adjudication—directly involves the Second Amendment and a related section of the GCA. Decided before the 2008 *Heller* opinion, this Fifth Circuit adjudication followed the precedent established by *Emerson* (2001), and it treated the Second Amendment as an individual right.

United States v. Everist (2004): Violating 18 U.S.C. §922 (g) (1) of the 1968 Gun Control Act

Having prior felony convictions for bank robberies, Joseph Everist was later charged with being a felon in possession of a firearm, in violation of 18 U.S.C. §922 (g) (1). Convicted, he received a sentence of 180 months. He requested that this sentence run concurrently with the 300-month sentence he had received for the bank robberies. When the district court allowed only sixty months to run concurrently, Everist appealed his gun conviction under 922 (g) (1), as well as the court's determination of his partial concurrent sentencing. Judge Jerry Smith wrote the opinion for the Fifth Circuit Court of Appeals.[17]

Judge Smith observed that

> Everist makes a facial constitutional charge to 922 (g) (1), arguing that the felon firearm possession statute deprives him of his constitutional right to keep and bear arms. In *United State v. Emerson* [Citation provided], we held that the Second

> Amendment "protects the rights of individuals, including those not then actually a member of any militia or engaged in active military service or training, to privately possess and bear their own arms." The Second Amendment right is subject to "limited to narrowly tailored specific exceptions or restrictions for particular cases that are reasonable."[18]

Continuing, Judge Smith asserted,

> It is not inconsistent with the Second Amendment to limit the ability of convicted felons to keep and possess firearms. Irrespective of whether his offence was violent in nature, a felon has shown manifest disregard for the rights of others. He may not justly complain of the limitation on his liberty when his possession of firearms would otherwise threaten the security of his fellow citizens. ... Accordingly, 922 (g) (1) represents a limited and narrowly tailored exception to the freedom to possess firearms, reasonable in its purposes and consistent with the right to bear arms protected under the Second Amendment.[19]

The court then considered Everist's sentencing arguments, but its Second Amendment relevance ended here. Its important conclusion that felons—violent or nonviolent—threaten the security of the community and thus justify 922 (g) (1) as a reasonable and narrowly tailored infringement on Second Amendment rights surfaces in future gun cases. In the Eleventh Circuit, for example, Christopher Rozier challenged the constitutionality of 922 (g) (1) six years later—after publication of the *Heller* opinion. The circuit court, referencing *Heller* and using reasoning similar to *Everist*, rejected his argument. Also in 2010, the Ninth Circuit used comparable arguments to uphold the constitutionality of 922 (g) (1) in *United States v. Vongxay*.[20] Given the cases' similarities, only *Rozier* is considered below.

United States v. Rozier (2010): Violating 18 U.S.C. 922 (g) (1) of the 1968 Gun Control Act

A felon with several prior drug convictions, Christopher Rozier got into an argument with Eenie Austin, the mother of his child. At some point, Austin attacked Rozier with a cement statute, and he responded by pulling out a handgun. Later that day, executing a search warrant, police found drugs, a sum of money, and ammunition in the house. In a shallow hole in his backyard, deputies uncovered a .38-caliber revolver. Rozier claimed the firearm was necessary for self-defense. Subsequently convicted of violating 18 U.S.C. 922 (g) (1)—possession of a firearm by a convicted felon—Rozier appealed his conviction and sentence.[21] The circuit court issued a *per curiam* opinion.

The court noted that Rozier

> challenges his conviction on the grounds that 922 (g) (1) is an unconstitutional invasion upon his Second Amendment right to bear arms. Rozier relies on the Supreme Court's recent ruling in *District of Columbia v. Heller*, wherein the Court

> held that "the Second Amendment conferred an individual right to keep and bear arms." [Citation given]. … One of the major thrusts of the Court's ruling was "the inherent right of self-defense, central to the Second Amendment right." Rozier argues that his case parallels the facts in *Heller*, in that his possession of a handgun was in the home and for the purposes of self-defense.[22]

The court continued,

> We accept Rozier's assertion that he possessed the handgun for self-defense; however, the motive behind Rozier's possession of the handgun is irrelevant. … Prior to taking into account Rozier's purpose for possessing the handgun, we must determine whether he is qualified to possess a hand gun. Rozier's Second Amendment right to bear arms is not weighed in the same manner as that of a law-abiding citizen, such as the appellant in *Heller*. While felons do not forfeit their constitutional rights … their status as felons substantially affects the level of protection those rights are accorded. The [Supreme] Court made this clear when it referred to those "disqualified from the exercise of Second Amendment rights." *Heller* stated that "nothing in our opinion should be taken to cast doubt on longstanding prohibitions on the possession of firearms by felons."[23]

The court further observed,

> This language suggests that statutes disqualifying felons from possessing a firearm under any and all circumstances do not offend the Second Amendment. Recently, in *United States v. White*, we held that *Heller* recognizes 922 (g) (1) as "a presumptively lawful longstanding prohibition." [Citation given]. Thus, statutory restrictions on firearm possession, such as 922 (g) (1), are a constitutional avenue to restrict the Second Amendment right of certain classes of people. Rozier, by virtue of his felony conviction, falls within such a class. Therefore, the fact that Rozier may have possessed the handgun for purposes of self-defense (in the home), is irrelevant.[24]

After finding "no merit" in Rozier's contentions that his sentence was in error, the court concluded, "We find 922 (g) (1) is a constitutional restriction on Rozier's Second Amendment right. The circumstances surrounding Rozier's possession of a firearm in violation of 922 (g) (1) are irrelevant. Finally, Rozier's sentence was constitutional and in accord with our precedent."[25] Thus, the circuit court affirmed the district court's rulings.

Six years later, the Third Circuit Court of Appeals confronted another challenge to the constitutionality of 922 (g) (1), but unlike *Rozier*, the crimes of the gun-prohibited felons in the case were state-level, nonviolent misdemeanors. Further, for decades after their initial convictions, both appellants had led crime-free lives. In deciding the case, the circuit court's *en-banc* opinion produced several partial concurrences and partial dissents among the jurists. The discussion below focuses on the majority opinion.

Binderup v. U.S. Attorney General (2016): Violating 18 U.S.C. 922 (g) (1) of the Gun Control Act

In 1996, Daniel Binderup, a 41-year-old bakery owner, had engaged in a consensual sexual relationship with a seventeen-year-old female employee. Although she was over the legal age of consent, she was still considered a minor, and in 1998 Binderup pled guilty to a misdemeanor charge of corrupting a minor in Pennsylvania state court. Though a misdemeanor, the charge carried a possible penalty of up to five years' imprisonment. However, Binderup was actually sentenced to three years' probation, and a $300 fine. Since that incident, Binderup had no subsequent charges.[26]

In 1990, Julio Suarez was stopped by Maryland police on suspicion of driving while intoxicated. During the stop, the police discovered that Suarez carried a .357 magnum firearm and two cartridge-loading devices. Having no permit for the firearm, Suarez pled guilty in state court to unlawfully carrying a handgun without a license. This misdemeanor charge carried a penalty of possible imprisonment for "not less than 30 days and not [more than] three years or a fine of not less than $250 and not [more than] $2500 or both."[27] Suarez's actual sentence was 180 days' imprisonment (suspended), a $500 fine, and a year of probation. Eight years after completing probation, Suarez was convicted of a state-level misdemeanor of driving under the influence. Suarez had no further legal incidents after that, later moved to Pennsylvania, and was able (as a consultant for a federal government contractor) to obtain a "Secret" security clearance.[28]

Having been barred from owning or possessing firearms because of their convictions, both Binderup and Suarez in 2009 successfully petitioned Pennsylvania courts to remove that state's firearms bar. But because of these convictions, *federal* law—922 (g) (1)—still prevented the two appellants from owning guns for self- and home-defense. Subsequently, in separate federal district courts, each brought a case seeking judicial relief. Both asserted that 922 (g) (1) did not apply to their convictions (as a matter of statutory construction), or, if it did, the statute was unconstitutional as applied. Both district courts rejected the appellants' statutory argument, but both held that 922 (g) (1) was unconstitutional as applied.[29]

In Binderup's case, the district court concluded that the statute was unconstitutional as applied "because he 'distinguished himself from those individuals traditionally disarmed as a result of prior criminal conduct and demonstrate[d] that he poses no greater threat of future violent criminal activity than the average law-abiding citizen.'"[30]

The district court in the Suarez case used a two-step test in evaluating his argument and concluded, "first that Suarez has Second Amendment rights notwithstanding his 1990 conviction because he demonstrated that 'he is no longer more dangerous than a typical law-abiding citizen.'"[31] For the second step, the court employed a "strict scrutiny" means-end analysis and decided that 922 (g) (1) was unconstitutional as applied to him "due to the severity of the burden it imposes."[32] The government appealed the two district judgments, and the circuit court consolidated the two cases for an *en banc* review. Judge Thomas Ambro delivered the court's majority opinion.[33]

Judge Ambro first addressed the appellants' statutory argument that their state misdemeanors (for technical reasons) were not subject to 922 (g) (1). The court disagreed, and rejected this argument. Turning to the case's constitutional issue, Judge Ambro began by asserting that, while the Third Circuit had established in *United States v. Barton* that 922 (g) (1) does not violate the Second Amendment facially, 922 (g) (1) "remains subject to as-applied constitutional challenges."[34] He also noted that the Third Circuit used a two-step framework as established in *United States v. Marzzarella* for deciding facial and as-applied Second Amendment challenges.[35]

Judge Ambro acknowledged that, as cited in *Heller* and *McDonald*, an individual's right to keep and bear arms did have exceptions (such as prohibitions on the possession of firearms by felons). But he asserted, "neither the Supreme Court nor any court of appeals has held that laws burdening Second Amendment rights evade constitutional scrutiny. Rather, when faced with an as-applied Second Amendment challenge, they agree that some form of heightened scrutiny is appropriate after it has been determined that the law in question burdens protected conduct."[36]

In explaining the court's approach to the case, Ambro stated,

> At step one of the *Marzzarella* decision tree, a challenger must prove, per *Barton*, that a presumptively lawful regulation burdens his Second Amendment rights. This requires a challenger to clear two hurdles: he must (1) identify the traditional justifications for excluding from Second Amendment protections the class of which he appears to be a member, and then (2) present facts about himself and his background that distinguish his circumstances from those of persons in the historically barred class. … [I]f the challenger succeeds at step one, the burden shifts to the government to demonstrate that the regulation satisfies some form of heightened scrutiny … at step two of the *Marzzarella* analysis.[37]

In applying this framework, Ambro observed that the maximum possible punishments for the appellants' crimes subjected them to a "presumptively lawful" (as per *Heller*) firearms ban. Thus, the court examined

> the historical justification for stripping felons … of their Second Amendment rights. "[M]ost scholars of the Second Amendment agree that the right to bear arms was tied to the concept of a virtuous citizenry and that, accordingly, the government could disarm 'unvirtuous citizens.' [Citations provided]. Several of our sister circuits endorse the "virtuous citizen" justification for excluding felons and felon-equivalents from the Second Amendment's ambit. [Citations given]."[38]

Continuing, the court stated,

> People who have committed or are likely to commit "violent offenses" … undoubtedly qualify as 'unvirtuous citizens' who lack Second Amendment rights. … But *Heller* recognized "longstanding prohibitions on the possession of firearms by felons," not just violent felons. The category of "unvirtuous citizens" is thus

> broader than violent criminals; it covers any person who has committed a serious criminal offense, violent or non-violent. … We agree with *Barton* … that a person who did not commit a serious crime retains his Second Amendment rights. … [It is] only the seriousness of the purportedly disqualifying offense [that] determines the constitutional sweep of statutes like 922 (g) (1) …. We now consider whether the Challengers have shown that their crimes are not serious.[39]

Judge Ambro first summarized the government's position—that all crimes subject to 922 (g) (1) are disqualifying because their maximum possible punishments are conclusive proof they are serious. However, he noted this view

> puts the rabbit in the hat by concluding that all felons and misdemeanants … lack the right to keep and bear arms when, despite their maximum possible punishment, some offenses may be "so tame and technical as to be insufficient to justify the ban." [Citation provided]. *Heller* confirms such a showing is possible, as it describes prohibitions … as only "presumptively lawful." Unless flagged as irrebutable, presumptions are rebuttable. … *Heller* requires us to consider the maximum possible punishment but not to defer blindly to it.[40]

After noting that no set criteria existed for determining if a crime's severity warranted revoking Second Amendment rights, the judge asserted, "we will presume the judgment of the legislature is correct and treat any crime subject to 922 (g) (1) as disqualifying unless there is a strong reason to do otherwise."[41] He continued,

> Here, upon close examination of the Challengers' apparently disqualifying convictions, we conclude that their offenses were not serious enough to strip them of their Second Amendment rights. … For starters, though the Challengers' crimes meet the generic definition of a felony … the Pennsylvania and Maryland legislatures enacted them as misdemeanors. … [A] state legislature's classification of an offense as a misdemeanor is a powerful expression of its belief that the offense is not serious enough to be disqualifying.[42]

Ambro further noted,

> Other considerations … confirm our belief that the Challengers' crimes were not serious. As explained above, violent criminal conduct—meaning a crime "in which violence (actual or attempted) is an element of the offense" [Citation provided]—is disqualifying. But neither Challenger's offense had the use or attempted use of force … [and] the lack of a violence element is a relevant consideration. Also important is that each Challenger received a minor sentence by any measure: Binderup was sentenced to three years' probation … while Suarez received a suspended sentence …. That is because severe punishments are typically reserved for serious crime. … With not a single day of jail time, the punishments here reflect the sentencing judges' assessment of how minor the violations were.

> Finally, there is no cross-jurisdictional consensus regarding the seriousness of the Challengers' crimes .... In sum, the Challengers have carried their burden of showing that their misdemeanors were not serious offenses despite their maximum possible punishment.[43]

Having concluded that the appellants were not from the class of individuals historically prohibited arms, the court moved to step two of the analytical framework, subjecting the government's statute to some suitable level of heightened scrutiny. Judge Ambro began by stating,

> "No doubt 922 (g) (1) is intended to further the government interest in promoting public safety .... But whether we apply intermediate scrutiny or strict scrutiny ... the Government bears the burden of proof on the appropriateness of the means it employs to further its interest. [Citations provided.] Here, the Government falls well short of satisfying its burden—even under intermediate scrutiny. The record ... contains no evidence explaining why banning people like them (*i.e.*, people who decades ago committed similar misdemeanors) from possessing firearms promotes public safety.[44]

Continuing,

> The Government claims that someone like Suarez is "particularly likely to misuse firearms" because he belongs to a category of "potentially irresponsible persons," and that someone like Binderup is "particularly likely to commit crimes in the future." But it must "present some meaningful evidence, not mere assertions, to justify its predictive [and here conclusory] judgments." [*Heller* citation.] In these cases, neither the evidence in the record nor common sense support those assertions. The Government relies on a number of off-point statistical studies to argue that it is reasonable to disarm the Challengers .... It is not helpful to draw inferences about the usefulness of disarming [the appellants] from those off-point studies. ... The Challengers' isolated, decades-old, non-violent misdemeanors do not permit the inference that disarming people like them will promote the responsible use of firearms.[45]

Judge Ambro concluded, "Without more, there is not a substantial fit between the continuing disarmament of the Challengers and an important government interest. Thus, 922 (g) (1) is unconstitutional as applied to them. ... Accordingly, we affirm the judgments of the District Courts."[46]

The *Binderup* opinion did not foreclose arguments about gun rights for non-violent felons, even in the Third Circuit. Four years later, the court encountered Lisa Folajtar, also a non-violent felon looking to have her Second Amendment rights restored. The court would come to a different conclusion. But even before that, in 2019, the influential District of Columbia Court of Appeals adjudicated a case somewhat similar to *Binderup*, but explicitly rejected *Binderup's* reasoning.

Medina v. Whitaker (2019): Challenging 18 U.S.C. 922 (g) (1) of the Gun Control Act

In 1990, Jorge Medina grossly falsified his income on a mortgage application at a California bank, which referred him for criminal prosecution. He admitted his crime, cooperated with investigators, and in 1991 pled guilty to a felony count of making a false statement to a lending institution. The crime had a maximum sentence of up to thirty years' incarceration, but Medina received a sentence of three years' probation, sixty days of home detention, and a fine. Based on recommendations from the US Attorney, the probation officer and others, Medina was released from probation after only one year. Later in the mid-1990s, he pled guilty to three misdemeanor counts of falsifying information on a Wyoming game license application. He received a fine and an eight-year hunting license revocation.[47]

Medina then had no further legal entanglements. He ran a successful business, supported a family, and made philanthropic contributions to his community. The California real estate licensing board continued to license him after his 1991 conviction, and the bank that had earlier referred him for prosecution offered him in 2005 a million dollar line of credit. Almost three decades after his felony conviction, wanting to own a gun for self-defense and recreation but prohibited by federal statute, Medina challenged that statute—18 U.S.C. 922 (g) (1). He argued that since he posed no greater danger of gun violence than the average citizen, applying the statute to him violated his Second Amendment rights. After the US District Court for the District of Columbia dismissed his case, he appealed to the circuit court. Senior Circuit Judge David Sentelle wrote the court's opinion.[48]

Judge Sentelle began by noting that

> Since 1968, anyone convicted of "a crime punishable by imprisonment for a term exceeding one year" is prohibited from owning firearms for life under 18 U.S.C. 922 (g) (1). … [This] practice of barring convicted felons from possessing firearms is a "presumptively lawful regulatory measure." [*Heller* citation]. Notwithstanding the Supreme Court's statements about felon disarmament, the constitutionality of 922 (g) (1) has been challenged several times. Litigation has taken the form of both facial challenges to the statute and challenges to the law's application in particular circumstances. Facial challenges to the statute's constitutionality have failed in every circuit to consider the issue. [Citations provided].[49]

Sentelle continued,

> As-applied challenges have fared only marginally better, and no circuit has held the law unconstitutional as applied to a convicted felon. The Ninth Circuit takes the view that "felons are categorically different from the individuals who have a fundamental right to bear arms." [Citation provided]. Four other circuits have, in a similar vein, also rejected as-applied challenges by convicted felons. [Citations provided]. … Only one court has held 922 (g) (1) unconstitutional in any of its

applications. [*Binderup* citation]. The court ultimately concluded that the law was unconstitutional as applied, but split sharply on the reasoning. The narrowest ground supporting the judgment held that those who commit serious crimes forfeit their Second Amendment right to arms [and] that the "passage of time or evidence of rehabilitation" could not restore the lost right; only the seriousness of the crime was relevant.[50]

Sentelle noted further,

Applying this reasoning, the misdemeanor crimes at issue in that case were not sufficiently serious to warrant disarmament. In a concurrence to the judgment, five judges disagreed with the seriousness test and took the view "that non-dangerous persons convicted of offenses unassociated with violence may rebut the presumed constitutionality of 922 (g) (1) on an as-applied basis." Finally, seven judges dissented from the judgment and would have rejected the as-applied challenge to 922 (g) (1) [because] they were satisfied that crimes encompassed by the statute were sufficiently serious to warrant disarmament.[51]

In analyzing the present case, the court first restated Medina's argument that

the district court was incorrect to conclude that "disregard for the law" was sufficient to justify disarmament [and that it] failed to conduct a sufficiently individualized assessment of his crime, his life, and his rehabilitation before deciding that he was not within the scope of the Second Amendment. … [O]nce he shows he is not dangerous, an outright prohibition on his right to possess firearms is indistinguishable from the ban struck down in *Heller* and fails under any form of scrutiny.[52]

Continuing, Sentelle noted, "The district court concluded that … his commission of a serious crime removes him from the category of 'law-abiding and responsible' citizens. In [Medina's] view, the scope of the Second Amendment only excludes dangerous individuals. Since the government cannot show that he is particularly dangerous, it offends the Second Amendment to bar him from possessing firearms."[53] In resolving the issue, the judge turned to tradition and history, starting with how felony crime was understood at the nation's founding. He observed, "At the time of the Second Amendment's ratification, nonviolent crimes such as forgery and horse theft were capital offenses. … Admittedly, the penalties for many felony crimes became less severe …. Nevertheless, felonies were—and remain—the most serious category of crime deemed by the legislature to reflect 'grave misjudgment and maladjustment.' "[54]

Next, the judge examined historical evidence relating to the disarming of only dangerous individuals, and concluded,

the public in the founding era understood that the right to bear arms could exclude at least some non-violent persons. A number of other circuits have also …

> concluded that history and tradition support the disarmament of those who were not (or could not be) virtuous members of the community. At least four circuits have endorsed the view that ... the right to bear arms was tied to the concept of a virtuous citizenry and that, accordingly, the government could disarm "unvirtuous citizens." [Citations provided]. Several circuits have relied on this theory to uphold ... laws banning the possession of firearms by illegal aliens and juveniles—classes of people who might otherwise show, on a case-by-case basis, that they are not particularly dangerous. [Citations provided]. While we need not accept this theory outright, its support among courts and scholars serves as persuasive evidence that the scope of the Second Amendment was understood to exclude more than just individually identifiable dangerous individuals.[55]

Sentelle concluded,

> On balance, the historical evidence and the Supreme Court's discussion of felon disarmament laws leads us to reject the argument that non-dangerous felons have a right to bear arms. ... Having established that a felony conviction removes one from the scope of the Second Amendment, Medina's claim presumptively fails .... Medina argues that an examination of his "present complete character" places him back within the class of "law-abiding, responsible citizens." We disagree. ... Medina would have to show facts about his conviction that distinguish him from other convicted felons .... Medina has not done so. He was convicted of felony fraud—a serious crime, *malum in se*, that is punishable in every state. ...Nor can Medina's present contributions to his community, the passage of time, or evidence of his rehabilitation, un-ring the bell of his conviction. While these ... may play a role in some as-applied challenges ... such as those brought by misdemeanants ... we hold that for unpardoned convicted felons such as Medina, they are not relevant. We therefore affirm the decision of the district court.[56]

With the *Medina* decision, the DC Circuit Court emphasized that all felony crimes are by their nature serious, and make the offenders "unvirtuous" individuals. Even if the felony is nonviolent, history and tradition suggest that felony offenders (as "unvirtuous" individuals) are outside Second Amendment protections and therefore can be disarmed. While the court acknowledged that the "virtuous citizen" theory was controversial, in the next case the Third Circuit would similarly call upon the theory in making its adjudication. Circuit Judge Thomas Ambro—author of the majority opinion in the *Binderup* case—also authored the majority opinion in *Folajtar*.

Folajtar v. U.S. Attorney General (2020): Challenging 18 U.S.C. 922 (g) (1) of the Gun Control Act

In 2011, Lisa Folajtar pled guilty to filing a fraudulent income tax return—a federal felony punishable by up to three years' incarceration and a fine of up to $100,000. Folajtar's actual sentence was three years' probation, three months of home confinement, and a fine of $10,000. Additionally, she had to reimburse the IRS over $250,000 in back taxes, penalties, and interest. Her felony conviction also triggered 18 U.S.C. 922 (g) (1), prohibiting her from possessing firearms for life.[57]

In 2018, she challenged that prohibition, asserting that the statute violated her Second Amendment rights. The district court dismissed her suit, accepting the government's argument that, as a felon, "she is categorically excluded from the class of citizens entitled to possess a firearm."[58] Folajtar then appealed to the circuit court. That court observed, "Consistent with our precedents, we hold that the legislature's designation of an offense as a felony is generally conclusive in determining whether that offense is serious. Because we determine the felony here is a serious crime, Folajtar is not protected by the Second Amendment, and her as-applied challenge to 922 (g) (1) fails."[59]

In supporting this determination, Judge Ambro cited *Heller*'s admonition that long-standing gun regulations (such as prohibitions on felons) are presumptively lawful and that every circuit court since *Heller* has rejected facial challenges to the statute. While acknowledging that "as-applied" challenges were possible regarding misdemeanor convictions, he noted,

> Until now, we have not had to decide whether 922 (g) (1) is unconstitutional as applied to a felony conviction. ... [W]e typically would proceed ... to determine ... whether Folajtar, as one convicted of a federal tax fraud felony, can distinguish herself from that class. ... Has the plaintiff overcome the generally conclusive rule that a felony conviction is serious, so that it falls outside the historical class of offenses that render felons excluded from Second Amendment protections?[60]

In examining the historical justification for limiting the right to bear arms, Ambro observed that many scholars contended that the right

> was tied to the concept of a virtuous citizenry ... accordingly, the government could disarm "unvirtuous citizens." [Citations provided]. We reasoned [in *Binderup*] that people who committed or were likely to commit violent offenses "undoubtedly qualify as 'unvirtuous citizens' [but] that the category of 'unvirtuous ciizens' is ... broader than violent criminals; it covers any person who has committed a serious criminal offense, violent or non-violent." Accordingly, we held that "persons who have committed serious crimes forfeit the right to possess firearms much the same way they forfeit other civil liberties."[61]

Ambro then emphasized, "While our dissenting colleague and Folajtar attempt to define the category of those excluded from Second Amendment protection solely by 'dangerousness,' we made clear in *Binderup* that the exclusion applies to all serious crimes ... not whether the offense is violent."[62] The judge further noted, "There are 'no fixed criteria for determining whether crimes are serious enough to destroy Second Amendment rights.' [*Binderup* citation]. ... Thus, the legislature's decision to label an offense as a felony is generally conclusive in our analysis of seriousness, and while we do not foreclose the possibility ... a 'non-serious felony' would be rare."[63]

After reviewing historical treatment of various felonies in England and early America—suggesting that non-violent felonies were also considered serious crimes—the judge noted, "even as the term evolved and expanded, felonies continued to reflect the category of serious crimes committed by those outside the virtuous citizenry."[64] He further observed,

> As felons are rarely protected by the Second Amendment, Congress is also normally entitled to require disarmament ... without engaging in an evaluation of each felon's rehabilitation and likelihood to engage in further criminal activity of any kind. [*Medina* citation]. ... Practical considerations confirm the wisdom of this approach ... district courts would face the unenviable task of weighing the relative dangerousness of hundreds of offenses already deemed sufficiently serious to be classified as felonies.[65]

The court elaborated on why "dangerousness" alone was too limited, indicating that such a focus was inconsistent with both established precedents and historical tradition. Ambro noted,

> Our Court has repudiated [this view] three times in just the last four years .... Ten of the fifteen judges to participate in *Binderup* rejected it [and] "agreed that the correct test ... is whether the offense is 'serious' not whether the offense is violent." ... [The] dangerousness standard is also inconsistent with history. ... While the dissent attempts to shoehorn all these proposals and laws [that the court previously reviewed] into the silo of dangerousness, a more accurate reading recognizes that while some ratification and legislative bodies at the Founding focused on the dangers that certain people posed, others disarmed a broader portion of the populace based on "virtuousness" and the seriousness of the crime .... The dissent's cherry-picked history only shows that dangerousness was one reason to restrict firearm possession, but it hardly was the only one.[66]

Asserting that Folajtar did not overcome the general rule that her felony is a serious crime, Judge Ambro concluded, "By making a tax return she knew to be false, Folajtar willfully deprived the government of its property. This act is no less serious than larceny, one of the nine common law felonies .... When Folajtar ... materially misstat[ed] her tax liability ... she removed herself from the constitutionally protected class of 'law-abiding citizens.' Thus her claim fails...."[67] With that, the circuit court affirmed the lower court's ruling.

For the Third Circuit, the *Folajtar* decision would not be its final examination of nonviolent felons. In 2023, Bryant Range would come before this appeals court, and in an *en banc* ruling, the court's majority would apply a different legal lens to the issue, and arrive at a different conclusion. And four days before the Third Circuit's *Range* decision, the Eighth Circuit examined the appeal of Edell Jackson, another nonviolent felon. This appeals court offered an opinion more in line with *Folajtar*, but used somewhat different reasoning.

United States v. Edell Jackson (2023): Challenging 18 U.S.C. 922 (g) (1) of the Gun Control Act

Responding to a report of "shots fired" and told that a suspect was in a parking lot, Minneapolis police officers approached Edell Jackson who was sitting in a vehicle in the lot. Jackson ran from the vehicle, shedding his jacket as he fled. The officers eventually apprehended Jackson, and later found a 9-mm firearm in his jacket pocket. Previously, Jackson had two convictions for drug sales, receiving multi-year sentences for each conviction. Consequently, Jackson was charged with violating 18 U.S.C. 922 (g) (1), the felon-in-possession statute.[68]

At trial, Jackson testified that when he was originally discharged from parole, his parole officer gave him discharge papers, said that his rights had been restored, that he could vote, and "do everything else as a productive citizen of society." He also testified that the parole officer did not provide specific guidance on the possession of firearms. Based on these exchanges, Jackson claimed that he believed his gun rights had been restored. However, a copy of Jackson's discharge papers, introduced by the government, noted that "your civil rights have been restored [but] if you have been convicted of a Crime of Violence under Minn. Statute 624.712 subd. 5, you cannot ship, transport, possess, or receive a firearm for the remainder of your lifetime."[69]

Found guilty, Jackson moved (before sentencing) to have the indictment dismissed. Citing *Bruen*, he argued that the felon-in-possession statute was unconstitutional on its face and as applied to him. The district court rejected that motion, sentencing Jackson to 108 months' imprisonment. Jackson appealed on two grounds. The first was that the district court erred in its jury instructions regarding the elements necessary for conviction under the felon-in-possession statute. The second was that 922 (g) (1) was unconstitutional as applied to him, because his drug offenses were nonviolent and thus did not indicate he was more dangerous than the average law-abiding citizen.[70]

Judge Steven Colloton authored the circuit court's opinion, dealing first with Jackson's arguments regarding various jury instruction errors. Colloton reviewed the district court's instructions, the relevant legal standards involved, and the guiding case law applicable to Jackson's arguments. He concluded that district court made no errors in its instructions to the jury or in its interpretation of the law.[71]

Turning then to Jackson's 922 (g) (1) argument, Colloton stated,

> We conclude that the district court was correct that 922(g)(1) is not unconstitutional as applied to Jackson based on his particular felony convictions. The Supreme Court has said that nothing in *Heller* [citation provided] … "should be taken to cast doubt on longstanding prohibitions on the possession of firearms by felons." *Id.* at 626; see *McDonald* [Citation provided]. The decision in *Bruen*, which affirmed that the right is "subject to certain reasonable, well-defined restrictions" … did not disturb those statements or cast doubts on the prohibitions.[72]

The judge continued,

> Given these assurances by the Supreme Court, and the history that supports them, we conclude that there is no need for felony-by-felony litigation regarding the constitutionality of 922(g)(1). History shows that the right to keep and bear arms was subject to restrictions that included prohibitions on possession by certain groups of people. There appear two schools of thought on the basis for these regulations. A panel of the Third Circuit recently surveyed the history in light of *Bruen* and concluded that legislatures have longstanding authority and discretion to disarm citizens who are not "law-abiding"—i.e., those who are "unwilling to obey the government and its laws, whether or not they had demonstrated a propensity for violence." [citation provided]. Jackson contends that a legislature's traditional authority is narrower and limited to prohibiting possession of firearms by those who are deemed more dangerous than a typical law-abiding citizen. While the better interpretation of history is debatable, we conclude that either reading supports the constitutionality of 922(g)(1) as applied to Jackson and other convicted felons, because the law "is consistent with the Nation's historical tradition of firearm regulation." *Bruen* [citation provided].[73]

After a brief historical review of early English and American statutes restricting the possession of firearms, Colloton noted that the Third Circuit interpreted this historical record to conclude that

> legislatures traditionally possessed discretion to disqualify categories of people from possessing firearms to address a threat purportedly posed by these people "to an orderly society and [to] compliance with its legal norms," and not merely to address a person's demonstrated propensity for violence. [Citation provided]. This conclusion was bolstered by the Supreme Court's repeated statements in *Bruen* that the Second Amendment protects the right of a "law-abiding citizen" to keep and bear arms. [Citations provided.] ... Congress did not violate Jackson's rights by enacting 922(g)(1). He is not a law-abiding citizen, and history supports the authority of Congress to prohibit possession of firearms by persons who have demonstrated disrespect for legal norms of society.[74]

The judge went further,

> If the historical regulation of firearms possession is viewed instead as an effort to address a risk of dangerousness, then the prohibition on possession by convicted felons still passes muster under historical analysis. Not all persons disarmed under historical precedents ... were violent or dangerous persons. The Third Circuit panel understood ... regulation was not limited to dangerousness. [Citation provided]. But if dangerousness is considered the traditional *sine qua non* for dispossession, then history demonstrates that there is no requirement for an individualized determination of dangerousness as to each person in a class of prohibited persons.

> Legislatures historically prohibited possession … based on a conclusion that the category as a whole presented an unacceptable risk of danger if armed.[75]

Colloton continued,

> The Supreme Court has observed that the purpose of the Safe Streets Act, as amended by the Gun Control Act, was to curb "lawlessness and violent crime." [Citation provided]. The "very structure of the Gun Control Act demonstrates that Congress … sought broadly to keep firearms away from persons Congress classified as potentially irresponsible and dangerous." [Citations provided]. … "Congress obviously determined that firearms must be kept away from persons, such as those convicted of serious crimes, who might be expected to misuse them." [Citation provided]. That determination was not unreasonable.[76]

Judge Colloton finished,

> In sum, we conclude that legislatures traditionally employed status-based restrictions to disqualify categories of persons from possessing firearms. Whether these actions are best characterized as restrictions on persons who deviated from legal norms or persons who presented an unacceptable risk of dangerousness, Congress acted within the historical tradition when it enacted 922(g)(1) and the prohibition on possession of firearms by felons. … [W]e conclude the statute is constitutional as applied to Jackson. The district court properly denied the motion to dismiss the indictment. For these reasons, the judgment of the district court is affirmed.[77]

Less than a week after the Eight Circuit filed the *Jackson* decision, the Third Circuit filed an *en banc* opinion in the *Range* case. Ironically, this opinion repudiated much of the reasoning Judge Colloton relied on in *Jackson* and provided a substantially different assessment of nonviolent felonies.

United States v. Bryan Range (2023): Challenging 18 U.S.C. 922 (g) (1) of the Gun Control Act

In 1995, Bryan Range lied about his income in order to obtain food stamps. Making about $9.25 an hour, with three young children, he and his wife struggled to raise a family on $300 per week. In their application for food stamps, Range's wife understated his income. Both she and Range signed the application, and although he did not recall reviewing the form, Range took full responsibility for the deception. The Pennsylvania court sentenced him to three years' probation (completed without incident), required him to pay restitution ($2,458), fined him ($100), and charged him court costs ($288.29). Since that period, Range's legal encounters only involved minor traffic and parking infractions and a summary offense for fishing without a license.[78]

Range's conviction involved a misdemeanor offense punishable by up to five years' imprisonment. Since federal law generally prohibits gun ownership by anyone convicted of a crime punishable with imprisonment exceeding one year, Pennsylvania's instant background check system rejected Range's attempt to purchase a firearm in 1998. Assuming the rejection was an error, Range's wife purchased a deer-hunting rifle for him as a gift. Some years later, Range again tried to purchase a firearm and again was unsuccessful. Prompted to investigate the basis for the denial, he discovered that his 1995 conviction barred him from buying or possessing firearms. Range then found a firearms dealer to purchase his deer rifle.[79]

Wanting firearms for hunting and home-defense, Range eventually sued in federal court, arguing that, as applied to him, §922 (g) (1) violated the Second Amendment. Referencing the then-controlling precedents of the Third Circuit, the district court found that Range's offense was serious enough to justify depriving him of his gun rights. The court considered five factors in forming this opinion: whether the crime was classified as a misdemeanor or a felony, whether it involved violence, the severity of the sentence imposed, the potential for physical harm to others, and the degree of cross-jurisdictional consensus regarding the crime's seriousness. While four of the factors favored Range—convicted of a nonviolent, non-dangerous, misdemeanor for which he was not jailed—the last factor did not. About forty jurisdictions would have considered his crime a felony. Noting that past precedents had rejected similar as-applied challenges using only one factor, the court determined that Range's conviction made him an "unvirtuous citizen" outside Second Amendment protections.[80]

Range appealed the decision, and with his appeal still pending, the Supreme Court ruled on *Bruen*. Then, when the circuit court's panel affirmed the district court's opinion, Range asked for a rehearing *en banc*. That petition was granted, vacating the panel's findings. Circuit Judge Thomas Hardiman wrote the majority opinion for the fifteen-member *en banc* court.[81]

Hardiman began his analysis by noting that many courts—including the Third Circuit—overinterpreted a comment in *Heller* suggesting that a two-step approach to Second Amendment cases was appropriate, with the second step involving a means-end analysis. Hardiman asserted, "*Bruen* rejected the two-step approach as 'one-step too many.' [Citation provided]. The Supreme Court declared: '*Heller* and *McDonald* do not support applying means-end scrutiny in the Second Amendment context.' Instead, those cases teach 'that when the Second Amendment's plain text covers an individual's conduct, the Constitution presumptively protects that conduct.' "[82]

The judge continued,

> Range's appeal ... requires us to examine *who* is among "the people" protected by the Second Amendment. ... Range claims that he is one of "the people" entitled to keep and bear arms and that our Nation has no historical tradition of disarming people like him. The Government responds that Range has not been one of "the people" since 1995, when he pleaded guilty ... to making a false statement on his food stamp application, and his disarmament is historically supported. ... We begin with ... whether Range is one of "the people" .... The Government contends

> that the Second Amendment does not apply to Range at all because "[t]he right to bear arms has historically extended to the political community of law-abiding, responsible citizens." [Citation provided]. So Range's 1995 conviction, the Government insists, removed him from "the people" protected by the Second Amendment.[83]

Hardiman observed further,

> The Supreme Court referred to "law-abiding citizens" in *Heller*. … [I]t explained that "the people" as used throughout the Constitution "unambiguously refers to all members of the political community, not an unspecified subset." [Citation given]. So, the Second Amendment right, *Heller* said, presumptively "belongs to all Americans." Range cites these statements to argue that "law-abiding citizens" should not be read "as rejecting *Heller's* interpretation of 'the people.' [Citation provided]. We agree with Range for four reasons.[84]

Elaborating, Hardiman noted that, first, the *Heller*, *McDonald*, and *Bruen* cases were not about criminal behavior, suggesting that references to "law-abiding, responsible citizens" were likely dicta. Second, other Constitutional provisions also reference "the people"—regarding voting; peaceable assembly; petitioning the government; and protection against unreasonable searches and seizures. Unless the meaning of "the people" varied from provision to provision—and the court saw no reason for such inconsistency—Range's exclusion from Second Amendment rights would exclude him from those rights as well. Third, past jurists (i.e., Judge Amy Barrett) have persuasively argued that, although the legislature may constitutionally ban arms from certain groups, "all people have the right to keep and bear arms."[85] [Citation provided].

Hardiman finally observed,

> Fourth, the phrase "law-abiding, responsible citizens" is as expansive as it is vague. Who are "law-abiding" citizens in this context? Does it exclude those who have committed summary offenses or petty misdemeanors which typically result in a ticket or a small fine? No, We are confident that the Supreme Court's references to "law-abiding, responsible citizens" do not mean that every American who gets a traffic ticket is no longer among "the people" …. As for the modifier "responsible," it serves only to undermine the Government's argument because it renders the category hopelessly vague. … Americans have widely divergent ideas about what is required for one to be considered a "responsible" citizen.[86]

The judge continued,

> At root, the Government's claim that only "law-abiding, responsible citizens" are protected by the Second Amendment devolves authority to legislators to decide whom to exclude from "the people." We reject that approach because such "extreme deference gives legislatures unreviewable power to manipulate the

> Second Amendment by choosing a label." [Citation provided]. And that deference would contravene *Heller's* reasoning that "the enshrinement of constitutional rights necessarily takes certain policy choices off the table." [Citations provided.] In sum, we reject the Government's contention that only "law-abiding, responsible citizens" are protected by the Second Amendment. ... Bryan Range remains among "the people" despite his 1995 false statement conviction.[87]

Having established that Range is one of "the people," and that his desire to buy and possess firearms is constitutionally protected by the Second Amendment, Hardiman then asked

> whether the government has justified applying §922(g)(1) to Range "by demonstrating that it is consistent with the Nation's historical tradition of firearms regulation." [Citation given.] We hold that the Government has not carried its burden. ... In attempting to carry its burden, the Government relies on the Supreme Court's statement in *Heller* that "nothing in our opinion should be taken to cast doubt on longstanding prohibitions on the possession of firearms by felons." [Citation provided.] ... And since 1961, "federal law has generally prohibited individuals convicted of crimes punishable by more than one year of imprisonment from possessing firearms." [Citation provided.][88]

The judge continued,

> But the earliest version of that statute, the Federal Firearms Act of 1938, applied only to *violent* criminals. [Citation provided.] As the First Circuit explained: "the current federal felony firearms ban differs considerably from the [original] version .... [T]he law initially covered those convicted of a limited set of violent crimes such as murder, rape, kidnapping, and burglary .... [Citations provided.]" Even if the 1938 Act were "longstanding" enough to warrant *Heller's* assurance—a dubious proposition given the *Bruen's* Court's emphasis on Founding- and Reconstruction-era sources—Range would not have been a prohibited person under that law. [Further] ... we are confident that a law passed in 1961 ... falls well short of "longstanding" for purposes of demarcating the scope of a constitutional right. So the 1961 iteration of §922(g)(1) does not satisfy the Government's burden.[89]

Hartiman also asserted that the government's older historical analogues were not sufficient. He noted that those earlier status-based arms restrictions—based on religion and race—were now not only unconstitutional, but that they also failed to address Range's specific circumstances. He observed,

> Founding era laws often prescribed the forfeiture of the weapon used to commit a fire-arms related offense without affecting the perpetrator's right to keep and bear arms generally. ... [A] felon could "repurchase arms" after successfully completing his sentence and reintegrating into society. [Citation provided.] That

> aptly describes Range's situation. ...The Government has not cited a single statute or case that precludes a convict who has served his sentence from purchasing the same type of object that he used to commit a crime. So the Government's attempt to disarm Range is not "relevantly similar" to earlier statutes allowing for execution and forfeiture. [Citation given.][90]

Addressing the government's last argument—that other circuit and district courts have categorically upheld the felon-in-possession prohibition—the judge observed,

> As impressive as these authorities [are], they fail to persuade. First, the circuit court opinions were all decided before *Bruen*. Second, the district courts are bound to follow their circuits' precedent. ... For the reasons stated, we hold that the Government has not shown that the Nation's historical tradition of firearms regulation supports depriving Range of his Second Amendment rights .... We will reverse the judgment of the District Court and will remand so the Court can enter a declaratory judgment in favor of Range.[91]

Given the various legal theories and differing determinations reflected in these cases, some future Supreme Court decisions will undoubtedly decide and resolve these felon-in-possession disagreements currently roiling the circuit courts.

1999–2023: Domestic Abusers as Dangerous Individuals

In 1996, Congress amended the GCA of 1968, adding sections (g)(8) and (g)(9) to 18 U.S.C. §922. The first section—(g)(8)—revoked the gun rights of individuals found (by a court restraining order) to be a credible threat to an intimate partner's (or child's) physical safety. The second section—(g)(9)—revoked the gun rights of individuals actually convicted of a domestic violence misdemeanor. Soon after the amendment's enactment, individuals challenged its constitutionality. Two early court cases—*Gillespie* and *Napier*—were decided before *Heller* codified the Second Amendment as an *individual* right. Since they offer only limited constitutional insight regarding sections (g)(8) and (g)(9), they are only briefly examined.

Gillespie v. City of Indianapolis (1999): Appealing a Violation of 18 U.S.C. §922 (g) (9) of the Gun Control Act

Jerald Gillespie filed suit against the city of Indianapolis in 1998 when he lost his job as a police officer. Having pled guilty to a misdemeanor battery charge involving his former wife, Gillespie could no longer carry a firearm, and the Indianapolis police department discharged him. When the district court rejected each of his constitutional arguments, Gillespie appealed, arguing (among other things) that the gun prohibition violated his Second Amendment protections. Adjudicated in 1999 before *Heller*, the circuit court held that the right to bear arms was a *collective* right and, "finding no constitutional defect in section 922(g)(9)," affirmed the dismissal of Gillespie's complaint.[92]

United States v. Napier (2000): Appealing a Violation of 18 U.S.C. §922 (g) (8) of the Gun Control Act

A year later, Harvey Napier fared no better in a different circuit court. Napier, the subject of two domestic abuse orders, was convicted of violating 18 U.S.C. §922(g)(8)—possession of firearms while under a domestic violence order. The police had found a handgun and ammunition in Napier's car after responding to an assault report by Napier's estranged wife. When the district court denied his various motions, he appealed. Among his arguments, Napier contended that (g) (8) violated his Second Amendment right to bear arms. Adjudicated in 2000, the circuit court also held that the Second Amendment was a collective right, and affirmed the district court's decision to overrule Napier's challenges, including his Second Amendment argument.[93]

The following five cases were all determined after *Heller*, and one after *Bruen*. Thus, the decisions in these cases provide more meaningful insight into the relationship between the gun statute's domestic abuse provisions and the right to bear arms. All five cases—*White*, *Skoien*, *Chester*, *Chovan*, and *Rahimi*—were adjudicated in different circuit courts. Four opinions cover the period from 2010 to 2013. The last case—*Rahimi*—was adjudicated in 2023, with the Supreme Court ultimately resolving that case in 2024.

United States v. White (2010): Appealing a Violation of 18 U.S.C. §922 (g) (9) of the Gun Control Act

In 2005, Ludivic White had been convicted of misdemeanor domestic violence—trying to choke his then live-in girlfriend. In 2007, responding to a loud-noise complaint in a high-crime area, Alabama police officers questioned four occupants of a parked vehicle matching the dispatch's description. One of the officers recognized White from previous encounters, and "patted him down for weapons ... for officer safety."[94] Upon discovering a black handgun, the officer arrested White when he could not produce a pistol permit. White was charged with violating 18 U.S.C. §922 (g) (9)—possession of a firearm by a person convicted of a misdemeanor crime of domestic violence.[95]

After the district court denied his various motions—including his motion to dismiss based on *Heller*—the jury found him guilty and White was sentenced to forty-six months' incarceration. He appealed, and the Eleventh Circuit Court of Appeals reviewed the case. Judge Eugene Siler authored the court's opinion. Siler first considered White's fourth amendment motion to suppress the gun as an illegal search. Siler held that the totality of the circumstances justified the pat-down search and affirmed the district court's denial of the motion. Next, he considered White's motion that his domestic violence conviction did not meet the criteria contained in (g)(9)—that is, that the conviction was not a "predicate offense" for purposes of the statute. The judge disagreed. After his legal analysis, Siler concluded that the district court was correct in determining that White's domestic violence conviction met the criteria contained in (g)(9) and was a predicate offense. [96]

Siler then turned to White's Second Amendment argument. He observed,

> Today we limit our holding to deciding whether § 922 (g)(9) may be properly included as a presumptively lawful "longstanding prohibition[] on the possession of firearms," a category of prohibitions the Supreme Court has implied survives Second Amendment scrutiny.[*Heller* citation]. ... While the Court did not specifically mention § 922 (g)(9), it included a footnote to clarify that the enumerated "presumptively lawful regulatory measures [are] only examples; [this] list does not purport to be exhaustive." [*Heller* citation]. We are called to decide whether ... § 922 (g)(9) warrants inclusion on *Heller's* list.[97]

The judge noted that Congress passed §922 (g) (9) because existing felon-in-possession laws were not keeping firearms from domestic abusers—these individuals often were not charged with felonies—and §922 (g) (9) was designed to remedy this problem. He observed,

> The federal ban on felons-in-possession in § 922 (g)(1)—a statute ... presumptively lawful—does not distinguish between the violent and non-violent offender. Thus, both an armed robber and a tax evader lose their right to bear arms under § 922 (g)(1). In contrast, a person convicted under § 922 (g)(9) must have first acted violently toward a family member .... Thus, although passed relatively recently, § 922 (g)(9) addresses ... a problem Congress recognized was not remedied by "longstanding" felon-in-possession laws. We see no reason to exclude § 922 (g) (9) from the list of longstanding prohibitions on which Heller does not cast doubt. [Citation provided].[98]

Siler concluded, "We now explicitly hold that § 922 (g)(9) is a presumptively lawful 'longstanding prohibition[] on the possession of firearms.' [*Heller* citation]. Given that *Heller* does not cast doubt on the constitutionality of § 922 (g)(9), we affirm White's conviction."[99]

About six months after Judge Siler decided that §922 (g) (9) did not violate the Second Amendment, the Seventh Circuit came to the same conclusion, for a different reason. Where the *White* opinion relied on logic and the similarity of §922 (g) (9) to §922 (g) (1)—a presumptively lawful prohibition—to uphold the statute, the Seventh Circuit in *Skoien* justified §922 (g) (9) as a proper exercise of Congress's power to enact categorical disqualifications on the right to keep and bear arms.

United States v. Skoien (2010): Appealing a Violation of 18 U.S.C. §922 (g) (9) of the Gun Control Act

Found in possession of several firearms after having been twice convicted of misdemeanor domestic violence, Steven Skoien was charged and convicted in district court of violating §922 (g) (9). Skoien appealed, arguing that his prior offenses were not felonies; and that §922 (g) (9) was not a "longstanding prohibition."[100]

Rejecting these arguments, Chief Judge Frank Easterbrook, writing for the circuit court, asserted that the legislative role in regulating firearm possession "did not end in 1791. That *some* categorical limits [on Second Amendment rights] are proper is part of the original meaning, leaving to the people's elected representatives the filling in of details. ... If convictions may be used to limit where sex offenders can live [Citation provided], a disqualification-on-conviction statute such as § 922 (g)(9) also is generally proper."[101] The court affirmed Skoien's conviction.

Six months after the *Skoien* opinion, a third circuit court issued an opinion on the statute. This case involved William Chester Jr., an individual previously convicted of domestic assault and battery.

United States v. Chester (2010): Appealing a violation of 18 U.S.C. §922 (g) (9) of the Gun Control Act

Subsequent to an earlier domestic assault and battery for which he was found guilty, William Chester's wife again reported him for domestic violence. Responding police officers found various firearms that Chester admitted were his. Charged with violating §922 (g) (9), Chester argued that the statute violated his Second Amendment rights. The district court dismissed this argument and convicted Chester. That court noted that "'the need to bar possession of firearms by domestic violence misdemeanants' is 'often far greater than that of the similar prohibition of § 922 (g)(1) on those who commit non-violent felonies,'" Chester appealed the conviction.[102]

The Fourth Circuit Court of Appeals summarized the case, "The sole issue ... is whether [his] conviction for illegal possession of a firearm under 18 U.S.C. § 922 (g) (9) abridges his right to keep and bear arms under the Second Amendment in light of *District of Columbia v. Heller* [Citation provided]."[103] Rejecting the approaches taken in *White* and *Skoien*, (i.e., relying on the presumptive validity of felon-dispossession laws and by linking §922 (g) (9) to (g) (1) by analogy), this circuit court asserted that a two-part analysis—as undertaken in *Mazzarella*—was appropriate. The court noted that the first step determines if the statute burdens Second Amendment rights, and if it does, the second step determines whether the government can justify the burden under an appropriate level of scrutiny.[104]

Using this approach, the circuit court's analysis concluded that §922 (g) (9) did burden Chester's gun rights, that the appropriate level of scrutiny to meet that burden was intermediate scrutiny, and that the government failed to carry that burden. The court stated, "we think it best to remand this case to afford the government an opportunity to shoulder its burden and Chester an opportunity to respond. Both sides should have an opportunity to present their evidence."[105] The court sent the case back to the district court for further proceedings. On remand, Chester's conviction was upheld.

In 2013, the Ninth Circuit also weighed in on §922 (g) (9), as it considered the appeal of Daniel Chovan. The case extensively reviewed similar cases in other circuits, and it captured the judicial reasoning during this period. Decided before the Supreme

Court's 2022 decision in *Bruen*, *Chovan* contrasts sharply with the approach and reasoning adopted post-*Bruen*, as seen in the chapter's last adjudication, the 2023 *Rahhimi* decision.

United States v. Chovan (2013): Appealing Violation of 18 U.S.C. §922 (g) (9) of the Gun Control Act

Found guilty in a California court of misdemeanor spousal abuse in 1996, Daniel Chovan attempted to purchase a firearm from a San Diego gun dealer in 2009. The required application form asked whether he had ever been convicted of a misdemeanor crime of domestic violence, to which he responded "no." The background check uncovered his 1996 conviction, resulting in a denial of his firearm purchase. While under California law, Chovan could legally purchase a gun—ten years had passed since his conviction and his civil rights were presumably restored—the federal statute nevertheless prohibited such a purchase.[106]

In 2010, after his estranged wife filed another report of violent abuse—Chovan had hit her with a cell phone and threatened to shoot her if she ever left him—law enforcement agents executed a search warrant of Chovan's home. They found several firearms and ammunition. Arrested, Chovan was indicted for violating the gun possession prohibition (i.e., §922 (g) (9)) and for making a false statement on his application to purchase a firearm. Chovan moved to dismiss the charges, arguing that §922 (g) (9) was unconstitutional both on its face and as applied to him—it violated his Second Amendment right to bear arms. Alternatively, he argued that the statute did not apply to him because his civil rights had been restored. When the district court concluded that the statute was a presumptively lawful prohibition as articulated in *Heller* and denied his motion, Chovan appealed. [107]

The appeals court first addressed Chovan's "civil rights restored" argument, noting that an earlier Ninth Circuit adjudication examined—and rejected—a similar argument. After reviewing that case, the present court concluded,

> Chovan's 1996 misdemeanor domestic violence conviction did not divest him of his civil rights because it did not divest him of the right to vote, the right to serve on a jury, or the right to hold public office. Because Chovan never lost these 'core' civil rights, he cannot qualify for the civil rights restored exception to § 922 (g) (9).[108]

The court then turned to Chovan's Second Amendment challenge, observing that it rested on the *Heller* decision.

After acknowledging that the Ninth Circuit had never addressed the constitutionality of §922 (g) (9), the court identified a number of other circuits that upheld the statute using various rationales. The Eleventh Circuit, in *White*, considered the constitutionality of §922 (g) (9) and concluded that the statute was similar to the "presumptively lawful longstanding prohibitions" discussed in *Heller*. Without additional constitutional analysis, that circuit upheld the statute.[109]

But the court noted that the Fourth Circuit (in *Chester*) criticized *White's* use of *Heller's* "presumptively lawful measures" as a seeming "safe harbor," justifying any unlisted gun regulation appearing similar to those listed in *Heller*. Instead, that court applied a two-part inquiry to the statute, concluding that §922 (g) (9) burdened Second Amendment rights. With this determination, the court asserted that intermediate scrutiny was appropriate and remanded the case back to the district court for further development.[110]

Turning to *Skoien*, the court observed that the Seventh Circuit also employed intermediate scrutiny to determine §922 (g) (9)'s constitutionality. Reviewing relevant studies, the *Skoien* court concluded that the empirical evidence demonstrated a substantial connection between the statute and the important government objective of preventing gun violence in domestic situations. Similarly, the First Circuit upheld §922 (g) (9) after determining that "social science research supported a finding of a 'substantial relationship between § 922 (g) (9)'s disqualification of domestic violence misdemeanants from gun ownership and the governmental interest in preventing gun violence in the home.'"[111] Additionally, the court cited a Fourth Circuit adjudication (decided after *Chester*) that also examined social science findings and concluded that the evidence established "a reasonable fit between the substantial government objective of reducing domestic gun violence and keeping firearms out of the hands of [domestic violence misdemeanants."[112]

After considering these adjudications, the *Chovan* court also adopted the two-step inquiry procedure. The court determined,

> At the first step ... we conclude that ... § 922 (g) (9) burdens rights protected by the Second Amendment. ... The government argues that § 922 (g) (9) is a presumptively lawful regulatory measure and ... is part of a "long line of prohibitions and restrictions on the right to possess firearms by people perceived as dangerous or violent." We disagree. First, it is not clear that such prohibitions are so longstanding. The first federal firearms restrictions regarding violent offenders were not passed until 1938.[113]

Noting the lack of relevant historical evidence, the court quoted *Chester*, "We must assume, therefore, that [Chovan's] Second Amendment rights are intact...."[114]

The court then moved to the second step. Emphasizing that the "core" of the Second Amendment was the right to use arms for home- and self-defense [*Heller* citation], the court noted,

> Section 922 (g)(9) does not implicate this core Second Amendment right because it regulates firearms possession for individuals with criminal convictions ... "we believe [Chovan's] claim is not within the core right identified in *Heller*—the right of a law-abiding, responsible citizen to possess and carry a weapon for self-defense—by virtue of [his] criminal history as a domestic violence misdemeanant." [*Chester* citation]. ... In sum, § 922 (g) (9) does not implicate the core Second Amendment right, but it does place a substantial burden on the right. Accordingly,

> we conclude that intermediate rather than strict scrutiny is the proper standard to apply.[115]

To survive intermediate scrutiny, the court stressed that the government's stated objective had to be important, and a reasonable fit had to exist between the challenged regulation and the government's objective. The court observed that the prevention of domestic gun violence was a self-evidently and important government objective. It further noted that §922 (g) (9)—by prohibiting firearms to domestic violent misdemeanants who were not prevented from gun possession by §922 (g) (1)—was a reasonable way to achieve that objective. The court finished, "Because § 922 (g) (9) is supported by an important government interest and substantially related to that interest, the statute passes constitutional muster under intermediate scrutiny."[116]

The court then moved to Chovan's "as-aplied" argument:

> Chovan argues that § 922 (g) (9) is unconstitutional as applied to him because his 1996 domestic violence conviction occurred fifteen years before his § 922 (g) (9) conviction, [and] he is unlikely to recidivate .... Chovan cites several statistics in support of his argument that he is at low risk .... Meanwhile, the government has referred to domestic violence studies mentioned by the *Skoien* court showing that the recidivism rates for individuals convicted of domestic violence is significant—between 35 and 80 percent. [*Skoien* citation]. Chovan also argues ... that a March 2021 domestic violence call made by his estranged wife ... should not be held against him because it did not result in a charge ... and amounts to "unsubstantiated allegations."[117]

Continuing, the court observed,

> Although Chovan was not arrested for domestic violence ... [t]he call is part of the record. And it should be considered, especially in light of one of the underlying rationales of § 922 (g) (9): acts of domestic violence are under-reported and often do not lead to arrest or conviction. ... In light of the domestic abuse call, § 922 (g) (9)'s application to Chovan is substantially related to the goal of reducing domestic gun violence. ... If Congress had wanted § 922 (g) (9) to apply only to individuals with recent domestic violence convictions, it could have easily created a limited duration rather than a lifetime ban. Or it could have created a good behavior clause .... But Congress did not do so. ... The breadth of the statute ... reflect[s] Congress's express intent to establish a "zero tolerance policy" towards guns and domestic violence.[118]

The court concluded, "For the foregoing reasons, we reject Chovan's 'civil rights restored' claim, hold that intermediate scrutiny is the proper standard to apply to his Second Amendment claim, and uphold § 922 (g) (9) and its application to Chovan under intermediate scrutiny. Affirmed."[119]

Constitutionally, the *Chovan* adjudication is noteworthy both for its treatment of *Heller's* ambiguous "presumptively lawful measures" and "longstanding prohibitions" guidance and for its use of intermediate scrutiny. A decade after *Chovan*, and a year after *Bruen*, the Fifth Circuit adjudicated another challenge to §922, this one focused on (g) (8)—possession of a firearm while under a domestic violence restraining order. While the issues in *Chovan* and *Rahimi* are similar, the constitutional analysis and outcomes are quite different.

United States v. Rahimi (2023): Appealing Violation of 18 U.S.C. §922 (g) (8) of the Gun Control Act

In February 2020, a Texas state court imposed an agreed civil protective order against Zackey Rahimi after he allegedly assaulted his ex-girlfriend. In addition to prohibitions on harassing or threatening the woman, the order specifically banned Rahimi from possessing a firearm. But between December 2020 and January 2021, Rahimi was involved in multiple shootings in Arlington, Texas—firing into a residence after a drug sale, at a car and driver after an accident, at a constable's vehicle, and in the air at a restaurant when a credit card was declined. After identifying Rahimi as a suspect, police searched his home, finding a pistol and a rifle that Rahimi admitted was his. A federal grand jury then indicted Rahimi for violating 18 U.S.C. §922 (g) (8).[120]

Rahimi moved to dismiss the indictment, arguing that §922 (g) (8) was unconstitutional. When the district court denied his motion—a precedential earlier case foreclosed his argument—he pled guilty but reiterated his constitutional challenge on appeal. Initially affirming the district court's ruling, the circuit court's original panel withdrew its opinion after the *Bruen* adjudication. The panel ordered an expedited hearing (before another Fifth Circuit panel) to consider Rahimi's current contention that "*Bruen* overrules our precedent and that under *Bruen*, § 922 (g) (8) is unconstitutional."[121] Circuit Judge Cory Wilson authored the opinion of this second panel.

Judge Wilson began by noting that the Fifth Circuit held in *Emerson* that the Second Amendment guaranteed an individual right to bear arms, but that §922 (g) (8) was nonetheless constitutional as it was " 'narrowly tailored' to the goal of minimizing 'the threat of lawless violence.' [*Emerson* citation]. After *D.C. v. Heller* [Citation provided] courts coalesced around a similar 'two-step inquiry for analyzing laws that might impact the Second Amendment.' [Citation provided]. … In *McGinnis*, this court upheld § 922 (g)(8) using this two-step framework. The initial panel in this case did likewise."[122]

Continuing, Wilson stated,

> Enter *Bruen*. Expounding on *Heller*, the Supreme Court held that "[w]hen the Second Amendment's plain covers an individual's conduct, the Constitution presumptively protects that conduct." [*Bruen* citation]. In that context, the Government bears the burden of "justify[ing] its regulation by demonstrating that

> it is consistent with the Nation's tradition of firearm regulation." Put another way, "the [G]overnment must affirmatively prove that its firearms regulation is part of the historical tradition that delimits the outer bounds of the right to keep and bear arms." ... the Court expressly repudiated the circuit courts' means-end scrutiny—the second step embodied in *Emerson* and applied in *McGinnis* .... *Bruen* clearly "fundamentally change[d]" our analysis of laws that implicate the Second Amendment, [citation provided], rendering our prior precedent obsolete.[123]

Judge Wilson then observed that

> to the Government, *Heller* and *Bruen* add a gloss on the Second Amendment that restricts its applicability to only "law abiding, responsible citizens," [*Heller* citation] and "ordinary, law-abiding citizens," [*Bruen* citation]. Because Rahimi is neither responsible nor law-abiding ... he falls outside the ambit of the Second Amendment. Therefore, argues the Government, § 922 (g)(8) is constitutional as applied to him.[124]

Wilson rejected this argument, asserting that it "fails because (1) it is inconsistent with *Heller*, *Bruen*, and the text of the Second Amendment, (2) it inexplicably treats Second Amendment rights differently than other individually held rights, and (3) it has no limiting principles."[125]

Wilson elaborated,

> *Heller* explained that the words "the people" in the Second Amendment have been interpreted throughout the Constitution to "unambiguously refer[] to all members of the political community, not an unspecified subset." ...*Heller's* exposition of "the people" strongly indicates that Rahimi is included in the "the people" and thus within the Second Amendment's scope. ... The Government's reading of *Heller* and *Bruen* also turns the typical way of conceptualizing constitutional rights on its head. "[A] person could be in one day and out the next: the moment he was convicted of a violent crime or suffered the onset of mental illness, his rights would be stripped as a self-executing consequence of his new status." [Citation provided]. This is "an unusual way of thinking about rights."[126]

The judge concluded his elaboration,

> Perhaps most importantly, the Government's proffered interpretation lacks any true limiting principle. ...Congress could remove "unordinary" or "irresponsible" or "non-law abiding" people—however expediently defined—from the scope of the Second Amendment. Could speeders be stripped of their right to keep and bear arms? Political non-conformists? People who do not recycle or drive an electric vehicle? ... Neither *Heller* nor *Bruen* countenances such a malleable scope of the Second Amendment's protections.[127]

Wilson then addressed whether §922 (g) (8) was a constitutional restriction on Rahimi's right to arms. Citing *Bruen*, the judge noted that if the Second Amendment's plain text covered an individual's conduct, the government had to justify the statute by showing a consistency with the country's historical tradition of firearm regulation. The absence of a similar historical regulation would indicate that the challenged statute violated the Second Amendment and is unconstitutional. Since

> Rahimi's possession of a pistol and rifle easily falls within the purview of the Second Amendment … the Second Amendment presumptively protects [his] right to keep the weapons officers discovered in his home. But Rahimi … may have forfeited his Second Amendment rights if his conduct ran afoul of a "lawful regulatory measure[]" "prohibiting the possession of firearms" [*Heller* citation] that is consistent with "the historical tradition …." [*Bruen* citation]. The question turns on whether § 922 (g)(8) falls within that historical tradition, or outside it.[128]

In answering that question, the judge asserted,

> The Government offers potential historical analogues to § 922 (g)(8) that generally fall into three categories: (1) English and American laws … providing for disarmament of "dangerous" people, (2) English and American "going armed" laws, and (3) colonial and early state surety laws. We discuss … why each of these historical regulations falter as "relevantly similar" precursors to § 922 (g)(8).[129]

Considering "dangerous" analogues, Wilson rejected the English Militia Act of 1662 that had allowed the Crown to seize the arms of people judged dangerous. He noted that the 1689 English Bill of Rights restricted the Militia Act's reach specifically to prevent politically motivated disarmaments.[130]

Regarding early American laws that disarmed classes of people considered dangerous, he observed that these laws "disarmed people by class or group, not after individualized findings of 'credible threats' to identified potential victims. … The purpose of these 'dangerous' laws was the preservation of political and social order, not the protection of an identified person from the specific threat posed by another."[131] Wilson similarly dismissed proposals from state ratification conventions that would have limited gun rights to peaceable citizens, noting that they were not enacted and thus cannot counter the Second Amendment's text.[132]

Turning to restrictions on "going armed" laws, the government offered examples from four different states. Unimpressed, Wilson asserted,

> These proffered analogues fall short … it is dubious these "going armed" laws are reflective of our Nation's historical tradition of firearm regulation, at least as to forfeiture of firearms. … North Carolina's law did not provide for forfeiture … fairly early on, Massachusetts and Virginia dropped forfeiture as a penalty …. It is unclear how long New Hampshire's "going armed" law preserved its forfeiture

> provision, but ... one outlier is not enough "to show a tradition of public carry regulation." [*Bruen* citation].[133]

Finally, Wilson considered the surety laws envoked by the government. He observed,

> The surety laws come closer to being "relevantly similar" to § 922 (g)(8) than the [other] laws discussed ... they are more clearly a part of our tradition of firearm regulation. And ... they were meant to protect an identified person (who sought surety) from the risk of harm posed by another identified individual (who had to post surety to carry arms). ... The surety laws required only a civil proceeding, not a criminal conviction. The "credible threat" finding required to trigger § 922 (g)(8)'s prohibition on possession of weapons echoes the showing that was required to justify posting of surety to avoid forfeiture. But ... historical surety laws did not prohibit public carry, much less possession of weapons, so long as the offender posed surety. ...At bottom, the historical surety laws did not impose "a comparable burden on the right of armed self-defense" as § 922 (g)(8). [*Bruen* citation].[134]

Judge Wilson ended,

> The Government fails to demonstrate that § 922 (g)(8)'s restrictions of Second Amendment rights fits within our Nation's historical tradition of firearm regulation. ... [W]e conclude that § 922 (g)(8)'s ban on possession of firearms is an "outlier that our ancestors would never have accepted." [*Bruen* citation]. Therefore, the statute is unconstitutional, and Rahimi's conviction under that statute must be vacated. Reversed; Conviction vacated.[135]

Considering the beneficial societal focus of §922 (g) (8), the circuit court's decision struck many observers as counterintuitive. But as the adjudication itself noted, the case was not about whether §922 (g) (8) represented a laudable policy goal; it was about whether the statute was constitutional under the Second Amendment. Attempting to apply the adjudicating standards contained in *Bruen*, the Fifth Circuit concluded it was not. Unsurprisingly, the state appealed the case to the Supreme Court, and in 2024 the Supreme Court rejected the Fifth Circuit's reasoning. The Supreme Court upheld the constitutionality of §922 (g) (8) and reinstated Rahimi's conviction. Chapter 9 examines the court's reasoning and analysis of the case.

Some Observations

As several of the cases in this chapter emphasized, the imposition of a lifetime weapons ban for felonious criminal behavior was a twentieth-century development. In the early days of the republic, that specific penalty was unknown, and while the state might have confiscated weapons from felons, such individuals were free to reacquire firearms after serving their sentences. Recognizing the severity of this gun-ban penalty, modern courts have devoted considerable effort in examining the constitutionality of such a harsh prohibition. Evident in *Binderup* and other adjudications, the notion of a "virtuous citizenry" has had a central role in determining its constitutionality.

While a certain vagueness surrounds the concept, the "virtuous citizen" argument asserted that civil society could trust only law-abiding and responsible individuals with firearms. "Unvirtuous" individuals—those who refused to abide by society's legal codes and expectations or who were irresponsible and reckless—posed a danger to the community and to themselves, and access to firearms significantly heightened that danger. Thus, from a "virtuous citizenry" perspective, depriving the unvirtuous of their gun rights was both justified and commonsensical. But was such a revocation constitutional, in light of the *people's* enumerated right to arms?

To answer this objection, the government asserted that unvirtuous individuals had no Second Amendment rights because they simply were not a part of those "people" protected by the amendment. This argument countered the initial constitutional objection, and also addressed potentially troubling distinctions of felonious "degrees." Because only unvirtuous individuals committed felonies, no meaningful distinction actually existed between violent and nonviolent felons. This reasoning supported the revocation of even the nonviolent felon's right to guns.

In addition to the "virtuous citizenry" argument supporting gun bans, the cases show two other approaches—lenses—for justifying such bans. One lens focuses on the "seriousness" of the individual's past crime, and the other focuses on the "violence/dangerousness" implicit in the crime. In weighing the societal implications (and fairness) of permanent bans for nonviolent felons—particularly for those whose crimes occurred decades earlier—the cases suggest the two lens lead to differing judicial orientations. In these cases, because the felon's crime was not violent or threatening, the "dangerous/violence" lens fosters lenient judgments about the crime and suggests the inappropriateness of a permanent ban. Judgments using the "seriousness" lens are more complicated. They likely encourage a harsher orientation and provide implicit support for the ban. After all, by definition, whether violent or nonviolent, felonies are always serious crimes.

Of course, regardless of which lens a court may adopt in approaching a challenge to a nonviolent felony gun ban, the ultimate determination still rests on the government's ability to demonstrate that the statute conforms to the nation's past history and traditions. As Chapter 9 suggests, the Supreme Court is likely to weigh in on the matter at some future point.

Notes

1 *Barrett v. United States, 423 U.S. 212 (1976)*. At https://caselaw.findlaw.com/court/us-supreme-court/423/212.html.

2 *"Does a customer have to be a certain age to buy firearms or ammunition from a licensee?"* At https://www.atf.gov/firearms/qa/does-customer-have-be-certain-age-buy-firearms-or-ammunition-licensee.

3 *Simpson v. State of Tennessee, 13 Tenn. (5 Yer.) 356 (1833).* At https://guncite.com/court/state/13tn356.html.
4 Ibid.
5 See *Range v. Lombardo, No. 21-2835 D.C. No. 5:20-CV-03488 (2023)*. p. 20. At https://www2.ca3.uscourts.gov/opinarch/212835pen.pdf.
6 *Huddleston v. United States, 415 U.S. 814 (1974).* At https://caselaw.findlaw.com/court/us-supreme-court/415/814.html.
7 Ibid.
8 Ibid.
9 Ibid.
10 Ibid.
11 Ibid.
12 Ibid.
13 Ibid.
14 Ibid.
15 Ibid.
16 Ibid.
17 *United States v. Everist 368 F. 3d 517 (2004).* At https://scholar.google.com/scholar_case?case=16252186800859977166&q=U.S.+v.+Everist+(2004)&hl=en&as_sdt=4006&as_vis=1.
18 Ibid.
19 Ibid.
20 *United States v. Vongxay*, 594 *F.3d 1111 (2010).* At https://cdn.ca9.uscourts.gov/datastore/opinions/2010/02/09/09-10072.pdf.
21 *United States v. Rozier, 598 F.3d 768 (2010).* At https://case-law.vlex.com/vid/u-s-v-rozier-886618306.
22 Ibid.
23 Ibid.
24 Ibid.
25 Ibid.
26 *Binderup v. Attorney General of the United States, No. 14-4549 (3d Circuit) (2016).* At https://law.justia.com/cases/federal/appellate-courts/ca3/14-4549/14-4549-2016-09-07.html.
27 Ibid.
28 Ibid.
29 Ibid.
30 Ibid.
31 Ibid.
32 Ibid.
33 Ibid.
34 Ibid.
35 Ibid.
36 Ibid.
37 Ibid.
38 Ibid.
39 Ibid.
40 Ibid.
41 Ibid.

42 Ibid.
43 Ibid.
44 Ibid.
45 Ibid.
46 Ibid.
47 *Medina v. Whitaker, 913 F.3d 152 (D.C. Cir. 2019).* At https://casetext.com/case/medina-v-whitaker.
48 Ibid.
49 Ibid.
50 Ibid.
51 Ibid.
52 Ibid.
53 Ibid.
54 Ibid.
55 Ibid.
56 Ibid.
57 *Folajtar v. Attorney General of the United States, No. 19-1687 (3d Circuit) (2020).* At https://law.justia.com/cases/federal/appellate-courts/ca3/19-1687/19-1687-2020-11-24.html.
58 Ibid.
59 Ibid.
60 Ibid.
61 Ibid.
62 Ibid.
63 Ibid.
64 Ibid.
65 Ibid.
66 Ibid.
67 Ibid.
68 *United States v. Edell Jackson, No. 22-2870 (8th Circuit) (2023).* At https://caselaw.findlaw.com/court/us-8th-circuit/2202882.html.
69 Ibid.
70 Ibid.
71 Ibid.
72 Ibid.
73 Ibid.
74 Ibid.
75 Ibid.
76 Ibid.
77 Ibid.
78 *United States v. Bryan Range, No. 21-2835 (3rd Circuit) (2023).* At https://www2.ca3.uscourts.gov/opinarch/212835pen.pdf.
79 Ibid.
80 Ibid.
81 Ibid.
82 Ibid.
83 Ibid.
84 Ibid.

85 Ibid.
86 Ibid.
87 Ibid.
88 Ibid.
89 Ibid.
90 Ibid.
91 Ibid.
92 *Gillespie v. City of Indianapolis, 185 F.3d 693 (7th Circuit) (1999).* At https://casetext.com/case/gillespie-v-city-of-indianapolis-2.
93 *United States v. Napier, 233 F.3d 394 (*6th *Circuit) (2000).* At https://casetext.com/case/us-v-napier-10.
94 *United States v. White, 593 F.3d 1199 (11*th *Circuit) (2010).* At https://www.courtlistener.com/opinion/78550/united-states-v-white/.
95 Ibid.
96 Ibid.
97 Ibid.
98 Ibid.
99 Ibid.
100 *United States v. Skoien, 614 F.3d 638 (7th Circuit) (2010).* At https://casetext.com/case/us-v-skoien-9.
101 Ibid.
102 *United States v. Chester, 628 F.3d 673 (4th Circuit) (2010).* At https://caselaw.findlaw.com/court/us-4th-circuit/1550305.html.
103 Ibid.
104 Ibid.
105 Ibid.
106 *United States v. Chovan, 735 F. 3d 1127 (9th Circuit) (2013).* At https://caselaw.findlaw.com/court/us-9th-circuit/1649926.html.
107 Ibid.
108 Ibid.
109 Ibid.
110 Ibid.
111 Ibid.
112 Ibid.
113 Ibid.
114 Ibid.
115 Ibid.
116 Ibid.
117 Ibid.
118 Ibid.
119 Ibid.
120 *United States of America v. Rahimi, No. 21-11001 (5th Circuit) (2023).* At https://www.ca5.uscourts.gov/opinions/pub/21/21-11001-CR2.pdf.
121 Ibid.
122 Ibid.
123 Ibid.
124 Ibid.
125 Ibid.

126 Ibid.
127 Ibid.
128 Ibid.
129 Ibid.
130 Ibid.
131 Ibid.
132 Ibid.
133 Ibid.
134 Ibid.
135 Ibid.

8

Dangerous People: The Risky and Irresponsible

> *It shall be unlawful for any person to sell ... any firearm or ammunition to any person [who is] a juvenile ... an unlawful user of or addicted to any controlled substance ... [who]has been adjudicated as a mental defective or who has been committed to a mental institution ... It shall be unlawful for [these individuals] to ... possess ... any firearm or ammunition; or to receive any firearm or ammunition.*
>
> 18 U.S. Code §922—Unlawful Acts[1]

In its efforts to protect American society from dangerous individuals, Congress did not just bar obviously violent felons from owning or possessing firearms. The Gun Control Act (GCA) of 1968 and its various amendments disarmed three other notable categories of people *potentially* dangerous due to likely diminished judgment. As the prior chapter indicated, the Act also prohibited anyone below the age of twenty-one from buying handguns, and anyone under the age of eighteen from purchasing rifles. The law likewise banned dealers from *selling* handguns and rifles to underage individuals. Additionally, the Act prohibited illegal users of controlled substances and drug addicts from owning or possessing firearms. Finally, the statute disarmed individuals previously committed to a mental institution.

Limiting the gun rights of underage and emotionally or mentally unstable individuals—persons likely to pose a danger to themselves or others—appears to be an appropriate societal policy. But are these prohibitions constitutional? The *Heller* decision suggested that such bans were "presumptively constitutional." But after the Supreme Court's *Bruen* decision in 2022, various district and circuit courts struggled with determining whether the Second Amendment allows the suspension of gun rights simply because individuals are below an arbitrarily specified age and are presumed irresponsible. Similarly, drug users and individuals once involuntarily committed for mental instability have challenged the constitutionality of the statutes' lifetime firearm prohibitions.

This chapter examines notable court decisions in each of these categories. The first section covers age-related adjudications, containing five cases spanning fifteen years and multiple jurisdictions. The second section focuses on four drug-user adjudications and also spans fifteen years and several circuits. The three adjudications in the last section center on gun prohibitions due to prior mental illness.

2009–25: Minors as Dangerous Individuals

This section's Second Amendment challenges to age-linked gun prohibitions cover two distinctive judicial periods. The first period is post-*Heller/McDonald* but pre-*Bruen*. These cases—*United States v. Rene* (2009) and *NRA v. BATFE* (2012)—illustrate how courts interpreted the ambiguous guidance regarding potentially unconstitutional gun laws contained in *Heller* and *McDonald*. The second period covers post-*Bruen* decisions. These three cases—*NRA v. Bondi* (2023), *Worth v. Harrington* (2023), and *Lara v. Commissioner Pennsylvania State Police* (2023)—highlight the judicial impact *Bruen* has had in this area.

United States v. Rene (2009): Violating 18 U.S.C. §922 (x) (2) of the 1994 Youth Handgun Safety Act

In 2008, the Central Maine Violent Crime Task Force learned that a juvenile—seventeen-year-old Rene E.—had possession of a handgun, a bulletproof vest, drugs, and stolen property. Arriving at the juvenile's residence, Rene's grandmother admitted the agents and led them to Rene's bedroom. After receiving permission from Rene, the agents searched his room, found marijuana and drug paraphernalia, stolen property, ammunition, and a silver-colored revolver. During the search, Rene fled the house and escaped, but turned himself in sixteen days later. After his arrest, the state transferred Rene's case to the Bureau of Alcohol, Tobacco, Firearms, and Explosives (BATFE). He was then charged "with an act of juvenile delinquency, the knowing possession of a handgun in violation of 18 U.S.C. §922 (x) (2) (A)."[2] When the district court denied his motions to suppress the evidence because the statute both exceeded Congress's power under the Commerce Clause, and violated the Second Amendment, Rene entered a conditional guilty plea but appealed the denials. Circuit Judge Kermit Lipez authored the opinion of the appeals court.[3]

After a brief review of the Second Amendment and the interpretive guidance provided in the *Heller* decision, Judge Lipez turned to Rene's argument that the federal ban on juvenile possession of handguns is unconstitutional as applied to him. The judge observed,

> [Rene] points out that, like the D.C. handgun ban invalidated in *Heller*, section 922(x)(2)(A) bans the mere possession of handguns, but suggests that it is "even more complete," because it applies "at all times, under all circumstances." Nor is it, he says, a "longstanding" prohibition having been enacted into federal law in 1994. [Citation provided.] He argues that the interest in self-defense he has as a seventeen-year-old is just as strong as the adult respondent in Heller.[4]

Lipez continued,

> In response, the government argues that there are "longstanding" prohibitions on the possession of firearms, since juveniles did not serve in militias and were

> the sort of "potentially irresponsible persons" historically targeted by restrictive gun laws. It suggests that the ban ... could survive even strict scrutiny, since the government's interest in regulating the illicit market in handguns is compelling and the ban narrowly tailored .... We agree with the government that *Heller* does not render section 922(x)(2)(A) unconstitutional as applied to appellant. We rest our conclusion on the existence of a longstanding tradition of prohibiting juveniles from both receiving and possessing hand guns .... We begin by examining the contemporary federal restrictions on firearm and handgun restrictions by juveniles, and then look to nineteenth-century state laws imposing similar restrictions, as the *Heller* Court did.[5]

The judge then reviewed congressional regulations limiting juvenile access to guns. He noted,

> Congress first restricted the transfer of weapons on the basis of age in 1968. See Omnibus Crime Control and Safe Streets Act of 1968 [Citation provided] (finding that there "is a causal relationship between the easy availably of firearms other than a rifle or shotgun and juvenile and youthful criminal behavior, and that such firearms have been widely sold to emotionally immature, or thrill-bent juveniles and minors prone to criminal behavior"); [Also] Gun Control Act of 1968 [Citation provided] (prohibiting the sale of rifles and shotguns to individuals less than eighteen years old). Congress's principal purpose in enacting these restrictions was "to keep firearms out of the hands of those not legally entitled to possess them because of age ...." [Citation provided].[6]

Continuing, Lipez stated,

> Handgun possession by juveniles, defined as those under eighteen years of age, was banned by federal law in 1994. See Youth Handgun Safety Act .... [This Act] was aimed at preventing juvenile misuse of handguns and associated crime: "[V]iolent criminals often start their criminal careers on the streets where the readily availability of guns to young people results in the acceptability of their random use. ... Inasmuch as illicit drug activity and related violent crime overflow State lines and national boundaries, the Congress has power, under the interstate commerce clause ... to enact measures to combat these problems. The Congress ... assist[s] the States in controlling crime by stopping the commerce in handguns with juveniles nationwide, and allowing the possession of handguns by juveniles only when handguns are possessed and used for legitimate purposes under appropriate conditions." [Citation provided].[7]

After additionally noting that section 922 (x) (2) (A) had several exception—contrary to Rene's claim that the statute's ban was even more absolute than the DC ban—Lipez reviewed state limitations on juvenile access to guns. He observed that state regulations also "sometimes reflected concerns that juveniles lacked the judgment necessary to safely possess deadly weapons, and that juvenile access to such weapons would increase crime. For example, in 1878, the Supreme Court of Tennessee suggested that a regulation criminalizing the sale of a pistol to a juvenile did not violate the Second Amendment and was wise public policy. [Citation provided]."[8] The judge then asserted that other states similarly restricted the transfer of lethal weapons (often handguns) to juveniles, citing examples from eight other states covering the period of 1858 through 1926.[9]

In addition to the referenced cases, Judge Lipez argued that the founding generation would likely have seen public-safety-based limitations on juvenile possession of firearms as permissible, given that generation's emphasis on the "virtuous citizen." Citing a 1995 law review paper, the judge quoted,

> "One implication of this emphasis ... on the virtuous citizen is that the right to bear arms does not preclude laws disarming the unvirtuous (i.e. criminals) or those who, like children or the mentally imbalanced, are deemed incapable of virtue."[10] Lipez asserted further, "In this sense, the federal ban on juvenile possession of handguns is part of a longstanding practice of prohibiting certain classes of individuals from possessing firearms—those whose possession pose a particular danger to the public."[11]

In ending his analysis of the constitutionality of U.S.C. §922 (x) (2) (A), the judge concluded,

> We have evaluated this prohibition in light of the state laws of the nineteenth century regulating juvenile access to handguns [finding] that their possession can pose a serious threat to public safety. We have evaluated evidence that the founding generation would have regarded such laws as consistent with the right to keep and bear arms. Therefore, we have concluded that this law, with its narrow scope and exceptions, does not offend the Second Amendment.[12]

While the *Rene* decision examined the constitutionality of a statute barring juveniles from *possessing* handguns, that next case additionally examined the constitutionality of a statute prohibiting federally licensed firearms dealers from *selling* handguns to individuals under the age of twenty-one. The constitutional issues remain the same, and the arguments and much of the reviewed legal and historical evidence overlap.

NRA v. BATFE (2012): Challenging 18 U.S.C. §§922 (b) (1) & (c) (1) of the 1968 Omnibus Crime Act

Three individuals between the ages of eighteen and twenty-one—Andrew Payne, Rebekah Jennings, and Brennan Harmon—and the National Rifle Association (NRA) challenged the constitutionality of 18 U.S.C. §§922 (b) (1) & (c) (1) and several associated regulations. These statutes prevented eighteen- to twenty-year-old NRA members from purchasing handguns from federal firearms licensees (FFLs), and also prevented FFLs from making such sales. The appellants argued that the statutes infringed on the Second Amendment rights of eighteen- to twenty-year-old adults to keep and bear arms and that the statutes violated the Fifth Amendment's Due Process Clause.[13]

In district court, the government argued that the appellants lacked standing to challenge the federal statutes and also that their constitutional claims failed on the merits. When the district court ruled that the appellants had standing, but had failed to make a viable Second or Fifth Amendment claim, the appellants appealed. Circuit Judge Edward Prado authored the appeals court opinion.[14]

Judge Prado first dealt with the question of standing, stating that the appellants had to show (1) they suffered a concrete injury, (2) that a causal link existed between their injury and the conduct complained of, and (3) that a favorable decision could redress the injury. After reviewing the statutory provisions at issue, he observed that the law allowed eighteen- to twenty-year-olds to possess and use handguns—for instance, as gifts from parents or guardians—and that eighteen- to twenty-year-olds could purchase handguns from unlicensed private sellers (i.e., non-FFls). He noted that they could also possess and purchase long guns from either FFls or non-FFLs. Responding to the government contention that the appellants—since they could still possess and use handguns—had not suffered an injury-in-fact, Prado disagreed, asserting that "by prohibiting FFLs from selling handguns to 18-to-20-year-olds, the law causes those persons a concrete, particularized injury—i.e., the injury of not being able to purchase handguns from FFLs."[15]

Turning to the appellants' Second Amendment argument, the judge stated, "No other circuit court has considered the constitutionality of the challenged federal laws in light of *Heller*. … Because we—unlike some of our fellow circuit courts—have yet to establish a framework for evaluating post-*Heller* Second Amendment challenges, we sketch a framework here."[16] After stating that *Heller* did not provide such an analytical framework, Prado observed that other circuit courts

> filled the analytical vacuum. A two-step inquiry has emerged … the first step is to determine whether the challenged law impinges upon a right protected by the Second Amendment … the second step is to determine whether to apply intermediate or strict scrutiny to the law, and then determine whether the law survives the proper level of scrutiny. [Citations provided]. We adopt a version of this two-step approach.[17]

Continuing, Prado stated,

> "To determine whether a law impinges on the Second Amendment right, we look to whether the law harmonizes with the historical traditions associated with the Second Amendment guarantee. [Citations provided]. If the challenged law burdens conduct that falls outside the Second Amendment's scope, then the law passes constitutional muster. [Citation given]. If the law burdens conduct that falls within the Second Amendment's scope, we then proceed to apply the appropriate

level of means-ends scrutiny. We agree … that the appropriate level of scrutiny "depends on the nature of the conduct being regulated and the degree to which the challenged law burden the right." [Citations given].[18]

The judge further noted,

A regulation that threatens a right at the core of the Second Amendment … triggers strict scrutiny. [Citations given]. A less severe regulation—a regulation that does not encroach on the core of the Second Amendment—requires a less demanding means-ends showing. [Citations provided]. This more lenient level of scrutiny could be called "intermediate scrutiny" [and] requires the government to demonstrate a "reasonable fit" between the challenged regulation and an "important" government objective. [Citations provided].[19]

Prado recognized a major issue with this approach. He wrote,

We admit that it is difficult to map H*eller's* "longstanding" "presumptively lawful regulatory measures" onto this two-step framework. It is difficult to discern whether "longstanding prohibitions on the possession of firearms by felons and the mentally ill, … or laws imposing conditions and qualifications on the commercial sale of arms," … either (i) presumptively fail to burden conduct protected by the Second Amendment, or (ii) presumptively trigger and pass constitutional muster under a lenient level of scrutiny. … For now, we state that a longstanding presumptively lawful regulatory measure … would likely fall outside the ambit of the Second Amendment; that is, such a measure would likely be upheld at step one of our framework. … We further state that a longstanding measure that harmonizes with the history and tradition of arms regulation … even if [it] advanced to step two … would trigger our version of "intermediate" scrutiny.[20]

The judge continued,

In addition, *Heller* demonstrates that a regulation can be deemed "longstanding" even if it cannot boast a precise founding-era analogue. … After all, *Heller* considered firearm possession bans on felons and the mentally ill to be longstanding, yet the current versions of these bans are of mid-20th century vintage. [Citations provided.] … [W]e reject the contention that every regulation impinging upon the Second Amendment right must trigger strict scrutiny. [Citation provided]. … [W]e believe that a law impinging upon the Second Amendment must be reviewed under … a level that is proportionate to the severity of the burden that the law imposes on the right.[21]

After reviewing the legislative background of the challenged laws, and observing that Congress's intent in passing those laws was to curb violent crime with age-based, categorical restrictions on handgun access, Prado moved to step one of the proposed two-step framework. In determining whether the statutes burdened Second Amendment-protected conduct, he first considered Founding-Era attitudes. He observed that around the time of the founding, the "historical record shows that gun safety regulation was commonplace … [and included] laws disarming certain groups and restricting sales to certain groups. [Citations provided]."[22]

Citing the classical republican theory of a "virtuous citizenry," Prado argued that this theory permitted laws disarming individuals deemed incapable of virtue, such as criminals, the mentally imbalanced, and "infants." He noted that, historically, the term "infant" applied to persons under the age of twenty-one. He concluded, "If a representative citizen of the founding era conceived of a 'minor' as an individual who was unworthy of the Second Amendment guarantee … then it stands to reason that the citizen would have supported restricting an 18-to-20 year-old's right to keep and bear arms."[23]

The judge then moved on to relevant evidence from the nineteenth century, remarking that by the end of this century, nineteen states had expressly restricted individuals under twenty-one from purchasing or using particular firearms, and by 1923, twenty-two states had such laws. Prado additionally observed that multiple nineteenth-century courts and influential commentators had upheld age-based restrictions on the purchase of firearms. These sources maintained that "restrictions on the ability of persons under 21 to purchase firearms comported with the Second Amendment guarantee. [Citations provided.]"[24]

Judge Prado concluded,

> We have summarized considerable evidence that burdening … the ability of 18-to-20-year-olds to purchase handguns from FFLs is consistent with a longstanding historical tradition, which suggests that the conduct at issue falls outside the Second Amendment's protection. … Nonetheless, we face institutional challenges in conducting a definitive review of the relevant historical record. Although we are inclined to uphold the challenged federal laws at step one … we proceed to step two.[25]

Step two requires the court to determine the level of scrutiny to employ in evaluating the severity of the laws' infringement on the Second Amendment and the "fit" between the law and the governmental objective. The judge asserted,

> Unquestionably, the challenged federal laws triggers nothing more than "intermediate" scrutiny. … The narrow ambit of the ban's target mitigates against strict scrutiny. … The Second Amendment, at its core, protects "law-abiding, '*responsible*' citizens. [*Heller* citation]. Congress found that persons under 21 to be relatively irresponsible and can be prone to violent crime …. [T]hese laws … do not prevent 18-to-20-year-olds from possessing and using handguns … they may acquire handguns from responsible parents or guardians; and they may possess, use, and purchase long-guns. Accordingly, the scheme is sufficiently bounded to avoid strict scrutiny."[26]

After additionally noting that the age laws had only a temporary effect, further reducing the burden they created, Prato then employed intermediate scrutiny to determine "whether there is a reasonable fit between the law and an important government objective."[27] His review of congressional concerns and the legislative background of the statutes indicated that

> the government has satisfied its burden of showing a reasonable means-ends fit between the challenged federal laws and an important government interest. First, curbing violent crime perpetuated by young persons ... constitutes an important government objective. [Citation provided]. Second, Congress selected means that were reasonably adapted to achieving that objective. ... We therefore hold that the challenged federal laws are constitutional under the Second Amendment. *Heller* does not cast doubt on them.[28]

The constitutional analyses used in the *Rene* and *NRA* decisions—with their reliance on *Heller*'s directive regarding "longstanding prohibitions"—characterized not just the federal judiciary's approach to age-based gun statutes. State-based adjudications also adopted this orientation. For instance, seventeen-year-old Alberto Aguilar, in a 2013 Illinois Supreme Court case, contested his conviction for violating an "unlawful possession of a firearm" statute. He argued that the state's abrogation of his ability to protect himself with a handgun infringed his Second Amendment rights. The state rejected this argument, citing *Heller*'s "longstanding prohibitions" directive.[29] But about a decade later, after clarifications contained in the US Supreme Court's *Bruen* decision, the judiciary adopted a different approach in adjudicating Second Amendment gun law challenges. The next case, *NRA v. Bondi*, highlights this approach.

NRA v. Bondi (2023): Challenging Florida Statute §790.065 (13) (High School Public Safety Act)

Reacting to a mass shooting at Marjory Stoneman Douglas High School in 2018, the Florida legislature enacted Florida Statute §790.065 (13), banning the sale of firearms to eighteen- to twenty-year-olds. The law attempted "to comprehensively address the crisis of gun violence, including but not limited to, gun violence on school campuses."[30] Arguing that the law violated the Second and Fourteen Amendments, the NRA challenged the statute but lost in district court. On appeal, the case came before a panel of the Eleventh Circuit, with Circuit Judge Robin Rosenbaum authoring the court's opinion.

Judge Rosenbaum began her analysis by noting,

> Even though 18-to-20-year-olds now account for less than 4% of the population, they are responsible for more than 15% of homicide and manslaughter arrests ... under-21-year-old gunmen continue to intentionally target others—now, with disturbing regularity, in schools. ... But State governments have never been required to stand idly by and watch the carnage rage. In fact, during the

> Reconstruction Era—when the people adopted the Fourteen Amendment, thereby making the Second Amendment applicable to the States—many States responded to gun violence by 18-to-20-year-olds by prohibiting that age group from even possessing deadly weapons like pistols.[31]

The judge continued,

> The Marjory Stoneman Douglas High School Public Safety Act ("the Act") precludes those under 21 only from buying firearms while leaving that age group free to possess and use firearms of any legal type. [Citation given]. That kind of law is consistent with our Nation's historical tradition of firearm regulation. Indeed, the Supreme Court has already identified "laws imposing conditions and qualifications on the commercial sale of firearms' as "longstanding" and therefore "presumptively lawful" firearm regulations. [*Heller* citation]. Florida's law does just that by imposing a minimum age as a qualification for buying firearms.[32]

After noting *Heller*'s admonition that gun rights were "not unlimited," Rosenbaum discussed the change the *Bruen* decision imposed on the judicial analysis of gun cases. *Bruen* made clear

> Now, "when the Second Amendment's plain text covers an individual's conduct, the Constitution presumptively protects that conduct." [*Bruen* citation]. To rebut that presumption, "the government must demonstrate that" a state's "regulation" of that conduct "is consistent with this Nation's historical tradition of firearm regulation." [*Bruen* citation]. ... Like the Fifth Circuit, we read *Bruen* as articulating two analytical steps. [Citation provided]. First, we consider the plain text of the Amendment, as informed by historical tradition. Second, we look for a historical analogue—not a historical "dead ringer" [*Bruen* citation].—of the challenged law.[33]

Rosenbaum then asserted,

> The Reconstruction Era historical sources are the most relevant to our inquiry on the scope of the right to keep and bear arms. That is so because those sources reflect the public understanding of the right to keep and bear arms at the very time the states made that right applicable to the state governments by ratifying the Fourteenth Amendment. ... [The] historical sources from the Reconstruction Era are more probative of the Second Amendment's scope than those from the Founding Era. ... [B]ecause the Fourteenth Amendment is what *caused* the Second Amendment to apply to the States, the Reconstruction Era understanding of the right to bear arms—that is, the understanding that prevailed when the States adopted the Fourteenth Amendment—is what matters.[34]

The judge further noted that, as the Supreme Court emphasized,

> "When it comes to interpreting the Constitution, not all history is created equal" [and that] "Constitutional rights are enshrined with the scope they were understood to have *when the people adopted them*." [*Bruen* citation]. ... The key takeaway ... is that the States are "bound to respect the right to keep and bear arms because of the Fourteenth Amendment, not the Second." [*Bruen* citation]. And so the understanding of the Second Amendment right that ought to control in this case—where a State law is at issue—is the one shared by the people who adopted "the Fourteenth Amendment, not the Second." [Citations provided].[35]

After acknowledging that the Supreme Court has generally "assumed" the scope of a right is determined by the public understanding of the right in 1791 (when Congress adopted the Bill of Rights), Rosenbaum observed, "But an assumption is not a holding ... [and] it makes no sense to suggest that the States would have bound themselves to an understanding of the Bill of Rights—including that of the Second Amendment—that they did not share when they ratified the Fourteenth Amendment."[36] Having determined that Reconstruction Era sources were more probative than Founding-Era sources, the judge then considered *Bruen*'s two analytical steps.

Regarding the first step, Rosenbaum noted that Florida did not contest the NRA's contention that eighteen- to twenty-year-olds were part of "the people" protected by the Second Amendment. She also noted she would assume the amendment's plain text covered their right to buy firearms. Then, moving to the second step, she stated this required Florida to demonstrate that its firearms regulation was part of a historical tradition—i.e., by showing that the modern statute was "relevantly similar" to historical regulations in how and why the statute curtailed a citizen's Second Amendment rights. She indicated that "the government need only 'identify a well-established and representative *analogue*, not a historical twin.' [*Bruen* citation]."[37]

Asserting that such representative historical analogues existed, she continued, "In fact ... regulations from the Reconstruction Era burdened law-abiding citizens' rights to armed self-defense to an even greater extent and for the same reason as the Act does. In other words, at *Bruen's* second step, Florida has satisfied its burden as to both 'how' and 'why.'" She noted that Alabama, Tennessee and Kentucky all passed laws prohibiting eighteen- to twenty-year-olds from buying (and sometimes possessing) firearms twelve years before ratification of the Fourteenth Amendment. Further, Rosenbaum observed that the Alabama and Tennessee laws also made it illegal to even *lend* arms to that age group—thus imposing a more severe restriction on the right to arms than the Florida statute.[38]

Turning to the "why" of these laws, the judge asserted that both the past and present statutes burden the Second Amendment for an identical reason: to enhance public safety. She pointed out that the Florida law addressed gun violence on school campuses, noting that public universities "have long prohibited students from possessing firearms on campus."[39] She cited an 1810 University of Georgia resolution that prohibited students from keeping firearms and other offensive weapons "in College or elsewhere"; she stated, "Just over a decade later, the University of Virginia passed a resolution—with supporting votes from Thomas Jefferson and James Madison—that prohibited students from keeping or using 'weapons or arms of any kind, or gunpowder' on school grounds."[40]

Continuing, Judge Rosenbaum observed,

> Between the Fourteenth Amendment's ratification and the close of the nineteenth century, at least sixteen states and the District of Columbia joined Alabama, Kentucky, and Tennessee—a total of at least twenty jurisdictions—in banning sales of firearms to 18-to-20-year-olds. These regulations, like their pre-ratification predecessors, were state responses to the problem of death and injuries that underage firearm users inflicted. ... Thus, we have no trouble concluding that the Reconstruction Era statutes serve as historical analogues for the Act. ... Our conclusion ... finds further support from Reconstruction Era newspapers. ... Based on newspapers from the Reconstruction Era, historians have confirmed that the public did not understand the right to keep and bear arms to protect the rights of 18-to-20-year-olds to purchase such weapons. In fact much of the public at the time supported such restrictions. [Citations provided].[41]

The judge additionally observed,

> The courts generally shared the public's approval of laws that prohibited providing handguns and other dangerous weapons to minors. Take the Supreme Court of Tennessee ... [in 1878] that same court described [a Tennessee statute]—which prohibited "the sale, gift, or loan of a pistol or other dangerous weapon to a minor"—as "not only constitutional ... but wise and salutary in all its provisions." [Citations provided]. ... [L]egal scholars [also] viewed the Reconstruction Era statutes as constitutional. Thomas Cooley "wrote a massively popular 1868 Treatise on Constitutional Limitations." [*Heller* citation]. Cooley's treatise espoused the view that states could use their police power to prohibit the sale of arms to minors. [Citation given].[42]

Asserting that these points all demonstrate the Florida statute's consistency with the country's historical tradition of firearms regulation, Rosenbaum then addressed the opposing argument advanced by the NRA. She stated,

> The NRA responds that Founding Era federal law obligated 18-to-20-year-olds to join the militia. [Citation provided]. ... the NRA contends that the fact that Congress required 18-to-20-year-olds to muster for the militia is compelling evidence that 18-to-20-year-olds had the right to an unimpeded ability to purchase firearms. The NRA's conclusion is incorrect. The NRA mistakes a legal obligation for a right. ... The fact that federal law obliged 18-to-20-year-olds to join the militia does not mean that 18-to-20-year-olds had an absolute right to buy arms. ... Congress imposed upon 18-to-20-year-olds a specific obligation to serve in the militia but did not give them all the rights associated with full citizenship (like, at that time, the right to vote). So we can't infer from the fact that 18-to-20-year-olds had a specific obligation that they had a specific right.[43]

Judge Rosenbaum concluded,

> Because Florida's Act is at least as modest as the firearm prohibitions on 18-to-20-year-olds in the Reconstruction Era and enacted for the same reason as those laws, it is "relevantly similar" to those Reconstruction Era laws. [*Bruen* citation]. And as a result, it does not violate the Second Amendment. We therefore affirm the district court's order granting summary judgment in Florida's favor. AFFIRMED.[44]

Not surprisingly, the NRA disagreed with the panel court's analysis and opinion and asked for (and was granted) an en-banc rehearing of the case. Thus, the whole Eleventh Circuit will at some point revisit the constitutionality of the Florida statute, but currently the outcome is pending.

The next case, originating in an Eighth Circuit US District Court in Minnesota, foreshadows a major issue the en-banc Eleventh Circuit will likely consider: which historical period—the Founding Era or the Reconstruction Era—should courts use in determining the "prevailing understanding" of the right to bear arms? Rosenbaum's analysis endorses the "prevailing understanding" reflected in Reconstruction Era historical documents and legislation. The Minnesota court endorses a Founding-Era perspective and arrives at a different conclusion.

Worth v. Harrington (2023): Challenging Minnesota's Gun Permit Age Requirement (§624.714)

For individuals who wish to carry a pistol in public, Minnesota statute §624.714 requires that they first obtain a permit. However, the statute makes otherwise permit-eligible individuals ineligible if they are not at least twenty-one years old. Kristin Worth (and other plaintiffs not yet twenty-one) wanted to carry a pistol for self-protection, and she challenged the statute as a violation of her Second Amendment rights. The case came before US District Judge Katherine Menendez, nominated to the federal judiciary by President Joe Biden.[45]

Judge Menendez began her analysis by briefly reviewing the impact of the *Heller*, *McDonald*, and *Bruen* rulings on the judiciary's understanding of Second Amendment jurisprudence. Observing that *Bruen* rejected the two-step, means-end scrutiny approach that federal appellate courts adopted after *Heller* and *McDonald*, she explained *Bruen*'s standard for determining a firearm statute's constitutionality: "plain text" analysis and "historical tradition" analysis. She asserted, "*Bruen* requires a court to conduct a 'textual analysis' that is 'focused on the "normal and ordinary" meaning of the Second Amendment's language.' [*Heller* citation]."[46]

Continuing, she stated,

> This inquiry into the "normal meaning" of the "words and phrases used" is … focused on what those words meant in 1791 when the Second Amendment was ratified …. A court … can employ several tools in discerning the text's normal and ordinary meaning. These may include: (1) comparison of a phrase within

> the Second Amendment to the same or similar language used elsewhere in the Constitution [*Heller* citation]; (2) consideration of historical sources ...; (3) evaluation of the historical background leading to the Second Amendment's adoption .... [Citations provided].[47]

Turning to historical tradition, the judge asserted,

> If the normal and ordinary meaning of the Second Amendment's text protects the individual's proposed course of conduct, then the Amendment "presumptively guarantees" the individual's right related to firearms, and the burden falls on the government to justify the challenged regulation. [*Bruen* citation]. However, *Bruen* held that this justification cannot be based on the policy reasons that motivated the regulation at issue. ... Instead, the government must show that the law is "consistent with this Nation's historical tradition of firearm regulation." [*Bruen* citation]. ... Courts applying Bruen must consider "whether modern and historical regulations impose a comparable burden on the right of armed self-defense and whether that burden is comparably justified." [*Bruen* citation].[48]

Applying this framework to Minnesota's age requirement, Menendez stated,

> Textual analysis requires the Court to consider the Plaintiff's "proposed course of conduct" and ask whether the Second Amendment's plain text "covers that conduct." [*Bruen* citation]. It is already settled that the plain text of the Second Amendment covers "carrying handguns publicly for self-defense" [*Bruen* citation] and here, the parties do not dispute that the course of conduct proposed by the Plaintiffs involves doing just that. ... But that clarity does not end the textual analysis. In this case, the dispute is not about whether the conduct is covered by the text, but whether the Plaintiffs are covered if they engage in that conduct. The parties disagree whether the Plaintiffs are among "the people" referred to in the Second Amendment's operative clause.[49]

The judge elaborated,

> Plaintiffs argue that the Second Amendment's reference to *the people* applies to *all* the people, including adults who are over the age of eighteen, but not yet twenty-one. Defendants argue that the plain and ordinary meaning of 'the people' as understood at the time the Second and Fourteenth were adopted, would not have included persons under twenty-one, and adopting the Plaintiffs' *all*-the-people reading too literally would lead to absurd results, such as allowing young children to publicly carry firearms. For the reasons that follow, the Court concludes that the Second Amendment's plain text is better read to include adults 18 and older in its protections.[50]

Menendez based this conclusion on four considerations. First, she noted that "Neither *Heller* nor *Bruen* addressed the specific issue of whether the Second

Amendment's text protects the rights of 18-to-20 year olds. But because the normal and ordinary meaning of 'the people' includes all Americans who are part of the national community, the right codified by the Amendment appears to include them. [Citations provided]."[51] Second, she observed that, despite the Founders placing age requirements in other parts of the Constitution, "neither the Second Amendment's text nor other provisions within the Bill of Rights include an age limit."[52] Third, the judge asserted, "the inclusion of 'the people' elsewhere in the Bill of Rights supports the interpretation that the Second Amendment extends to individuals over the age of 18. ...Although one can find certain limitations upon the rights of young people secured by both the First and Fourth Amendments, neither has been interpreted to exclude 18-to-20 year olds from their protection."[53]

Menendez's last consideration focused on Founding-Era militia laws. She asserted that these laws

> lend support to the understanding that "the people" ... includes18-to-20 year olds. ... [T]he majority of pre-ratification and post-ratification militia laws suggest that persons between the ages of 18 and 20 were expected to supply their own weapons in connection with militia service. [Citation provided]. ... Founding-era militia laws requiring service in the militia by 18-to-20 year olds who are responsible for supplying their own weapons is consistent with a contemporary understanding that this age group was not excluded from the class of persons who had the right to keep and bear arms.[54]

Addressing the defendants' argument that the militia laws' imposition of a *duty* to bear arms does not necessarily confer an individual *right*, Menendez responded, "While true, the significance of the ... founding-era militia laws ... is not that they *created* a right to keep and bear arms ... [but] that they provide some indication that the existing right to keep and bear arms likely included those who were included in the already existing militia."[55] Determining that the Second Amendment presumptively guaranteed the Plaintiffs' right to publicly carry a handgun for self-defense, the judge indicated that, under *Bruen*, the defendants now had to demonstrate that the statute's age requirement was consistent with the nation's history and tradition of firearms regulation.

On this point, she concluded,

> Based on a careful review of the record, the Court finds that Defendants have failed to identify analogous regulations that show a historical tradition in America of depriving 18–20-year-olds the right to publicly carry a handgun for self-defense. ... In searching for historical analogues, the Court must first decide where to look. ... Plaintiffs insist that 1791, when the Second Amendment was ratified, and the nearby years of the founding era are the most relevant historical reference points for finding analogous firearms regulations. In contrast, the Commissioner argues the years surrounding 1868, the year the Fourteenth Amendment was ratified, mark the correct period.[56]

Menendez then noted that the Eleventh Circuit also confronted this issue in *Bondi* (2023), and concluded that the 1868 period was the more relevant period. Despite being sympathetic to that court's arguments, Menendez disagreed.

She argued,

> But, in this Court's view, *Bondi* declined to follow rather clear signs that the Supreme Court favors 1791 as the date for determining the historical snapshot of "the people" whose understanding of the Second Amendment matters. *See Bruen* at 2137 ("And we have generally assumed that the scope of the protection applicable to the Federal Government and States is pegged to the public understanding of the right when the Bill of Rights was adopted in 1791."). *Bondi* does not mention the *Bruen* Court's warning to "guard against giving post-enactment history more weight than it can rightly bear." … This reasoning makes it difficult to agree with the Commissioner's position that 1868 should control. Other courts applying *Bruen's* second step have similarly placed particular emphasis on founding-era analogues. [Citations provided].[57]

Specifically considering the defendants' historical analogues, the judge rejected as not "relevantly similar" early college campus restrictions on student possession of firearms. She argued, "none of these proposed analogues appears to be the product of a legislative body elected by founding-era voters … [and] identifying that a proposed analogue and a modern regulation are both aimed at promoting safety … is not enough to suggest that the campus rules are 'distinctly similar' historical analogues."[58] She further noted that the two Founding-Era municipal laws cited were not relevantly similar because "they burden the right to bear arms for different reasons and in different ways than Minnesota's age requirement. … they place restrictions on the discharge of firearms, but do not ban carrying them outright … [and] both the laws governed conduct regardless of age, prohibiting conduct of adults of any age."[59]

Menendez also found the defendants' Reconstruction-era analogues insufficient. She noted that the cited laws

> were enacted decades over the founding [and] none of these regulations is "relevantly similar" to the age requirement in Minnesota's permit-to-carry law. Several … prohibited sales of firearms to minors but did not place restrictions on minors receiving them from parents or even employers. And other proffered laws limited firearm possession by those under the age of 16, but not the 18-to-20-year-old cohort at issue in Minnesota's law. [Citations provided]. … These restrictions do not burden the Second Amendment right in a manner distinctly similar to the age requirement.[60]

Menendez concluded her analysis by stating that the plaintiffs were entitled to judgment as a matter of law. She asserted, "Based on the record here, the Court grants Plaintiffs' motion for summary judgment …. Because the Court has concluded that the age requirement is unconstitutional, Defendants will ultimately be enjoined from denying a permit to carry a pistol from an otherwise-qualified applicant who is at least 18 years old."[61]

Minnesota appealed the court's decision, but in July of 2024, the Eighth Circuit, after reviewing the evidence, also concluded the statute was unconstitutional and affirmed the district court's ruling. Further, Judge Menendez's analysis and application of *Bruen* had already influenced other federal courts. Just two months after publication, a US district court in Virginia adjudicated (in *Fraser v. BATFE)* a similar constitutional challenge to the age-related restriction contained in 18 U.S.C. §922. Examining many of the same arguments raised in *Worth*, that court observed, "The analysis in *Worth* is an especially well-reasoned approach."[62] After applying the guidance elaborated in *Bruen*, the *Frazer* court also found that statute's age restriction unconstitutional. The last case in this section—a Third Circuit Court of Appeals adjudication—continues in this vein.

Lara v. Commissioner PA State Police (2024/5): Challenging PA's Uniform Firearms Act

The Pennsylvania Uniform Firearms Act (UFA) forbids individuals from carrying a concealed firearm without a license, and it requires them to be at least twenty-one years old to apply for a license. Pennsylvanians without a license can normally carry openly, except during proclaimed states of emergency. Taken together, and considering that Pennsylvania had been under a state of emergency for nearly three years when the plaintiffs filed suit, these regulations had the effect of preventing eighteen- to twenty-year-olds from carrying firearms in public places. Wanting to carry for self-defense, Madison Lara and two other plaintiffs challenged the enforcement of the statutes as a violation of the Second Amendment. When the district court dismissed their case, they appealed to the circuit court. Circuit Judge Kent Jordan, nominated to the federal judiciary by President George W. Bush, wrote the opinion for the court.[63]

After observing that the *Bruen* opinion rejected the means-end analytical approach courts had previously used in evaluating gun regulation challenges, Jordan explained the two-step procedure contained in *Bruen*: "plain text" analysis and "historical tradition" analysis. He stated that, if the "'normal and ordinary' meaning of the Second Amendment's language ... applies to the conduct at issue, 'the Constitution presumptively protects that conduct.' [*Bruen* citation]. At the second step, a court determines whether the regulation in question 'is consistent with the Nation's historical tradition of firearm regulation.' [*Bruen* citation]."[64] The judge further explained that "the government bears the burden of identifying a 'founding-era' historical analogue to the modern firearm regulation ... because '[c]onstitutional rights are enshrined with the scope they were understood to have when the people adopted them.' [*Bruen* citation]."[65]

In assessing the similarity of current regulations to their potential historical analogues, Jordan observed that courts had to "consider both 'how and why the regulations [being compared] burden a law-abiding citizen's right to armed self-defense.' [*Bruen* citation]."[66] Continuing, the judge noted, "In defense of the Pennsylvania statutes, the Commissioner first argues that 18-to-20-year-olds are not among 'the people' protected by the Second Amendment and the Appellants' challenge therefore fails the first step of the *Bruen* test. ... To succeed on this argument, the Commissioner must overcome the strong presumption that the Second Amendment applies to 'all Americans.' [*Heller* citation]."[67]

After citing a past adjudication—*Range v. Attorney General*—that interpreted "the people" quite broadly, Jordan observed, "The Commissioner endeavors to argue around that conclusion by saying that, '[a]t the time of the Founding—and, indeed, for most of the Nation's history—those who were under the age of 21 were considered "infants" or "minors" in the eyes of the law ... mean[ing] they had few independent legal rights.' "[68] The judge dismissed this argument for three reasons. He argued, "First, it supposes that the first step of a *Bruen* analysis requires excluding individuals from 'the people' if they were so excluded at the founding. That argument conflates *Bruen's* two distinct analytical steps."[69]

He continued,

> Although the government is tasked with identifying a historical analogue at the second step ..., we are not limited to looking through that same retrospective lens at the first step. If, at step one, we were rigidly limited by eighteenth century conceptual boundaries, "the people" would consist of white, landed men, and that is obviously not the state of the law. ... Second, it does not follow that, just because individuals under the age of 21 lacked certain legal rights at the founding, they were ex ante excluded from the scope of "the people." As then-Judge Barrett explained, "[n]either felons nor the mentally ill are categorically excluded from our national community." [Citation provided].[70]

Regarding the last reason, Jordan noted,

> Third, consistency has a claim on us. It is undisputed that 18-to-20-year-olds are among "the people" for other constitutional rights .... As we recently observed in *Range*, there is "no reason to adopt an inconsistent reading of 'the people.'" Indeed, wholesale exclusion of 18-to-20-year-olds from the scope of the Second Amendment would impermissibly render "the constitutional right to bear arms in public for self-defense ... 'a second-class right subject to an entirely different body of rules than the other Bill of Rights guarantees.' [*Bruen* citation, quoting *McDonald*]."[71]

The judge then concluded, "We therefore hold that 18-to-20-year-olds are, like other subsets of the American public, presumptively among 'the people' to whom Second Amendment rights extend. If ... the Commonwealth can restrict the rights of 18-to-20-year-olds with respect to firearms ... the Commissioner must make that argument by showing that such restrictions are part of the nation's historical tradition of gun regulation."[72]

Before considering the Commissioner's historical arguments, Jordan addressed the issue of determining the relevant historical timeframe involved: 1791, when the

Second Amendment was ratified, or 1868, when the Fourteenth Amendment was ratified. He observed,

> While the Supreme Court has not held that all constitutional rights that have been made applicable to the states must be construed according to their public meaning in 1791, the Commissioner has not articulated a theory for defining some rights according to their public meaning in 1791 and others according to their public meaning in 1868. Moreover, *Bruen* has already instructed that historical evidence from 1791 is relevant to understanding the scope of the Second Amendment as incorporated against the states. [*Bruen* citation]. Accordingly … we hold that the Second Amendment should be understood according to its public meaning in 1791.[73]

The judge continued,

> We thus set aside the Commissioner's catalogue of statutes from the mid-to-late nineteenth century, as each was enacted at least 50 years after [1791]. What is left is an eighteenth century statute … which prohibited "carry[ing] any gun or hunt[ing] on the improved or inclosed lands of any plantation other than his own[.]" But we can discern no near equivalence or significant analogue between the burdens imposed by that statute and those at issue here. … to the extent the statute did burden the right to carry a gun in public, it did so without singling out 18-to-20-year-olds.[74]

Jordan contrasted the "conspicuously" sparse record of state regulations focused on eighteen- to twenty-year-olds during this period with the Second Militia Act of 1792. He noted, "The Act required all-able bodied men to enroll in the militia and arm themselves upon turning 18. [Citation provided]. That young adults had to serve in the militia indicates that founding-era lawmakers believed those youths could, and indeed should, keep and bear arms."[75]

Addressing some issues and implications raised by the Commissioner regarding the Militia Act, the judge stated, "No doubt the Commissioner is correct that a duty to possess guns in a militia or National Guard setting is distinguishable from a right to bear arms unconnected to such service. … Still, the Second Militia Act is good circumstantial evidence of the public understanding [in 1791] … as to whether 18-to-20-year-olds could be armed."[76]

After considering and ruling on several non-Second Amendment questions associated with the case, Jordan concluded, "we will reverse the decision of the District Court and remand with instructions to enter an injunction forbidding the Commissioner from arresting law-abiding 18-to-20-year-olds who openly carry firearms during a state of emergency declared by the Commonwealth."[77] The state appealed Judge Jordan's ruling to the Supreme Court for certiorari review, which that court eventually granted.[78]

But before this review, the Supreme Court adjudicated *United States v. Rahimi*—an opinion that reversed a lower-court opinion and upheld the constitutionality of a related federal firearms regulation (see Chapters 7 and 9). Turning then to the Third Circuit's *Lara* opinion, the Supreme Court vacated Jordan's initial ruling and remanded the case back to the Third Circuit for further consideration in light of *Rahimi*.[79]

On remand, after reiterating much of its earlier analysis and examining the *Bruen* analytic clarifications contained in *Rahimi*, the circuit court concluded that "our prior analysis reflects the approach taken in *Bruen* and clarified in *Rahimi*. ... Having determined that Rahimi sustains our prior analysis, we will again reverse and remand the District Court's judgment."[80]

Taken as a set, these adjudications clearly highlight the impact the *Bruen* decision has had on age-related Second Amendment questions. Prior to *Bruen*, intermediate scrutiny typically supported the constitutionality of age-related restrictions. But with *Bruen*'s emphasis on demonstrating a tradition of at least relevantly similar historical analogues, and with interest-balancing no longer a consideration, the constitutionality of such restrictions has become uncertain. Even in the post-*Bruen Bondi* opinion upholding such restrictions, the decision centered on the use of Reconstruction-era analogues. Given the Supreme Court's expressed skepticism about the relevance of evidence from this period, it seems unlikely that this opinion will stand.

2009–24: Drug Users as Dangerous Individuals

The "text, history and tradition" analytical approach emphasized in *Bruen* (and implied earlier in *Heller* and *McDonald*) did not just called into question the constitutionality the age-related statutes discussed above. Defendants also began to challenge the constitutionality of gun prohibitions imposed on drug addicts and other habitual users of illegal substances. Contained in the Gun Control Act of 1968, the initial prohibiting statute—18 U.S.C. §922 (h) (3)—made it illegal for an individual who was "an unlawful user of or addicted to marihuana or any depressant or stimulant drug ... or narcotic drug" to receive a firearm. Amended by the 1986 Firearm Owners' Protection Act, the statute moved to subsection (g)(3), and further forbade the *possession* of a firearm by such individuals.

Many of the pre-*Heller* challenges to 18 U.S.C. §922 (g) (3) were not based on the Second Amendment. In 1999, Jason Edwards appealed his conviction for possessing a firearm while being an unlawful user of a controlled substance on the grounds that the phrase "unlawful user of a controlled substance" was unconstitutionally vague—it failed to specify a time frame regarding the use of the controlled substance and the possession of the firearm. The Fifth Circuit Court of Appeals rejected this argument and affirmed conviction.[81] Similarly, in 2001, Ronnie Purdy also challenged the statute as unconstitutionally vague, as applied to him. The Ninth Circuit Court of Appeals disagreed and affirmed his conviction.[82] The Fourth Circuit Court of Appeals[83] in 2002 and the Eighth Circuit[84] in 2003 also rejected "vagueness" challenges to 18 U.S.C. §922 (g) (3).

In 2005, Nolon Patterson likewise appealed a conviction based on this statute. But he argued that the statute was both vague and overbroad *and* that it violated the

Second Amendment. In rejecting his contentions, the Fifth Circuit Appeals Court noted that the

> right to bear arms is subject to "limited, narrowly tailored specific exceptions … that are reasonable and not inconsistent with the right of Americans generally to individually keep and bear their private arms as historically understood …." (*Emerson* citation.) Congress may prohibit those who pose a risk to society, like felons, from exercising the right to bear arms [and] unlawful users of controlled substances pose a risk to society if permitted to bear arms.[85]

The *Patterson* adjudication, relying on reasoning in *Emerson*—an opinion that foreshadowed the Supreme Court's *Heller* decision—provides the background for the four cases considered in this section. The first two—*Richard* (2009) and *Seay* (2010)—are post-*Heller* opinions influenced by that decision. The next two—*Daniels* (2023) and *Veasley* (2024)—are post-*Bruen* opinions shaped by that adjudication.

United States v. Richard (2009): Challenging18 U.S.C. §922 (g) (3) (Gun Possession by Drug User)

Federal agents executing a search warrant seized drug paraphernalia and a rifle from Adam Richard's bedroom in a residence where he lived with his parents. Shortly afterward, Richard voluntarily met with members of various law enforcement agencies for an interview regarding the seized items. During the interview, he admitted to using methamphetamine for several years, consuming up to a gram each time, every other day or so. He also admitted his last usage had been a few days before the interview and that the rifle was a gift from his uncle. Richard said he possessed the rifle for about two years, and had last shot it about six months before.[86]

Subsequently, Richard was indicted and found guilty on one count of being a drug user in possession of a firearm, in violation of 18 U.S.C. §922 (g)(3). On appeal to the Tenth Circuit, Richard made several arguments, including (1) that the district court should have suppressed the evidence obtained due to lack of probable cause; (2) that he was denied due process; (3) that the statute was unconstitutionally vague as applied to him; and (4) that the statute violated his Second Amendment right to keep and bear arms. Circuit Judge Stephen Anderson, nominated to the federal judiciary by President Ronald Reagan, authored the opinion for the court.[87]

After a review of the relevant evidence, Anderson rejected Richard's first argument, concluding the "affidavit provided probable cause to believe that evidence of Mr. Richard's criminal activity would be found at [his] residence."[88] Regarding Richard's due-process argument, the judge chastised the agents' interviewing procedures, but he asserted, "the government's treatment of defendant was high-handed and arrogant [and] while definitely not commendable, the government's conduct did not amount to bad faith. We accordingly affirm the district court's denial of … acquittal on the ground that the Due Process clause of the Constitution was violated."[89]

Turning to Richard's contention that the statute was unconstitutionally vague as applied to him, the judge observed,

> In particular, [Richard] asserts that § 922 (g) (3) fails to apprise what conduct is prohibited and fails to establish minimal guidelines to govern law enforcement. … [He] argues that the government failed to prove he was an unlawful user of a controlled substance during the time period the firearm was in his bedroom and, additionally, that the government failed to prove a nexus between the unlawful use of a controlled substance (methamphetamine) and the possession of the firearm.[90]

Anderson dismissed this argument, referencing Richard's admissions to law enforcement officials. Given these admissions, the judge asserted, "the jury could reasonably infer that Mr. Richard possessed the firearm during the same period he was a regular and ongoing user of a controlled substance. We accordingly conclude the evidence was sufficient to support the jury's verdict."[91]

Finally, considering Richard's Second Amendment contention, Judge Anderson noted,

> In *District of Columbia v. Heller* (2008), the Supreme Court … specifically stated in *Heller* that "nothing in our opinion should be taken to cast doubt on longstanding prohibitions on the possession of firearms by felons and the mentally ill, or laws forbidding the carrying of firearms in sensitive places like schools and buildings." [Citations provided]. The Court also specifically stated its intention that such "presumptively lawful regulatory measures [act] only as examples; our list does not purport to be exhaustive." [*Heller* citation.] Accordingly, the individual right to bear arms protected by the Second Amendment is subject to appropriate restrictions like those contained in 18 U.S.C. § 922 (g) (3).[92]

Less than a year later, the Eighth Circuit considered a Second Amendment challenge to the statute, this challenge arguing that §922 (g) (3) was not just unconstitutional "as applied," but unconstitutional "facially." As Adam Richard did, Andrew Seay argued that the Second Amendment and *Heller* protected his right to arms. But the Eighth Circuit, like the Tenth, disagreed.

United States v. Seay (2010): Challenging 18 U.S.C. §922 (g) (3) (Gun Possession by Drug User)

Andrew Seay was on probation after a conviction for distribution and possession with intent to distribute marijuana. When a probation search of his vehicle and residence uncovered four firearms and marijuana, he was arrested and later indicted by a federal grand jury for violating 18 U.S.C. §922 (g) (3). He moved to dismiss the indictment on two grounds. One was a technical argument that the government unnecessarily delayed presenting his case to the grand jury; the other was that the indictment violated his Second Amendment rights. Seay eventually pled guilty to the charges, but after imposition of a nine-month sentence, he filed an appeal. Circuit Judge Bobby Shepherd, nominated to the federal judiciary by President George W. Bush, wrote the opinion for the Eighth Circuit.[93]

Shepherd first decided whether Seay, having already pled guilty, waived his right to bring an appeal. He noted that, by legal principle, a valid guilty plea is an admission of guilt that waives all non-jurisdictional defenses. Since Seay's "unnecessary delay" contention was non-jurisdictional in nature, that argument was waived and lost by his guilty plea. Turning to Seay's Second Amendment contention, Shepherd stated, "This is not an as-applied challenge; rather, Seay argues § 922(g) (3) is unconstitutional in all instances. ... We have previously held that such facial attacks are jurisdictional in nature and survive a valid guilty plea. ... [Since] Seay's constitutional argument survives his guilty plea, we now turn to the merits of his claim."[94]

After a brief overview of *Heller* and the Second Amendment, the judge asserted,

> In dicta, the [Supreme] Court emphasized that, "Like most rights, the right secured by the Second Amendment is not unlimited ... nothing in our opinion should be taken to cast doubt on longstanding prohibitions on the possession of firearms by felons and the mentally ill ....' "[*Heller* citation]. The Court noted that its list of presumptively valid law "does not purport to be exhaustive." ... Following *Heller*, many defendants have argued that 18 U.S.C. § 922(g), or some subsection thereof, violates the Second Amendment. To date none have succeeded.[95]

After listing seven federal adjudications supporting this assertion, Shepherd then focused specifically on §922 (g) (3). He continued,

> one circuit and several district courts have upheld § 922(g) (3) against Second Amendment attack. *See e.g., United States v. Richard ...; United States v. Korby ...; United States v. Lacy ...; United State v. Carter ...; United States v. Prince ...; United States v. Yancey...; see also United States v. Patterson* .... Nothing in Seay's argument convinces us that we should depart company from *every* other court to examine § 922(g) (3) following *Heller*. Further, § 922(g) (3) has the same historical pedigree as other portions of § 922(g) which are repeatedly upheld by numerous courts since *Heller*.[96]

Judge Shepherd concluded, "Moreover, in passing § 922(g) (3), Congress expressed its intention to 'keep firearms out of the possession of drug abusers, a dangerous class of individuals.' [Citation provided]. As such, we find that § 922(g) (3) is the type of 'longstanding prohibition[] on the possession of firearms' that *Heller* declared presumptively lawful. Accordingly, we reject Seay's facial challenge to § 922(g) (3)."[97]

As Shepherd asserted, despite *Heller*'s confirmation of an individual right to arms, that opinion's endorsement of "longstanding prohibitions" as "presumptively lawful" effectively foreclosed successful Second Amendment challenges to 18 U.S.C. §922

(g) (3). As the next two cases show—*Daniels* in 2023 and *Veasley* in 2024—the 2022 *Bruen* decision radically altered the legal landscape in this area.

United States v. Daniels (2023): Challenging 18 U.S.C. §922 (g) (3) (Gun Possession by Drug User)

In 2022, Patrick Daniels Jr. was stopped for driving without a license plate. When one of the officers, a Drug Enforcement Agent (DEA), smelled marijuana and searched the car, he found marijuana butts in the ashtray, a loaded 9-mm pistol, and a loaded semiautomatic rifle. Taken into custody at the local DEA office, Daniels admitted that he had been a regular user of marijuana since high school, and that he used the drug about every other day. The officers did not indicate that Daniels appeared intoxicated, he was never asked if he was under the influence, and he was not given a drug test. But based on his admissions, Daniels was charged with violating 18 U.S.C. §922 (g) (3).[98]

Daniels was still under indictment when the Supreme Court decided *Bruen*. He moved to dismiss the indictment, arguing that the statute failed *Bruen*'s new "history and tradition" standard, making it unconstitutional. The district court rejected this argument, and he was convicted of violating the gun statute in a jury trial. Daniels appealed, and Circuit Judge Jerry Smith, a Yale Law School graduate appointed to the federal judiciary by President Ronald Reagan, wrote the opinion for the Fifth Circuit.[99]

Smith stated that the gun statute made it illegal for "an unlawful user of ... any controlled substance ... to ... possess any firearm."[100] Observing further that an "unlawful user" was someone who used illegal drugs "regularly and in some temporal proximity to the gun possession,"[101] the judge noted that the district court had concluded Daniels was not a "law abiding, responsible citizen" and thus unlikely to be part of "the people" protected by the Second Amendment. That court further asserted, even if Daniels had a right to arms, §922 (g) (3) was a long-standing firearms regulation, similar "to laws disarming felons and the mentally ill that *Heller* called 'presumptively lawful.' [*Heller* citation]."[102]

Commenting on the district court's reasoning, Smith stated, "It engaged with few historical sources from the Founding or Reconstruction, but it relied on statements from other courts—notably all predating *Bruen*—that § 922(g) (3) was supported by the historical practice of disarming those who 'exhibit a dangerous lack of self-control.' [Citation provided]."[103] The judge then briefly reviewed how federal courts handled gun law challenges before *Bruen*, that is, using some level of means-end scrutiny.

He asserted,

> *Bruen* decisively rejected that kind of analysis. In place of means-end balancing, *Bruen* "requires" us to interpret the Second Amendment in light of its original public meaning. [*Bruen* citation]. As the Court explained, the Second Amendment codified a "*pre-existing* right" with pre-existing limits. To ascertain those limits, history is our heuristic. Because historical gun regulations evince the kind of limits that were well-understood at the time the Second Amendment was ratified,

> a regulation that is inconsistent with those limits is inconsistent with the Second Amendment.[104]

The judge then reviewed the two steps of the *Bruen* procedure—whether the amendment's plain text covers the individual's conduct; and if so, whether the modern gun restriction comports with the country's historical tradition of firearm regulation. He continued, "Only by showing that the law does not tread on the historical scope of the right can the government 'justify its regulation' [*Bruen* citation]."[105]

Addressing the difficulty of determining whether a historical regulation was meaningfully similar to a modern regulation, Smith asserted, "What matters is whether a conceptual fit exists between the old law and the new. ...they must both address a comparable problem (the 'why') and place a comparable burden on the rightsholder (the 'how'). [*Bruen* citation]. ... Deciding whether there is a match ... requires the exercise of both analogical reasoning and sound judgment."[106]

In considering whether the Second Amendment applied to Daniels, the judge observed that the right to bear arms was held by "the people," and that both *Heller* and the Bill of Rights indicated the term referred "to all members of our political community, not a special group of upright citizens. ...Even as a marijuana user, Daniels is a member of our political community. Therefore, he has a presumptive right to bear arms. By infringing on that right, § 922(g) (3) contradicts the plain text of the Second Amendment."[107]

Judge Smith acknowledged that both *Heller* and *Bruen* describe the Second Amendment as applying to "law-abiding, responsible citizens." He continued,

> The government seizes on that language and insists that that the Second Amendment does not extend to Daniels because he is a criminal. But we cannot read too much into the Supreme Court's chosen epithet. More than just "model citizens" enjoy the right to bear arms. [*Rahimi* citation]. Indeed, *Rahimi* ... reasoned that when *Heller* and *Bruen* used the phrase "law-abiding," it was just "shorthand" to "exclude from the ... discussion" the mentally ill and felons, people who were historically "stripped of their Second Amendment rights." [*Rahimi* citation]. All others are presumptively included in the Second Amendment's ambit.[108]

Concluding that Daniels had a presumptive right to arms, Smith shifted focus to whether history and tradition upheld §922 (g) (3). Noting that few drug regulations existed until the late nineteenth century, he asserted that laws regarding alcohol intoxication offered the closest similarity to §922 (g) (3). The judge stated that Founding-Era statutes relating to firearms and alcohol were few in number, and limited in scope and duration. They primarily centered on either the misuse of weapons while intoxicated or on prohibitions during militia duty. In the first category, Smith cited a 1656 Virginia statute that banned shooting while drinking, and a 1771 New York law that prohibited the firing of guns from December 31 to January 2.[109]

Regarding the Virginia statute, Smith stated that it was explicitly passed to conserve gun powder and because random gunshots could mistakenly convey an Indian attack. The judge noted, "Not only was the statute enacted for a different purpose, but it did not even ban gun possession or carry—it only prevented the colonists from misusing the guns they did have during bouts of drinking."[110] Similarly, he observed that the New York law only banned the firing of guns during drunken New Year's celebrations. While the statute focused on preventing public harm—like §922 (g) (3)—the judge asserted, "The law was strikingly narrow. It applied on only three days ...; it only prevented firing guns (not possessing them); and it applied only to those under the influence, not habitual drinkers. Beyond [these regulations] ... the government identifies no Founding era law or practice of disarming ordinary citizens for drunkenness, even if that intoxication was routine."[111]

Turning to the statutes regulating militia service, Smith observed that New Jersey (and Pennsylvania) could "disarm" soldiers who appeared for militia service "disguised in liquor" and that dram shops were banned from selling liquor to local soldiers. But he stated,

> Those laws ... are even less probative. For one thing, their purpose is different. They exist to insure a competent military .... Furthermore, the limitations applied only to the militia; none of the laws spoke to the ability of militiamen to carry outside of their military service. ... [R]estrictions on the liberties of servicemen tell us little about the limits acceptable for the general public.[112]

Judge Smith then considered the government's Reconstruction-era evidence, observing that three states between 1868 and 1883 prohibited carrying firearms while intoxicated. He stated,

> Those laws come closer to supporting § 922(g) (3), but they are notably few. The *Bruen* Court doubted that three colonial-era laws could suffice to show a tradition, let alone three laws passed eighty to ninety years after the Second Amendment was ratified. [*Bruen* citation]. More fatally, § 922(g) (3) is substantially broader than the postbellum intoxication laws. ... At most, the postbellum statutes support banning the *carry* of firearms *while under the influence*. Section 922(g) (3) bans all possession, and it does so for an undefined set of 'user[s]' even if they are not under the influence.[113]

The judge elaborated,

> As applied to Daniels, § 922(g) (3) is a significantly greater restriction of his rights than were any of the 19th-century laws. ... [T]here is a considerable difference between someone who is actively intoxicated and someone who is an "unlawful user" under § 922(g) (3). The statutory term "unlawful user" ... does not specify how recently an individual must "use" drugs to qualify for the prohibition. Daniels himself admitted to smoking marihuana fourteen days a month, but we do not know how much he used at those times, and the government presented no evidence that Daniels was intoxicated at the time he was found with a gun. Indeed, under

> the government's reasoning, Congress could ban gun possession by anyone who has multiple alcoholic drinks ... based on the postbellum intoxicated carry laws.[114]

Continuing, Smith asserted,

> A further problem with the Reconstruction-era statutes is precisely that they emerged during and after Reconstruction. ... A tradition cannot inform the original meaning of the Bill of Rights if it emerges one hundred years later. ... Even if the public understanding of the right to bear arms *did* evolve, it could not change the meaning of the Second Amendment, which was fixed when it first applied to the federal government in 1791.[115]

The judge then noted, "As an alternative, the government posits that the tradition of disarming the mentally ill supports § 922(g) (3). ... Those who are 'briefly mentally infirm as a result of intoxication' are similar to those 'permanently mentally infirm' because of illness or disability. [Citation provided]."[116]

Smith countered,

> [Even if] we assume that intoxication with marihuana is analogous to short time mental illness ... that comparison could justify disarming a citizen only while he is in a state comparable to lunacy. ... there is no tradition that supports disarming a sober citizen who is not currently under an impairing influence. ... The Founders ... allowed alcoholics to possess firearms while sober. We must ask ... which is Daniels more like: a categorically 'insane' person? Or a repeat alcohol user? Given his periodic marihuana usage, Daniels is firmly in the latter camp. ... In short, neither the restrictions on the mentally ill nor the regulatory tradition surrounding intoxication can justify Daniels' conviction.[117]

Judge Smith then addressed the argument that Congress could disarm individuals considered "dangerous" to public peace or safety. He observed, "[The government] contends that principle was well understood when the Second Amendment was ratified. And it posits that Daniels—a repeat marihuana user—was presumptively dangerous enough to be disarmed."[118] While Smith acknowledged that some historical evidence supported this position, he nonetheless concluded, "the historical examples of danger-based disarmament do not justify § 922(g) (3)'s application here."[119]

He noted that the government's examples were of two kinds—(1) states barring political dissidents (e.g., Loyalists) from owning guns during periods of conflict and (2) governments (both British and American) disarming religious minorities (e.g., Catholics). While accepting that these laws were based on concerns for public safety, he asserted, "Founding-era governments did not disarm Loyalists [and religious minorities] because they were thought to lack self-control; it was because both were viewed as potential threats to the integrity of the state."[120]

Smith also rejected the government's argument that the Militia Act of 1662—allowing the Crown to disarm individuals judged dangerous to the peace of the kingdom—as relevant. He noted that the Act was never integrated into American law and that the American right to bear arms was purposely made broader than its British predecessor. Similarly, he dismissed the government's contention that Congress could disarm dangerous citizens based on discussions limiting gun rights during the Constitution's ratification process. He countered, "Yet that language was not adopted. Instead, the People ratified the unqualified directive: 'shall not be infringed.' "[121]

The judge elaborated further,

> Assuming the Second Amendment encodes some government power to disarm the dangerous, the question becomes: At what level of generality may we implement that principle? … the legislature cannot have unchecked power to designate a group of persons as "dangerous" and thereby disarm them. Congress could claim that immigrants, the indigent, or the politically unpopular were presumptively "dangerous" and eliminate their Second Amendment rights …. To remain faithful to *Bruen*, the solution is to analogize to particular regulatory traditions instead of a general notion of "dangerousness." …We must ask: *Why* was the group considered dangerous at the time of the Founding … [and] *how* did the historical regulation limit the rights of the dangerous class? And [why] and how does the modern regulation do so?[122]

Smith concluded,

> Applying *Bruen's* framework … the government's theory of danger-based disarmament falls apart. … Daniels is not like the minorities who the Founders thought threatened violent revolt. … As applied in this case, the government has not shown how Daniels's marihuana use predisposes him to armed conflict or that he has a history of drug-related violence. … Daniels's § 922(g) (3) conviction is inconsistent with our "history and tradition" of gun regulation. [*Bruen* citation]. … We do not invalidate the statute in all its applications, but, importantly, only as applied to Daniels. Nor do we suggest that a robust Second Amendment is incompatible with other reasonable gun regulations. Such statutes just need to be consonant with the limits the Founding generation understood …. The judgment of conviction is therefore REVERSED, and a judgment dismissing the indictment is RENDERED.[123]

Judge Smith emphasized the narrowness of this Fifth Circuit "as-applied" opinion, and less than a year later the Eighth Circuit's *Veasley* opinion proved his point. Focused on the same statute found unconstitutional as applied to Daniels, Veasley's "*facial*" challenge to the law was rejected by the appeals court.

United States v. Veasley (2024): Challenging 18 U.S.C. §922 (g) (3) (Gun Possession by Drug User)

After shooting at his dealer in a drug dispute, Devonte Veasley was charged with violating § 922 (g) (3), and he pled guilty shortly before the *Bruen* case was adjudicated. Following the *Bruen* decision, Veasley appealed. He argued that, in light of *Bruen*, the district court should have dismissed the indictment or permitted him to withdraw his guilty plea. When that court did neither, Veasley then challenged the "facial" constitutionality of § 922 (g) (3). Circuit Judge David Stras, nominated to the federal bench by President Donald Trump, authored the opinion for the Eighth Circuit.[124]

Judge Stras began by noting the practical difference between a *facial* and an *as-applied* constitutional challenge. While an "as-applied" challenge examines the constitutionality of a law based on the individual's own specific circumstances, a "facial" challenge contends that a statute is unconstitutional in *all* circumstances—there are no conditions where the law would be valid. As Stras observed, "The stakes are higher in a facial challenge .... If some applications are constitutional, then facially speaking, the statute is too. ... To counter a facial challenge ... all the government must do is identify constitutional applications—even if they are unrelated to Veasley's conduct—using [*Bruen*'s] same text-and-historical-understanding framework. [*Bruen* citation]."[125] Because his earlier guilty plea judicially prevented an as-applied challenge, a facial challenge to the statute was Veasley's only constitutional option.[126]

Stras asserted that the court was willing to assume that drug users were part of "the people" protected by the Second Amendment, and that handguns were commonly used weapons. Thus, the central issue the court had to resolve was whether the country's historical tradition of gun regulation supported §922 (g) (3). Stating that alcohol and drug abuse have been societal problems for centuries, he concluded that statues regulating intoxicating substances could provide relevant historical analogues. He wrote, "Our task is to figure out whether § 922(g) (3) looks like anything that 'earlier generations' did to keep firearms out of the hands of drug and alcohol users. [*Bruen* citation]."[127]

Continuing, the judge observed, "For drinkers, the focus was on the use of a firearm, not its possession. And the few restrictions that existed during colonial times were temporary and narrow in scope. One came from Virginia, which banned [shooting while drinking]. Another from New York, which prohibited firing guns for the three days bracketing New Years .... [Citations provided]. Disarmament, on the other hand, was not an option. [*Daniels* citation]."[128]

Stras further noted,

> There was even less regulation when it came to drugs. ... Despite the widespread use of opium in particular, the government concedes that its "review of early colonial laws has not revealed any statutes that prohibited [firearm] possession' by drug users. In fact, the 'general societal problem" of drug addiction did not receive congressional attention until 1909. [Citations provided]. And drug use went unmentioned in the National Firearms Act ... passed almost 25 years later. [Citation provided]. Instead, it took until 1968, with the passage of § 922(g) (3), for Congress to keep guns away from drug users and addicts.[129]

He concluded,

> The lesson here is that disarmament is a modern solution to a centuries-old problem. The fact that "earlier generations addressed the societal problem ... through materially different means ... [is] evidence that" disarming *all* drug users, simply because of who they are, is inconsistent with the Second Amendment. [*Bruen* citation.] The key word is *all*. ... Today's drugs are different than the opiates and cannabis of the past. They are, in a word, "unprecedented." [*Bruen* citation]. When it comes to regulations "implicating unprecedented societal concerns" *Bruen* is clear that ... we must take "a more nuanced approach," again "reasoning by analogy," to determine whether there is "a well-established and representative historical analogue" that could make § 922(g) (3) constitutional in some of its applications. [*Bruen* citation]. It turns out there is.[130]

Judge Stras pointed to historical regulations centered on the mentally ill. While acknowledging that mental illness and drug use were not identical, he asserted that a similarity existed in their behavioral effects—impairment in attention and control, deficits in reasoning and working memory, ineffective problem-solving and decision-making, and so forth. [References provided]. He then argued, "The fact that the analogy works for some, and that the mentally ill sometimes lost their guns, means that § 922 (g) (3) cannot be facially unconstitutional."[131]

The judge elaborated,

> The legal view of mental illness in the 18th century was different than it is now. Many believed it was a transitory condition, just like intoxication. ... Under that view, [the mentally ill] were never "looked upon as irrecoverable." [Citations provided]. The law described intoxication in the same rudimentary way, with almost identical terminology. [Citations provided]. The same went for drug addiction, even though the scientific understanding of it was still evolving. [Citation provided]. The similarities did not stop there. Just like the intoxicated kept their civil liberties, including the right to keep firearms, the mentally ill frequently did too. Those who posed no danger stayed at home with their families, and their civil liberties remained intact. [Citation provided].[132]

Stras emphasized that this was not the case for persons who were both mentally ill and dangerous. These people

> "were confined in barred cells in the basement" and "particularly violent individuals" were "restrained ... using a 'strait-waistcoat' ... or heavy arm and leg chains." [Citations provided]. ... Justices of the peace and other officials had a lot of discretion when deciding whether to confine the mentally ill. [Citations provided]. ... Initially, the colonies had no place for them. Sometimes, the solution was jail. [Citation provided]. Other times, building a one-person asylum. ... Mental

> hospitals later became the norm. … "They were not medical facilities designed for treatment; rather they intended to separate those suffering from mental illness from the rest of society." [Citations provided].[133]

The judge continued,

> Confinement led to the loss of liberties. … Gun rights were no exception. … By the late 1800s, state legislatures allowed the prosecution of people who gave guns to the mentally ill. … Along with the even longer tradition of confinement, these laws suggest that society made it a priority to keep guns out of the hands of anyone who was mentally ill and dangerous. … The "burden" imposed by § 922(g)(3) is "comparable," if less heavy-handed than Founding-era laws governing the mentally ill. … confinement with straitjackets and chains carries with it a greater loss of liberty than a temporary loss of gun rights. And the mentally ill had less of a chance to regain their rights …. Stopping the use of drugs, after all, restores gun rights under § 922(g) (3). The justification, which is to "keep guns out of the hands of presumptively risky people," is also comparable.[134]

Stras rejected Veasley's argument that the analogy was flawed because mental confinement has always required a judicial finding while §922 (g) (3) provides no warning that drug users are ineligible to possess a firearm. The judge observed that, given the wide latitude afforded justices of the peace, confining the mentally ill historically involved only limited due process. Further, he noted §922 (g) (3) did require a judicial finding, but that it came later: conviction of "regular" drug use during the time period of gun possession. He stated, "The procedure may not be identical, but it does not have to be. *See Bruen*."[135]

Judge Stras concluded,

> To be sure not every drug user or addict will terrify others, even with a firearm. … But those are details relevant to an as-applied challenge, not a facial one. For our purposes, all we need to know is that at least some drug users and addicts fall within a class of people who historically have had limits placed on their right to bear arms. Consistent with *Seay*, "we reject [Veasley] facial challenge to § 922(g) [(3)]." … [F]or some drug users, § 922(g) (3) is "analogous enough to pass constitutional muster." [*Bruen* citation]. Whether it is for others is a question for another day.[136]

As these cases show, generalizations about Second Amendment challenges to drug-related gun prohibitions are complicated by the specific details of the individual case and by the type of challenge raised—facial or as applied. The general impact of *Bruen*'s, "text, history, and tradition" framework on these statutes is still evolving.

No published court opinions have examined the Second Amendment rights of the (formerly) mentally ill since the *Bruen* decision. Thus, the cases in the next section were all adjudicated prior to that decision, and similar uncertainty surrounds *Bruen*'s eventual effect on these statutes.

2016–20: The Mentally Unstable as Dangerous Individuals

Judge Stras's discussion of the country's early regulations regarding intoxication and the treatment of the mentally ill in *Veasley* offers some historical background to the cases in the chapter's final section. In these three post-*Heller*, pre-*Bruen* adjudications—*Tyler* (2016), *Beers* (2019), and *Mai* (2020)—three different circuit courts came to different conclusions concerning the constitutionality of 18 U.S.C. §922 (g) (4), the statute that prohibits individuals once committed to a mental institution from buying or possessing firearms.

Tyler v. Hillsdale County Sheriff's Department (2016): Challenging 18 U.S.C. §922 (g) (4)

In 2011, Clifford Tyler attempted to purchase a firearm, but was refused because the criminal background check system (i.e., NICS—National Instant Criminal Background Check System) indicated he was a prohibited person under 18 U.S.C. §922 (g) (4). This statute bans anyone who has been involuntarily committed to a mental institution from possessing a firearm, and Tyler had undergone such an involuntary commitment in 1985.[137]

Background information in a 2012 substance abuse evaluation indicated that, in 1985, his wife of twenty-three years left him for someone else, depleted his finances, and served him with divorce papers. He became depressed, emotionally distressed, and exhibited troubling behaviors. His daughters (worried that he might hurt himself) contacted the police who arranged for a psychological evaluation. The examiner determined that Tyler needed hospitalization and the probate court, based on the presented evidence, concluded that Tyler posed a danger to himself and others. Given the severity of his mental illness, the court agreed that hospitalization was required. The court committed Tyler to Ypsilanti Regional Center for thirty days, with further follow-up treatment extending an additional ninety days.[138]

Because actual hospitalization records for this period were no longer available, the 2012 evaluation relied mostly on patient-supplied information. It indicated that Tyler had arrived at the Center depressed and with self-inflicted bruises on his hands and face. He remained an in-patient for several weeks but declined medication, fearing it would distort his thinking. After returning home, he successfully held a job, remarried in 1999, maintained a close relationship with his daughters, and mended his relationship with his former spouse. Further, Tyler stated that he had not experienced a depressive episode since the one triggered by his divorce.[139]

The evaluation further noted that Tyler showed no signs of thought disorder or cognitive disability and that his personal physician reported no signs of mental illness. The examiner concluded that Tyler's response to his divorce was a brief reactive episode—that he no longer presented any evidence of mental illness and that the evaluation revealed no problems with drug or alcohol abuse, or with past legal entanglements.[140]

When the FBI's NICS section denied his appeal of the 2011 decision, Tyler sued in federal court. He alleged that §922 (g) (4) was unconstitutional as applied to him because it operated as an essentially permanent ban on his Second Amendment right to arms. The government defendants moved to dismiss Tyler's complaint for failure to state a claim, and the district court granted that motion. The court relied on *Heller*'s observation that firearms prohibitions on the mentally ill were presumptively lawful, and that put Tyler outside Second Amendment protection. It also asserted that §922 (g) (4) would survive intermediate scrutiny. Tyler appealed this ruling, and a Sixth Circuit *en-banc* adjudication examined his claim. Circuit Judge Julia Gibbons, a President Reagan nominee to the federal judiciary, wrote the opinion for the circuit court.[141]

Judge Gibbons noted that the court's review centered on the district court's dismissal for failure to state a claim. She observed that Tyler's challenge to the "presumptively lawful" §922 (g) (4) centers on his assertion that "the Second Amendment forbids Congress from permanently prohibiting firearm possession by currently healthy individuals who were long ago committed to a mental institution."[142] After stating that she would follow other circuit courts and use a two-step framework for resolving the challenge, the judge then raised a "threshold question: To what extent does *Heller* itself provide an answer to the constitutionality of § 922(g) (4) as applied to Tyler?"[143]

She observed that the *Heller* Court's discussion of "presumptively lawful" long-standing prohibitions confirmed that

> the Second Amendment is not an absolute barrier to congressional regulation of firearms and that some categorical prohibitions are assumed to be constitutional … [but that] in making this observation, the Court expressly noted that it was not "clarify[ing] the entire field" of the Second Amendment and, importantly, the Court reserved for later cases an exploration of the historical justifications for its enumerated prohibitions. [*Heller* citation].[144]

Continuing, Gibbons wrote,

> *Heller* does not resolve this case on its own terms. … *Heller* only established a presumption that such bans were lawful; it did not invite courts onto an analytical off-ramp to avoid constitutional analysis. … We do not take *Heller's* "presumptively lawful" dictum to foreclose § 922(g) (4) from constitutional scrutiny. The mere fact that Congress created a categorical ban does not give the government a free pass; it must still be shown that the presumption applies in the instant case. [Citation provided]. As the Seventh Circuit has recognized, the *Heller* Court's observation regarding the presumptive lawfulness of longstanding bans is precautionary, not conclusive. [Citation provided].[145]

The judge further asserted,

> Refusing to give *Heller* conclusive effect is particularly proper given § 922(g) (4)'s lack of historical pedigree. ... "legal limits on the possession of firearms by the mentally ill ... are of 20th Century vintage." [Citation provided]. Indeed, § 922(g) (4) was not enacted until 1968. ... *Heller* spoke of bans on "the mentally ill." ... Prior involuntary commitment is not coextensive with current mental illness: a point the government concedes in its brief and a point Congress recognized when it ... allow[ed] states to restore the right to possess a gun to persons previously committed. ... To rely solely on *Heller's* presumption here would amount to a judicial endorsement of Congress's power to declare, "Once mentally ill, always so." This we will not do.[146]

Gibbons then began the two-step analysis used to resolve Tyler's challenge. She observed that the first step requires the government to show that the statute impacts persons historically understood to be unprotected. After reviewing the historical sources and other evidence cited by the government, the judge agreed with the district court that the evidence "does not directly support the proposition that persons who were once committed due to mental illness are forever ineligible to regain their Second Amendment rights. [Citation given]."[147]

Gibbons also rejected the government's argument (accepted by the district court) that *Heller's* "presumptively lawful" dictum was sufficient to establish that the Second Amendment as historically understood did not apply to Tyler. She noted, "In the face of what is at best ambiguous historical support, it would be peculiar to conclude that § 922(g) (4) does not burden conduct within the ambit of the Second Amendment as historically understood based on nothing more than *Heller's* observation that such a regulation is 'presumptively lawful.' "[148]

Moving to the second step of the analysis, the judge had to determine the appropriate level of scrutiny—strict or intermediate—to use in examining the government's justification for restricting Tyler's Second Amendment rights. She noted that Tyler argued for strict scrutiny, since §922 (g) (4) permanently denied his core right to use a firearm for hearth and home defense. While acknowledging that the statute severely restricted Tyler's right, she argued that it only burdens a narrow class of individuals who are not at the core of the Second Amendment (i.e., individuals previously involuntarily committed), not the general public. Thus, she opted for intermediate scrutiny, noting that several other circuits also held that level as appropriate.[149]

Gibbons observed that the government offered two specific justifications for §922 (g) (4), in addition to the general interest in keeping guns from presumptively risky people: preventing crime and preventing suicide. Given these compelling objectives, she noted that intermediate scrutiny then required the government to show a

> reasonable fit between [these goals] and its permanent ban on the possession of firearms by persons adjudicated to be mentally unstable, some of them long ago. ... In discharging this burden the government can rely on a wide range of sources ...

> but it may not "rely upon mere 'anecdote and supposition.'" [Citation provided]. ... The government relies on both legislative history and empirical evidence to support § 922(g) (4). First, it points to legislative observations about the role of mental illness in two public tragedies .... This is compelling evidence of the need to bar arms from those currently suffering mental illness and those just recently removed from an involuntary commitment.[150]

She continued, "It does not, however, answer why Congress is justified in permanently barring anyone who has been previously committed, particularly in cases like Tyler's, where a number of healthy, peaceable years separate the individual from their troubled history."[151] The judge then considered submitted studies showing that individuals who previously attempted suicide were more likely to commit suicide in the future and that a gun was the method typically used. She wrote,

> This evidence helps to explain why it might be reasonable to prevent those with a past suicide attempt from ever possessing a firearm, but it does not fully justify the need to permanently disarm anyone who has been involuntarily committed for whatever reason. Importantly, nothing in this record suggests that Tyler has ever attempted suicide, or that a significant proportion of individuals prohibited by § 922(g) (4) have attempted suicide.[152]

After considering additional governmental evidence examining connections between involuntary commitment, suicide, and violent crime, Gibbons concluded,

> The government has not presented sufficient evidence of the continued risk presented by persons who were previously committed. Such evidence has been integral in decisions upholding other portions of § 922(g) that impose permanent bans. [Citations provided.] ... Relatedly, the temporal limitation of other § 922(g) bans has been a key consideration in finding that those regulations pass muster under heightened scrutiny. [Citations provided.] None of the government's evidence squarely answers [whether it is] reasonably necessary to forever bar all previously institutionalized from owning a firearm. But perhaps the biggest problem for the government is Congress's most recent answer to this very question: No, it is not.[153]

Gibbons elaborated, noting that in 2008 Congress enacted the NICS Improvement Amendments Act. This legislation provided federal grants to help states improve the NICS instant background check system. But to receive a grant, a state had to create a relief-from-disabilities program that allowed §922 (g) (4) individuals to apply to have their rights restored. She asserted, "[This Act] is a less restrictive alternative to the permanent bar created by § 922(g) (4). It is a clear indication that Congress does not believe that previously committed persons are sufficiently dangerous as a class to permanently deprive all such persons of their Second Amendment right to bear arms."[154]

Judge Gibbons summarized,

> We cannot conclude, based on the current record, that the government has carried its burden .... Thus, we conclude that Tyler has a viable claim under the Second Amendment and that the government has not justified a lifetime ban on gun possession by anyone who has been "adjudicated as a mental defective" or 'committed to a mental institution." ... It seems therefore that, given the [multiple] views of the court, the proper resolution of the case is to reverse and remand to the district court for the application of intermediate scrutiny to determine the statute's constitutionality as applied to Tyler.[155]

Despite the *en-banc* court's mixed opinions associated with this ruling—ten judges supported reversing the district court while six did not—the Sixth Circuit's treatment of *Heller*'s "presumptively lawful" dicta is notable. As Judge Gibbons observed, are such "presumptively lawful" statutes constitutional because they have been already assessed, and are now accepted as not infringing on Second Amendment protection? Or are they simply regulations that are *likely* (i.e., "presumptively") to satisfy some form of heightened means-end scrutiny on examination? In the *Tyler* case, Gibbons opted for this second interpretation. Three years later, in the *Beers* case, the Third Circuit would disagree.

Beers v. Attorney General United States (2019): Challenging 18 U.S.C. §922 (g) (4)

In December 2005, after Bradley Beers inserted a gun in his mouth and told his mother he was suicidal, he was involuntarily committed to a psychiatric hospital for up to five days. There, an evaluation confirmed that Beers was suicidal and required inpatient treatment for his safety. During treatment, the Bucks County Court of Common Pleas determined that Beers was severely mentally incapacitated, continued to present a danger to himself and others, and extended his five-day involuntary commitment twice. Discharged in 2006, Beers received no further mental health treatment. Shortly after his discharge, he attempted to buy a firearm, but failed the background check because of his involuntary commitment.[156]

In 2013, a physician's evaluation concluded that Beers could again safely handle firearms and that he posed no risk of harm to others or himself. Subsequently, Beers challenged the involuntary commitment statute—18 U.S.C. §922 (g) (4)—as unconstitutional as applied to him. The federal district court, using the two-part procedure earlier developed in *Marzzarella* and *Binderup*, concluded that Beers was unable to distinguish his specific circumstances from mentally ill individuals also banned from gun possession. Citing *Binderup*, the court further held that evidence of rehabilitation was irrelevant and that Beers could not use such evidence as a distinguishing factor.[157]

The district court consequently ruled that 18 U.S.C. §922 (g) (4) did not infringe on conduct falling within the Second Amendment's scope and that the statute was thus constitutional as applied to Beers. Beers then appealed this rejection to the circuit court. Circuit Judge Jane Roth, nominated to the federal bench by President Ronald Reagan, authored the opinion for this court.[158]

After noting Beers's contention that his rehabilitation separates his circumstances from the historically barred class, Judge Roth summarized the case focus: "whether passage of time and evidence of rehabilitation are relevant to our inquiry concerning the constitutionality of the prohibition of the possession of firearms by Beers."[159] In determining this issue, she noted that earlier Third Circuit precedents required the court to conduct the same type of two-step inquiry as followed by the district court. Could Beers distinguish his situation from others in the barred class, and if so, could the government then justify the challenged statute under some form of heightened scrutiny?[160]

The judge then elaborated on the two-part test used by the Third Circuit in analyzing Second Amendment challenges, citing *Mazzarella* and *Barton.* She observed,

> In *Mazzarella*, we held that even if a law did impose a burden on protected content, in view of the government's interest in tracing weapons through serial numbers, the law survived intermediate scrutiny. ... In *Barton*, we determined that, even though felon dispossession statutes were presumptively lawful under *Heller*, § 922(g) (1) could still be challenged as it applied to individuals. In evaluating such a challenge ... the challenger had to distinguish his circumstances from those of persons historically-barred from possession of a firearm by demonstrating either (1) he was convicted of a minor, non-violent crime and thus "he is no more dangerous than a typical law-abiding citizen;" or (2) that a significant time has passed so that he has been "rehabilitated" and "poses no continuing threat to society."[161]

Roth then explained that in a later Third Circuit adjudication—*Binderup*—the court

> overruled *Barton* insofar as ... it allowed the challenger to distinguish himself ... by demonstrating the passage of time or evidence of rehabilitation. As we noted in *Binderup*, the historical justification for disarming felons was that they were "unvirtuous," a term historically applied to individuals who had committed "serious" crimes. Where the historical justification for disarming felons was because they had committed serious crimes, risk of violent recidivism was irrelevant .... We therefore emphasized that neither passage of time nor evidence of rehabilitation "can restore Second Amendment rights that were forfeited.'[162]

The judge then tied this discussion to Beers. She asserted,

> Even though he claims to be rehabilitated, Beers cannot distinguish himself from the historically-barred class of mentally-ill individuals who were excluded from Second Amendment protection because of the danger they posed to themselves and to others. ... Beers only bases for distinguishing himself ... are that a

> significant amount of time has passed since he was institutionalized and that he is now rehabilitated. We established in *Binderup* that neither passage of time nor evidence of rehabilitation "can restore Second Amendment rights that were forfeited." There was no historical support for the proposition that forfeited rights could be restored.[163]

Roth continued,

> The historical underpinnings of § 922(g) (4) were to keep guns from individuals who posed a danger to themselves or to others. Beers was committed to a mental institution for this very reason: he was suicidal and … a danger to himself or to others. … the only way Beers can distinguish his circumstances is by demonstrating that he was never determined to be a danger to himself or to others. This Beers cannot do. … Because Beers cannot distinguish his circumstances, we conclude that § 922(g) (4) as applied to him does not burden conduct falling within the scope of the Second Amendment. Beers therefore fails to surpass the first step of our Second Amendment framework, and we need not proceed to step two. … For the foregoing reasons, we will affirm the judgment of the District Court.[164]

In finding that Beers stood outside Second Amendment protection, Judge Roth made it clear that the ruling was not a rejection of Beers's possible rehabilitation, but rather it is the result of historical analysis that showed "our forebears saw a danger in providing mentally ill individuals the right to possess guns. That understanding require[d] us to conclude that § 922(g) (4) is constitutional as applied to Beers."[165] Roth acknowledged that the Sixth Circuit in *Tyler* reached the opposite conclusion, but she disagreed with that court's assessment of the historical evidence. In the chapter's final case, the Ninth Circuit notes these contradictions and offers a third perspective on the relationship between §922 (g) (4) and the Second Amendment.

Mai v. United States (2020): Challenging 18 U.S.C. §922 (g) (4)

In 1999, seventeen-year-old Duy Mai threatened to harm himself and others. A Washington State court concluded that he was mentally ill and dangerous, and involuntarily committed him for treatment. His treatment spanned more than nine months, with his release occurring in mid-2000. Since release, Mai reported that he earned a GED, and both undergraduate and graduate degrees. He also obtained gainful employment, fathered two children, and was free of mental illness. He noted that he now lives a "socially-responsible, well-balanced, and accomplished life."[166]

Having been involuntary committed, Washington law prohibited Mai from possessing a firearm. But in 2014, he petitioned the state court for relief. The court found that he no longer required treatment, that he had successfully managed his former condition, that he was no longer a danger to himself or to others, and that his former symptoms were not likely to occur. Accordingly, the court granted Mai relief from the state's gun prohibition. However, that relief did not extend to the similar gun ban imposed by federal law, that is, 18 U.S.C. §922 (g) (4). While alternative procedures for obtaining relief from the federal ban were nominally available, for various administrative reasons Mai could not access these procedures. With no other way to escape §922 (g) (4)'s gun prohibition, in 2017 Mai filed suit in federal court when the statute prevented his potential purchase of a firearm.[167]

Mai alleged that the government, in preventing him from possessing firearms, violated his right to bear arms and his right to due process. In turn, the government moved to dismiss Mai's suit for failure to state a claim. Ruling that §922 (g) (4) was categorically constitutional under the Second Amendment and that, alternatively, the statute would pass intermediate scrutiny, the district court granted the government's motion. Mai appealed to the circuit court, and Circuit Judge Susan Graber, nominated to the federal bench by President Bill Clinton, authored the opinion for the court.[168]

Judge Graber noted that Mai advanced only his Second Amendment claim in the appeal. Consequently, while pointing out Mai might have advanced other legal arguments in support of his challenge, the judge asserted her analysis would focus only on "whether the Second Amendment requires that Plaintiff be allowed to possess firearms."[169] After emphasizing that both *Heller* and *McDonald* discussed long-standing prohibitions on gun possession that were presumptively lawful, Graber explained the two-step procedure courts typically used in assessing potential Second Amendment violations: Does the challenged law burden conduct protected by the amendment; and if so, can the law pass an appropriate level of scrutiny?[170]

Acknowledging that Mai's challenge to §922 (g) (4) was "an issue of first impression in this circuit" (i.e., a new legal issue that the court had not previously addressed), the judge briefly reviewed decisions in similar contexts, citing *Chovan*, *Vongxay*, *Beers*, and *Tyler*. She then offered the court's own analysis, beginning with whether §922 (g) (4) burdens Second Amendment rights. Noting that this determination requires a historical understanding of the scope and reach of the Second Amendment, Graber asserted that "the government has presented a strong argument that … support[s] the conclusion that § 922(g) (4) does not burden Second Amendment rights."[171]

Continuing, she wrote, "In *Vongxay*, [citation provided] we held that § 922(g) (1)—the federal prohibition on the possession of firearms by felons—fell within *Heller's* 'presumptively lawful' category. … Similarly, historical evidence supports the view that society did not entrust the mentally ill with the responsibility of bearing arms. See e.g., *Beers*, [citation provided] (summarizing the historical evidence)."[172]

The judge observed that Mai conceded that a gun ban for those *presently* mentally ill and dangerous did not violate the Second Amendment, but contended that both *Heller* and the historical evidence only supported a ban for that limited group. Graber wrote, "He urges the court to agree with the Sixth Circuit that 'historical evidence … does not directly support the proposition that persons who were once committed due to mental illness are forever ineligible' to possess a firearm. [*Tyler* citation]."[173] Rather than decide whose interpretation of the historical evidence—the government's or Mai's—was more compelling, Graber opted to "assume, without deciding, that § 922(g) (4), as applied to the Plaintiff, burdens Second Amendment rights."[174]

The judge then indicated the next step was to determine how close the statute came to the "core" of the Second Amendment right and the severity of the imposition on the right. She observed that most post-*Heller* judicial decisions suggested that intermediate scrutiny was appropriate in evaluating these two concerns, and that Mai himself recognized that intermediate scrutiny applied. Citing *Tyler*, she argued that §922 (g) (4) impacted only a narrow class of individual not at the core of the amendment and that prior courts (e.g., *Chovan*) used intermediate scrutiny in assessing the other lifetime bans contained in §922 (g). She concluded intermediate scrutiny was also appropriate in Mai's case.[175]

In applying intermediate scrutiny, Graber noted that the government's interest in imposing §922 (g) (4)'s firearms ban was to prevent crime and prevent suicide. She wrote, "We agree with the Sixth Circuit that those two interests 'are not only legitimate, they are compelling.' [*Tyler* citation]."[176]

The judge then reviewed the government's scientific evidence showing that individuals released from involuntary commitment present an increased risk of violence. She acknowledged Mai's assertion that the cited evidence did not sufficiently match his circumstances: the studies examined outcomes for only up to 8.5 years after commitment, while Mai had been released for two decades. Nonetheless, she rejected his argument that the studies were not enough to support "the congressional judgment that he poses an increased risk of suicide."[177]

Elaborating, Graber wrote,

> In assessing congressional judgment, "we do not impose an 'unnecessarily rigid burden of proof' and we allow [the government] to rely on any material 'reasonably believed to be relevant' to substantiate its interests." [Citation provided]. ... We cannot conclude that, because no one apparently has published a study beyond 8.5 years after the participants' release from involuntary commitment, Congress may not infer that the increased risk of violence continues after that time period. ... Plaintiff has asserted that, because *he* was released from commitment years ago, no longer suffers from mental illness, and has been peaceable in recent years, the Second Amendment requires that he be allowed to possess firearms. But we emphasize that we are assessing congressional judgment about a category of persons, not about Plaintiff himself.[178]

Continuing, the judge observed, "But even if we were to consider his personal situation ... his history of mental illness remains a scientifically recognized factor in evaluating his current level of risk. ...nothing in the record suggests that Plaintiff's level of risk is nonexistent or that [it] matches the risk associated with a similarly situated person who lacks a history of mental illness."[179] She further asserted that the passage of U.S.C. §40915—legislation that allowed states to create "relief from disabilities" programs—did not suggest (as the Sixth Circuit in *Tyler* had argued) that Congress had reconsidered §922 (g) (4)'s firearms ban. She stated that the legislation was "part of a political compromise aimed at preventing gun violence [that] does not affect our constitutional analysis."[180]

After reiterating that intermediate scrutiny only required a "reasonable fit," the judge concluded that §922 (g) (4) reasonably fit the congressional goal of limiting gun violence. Noting the horrific impact suicide has on the victim and on family and friends, Graber asserted,

> Even a small decrease in the number of suicides is, therefore, a significant public benefit. ... The federal prohibition on Plaintiff's possession of firearms because of his past involuntary commitment withstands Second Amendment scrutiny. Those who are no longer mentally ill, but who were committed involuntarily years ago, unquestionably pose less risk of violence now ... but scientific evidence reasonably supports the congressional judgment that they still pose an increased risk .... The Second Amendment allows Congress to further its goal of preventing gun violence by barring Plaintiff from possessing a firearm. ... AFFIRMED.[181]

Given the divided opinions reflected in these cases (and noting that all three decisions were pre-*Bruen*), it seems likely the Supreme Court itself will eventually examine the constitutionality of §922 (g) (4).

Some Observations

Several aspects of the opinions in this chapter underscore the inherent ambiguity and complexity in judicial interpretation, even in areas that are seemingly straightforward. The disagreement about the implications of the Supreme Court's references to "law-abiding and responsible" individuals is an example. Does the phrase signify a meaningful legal division between people—substantial enough to uphold individuals' self-defense rights on one side, and strip those rights on the other side? Or is the phrase little more than a literary flourish, not meant to have any legal import? Some commentators argue that every word in a court opinion has significance, but even Supreme Court justices presumably have a right to a literary flourish every so often. Not surprisingly, lower court judges may differ over what is substantive and what is merely a flourish.

The courts' differing interpretations of "presumptively lawful" and "long-standing" provide another example. Until the Supreme Court's additional guidance in opinions after *Heller*, the varying meanings given to these straightforward (but nonspecific) phrases produced conflicting legal opinions on virtually identical gun questions. It would be a mistake to attribute such problems to a "flawed" judiciary or legal system. The problem here is not centered in the law, but in language. Rich in nuance, most English words have multiple meanings and interpretations, and this quality virtually insures that multiple judges will have multiple interpretations of such nonspecific phrases.

Court disagreements around the appropriate era—1791 or 1868—for determining historical analogues is a third example of interpretive complexity. Despite the Supreme Court's clear indication that Founding-Era historical evidence is determinative, Judge

Rosenbaum's reasoning in *NRA v. Bondi* offers a potent logical argument for why Reconstruction-era evidence may be better. Because this argument ultimately results in a two-tiered understanding of the Second Amendment—one meaning applicable to the federal government and another applicable to the states—Rosenbaum's reasoning creates other logical issues. In the end, simply settling the question by Supreme Court fiat perhaps offers the best—and most practical—solution.

Notes

1 18 U.S. Code §922—Unlawful Acts. Cornell Law School Legal Information Institute. At https://www.law.cornell.edu/uscode/text/18/922.
2 *United States v. Rene, 583 F.3d 8 (First Circuit) (2009).* At https://caselaw.findlaw.com/court/us-1st-circuit/1593627.html.
3 Rene also challenged the sentencing guideline the district court followed, but that challenge became moot when he turned eighteen.
4 *United States v. Rene, 583 F.3d 8 (First Circuit) (2009).*
5 Ibid. After this conclusion, the court also analyzed Rene's Commerce Clause and sentencing arguments—rejecting both.
6 Ibid.
7 Ibid.
8 Ibid.
9 Ibid.
10 Ibid.
11 Ibid.
12 Ibid.
13 *NRA v. BATFE, 700 F. 3d 185 (Fifth Circuit) (2012).* At https://www.ca5.uscourts.gov/opinions%5Cpub%5C11/11-10959-CV0.wpd.pdf.
14 Ibid.
15 Ibid.
16 Ibid.
17 Ibid.
18 Ibid.
19 Ibid.
20 Ibid.
21 Ibid.
22 Ibid.
23 Ibid.
24 Ibid.
25 Ibid.
26 Ibid.
27 Ibid.
28 Ibid. The court then considered the appellants' Fifth Amendment Due Process argument, also rejecting it.
29 *State of Illinois v. Alberto Aguilar, 2 N.E. 3d 321 (Illinois) (2013).* At https://law.justia.com/cases/illinois/supreme-court/2013/112116-0.html.

30 *NRA v. Bondi 61 F. 4th 1317 (Eleventh Circuit) (2023).* At https://scholar.google.com/scholar_case?case=17616517880385249927&hl=en&as_sdt=4006.
31 Ibid.
32 Ibid.
33 Ibid.
34 Ibid.
35 Ibid.
36 Ibid.
37 Ibid.
38 Ibid.
39 Ibid.
40 Ibid.
41 Ibid.
42 Ibid.
43 Ibid.
44 Ibid.
45 *Worth v. Harrington, 21-cv-1348 (KMM/LIB) (D. Minnesota) (2023).* At https://casetext.com/case/worth-v-harrington.
46 Ibid.
47 Ibid.
48 Ibid.
49 Ibid.
50 Ibid.
51 Ibid.
52 Ibid.
53 Ibid.
54 Ibid.
55 Ibid.
56 Ibid.
57 Ibid.
58 Ibid.
59 Ibid.
60 Ibid.
61 Ibid.
62 *Fraser v. BATFE, 3:22-CV-410 (D. Virginia) (2023).* At https://caselaw.findlaw.com/court/us-dis-crt-e-d-vir/2200469.html.
63 *Lara v. Commissioner PA State Police, 21-1832 (Third Circuit) (2024).* At https://law.justia.com/cases/federal/appellate-courts/ca3/21-1832/21-1832-2024-01-18.html.
64 Ibid.
65 Ibid.
66 Ibid.
67 Ibid.
68 Ibid.
69 Ibid.
70 Ibid.
71 Ibid.
72 Ibid.
73 Ibid.

74 Ibid.
75 Ibid.
76 Ibid.
77 Ibid.
78 *Lara v. Commissioner PA State Police, 21-1832 (Third Circuit) (2025).* At https://law.justia.com/cases/federal/appellate-courts/ca3/21-1832/21-1832-2025-01-13.html.
79 Ibid.
80 Ibid.
81 *United States v. Edwards, 98-50320 (Fifth Circuit) (1999).* At https://caselaw.findlaw.com/court/us-5th-circuit/1147924.html.
82 *United States v. Purdy, 00-30168 (Ninth Circuit) (2001).* At https://caselaw.findlaw.com/court/us-9th-circuit/1040384.html.
83 *United States v. Jackson, 01-4004 (Fourth Circuit) (2002).* At https://caselaw.findlaw.com/court/us-4th-circuit/1232930.html.
84 *United States v. Turnbull, 03-1633 (Eighth Circuit) (2003).* At https://caselaw.findlaw.com/court/us-8th-circuit/1173754.html.
85 *United States v. Patterson, 04-41077 (Fifth Circuit) (2005).* At https://caselaw.findlaw.com/court/us-5th-circuit/1205292.html.
86 *United States v. Richard, 08-6243 (Tenth Circuit) (2009).* At http://www.ecases.us/case/ca10/c3548913/united-states-v-richard.
87 Ibid.
88 Ibid.
89 Ibid.
90 Ibid.
91 Ibid.
92 Ibid.
93 *United States v. Seay, 620 F.3d 919 (Eighth Circuit) (2010).* At https://casetext.com/case/us-v-seay-3.
94 Ibid.
95 Ibid.
96 Ibid.
97 Ibid.
98 *United States v. Daniels, 22-60596 (Fifth Circuit) (2023).* At https://www.ca5.uscourts.gov/opinions/pub/22/22-60596-CR0.pdf.
99 Ibid.
100 Ibid.
101 Ibid.
102 Ibid.
103 Ibid.
104 Ibid.
105 Ibid.
106 Ibid.
107 Ibid.
108 Ibid.
109 Ibid.
110 Ibid.
111 Ibid.
112 Ibid.

113 Ibid.
114 Ibid.
115 Ibid.
116 Ibid.
117 Ibid.
118 Ibid.
119 Ibid.
120 Ibid.
121 Ibid.
122 Ibid.
123 Ibid.
124 *United States v. Veasley, 23-1114 (Eighth Circuit) (2024).* At https://caselaw.findlaw.com/court/us-8th-circuit/116062347.html.
125 Ibid.
126 Ibid.
127 Ibid.
128 Ibid.
129 Ibid.
130 Ibid.
131 Ibid.
132 Ibid.
133 Ibid.
134 Ibid.
135 Ibid.
136 Ibid.
137 *Tyler v. Hillsdale County Sheriff's Department, 837 F.3d 678 (6th Circuit) (2016).* At https://casetext.com/case/tyler-v-hillsdale-cnty-sheriffs-dept-2.
138 Ibid.
139 Ibid.
140 Ibid.
141 Ibid.
142 Ibid.
143 Ibid.
144 Ibid.
145 Ibid.
146 Ibid.
147 Ibid.
148 Ibid.
149 Ibid.
150 Ibid.
151 Ibid.
152 Ibid.
153 Ibid.
154 Ibid.
155 Ibid.
156 *Beers v. Attorney General United States, 927 F.3d 150 (Third Circuit) (2019).* At https://casetext.com/case/beers-v-attorney-gen-united-states.
157 Ibid.

158 Ibid.
159 Ibid.
160 Ibid.
161 Ibid.
162 Ibid.
163 Ibid.
164 Ibid.
165 Ibid.
166 *Mai v. United States, 952 F.3d 1106 (Ninth Circuit) (2020).* At https://casetext.com/case/mai-v-united-states-1.
167 Ibid.
168 Ibid.
169 Ibid.
170 Ibid.
171 Ibid.
172 Ibid.
173 Ibid.
174 Ibid.
175 Ibid.
176 Ibid.
177 Ibid.
178 Ibid.
179 Ibid.
180 Ibid.
181 Ibid.

9

The Second Amendment: A Summing Up

The President and the Congress are all very well in their way. They can say what they think they think, but it rests with the Supreme Court to decide what they have really thought.

Theodore Roosevelt[1]

In an early critique of the *Heller* decision, a legal scholar argued that the opinion was internally inconsistent and somewhat contradictory. He faulted the Supreme Court for failing to fully explain not just *what* it decided, but *why* it decided it.[2] In a broad way, the same criticism might be leveled at the whole body of judicial opinions attempting to clarify the right to bear arms. As the prior chapters have demonstrated, while the arguments developed in any particular opinion may not be contradictory or inconsistent, conflicts and contradictions certainly abound across the entire corpus of court rulings defining the Second Amendment. What general conclusions about the right to arms can a person draw from these clashing court opinions?

A possible answer to this question emerges by looking beyond the individual details and specific rulings of the cases. By identifying particular judicial concerns swirling around guns in specific periods, a more coherent understanding of the amendment appears. Based on the opinions examined in the book, four such broad concerns appear to have influenced the courts' varying interpretation of the right to keep and bear arms. While obviously interrelated, these concerns centered on (1) individual versus collective rights, (2) the incorporation issue, (3) the infringement dispute, and (4) the evaluative standards question.

Beyond these concerns, the varying array of judicial opinions suggests an even more fundamental issue. If the Constitution—the standard against which all legislation is weighed and evaluated—actually permits such a range of disagreeing rulings, how is a citizen *ever* able to determine the practical meaning of a law (or an amendment) with any confidence? The stock response to this query is a reference to the US Supreme Court as the ultimate referee of constitutional meaning. And while that court may provide *judicial* closure on differing interpretations, *societal* disagreements often still exist. Thus, a full appreciation of the Second Amendment also requires a consideration and an understanding of the Supreme Court—both as a judicial referee and as a political entity.

Finally, having extensively examined the Second Amendment's past, it seems fitting to close the book with a look at the amendment's future. One especially intriguing aspect of that future is identifying ongoing Second Amendment cases and weighing their likely judicial outcomes when finally adjudicated. Given the nature of firearms litigation, such speculations are always perilous, but hard to resist. The next sections consider each of these areas.

Making Sense of Judicial Disagreement: Four Issues That Shaped Opinions

In adjudicating a Second Amendment firearms case, the judicial procedure seems straightforward. The court examines case facts, considers the circumstances surrounding the issue, interprets the law in light of past precedents and legislative intent, and finally renders a verdict in that case. But since individual circumstances differ, statute interpretations vary, and precedents change, finding a larger pattern in a wide set of specific rulings—even when the rulings are all focused on a common area—is difficult. An alternative approach is to ignore the specific opinions and see if a common "theme"—a more general question or issue—links the different cases. As noted, four different themes appear to link Second Amendment gun cases.

The Individual/Collective Right Dispute

The question of whether the Second Amendment protects a personal right to firearms has shaped a majority of mid-twentieth-century gun cases, and it is probably the most prominent issue that has impacted current Second Amendment jurisprudence. While the idea that the amendment protects the states' right to arm a militia first surfaced in the *Buzzard* case in 1842 and the *Blaksley* case of 1905, this collective right interpretation only truly gained traction in 1939, with the US Supreme Court's *Miller* decision. Federal courts cited this opinion in denying gun law challenges for much of the rest of the twentieth century.

A judicial examination of the Second Amendment limited to this seventy-year period would likely conclude that the "individual right" understanding of the amendment is an aberration. This conclusion would be mistaken. The amendment's "individual right" interpretation claims a pedigree even before 1842, with the 1822 *Bliss* court asserting that *any* restriction on a person's right to arms is unconstitutional. While other nineteenth-century court rulings were not as extreme—they usually upheld restrictions on concealed pistols or unusual knives—they all implicitly endorsed the Second Amendment as protecting an individual right.

The notion of the Second Amendment as an individual right again took center stage early in the twenty-first century. Rejecting the 1939 *Miller* opinion as inconclusive, the *Emerson* ruling in 2001 held that the Second Amendment did, in fact, protect an individual right. When other federal courts (e.g., *Silveria* in 2002, *Warin* in 2006) rejected that court's analysis and continued to treat the amendment as protecting only a collective right, the Supreme Court finally resolved the matter. In a series of Supreme Court opinions (i.e., *Heller*, 2008; *McDonald*, 2010; and *Bruen*, 2022) the idea that the amendment protected an individual right to arms became the law of the land.

The Incorporation Question

A second issue that has shaped Second Amendment jurisprudence is the amendment's relationship to the states: Does the amendment also apply to state governments or does it only restrict the power of the federal government? After the Supreme Court had concluded (in its 1833 *Barron* opinion) that the Bill of Rights was not applicable to the states, many courts (e.g., *Andrews* in 1871, *Cruikshank* in 1875, *Shelby* in 1886, *Miller* in 1894) later in the century dismissed Second Amendment-based gun law challenges on this basis alone.

Not every court invoked lack of incorporation to dismiss Second Amendment challenges (e.g., see *Nunn* in 1846, *English* in 1872, *Wilforth* in 1881). And, even among those that did, the court often adjudicated the individual's legal challenge using the state constitution's Second Amendment analogue to render an opinion. Generalizations from these state-based rulings provided indirect insights into the nature of the federal Second Amendment. Nonetheless, until the Supreme Court's *McDonald* opinion in 2010 clearly established that the amendment also restrains state powers, the incorporation question (together with the individual/collective right dispute) forestalled the emergence of a consistent and uniform judicial interpretation of the amendment.

The Infringement Issue

A core difficulty for courts analyzing the "meaning" of the Second Amendment revolves around the founders' hyperbole in phrasing the protections it provides. Taken literally, the notion that the right to arms "shall not be infringed" means that (as the *Bliss* opinion suggested) *any* encroachment on the right—no matter how small or reasonable—violates the amendment. Despite *Bliss*, it seems unlikely that the founders saw the amendment as protecting, for example, the right of an inaccurate gun owner to target practice in an open, crowded, urban environment. On the other hand, if "shall not be infringed" actually allows for some constraints, what logic and standards should courts use in separating acceptable restrictions from unconstitutional infringements?

Nineteenth-century courts provided a range of rationales for concluding that certain gun restrictions were permissible. The *Aymette* court distinguished between militia firearms used in common defense and concealed weapons typically used in personal quarrels. Noting that concealed weapons were useless in common defense, the court ruled that such weapons were outside the amendment's protection. Similarly, the *Buzzard* court also upheld a concealed-carry statute. In addition to a militia-linked argument, that court also offered a logical justification for the statute's constitutionality, noting that without some restrictions on individual rights, effective civil governance would be impossible.

Since many state constitutions contained Second Amendment analogues, even courts dismissing federal Second Amendment infringements as inapplicable often needed to justify their gun prohibitions. These opinions typically upheld gun prohibitions using arguments similar to those found at the federal level. For instance, the *Fife* court in 1876 upheld a pistol-carrying prohibition because it outlawed only guns not useful for common defense (e.g., pocket pistols)—a prohibition that the court maintained was within the police powers of the state.

Later courts encountered Second Amendment challenges to restrictions that went beyond the type and function of the firearm, or how the gun might be carried. Judges had to determine whether the amendment allows permitting and licensing statutes (e.g., *Rosenthal* in 1903, *Darling* in 1913), and if so, whether "proper cause" requirements are constitutional (e.g., *Moore* in 1943, *Klenosky* in 1980, *Peruta* in 2014/16). After the federal government began regulating guns, courts had to adjudicate other potential infringements. Does the amendment allow the imposition of lifetime firearm bans on felons (e.g., *Everist* in 2004, *Rozier* in 2010, *Jackson* in 2023) or on those guilty of domestic violence (e.g., *White* in 2010, *Chovan* in 2013)?

Similarly, judges had to weigh whether the Second Amendment allows age restrictions on the possession and use of firearms (e.g., *Rene* in 2009, *NRA v. BATFE* in 2012). Are prohibitions on the possession of guns by illegal drug users and addicts constitutional (e.g., *Richard* in 2009, *Daniels* in 2023)? Do lifetime gun restrictions imposed on the formerly mentally unstable infringe the Second Amendment (e.g., *Tyler* in 2016, *Mai* in 2020)?

In analyzing these questions, courts often used a means-end balancing test to assess whether a challenged law was a permissible infringement on the Second Amendment. If the presumed social benefits of the statute were sufficiently high, courts usually ruled the potential infringement constitutional. The 2008 Supreme Court *Heller* opinion questioned this means-end approach to determining the constitutionality of possible Second Amendment violations, and the court's 2022 *Bruen* opinion repudiated it entirely. This change in how courts analyze Second Amendment violations also contributed to inconsistent interpretations of the amendment.

The Evaluative Standards Question

Even before *Bruen*, courts had disagreed on how to determine if a specific gun statute infringed the Second Amendment. In the twentieth century, with the 1939 *Miller* opinion implying that the Second Amendment was a state right and *not* an individual right, such determinations were generally straightforward. Arguments that a gun law "infringed" a *person's* Second Amendment rights made no legal sense; and early courts easily dismissed such contentions (e.g., *Tot* in 1942, *Case* in 1942). Later courts relied on and simply re-cited these cases to support their own dismissals of potential Second Amendment infringements (e.g., *Cody* in 1972, *Warren* in 1976, *Oakes* in 1977, *Hickman* in 1996).

Questioning this interpretation of *Miller*, courts in the twenty-first century disputed the notion that the Second Amendment is merely a collective right (e.g.,

Emerson in 2001, *Parker* in 2007); and when the Supreme Court confirmed the Second Amendment as an individual right (*Heller* in 2008), identifying standards for determining infringements took on increased significance. But after outlining some broad examples (referencing the amendment's text and the historical traditions of Founding-era gun regulations), neither *Heller* nor *McDonald* (in 2010) provided detailed guidance in the use of these new standards.

Lower courts handled the ambiguity in different ways. Some courts (e.g., *Richard* in 2009, *Rozier* in 2010, *Seay* in 2010, *Folajtar* in 2020) relied on *Heller*'s statements that the opinion did not call into question long-standing firearms prohibitions. They used that argument in upholding various gun statutes, and side-stepped a text-history-tradition analysis. Other courts (e.g., *NRA* in 2012, *Tyler* in 2016, *Mai* in 2020, *Miller* in 2021) adopted a two-step analytical framework. They first determined whether the challenged statute actually impinged on an individual's Second Amendment rights. If it did, they then determined if the statute could survive the appropriate level of scrutiny. Infringements striking at the core of the amendment required strict scrutiny, but less severe encroachments needed only intermediate scrutiny—a more lenient means-ends test. For most gun cases, courts found that intermediate scrutiny was the appropriate standard.

In rejecting this two-step framework, the Supreme Court's *Bruen* decision in 2022 re-emphasized that means-end balancing was not an acceptable yardstick for evaluating the constitutionality of firearms statutes; and instead admonished courts to use the text-history-tradition approach presented in earlier opinions. Using this approach, whenever the plain text of the Second Amendment protects an individual's conduct, the government has to justify the challenged statute by showing its consistency with the country's historical tradition of gun regulation. What outcome did the legislature attempt to achieve with a particular restriction (i.e., the "why" of the historical restriction)? And what method did the legislature use to accomplish this end (i.e., the "how" of the historical law)? Finally, how similar is the "how" and "why" of the current law to the Founding-era analogue?

But this new framework can also produce substantially different assessments of a statute's constitutionality (e.g., *Jackson* in 2023, *Range* in 2023, *Rahimi* in 2023). Judicial interpretations can vary in the depth of the historical analysis conducted and in judgments regarding the probative value of possible historical analogues. Courts also can differ in their choice of the relevant historical period to examine—the Founding period (e.g., *Worth* in 2023, *Lara* in 2024, *Daniels* in 2023) or the Reconstruction period (e.g., *NRA* in 2023). Thus, despite *Bruen*'s clarification of the appropriate standards to use in weighing Second Amendment infringements, the complexities associated with this assessment still abound.

The Supreme Court: Judicial Referee and Political Entity

As the country's ultimate legal referee, the Supreme Court is the responsible body tasked with resolving constitutional ambiguities created by judicial disagreements.

In theory, the refereeing role appears straightforward: the court examines the conflicting opinions and their supporting evidence, consults the relevant provisions of Constitution, verifies which opinion adheres more closely to these provisions, announces its conclusion, and resolves the conflict—if not to everyone's satisfaction, at least to everyone's understanding. In practice, because several of these steps are highly interpretive, the process is significantly more convoluted.

Additionally, while we may expect justices to be unbiased decision-makers, putting aside personal beliefs and remaining "above the fray," they nonetheless are individuals having personal values and opinions. As individuals, they are also surely aware that court rulings have wide-ranging political implications. These considerations (consciously or unconsciously) impact a justice's understanding of the Constitution. Thus, some decision-making subjectivity in court decisions is inevitable despite a vetting process that attempts to insure only "honest brokers" sit on the court. The next sections consider the Second Amendment implications of these various factors.

The Court as Unbiased Referee

Second Amendment gun cases essentially present a history of the country's ongoing attempt to balance an individual's right to arms with the community's need to contain gun misuse—that is, criminal and negligent behavior. In resolving these seemingly conflicting goals, courts at different times have varied widely in the emphasis placed on each goal. If seen as arbitrary, this variation raises questions about the judiciary's role as a neutral and unbiased referee, and perhaps about the Constitution as a fixed document offering an unchanging standard for assessing a statute's legality. A more benevolent view is that the highly interpretive nature of case assessment accounts for the inconsistencies that give rise to these perceptions of bias.

Unlike sports contests where rule violations are generally easy to spot and resolve, the range of relevant information in gun law challenges is substantial. In processing this information, different jurists can disagree on which bits of information take precedence and are determinative. For instance, one jurist may place considerable emphasis on the individual's status as a convicted felon; another may see the individual's decades of post-conviction law-abiding behavior as especially significant. Jurists have some leeway in deciding which facts to emphasize and, reflecting this leeway, different courts reach different conclusions.

Additionally, the Constitution itself—the rule book—demands interpretation. With the words "fixed" in the eighteenth century when the document was written, the Constitution's continuing role as the "law of the land" has required it to address issues unforeseen and unanticipated in the 1700s. Addressing such issues inherently entails extrapolating into unspecified areas and determining the Constitution's intent indirectly. Indeed, one need only look to the conflicting interpretations of the Second Amendment at various historical periods as evidence of this. Does the amendment protect an individual right? Does it protect only militia-type arms? Does it allow for lifetime bans on the right to arms? The amendment is sufficiently ambiguous that numerous jurists in diverse eras have interpreted the amendment and have answered those questions differently.

Further, even after the judicial process appears to have resolved the initial constitutional question, practical issues often remain that require (or allow) interpretive leeway. Decades after the Supreme Court clarified the nature of the Second Amendment with the *Heller* ruling, lower courts continued to struggle with the applied implications of that decision. What is the appropriate procedure for determining a gun statute's constitutionality? Did the amendment allow trade-offs between beneficial societal goals and individuals' gun rights? If so, what factors should influence relative balance between goals and rights? Needing practical resolutions to these unaddressed questions, courts crafted their own—sometimes conflicting—answers.

Finally, even after a series of court determinations have established a common orientation around a Second Amendment issue, judicial disagreement may still exist. The Founding-era versus the Reconstruction-era timeframe debate illustrates this. Despite the Supreme Court's emphasis on 1791 as the relevant historical period for specifying firearm laws or analogues, particular courts may still choose—presumably because of special case circumstances—to offer Reconstruction-era evidence as a more suitable historical choice. More broadly, even Supreme Court justices may strongly question their colleagues' interpretation of the amendment, even asserting the interpretation has no basis in the Constitution.[3]

All these considerations presume that the Supreme Court (and the judiciary generally) functions as an honest referee, and any perceived biases and inconsistencies in court rulings result from legitimate interpretive differences among impartial jurists. A more disturbing presumption is that judicially irrelevant political considerations critically impact judicial interpretation and shape important opinions—especially at the Supreme Court level.

The Court as Political Entity

Some recent political polls have documented a growing tendency in American society to see the judiciary as a political entity rather than as a neutral constitutional arbiter. A Quinnipiac survey in 2021 reported that 61 percent of Americans thought that the Supreme Court was mainly motivated by politics. Only 32 percent of respondents thought that the court ruled based on law.[4] Two years later, the same survey reported that these beliefs had worsened, now with 68 percent of respondents seeing court rulings as mainly reflecting politics and only 25 percent believing the law motivated the court.[5] Further, Americans apparently saw a politicized court as a cause for concern, accompanying these perceptions with a job disapproval rating of 58 percent.[6]

Political analysts have also weighed the influence partisan considerations have on Supreme Court opinions. Their assessments are more nuanced. As one commentator noted,[7] an opinion coinciding with a justice's presumed policy preferences is not necessarily evidence that the opinion was inherently political. The decision may have simply reflected legitimate textual or statutory considerations. Additionally, since most of the court's cases are not centered on divisive social issues, it seems unlikely that politics or personal preferences bias these decisions.

Nonetheless, as the commentator acknowledged, in a number of high-profile cases, the justices' opinions—whether individually conservative or liberal—have aligned dependably with their political views. Consequently, "when the political affiliations of the Court's members change, the Court's view of the Constitution—and fundamental rights—often changes. … Indeed, when the Court accepts for review cases involving [highly divisive] issues, most people know exactly how the justices will vote. They know that the justices will reach outcomes that so conveniently comport with their policy preferences."[8] The analyst argues that these perceptions of a partisan court undermines the court's legitimacy and negatively impact its institutional authority.

Another analyst[9] has suggested that, historically, the Supreme Court *typically* has been a highly political and partisan institution, and the notion of an apolitical Supreme Court is a relatively modern idea. As he has put it, "The notion that justices should be political saints, innocent of partisanship, would have been considered odd, if not risible."[10] But putting history aside, this commentator has also recognized that Americans expect the court to be a neutral arbiter of the law, with justices acting as unbiased umpires "who just call 'balls and strikes.'"[11]

Concluding, he noted,

> Americans from across the political divide regard the court as a political body that wraps ideology in legal garb. There is a reasonable concern that the Supreme Court might lose its legitimacy …. But maybe that's not a bad thing. You can't address a problem until you acknowledge it exists. We have pretended over the past fifty years that the Supreme Court is an apolitical institution. It never really was, and it isn't today.[12]

Still another analyst[13] has questioned Associate Justice Amy Barrett's defense of the impartiality of the Supreme Court. Responding to her assertion that "this court is not comprised of a bunch of partisan hacks. Judicial philosophies are not the same as political parties," he quoted Shakespeare—"the lady doth protest too much." He suggested that her own elevation to the court disproved her argument and added to the impression of a highly politicized court. Lamenting a court "poised to scrap, gut, or rewrite [important laws and policies] on the basis of novel, often dubious, legal theories"[14] he has advocated the use of broad congressional legislation to reform the court and bring it into line with the civics class model of impartial adjudicator.[15]

The research and summarization of yet another analyst[16] are pertinent here:

> The court is a political institution operating in a political environment, often surrounded by controversy …. The justices are individuals subject to political influences and processes that then influence decision-making. [They] each became decision-makers through political appointment processes after having been socialized, politically, just as their colleagues and all people are. And they are subject to the same emotional turmoil and political opinion storms as are we all.[17]

From this perspective, attempting to cleanly separate justices as "honest brokers" from justices as "biased partisans" is not realistic. As noted, even when specifically wanting to act as neutral arbiters, justices undoubtedly encounter interpretive complexities that permit the emergence of unintentional biases.

These ideas also clarify why conflicting rulings are not as discouraging as they might seem. Disagreement between different courts, even in highly similar cases, can reflect legitimate interpretive differences in analyzing constitutional or statutory material.[18] Desiring the "law" to be clear, simple, and straightforward is understandable, but if the law is to be seen as fair and just, statutes must be sufficiently complex to cope with the spectrum of human situations. With that complexity comes the need for judicial interpretation—for both clarity and fairness. Thus, interpretive disagreements about the meaning of the Second Amendment and its application in specific gun cases are not necessarily indicative of some "failure" in the legal process. Such disagreements often reflect firearm issues requiring additional review—typically provided and resolved by higher-level courts.

Nonetheless, this benign interpretation of contradictory opinions is severely undercut when the Supreme Court is viewed as just another political power player. Completely eliminating unavoidable and unconscious biases from court rulings is not possible, but this recognition cannot justify the substitution of deliberately partisan court opinions for neutral legal interpretations. In the Second Amendment context, the question of partisan rulings is especially salient. Firearms policy is a socially divisive issue in America, and the two defining Supreme Court opinions—*Miller* (1939) and *Heller* (2008)—on the Second Amendment seemed to have reached radically different conclusions about the right to bear arms. Might we justifiably conclude that either—or both—were deliberately partisan and biased?

The only objective behavioral evidence of questionable judicial partisanship is an unvarying liberal or conservative consistency in a justice's voting pattern, regardless of the specifics of particular cases.[19] While such consistency is not conclusive—it still may simply reflect the justice's particular understanding of the law—it at least suggests a potential issue. Similarly, the research conclusions of legal scholars—particularly those with some temporal distance from a suspect opinion—can also suggest partisanship.

Along these lines, one scholar—Brian Frye—examined the political environment leading up to the 1939 *Miller* opinion, and the peculiar legal road the case traveled in arriving at the Supreme Court. He has implied that partisan politics probably was influential in the case.[20] Similarly, another scholar—Carlton Larson—critiqued the 2008 *Heller* decision, focusing specifically on the several "presumably lawful" firearms prohibitions that *Heller* allowed. He concluded that these Second Amendment "exceptions" were *ad-hoc* prohibitions with no historical support warranting a constitutional exception. He suggested that they resulted from internal court politics.[21]

Such observations suggest that factors greater than mere differences in legal philosophy shaped the two opinions. Yet, neither of these analysts categorically dismissed the particular ruling as biased or partisan. As with justices' voting patterns, drawing a conclusive inference about partisanship from complex rulings that are unclearly presented or inconsistently argued is not possible. And to a large degree, it may not matter. Whether a Second Amendment opinion truly *is* partisan or merely *appears* partisan, the societal damage is identical. Individuals reject the legitimacy of the ruling, and disparage as incorrect its associated assertions about the meaning of the "right to keep and bear arms." Indeed, popular perceptions of bias and partisanship in gun opinions have even given rise to calls for repealing the amendment.

Repealing the Second Amendment?

Demands for repeal are an extension of the perceived politicization of judicial gun rulings. As proponents of gun control have questionably asserted, if the courts and arch-conservative justices can invent "for the first time in American history a constitutional right to own a gun for self-defense … and then pretend like it's always been there,"[22] then perhaps it is time for the country to consider abolishing the amendment.

Particularly after *Heller*, and frustrated by the perceived lack of judicial support for upholding "common sense" regulation, gun control activists have identified the Second Amendment as a major roadblock in protecting the country from firearm violence. Especially after mass shootings and other gun tragedies, editorials and opinion pieces arguing to abolish the amendment proliferate. Sometimes a commentator does not directly fault the amendment itself, noting that "the right to lock and load, any time, any place, is not protected by the Second Amendment—it's protected by the Republican interpretation of the Second Amendment."[23]

Other pundits do directly indict the amendment. One commentator described the amendment as an "anachronistic byproduct of an 18th century effort to avoid the need to raise and fund a federal army [and whose repeal] would finally remove what has become an intractable barrier to sensible regulation."[24] Another simply argued, "The hard truth is that the core problem is the Second Amendment itself. And America is going to reel from one mass murder to another unless the Second Amendment is repealed."[25]

Abolishing the amendment has also been endorsed by former Supreme Court justices. For instance, labeling the amendment as a relic of the eighteenth century, John Paul Stevens suggested that gun control demonstrators "should seek more effective and more lasting reform [and] should demand a repeal of the Second Amendment."[26] Similarly, Warren Burger stated, "If I were writing the Bill of Rights now, there wouldn't be any such thing as the Second Amendment."[27]

Many of those calling for repeal have done so because they believe the Supreme Court has misinterpreted the amendment's meaning, both as an individual right to possess firearms and as to who can possess a gun. As one person sarcastically wrote, "The Supreme Court has decided that 'a well-regulated militia' includes gang bangers and wild-eyed loners with a grudge."[28] But even some individuals who believe the court's *Heller* interpretation is likely correct have advocated for repeal. One such commentator has argued that, even if the amendment does protect an individual right to arms, the country can still simply conclude "the Founders were wrong about the importance of guns to a free society." He proposed repealing "the damned thing."[29]

The frustration embodied in these demands for repeal did not just arise with the *Heller*, *McDonald*, and *Bruen* decisions. While these opinions amplified Second Amendment uneasiness in segments of the American public, such hostility has long predated the court rulings. Cities and heavily populated urban areas have frequently asserted that only stringent regulations can reduce rampant gun carnage and insure public safety. Additionally, proponents for stringent gun controls have often looked to Western Europe and other "first world" nations for guidance, citing their regulations and much lower gun-related death rates relative to the United States. They pointedly have noted that none of those nations have a constitutional provision enshrining an individual right to arms.[30] Thus, calls to abolish the amendment go beyond perceptions of a partisan judiciary.

On a pragmatic level, repealing the amendment requires either Congress—or a Constitutional Convention—to enact an amendment that rescinds the Second. While possible, most experts consider either scenario highly unlikely.[31] Despite the low present-day probability, some advocates for repeal see value in the effort, even if the task is "a 50 year job."[32] Others have argued that even if repeal never happens, such calls might spur "the predictable debates over limited anti-gun legislation" to focus on "truly disarming America."[33] Still others, anticipating that repeal might take decades, see demands for repeal as a useful tactic for gaining "victories along the way." Specifically, such demands can make initially seeming radical gun control proposals appear more moderate, thus increasing their likelihood of enactment.[34]

Given the multiple motivations underlying calls for repeal, but the low likelihood of repeal actually happening, such calls imply that proponents will likely search for other novel ways to regulate an individual's right to arms. For instance, California governor Gavin Newsom has recently proposed an amendment to the US Constitution that he asserts will lower gun violence, "while leaving the Second Amendment unchanged and respecting America's gun-owning tradition."[35] His proposed amendment would permanently enshrine several well-known but controversial gun control principles into the Constitution, as well as affirm the ability of Congress, the states, and local governments to "enact additional common-sense gun safety regulations that save lives."[36]

The governor did not explain why this amendment might have a greater chance of enactment than one simply repealing the Second, or how the courts might resolve likely conflicts between the two amendments. But if actually enacted—a highly unlikely possibility—the amendment would undoubtedly circumscribe firearm-related behaviors currently protected by the Second Amendment.

More broadly, the desire of a sizable cohort of citizens to abolish an enumerated right is noteworthy. This willingness to overturn the amendment has serious societal consequences and important implications for the type of governing that might evolve. As one editorial board noted, "there will always be a fringe minority out there yapping for scrapping the Second Amendment. Or the Third Amendment. Or the Fourth Amendment. Or the ... You get the point."[37] Even assuming that more Americans support stringent gun regulation than oppose it, the US Constitution currently protects the fundamental rights of an even unpopular minority from the potential tyranny of the majority. The firearms debate and demands for repeal imply that this protective constitutional function is suspect. Referencing the claimed "overwhelming support"[38] for stringent gun regulation, the tone of many repeal demands appear to favor an unchecked "majority rule" approach to governing.

Providing a more cautious perspective on repeal, another commentator questioned whether even judges should "be in charge of stripping disfavored rights from the Constitution. If the courts can simply make gun rights disappear, what happens when the First Amendment becomes embarrassing or inconvenient? It corrodes the very idea of a written Constitution."[39] While supporting gun regulation, he nevertheless asserted that the desire for gun control should not compromise constitutional legitimacy.

Ultimately, demands for repeal of the Second Amendment are not important because repeal is a serious possibility but because they underscore a fracture in American society regarding the right to bear arms. Regardless of its judicial interpretation, the amendment has come to symbolize both a defining American strength for those individuals favoring gun rights and a reprehensible American failing for those wanting gun control. Under these circumstances, we anticipate that the future will likely look much like the past. Gun control proponents will surely keep attempting to limit the Second Amendment and regulate firearms, while gun rights advocates will as surely keep attempting to expand firearm rights and defend the amendment.

Current Firearms Challenges: Recent Clarifications

If the prediction above is accurate, with constitutional clashes over firearms ongoing, both the Supreme Court and federal appeals courts will continue to clarify the right to keep and bear arms. Along these lines, the Supreme Court in 2024 issued an important decision regarding disarming domestic abusers. The opinion focused on the *Rahimi* (2023) case discussed earlier. The court reversed the circuit court's determination that had upheld Rahimi's gun rights despite his status as a convicted violent felon.

United States v. Rahimi (2024)

As noted in Chapter 7, the Fifth Circuit had upheld Zackey Rahimi's challenge to the constitutionality of 18 U.S.C. §922 (g) (8), the statute prohibiting an individual subject to a domestic violence restraining order from possessing a firearm, if that individual represented a credible threat to the safety of an intimate partner. Rahimi, an illegal drug dealer, had a police history of gun violence and had threatened to shoot his intimate partner on at least one occasion. She obtained a restraining order against him, which included a finding that he had committed family violence that was likely to occur again and that he posed a credible threat to the physical safety of her and their child.[40]

After Texas police identified Rahimi as a suspect in a number of shootings, they obtained a warrant and searched his residence, where they found firearms, ammunition, and a copy of the restraining order. Indicted and convicted of violating 18 U.S.C. §922 (g) (8), Rahimi moved to dismiss the indictment, arguing that the statute violated the Second Amendment. On appeal, the Fifth Circuit, citing *Bruen*, concluded that the government's evidence was not persuasive in showing that the challenged statute fit within the country's tradition of gun regulation. The panel overturned Rahimi's conviction. Appealed then to the Supreme Court, Chief Justice John Roberts authored the majority opinion for the court.[41]

Chief Justice Roberts began by noting,

> Since the founding our Nation's firearm laws have included provisions preventing individuals who threaten physical arm to others from misusing firearms. As applied to the facts of this case, Section 922 (g) (8) fits comfortably within this tradition. ... At the founding, the bearing of arms was subject to regulations ranging from rules about firearm storage to restrictions on gun use by drunken New Year's Eve revelers. [Citations provided]. Some jurisdictions banned the carrying of 'dangerous and unusual' weapons. [Citations provided]. Others forbade carrying concealed weapons. [Citation provided].[42]

Roberts continued,

> As we explained in *Bruen*, the appropriate analysis involves considering whether the challenged regulation is consistent with the principles that underpin our regulatory tradition. [*Bruen* citation]. A court must ascertain whether the new law is "relevantly similar" to laws that our tradition is understood to permit .... Why and how the regulation burdens the right are central to this inquiry. For example, if laws at the founding regulated firearm use to address particular problems, that will be a strong indicator that contemporary laws imposing similar restrictions for similar reasons fall within a permissible category of regulations.[43]

He noted further,

> Even when a law regulates arms-bearing for a permissible reason, though, it may not be compatible with the right if it does so to an extent beyond what was done at the founding. And when a challenged regulation does not precisely match its historical precursors, "it still may be analogous enough to pass constitutional muster." [*Bruen* citation]. The law must comport with the principles underlying the Second Amendment, but it need not be a "dead ringer" or a "historical twin."[44]

Using these principles, the court evaluated Rahimi's argument.

In reviewing the history of early American gun laws, Roberts first observed that English common law dating back to the 1328 Statute of Northampton had typically included regulations barring individuals from misusing weapons to harm or frighten others. In eighteenth- and nineteenth-century America, the nation relied on both "surety laws" and "going armed" laws to address gun violence. Under the first, magistrates could require individuals suspected of possible future misbehavior to post a bond or be jailed. The individual forfeited the bond if he later broke the peace. Roberts asserted, "Well entrenched in the common law, the surety laws could be invoked to prevent all forms of violence, including spousal abuse."[45] Wives might demand sureties against their husbands, and husbands against their wives.

Additionally, the surety laws also regulated the misuse of firearms. They authorized magistrates to detain individuals who went about "armed offensively," and required them to post bonds to insure their keeping the peace. Roberts noted that significant procedural protections generally accompanied these laws.

> Before the accused could be compelled to post a bond … a complaint had to be made to a judge … by "any person having reasonable cause to fear" that the accused would do him harm or breach the peace. [Citation provided]. The magistrate would take evidence, and—if he determined that cause existed for the charge—summon the accused who could respond to the allegations. Bonds could not be required for more than six months at a time.[46]

The second mechanism used to address gun violence in early America was "going armed" laws. While the surety laws attempted to forestall violence before it happened, the "going armed" laws (a subset of ancient common-law prohibitions on affrays) sanctioned the punishment of individuals using firearms to menace others. Roberts wrote, "the going armed laws prohibited 'riding or going armed, with dangerous or unusual weapons, [to] terrify[] the good people of the land.' [Citation provided]. Such conduct disrupted the 'public order' and 'le[d] almost necessarily to actual violence.' [*Huntly* 1843 citation]. Therefore, the law punished these acts with 'forfeiture of the arms … and imprisonment.' [Citation given]."[47]

The chief justice concluded his historical review, asserting,

> Taken together, the surety and going armed laws confirm what common sense suggests: When an individual poses a clear threat of physical violence to another, the threatening individual may be disarmed. Section 922 (g) (8) is by no means identical to these founding era regimes, but it does not need to be. [*Bruen* citation]. Its prohibition on the possession of firearms by those found by a court to present a threat to others fits neatly within the tradition the surety and going armed laws represent. Like [these laws], Section 922 (g) (8) (C) (i) applies to individuals found to threaten the physical safety of another. This provision is "relevantly similar" to those founding era regimes in both why and how it burdens the Second Amendment right.[48]

Roberts further elaborated,

> Unlike the regulation in *Bruen*, Section 922 (g) (8) does not broadly restrict arms use by the public generally. … [Also] we note that Section 922 (g) (8) applies only once a court has found that the defendant "represents a credible threat to the physical safety" of another. §922 (g) (8) (C) (i). That matches the surety and going armed laws …. Moreover, like surety bonds of limited duration, Section 922

> (g) (8)'s restriction was temporary as applied to Rahimi. Section 922 (g) (8) only prohibits firearm possession so long as the defendant "is" subject to a restraining order. … Finally, the penalty—another relevant aspect of the burden—also fits within the regulatory decision. The going armed laws provided for imprisonment … then the lesser restriction of temporary disarmament that Section 922 (g) (8) imposes is also permissible.[49]

Roberts ended the court's opinion by considering the contrary view of Justice Thomas and the earlier ruling of the Fifth Circuit. He wrote,

> The dissent reaches a contrary conclusion, primarily on the ground that the historical analogues for Section 922 (g) (8) are not sufficiently similar to place that provision within our historical tradition. The dissent does, however, acknowledge that Section 922 (g) (8) is within that tradition when it comes to the "why" of the appropriate inquiry. The objection is to the "how." [Citation to Thomas Dissent]. For the reasons we have set forth, however, we conclude that Section 922 (g) (8) satisfies that part of the inquiry as well. As we said in *Bruen*, a "historical twin" is not required.[50]

Turning to the circuit court's earlier ruling, he asserted,

> The Fifth Circuit made two errors. First, like the dissent, it read *Bruen* to require a "historical twin" rather than a "historical analogue." Second, it did not correctly apply our precedents governing facial challenges. [Citation provided]. As we have said in other contexts, "[w]hen the legislation and the Constitution brush up against each other, [a court's task] is to seek harmony, not to manufacture conflict." [Citation provided]. Rather than consider the circumstance [where the statute] was most likely to be constitutional, the panel instead focused on hypothetical scenarios where Section 922 (g) (8) might raise constitutional concerns. [Citation provided]. That error left the panel slaying a straw man.[51]

Roberts closed the opinion by asserting that prior court rulings—*Heller*, *McDonald*, and *Bruen*—did not present an exhaustive analysis of the Second Amendment's full scope, and neither did this opinion. He continued,

> Rather, we conclude only this: An individual found by a court to present a credible threat to the physical safety of another may be temporarily disarmed consistent with the Second Amendment. The judgment for the Court of Appeals for the Fifth Circuit is reversed, and the case is remanded for further proceedings consistent with this opinion. *It is so ordered*.[52]

As the next section indicates, *Rahimi* is not the only circuit court decision that the Supreme Court is likely to soon address.

Future Firearms Challenges: Continuing Debates

In addition to gun issues already examined, future courts are likely to encounter Second Amendment gun clashes in at least four broad areas. The first revolves around the legality and possession of potentially dangerous gun "accessories" (e.g., large-capacity magazines (LCMs) and forced reset triggers (FRTs)). The second centers on the constitutionality of prohibiting certain types of firearms (e.g., unserialized "ghost" guns and "assault" weapons). The third focuses on firearms in prohibited areas and the acceptable specifications of such areas. Presently, "gun-free" zones are often extensive, covering public housing, congested urban spaces, schools and churches, and government buildings. The fourth area involves the constitutional boundaries of handgun permit requirements, post *Bruen*.

Large-Capacity Magazines

LCMs are commonly defined as magazines capable of holding more than ten or fifteen cartridges—the actual number varies from state to state. Gun rights proponents have long asserted that statutes restricting the ammunition capacity of these devices are unconstitutional, but at least fourteen states have prohibitions on the purchase of LCMs.[53] Federal circuit courts across multiple regions have upheld these prohibitions, but these rulings all occurred prior to *Bruen* and used means-end scrutiny in determining the constitutionality of the statutes. A ruling in a 2023 California case now suggests these prior decisions may not stand.[54]

In a remanded case that has been in litigation since 2017, US District Judge Roger Benitez determined that a California ban on the possession of magazines holding more than ten rounds (California Penal Code § 32310) was unconstitutional. In his ruling, Benitiz first provided a review of the case background; then discussed the applicable constitutional standards as promulgated in *Heller*, *McDonald*, and *Bruen*; and finally assessed the implications of the historical evidence. Contrary to the state's position, he concluded that LCMs are "arms" under the Second Amendment and that they are "presumptively protected." As such, the judge observed, "Under *Bruen*, the government must affirmatively prove that its firearm regulation is part of a constitutional historical tradition."[55]

Benitez noted that, pre-*Bruen*, the court had previously determined a LCM ban lacked a "historical pedigree," and had directed the state to create a list of relevant laws showing "a national 'historical tradition of firearm regulation.' "[56] The laws were to cover the period of 1791 (enactment of the Second Amendment) up to 1888 (twenty years after passage of the Fourteenth Amendment)—the most relevant timeframe according to *Bruen*. Instead, the state generated a list of 316 laws, dating from 1383 to 1933.[57]

Dismissing many of these laws as coming much earlier or much later than the significant time period, or because they were restrictions on use rather than on possession, the judge examined those laws the state considered most relevant. He concluded,

> Based on a close review of the State's law list, and the Court's own analysis, Plaintiffs are correct in asserting there are no Founding-era categorical bans on firearms in this nation's history. … the State has not identified any law, anywhere, at any time, between 1791 and 1868 that prohibited simple possession of a gun or its magazine or any container of ammunition.[58]

Benitez further asserted, "From the adoption of the Second Amendment through the next 50 years, there were no firearms restrictions in any states north of the Mason-Dixon Line. … The same was largely true south of the Mason-Dixon Line (disregarding laws targeting slaves and Indians, neither of which were considered to be citizens by lawmakers.)"[59] Concerning the state's best historic analogue—a New York City gunpower storage law limiting the amount of powder that could be stored within a city building—Benitez was dismissive. He argued, "The gunpowder storage law has nothing to do with gun violence. It was *a fire safety regulation*. … enacted after New York City suffered two great fires."[60]

Similarly, he dismissed the state's next-best historic analogues, laws regulating the concealed carrying of Bowie knives, dirks, sword canes, and some pistols. He observed, "*Bruen* says the state's burden is to identify a historical *firearm* regulation, not a knife regulation."[61] Regarding pistols, the judge argued,

> Historic concealed carry laws for pistols have a different "why" and "how" than do the State's large capacity magazine ban. The "why" of a concealed carry law was to prevent unfair surprise attacks …. The "how" … was to proscribe the manner of carrying a pocket pistol and only when in public. … concealed carry prohibitions are not nuanced analogues … as they are not relevantly similar.[62]

Ending his opinion by reiterating that magazines are presumptively protected, and that no American tradition exists in regulating firearms based on the number of rounds they can shoot, Judge Benitez declared the California LCM statute unconstitutional.

Benitez's ruling directly clashes with a July 2024 opinion regarding the constitutionality of LCMs rendered by US District Judge Peter Sheridan.[63] In this New Jersey case, the plaintiffs challenged the state's ban on both the Colt AR-15 rifle and LCMs. While he found the rifle ban unconstitutional, Judge Sheridan upheld New Jersey's ban on LCMs. He acknowledged that LCMs were "arms" covered by the Second Amendment, and that they are commonly owned. However, he observed that "the question of magazine capacity is directly related to the mass shooting issue [and] bears strongly upon the lethality and accuracy of modern firearms; where mass shootings have become a societal scourge, the very practical issue of ways to prevent—or alternatively, to limit—their lethality is before the Court."[64]

Citing specifically the "accurate brutality exacted today by mass shooters," Sheridan continued, "For these reasons, the nuanced historical analysis discussed within *Bruen*—which called for nuanced 'analogical reasoning' to determine whether historical analogues are 'relevantly similar' in unprecedented circumstances—is appropriate."[65] After reviewing various historical evidence, the judge indicated that the "apt historical analogues here are other firearms (specifically pistols) and the Bowie knife. With respect to pistols, the relevant restrictions provided by the State Defendants are largely contemporary. … The most analogous comparison to the regulation at issue here is the Bowie knife, which—like many knives—'were [historically] often regulated like handguns[.]' [Citation provided]."[66]

Sheridan then noted that, by the mid-1800s, "Once Bowie knives' potential misuse became apparent, restrictions were enacted"[67] in virtually all states and territories, and "like these restrictions, the LCM Amendment is precisely that—a restriction responding to safety concerns present in our time. As to the 'whys' for the LCM Amendment, there is significant data that large capacity magazines increase the lethality of mass shooting events."[68] Asserting that the LCM restriction responded to a current societal problem similarly to the way the nation had addressed such problems in the past, and that the law burdened an individual's right to self-defense no more than past historical laws, the judge upheld the LCM ban.

The legality of LCMs is also receiving attention at the state level. Gary Bashor, a Superior Court Judge in Cowlitz County, Washington, determined in April 2024 that the state's prohibition on the sale of LCMs violated both the federal Second Amendment and part of Washington's own state constitution. At the state attorney's request, Washington's Supreme Court has already agreed to review Bashor's opinion.[69] Similarly, circuit court reviews are likely outcomes for both the California and New Jersey district court LCM opinions. If the divergent conclusions regarding the constitutionality of LCMs are not resolved at this level, it is probable the Supreme Court will address the issue.

Forced Reset Triggers

An FRT modification allows the trigger of a semiautomatic firearm to reset faster than it would using a standard trigger-return spring. Because of the quicker reset, a shooter is able to fire the gun at a greater rate than with a standard trigger. In 2018, the Bureau of Alcohol, Tobacco, Firearms and Explosives (BATFE) revised its definition of "machinegun" and determined that firearms using an FRT mechanism were illegal machineguns under the revised definition. BATFE's determination, in effect, prohibited the possession, transfer, or manufacture of FRTs. Alleging that BATFE's revised definition of "machinegun" conflicted with the term's statutory definition, gun rights activists and manufacturers of FRTs challenged the legality of BATFE's classification. [70]

US District Judge Reed O'Connor received the case and, after reviewing the relevant filings and applicable law, determined that BATFE "engaged in unlawful agency action taken in excess of their authority."[71] In his decision, he emphasized that, even when firing multiple shots using an FRT, "the trigger must still reset after each round is fired and must separately function to release the hammer by moving far enough to the rear in order to fire the next round."[72] In contrast, O'Connor observed,

> As the Supreme Court agreed, a weapon that qualifies as a machinegun under §5845(b) of the NFA [National Firearms Act] must be capable of (1) firing multiple

rounds by a single function of the trigger and (2) do so automatically. [*Cargill* citation[73]]. In other words, the NFA unambiguously defines a machinegun as a weapon that fires automatically once the trigger performs a single function.[74]

Elaborating on the *Cargill* decision, the judge asserted,

> Similar to FRTs, a bump stock is an accessory that attaches to a semi-automatic weapon to increase the rate of fire. … Yet, despite this increase in firing speed, *Cargill* determined that bump stocks are not machine guns because the device does not meet both elements of the statutory definition: (1) capable of firing multiple rounds by a single function of the trigger and (2) operate automatically. … Applying the guidance from [*Cargill*] here, FRTs do not fire multiple rounds with a single function of the trigger and, thus, do not qualify as machine guns. For each and every round fired … the trigger of an FRT-equipped firearm functions for each shot fired [and that] disqualifies it as a machinegun under the current statutory definition.[75]

Judge O'Connor also faulted BATFE for not following the required processes outlined in the Administrative Procedures Act (APA) for promulgating or modifying substantive regulations. He noted that the agency's failure to follow required practices would be additional cause for setting aside the agency's action. After vacating BATFE's "unlawful classification of FRTs as 'machine guns,'" he then concluded that the case "is emblematic of a devastating problem that increasingly rears its head in federal courts: rampant evasion of the democratic process [in enacting laws on important societal issues]."[76]

Another case involving FRTs—*United States v. Rare Breed Triggers*[77]—is also wending its way through the judicial system. While the substantive issues in both these cases are technical and procedural in nature, the opinions have clear Second Amendment implications by determining whether a firearm falls under NFA restrictions. Both cases are likely to undergo higher court review. Given the Supreme Court's determination in *Cargill* that bump stocks do not transform a semiautomatic firearm into an illegal automatic machine gun, it seems likely that review courts will reach the same conclusion about FRTs and uphold their legality.

Ghost Guns

The Gun Control Act of 1968 requires that all commercially manufactured and sold firearms have a serial number, but privately made and kept firearms are currently not subject to this requirement. These guns—since they have no identifying number—are commonly called "ghost" guns because they are typically impossible for law enforcement to trace. The most conventional ways of creating ghost guns are through 3D printing or through the purchase of a commercially prepared "parts" kit that allows the buyer to finish assembling the firearm with some additional effort. A third way of creating a ghost gun is by obliterating or removing the serial number from a commercially manufactured weapon but, unlike the first two methods, such an alteration makes the gun illegal.

The existence of unserialized guns has always been a contentious point between gun rights advocates and gun control proponents. Gun control supporters argue that requiring serial numbers on all firearms is a necessary step in insuring that guns are kept out of the hands of dangerous individuals. Additionally, they assert that serial numbers are highly useful in solving gun crimes. In contrast, gun rights supporters argue that requiring serial numbers on privately created and kept firearms is government overreach, and an infringement on the Second Amendment. They also note that the argued benefit of serial numbers—solving gun crimes—is exaggerated, with traces typically identifying an owner who lost the gun or had it stolen.[78]

From a Second Amendment perspective, the immediate controversy centers on the constitutionality of 18 U.S.C. §922 (k)—the statute that prohibits possession of a firearm with an altered, obliterated, or removed serial number. In 2022, Randy Price, a convicted felon, was indicted "for being a felon in possession of a firearm … and for possession of a firearm with an obliterated serial number."[79] Regarding the obliterated serial number, US District Judge Joseph Goodwin noted that §922 (k) criminalized the mere *possession* of such a firearm—and concluded, "that is the definition of an infringement on one's right to possess a firearm."[80]

Goodwin emphasized that this made the statute "presumptively unconstitutional" and required the government to "show that 'it is consistent with the Nation's historical tradition of firearm regulation.' [*Bruen* citation]."[81] After reviewing the evidence, the judge determined, "The Government has not done so here [i.e., has not shown that the law was consistent with historical tradition] and I have no choice but to find 18 U.S.C. §922 (k) unconstitutional."[82] However, this decision is not be the final word regarding obliterated serial numbers: the government has already appealed the ruling to the Fourth Circuit *en banc* Court.

On another front of the ghost gun controversy, the Biden administration's attempt to regulate the treatment of commercially sold gun parts kits (typically used for assembling homemade AR-15 type rifles) will also receive further judicial scrutiny. As noted in *Vanderstok v. Garland* (2023),[83] these parts kits contain a partially machined billet of metal (i.e., an "80% receiver" in industry terms) that requires the buyer to drill a precise series of holes to finish the part and allow it to serve as a functional firearm. Another kit (usually supplied and purchased from another manufacturer) contains the guides, measurements, tools, and instructions for transforming 80 percent receivers into functional parts.

In 2023, the BATFE promulgated new rules treating such kits as actual firearms. As firearms, the kits are required to have serial numbers, and kit sellers are required to run background checks and keep records on purchasers. While the new regulations are not directly Second Amendment-related, they have obvious Second Amendment-implications, and gun rights activists immediately sued the agency to rescind them.

By treating 80 percent receiver kits as actual guns, the activists argued that BATFE's new regulations essentially expanded the definition of firearms—an expansion going far beyond the agency's statutory authority. A US district judge in Texas, Judge Reed

O'Connor (the same judge who handled the FRT case discussed above) agreed and blocked BATFE from enforcing the new rules.[84] On appeal to the Fifth Circuit, the circuit court upheld O'Connor's decision.

Making an emergency appeal to the Supreme Court, the government then asked that court to treat these "unassembled ghost guns" as it would an assembled gun. In a 5–4 split decision, the court voted to allow BATFE to implement the new regulations while legal challenges to it continued in the lower courts. Depending on how these courts rule, the Supreme Court may revisit the issue.

Ironically, while gun rights' proponents were claiming that BATFE *exceeded* its statutory authority regarding 80 percent receivers, the State of California was arguing that the agency *failed* to meet its statutory obligations regarding such receivers. Specifically, California has disputed BATFE's technical determination that 80 percent receiver kits sold without jigs or the tools necessary to complete the receiver are *not* firearms, while kits sold with the necessary tools *are* firearms. California has contended that, given the ease with which an individual can obtain the instructions and tools needed to convert an 80 percent receiver into a fully functional component, BATFE should also classify these receivers as firearms, even when sold without instructions or tools.

After reviewing the arguments and submitted evidence, in 2024, US District Judge Edward Chen accepted California's position that BATFE ignored relevant data when it failed to classify receiver kits without jigs as firearms. Citing the evidence that parts, guides, and information were readily available for a kit buyer to convert an 80 percent receiver into a functioning receiver, Chen concluded that the agency's determination was arbitrary and capricious, and vacated that aspect of the regulation.[85] It is likely that the Supreme Court will ultimately address the issues raised in both the Texas and California cases.

Assault Weapons

While definitions vary from state to state, "assault" weapons are typically defined as military-style semiautomatic rifles (or pistols) having certain characteristics, such as folding stocks, flash suppressors, detachable magazines, fixed magazines holding more than ten rounds, and so forth. Legislatures often list and identify proscribed firearms by type (e.g., the AR-15, the AK-47, the TEC-9) and include "copycat" variants of firearms specified in the ban. While the federal assault weapons ban expired in 2004, currently ten states have enacted prohibitions on such firearms.[86]

As discussed in Chapter 6, US District Judge Roger Benitez—the judge who also ruled against California's LCM ban in 2023—had determined that California's assault weapons ban was unconstitutional as early as 2021. The Ninth Circuit Court of Appeals stayed that decision. Later, in light of the 2022 *Bruen* opinion, the circuit court remanded the case back to the district court, and Benitez—seeing nothing in *Bruen* that contradicted his original ruling—again determined that the California statute was unconstitutional.[87] Given *Bruen*'s heavy emphasis on "text, history, and tradition" in determining the constitutionality of firearm statutes, that opinion certainly appears to offer strong support for Benitez's opinion that assault weapons bans violate the Second Amendment.

Similarly, in the New Jersey LCM case discussed above, Judge Sheridan also concluded that the state's ban on AR-15 rifles was unconstitutional. He noted that AR-15 rifles were commonly used for self-defense, and Supreme Court precedent made a categorical ban on such weapons unlawful.[88] Nonetheless, multiple states (i.e., California, Connecticut, Delaware, Hawaii, Illinois, Maryland, Massachusetts, New Jersey, New York, and Washington)[89] have—and seem willing to defend—such bans in court.

For instance, California has appealed Benitez's ruling, and Sheridan specifically limited his decision to only the Colt AR-15. He let stand the ban on the rest of the statute's list of prohibited firearms, thus making additional challenges likely. Also, in contrast to the California and New Jersey decisions, the Fourth Circuit Court of Appeals in August 2024 *upheld* Maryland's prohibition on the sale and possession of military-style assault weapons.[90] Overall, it seems clear that courts will continue to encounter tests of assault weapons bans until the Supreme Court more directly clarifies the issue.

Gun-Free Zones

Restrictions on carrying firearms in certain locations—for example, polling locations and courtrooms—date back to colonial times, but the passage of the Gun-Free School Zone Act in 1990 marked the modern genesis of prohibitions on gun-carrying in specially designated areas. Also referred to as "sensitive" or "restricted" locations, the premise underlying gun-free zones is that such prohibitions may increase public safety in highly congested locales (e.g., theaters, subways) and may protect particularly "vulnerable" populations (e.g., school children; hospital patients) in other special settings.

As a response to the 2022 *Bruen* decision that effectively invalidated or weakened many state firearms restrictions, a number of these states—for exampe, California, Maryland, New Jersey, New York—passed legislation greatly expanding the state's gun-free areas. Seen as an attempted "end-run" around the gun-bearing implications of *Bruen*, gun rights activists promptly challenged these restrictions in court. At this point, lower courts have come to different conclusions regarding the constitutionality of carry restrictions in these newly designated gun-free zones.

For instance, in early December 2023, the US Court of Appeals for the Second Circuit reviewed—and generally reversed—lower-court rulings that had found most of New York's new regulations likely unconstitutional and had enjoined enforcement of these provisions. In contrast, in late December, 2023, a US District Court of California reviewed a challenge to a recent California statute containing provisions virtually identical to the New York law. That court concluded the California statute turned nearly every public place in California into a "sensitive place" and, in effect, abolished the Second Amendment. The judge granted the preliminary injunction that the plaintiffs sought. Each of these cases are briefly described below.

In the New York case, *Antonyuk et al. v. Chiumento et al.*,[91] the Second Circuit reviewed four district court cases all challenging numerous provisions of the state's recently enacted Concealed Carry Improvement Act (CCIA). After *Bruen* invalidated New York's concealed carry "proper cause" requirement, the CCIA made it a crime (even for concealed-carry license holders) to carry a firearm in six categories of "sensitive locations." The Act also prohibited carrying firearms in "restricted locations"—that is, any private property, including property generally open to the public—unless the property owner provided affirmative express consent to armed entry. In the case of private property open to the public (e.g., grocery stores, gas stations), affirmative consent required the posting of conspicuous signage indicating armed entry was permitted.[92]

Sensitive locations included (1) medical and health treatment centers, (2) places of worship, (3) parks and zoos, (4) premises serving alcohol, (5) theaters, conference centers, and banquet halls, and (6) "First Amendment" gathering places. The four district courts had concluded the CCIA's provisions violated the various plaintiffs' Second Amendment rights and granted preliminary injunctions against enforcement. The circuit court—accepting the state's historical analogues—disagreed and reversed most of these rulings.[93]

Concerning treatment centers, the state's historical analogues consisted of militia laws from Maine, Massachusetts, and Rhode Island that excluded people with intellectual disabilities, mental illness, and alcoholism from militia duty. The state also pointed to the tradition of limiting firearms in areas crowded with "vulnerable" groups, such as school children. The district court rejected these mid-nineteenth-century militia regulations as insufficiently similar to the CCIA's challenged provisions, noting they differed both in purpose and in scope.[94]

In contrast, the circuit court concluded that "the laws [were] sufficiently established and representative to stand as analogues. ... [Just as the current provision] aims to protect 'vulnerable or impaired people who either cannot defend themselves or cannot be trusted to have firearms around them safely' [Citation provided] ... the 19th century state militia laws ... were aimed at protecting vulnerable populations from either misusing arms or having arms used against them."[95] The circuit court determined that the analogues reflected the "Nation's tradition of firearm regulation in locations where vulnerable populations are present. ... The three militia laws and the tradition of prohibiting firearms in schools are each 'relevantly similar.'"[96]

Asserting that the district court erroneously concluded that the state's evidence was insufficiently analogous, the circuit court vacated the district court's preliminary injunction against CCIA's treatment centers provision.

The circuit court's review of the other challenged CCIA provisions followed a similar pattern, with the circuit court typically concluding that the historical analogues questioned by the district courts were, in fact, "relevantly similar." For instance, in a challenge to the CCIA's parks and zoos provision, the district court rejected an 1870 Texas law and an 1883 Missouri law offered as historical analogues to the current statute. The court asserted that just two laws could not establish a tradition and that the statutes were not representative, covering only 6.6 percent of the nation's population at that time. The court also noted that neither statute specifically prohibited firearms in public parks and that the historical record contained no statutes banning firearms in similar areas (e.g., "commons" and "greens").[97]

The circuit court, however, accepted the state's contention that a tradition of regulating firearms (dating back to the 1328 Statute of Northampton) "in quintessential public forums, such as fairs and markets,"[98] justified regulating firearms in public parks, which also often serve as public forums. Additionally, the circuit court accepted the state's argument that the parks and zoo statute "endeavors to protect children who often frequent public parks from firearms and is thus consistent with the tradition of regulating firearms in areas frequented by children."[99]

The circuit court asserted, "We differ with the district court … because the district court erroneously discounted many of the State's proffered analogues," concluding that "the State has carried its burden by placing the regulation within a national traditional of regulating firearms in often-crowded public squares, including, specifically, city parks."[100] The court then vacated the district court's preliminary injunction concerning parks. Similarly, the circuit court also determined that "prohibiting firearms at zoos is consistent with the country's tradition of regulating firearms in places of educational and scientific opportunity, places heavily trafficked by children, and places that are densely crowded."[101]

Finding the state's historical analogues "analogous enough to pass constitutional muster"[102] [*Bruen* citation], the circuit court also vacated the preliminary injunctions against firearms prohibition in places of worship (with one church excepted), in alcohol-serving premises, and in theaters and conference centers. For banquet halls and First Amendment gatherings (e.g., protests), the court cited the plaintiffs' lack of standing for vacating the challenges.

Turning to "restricted locations," the circuit court asserted that the state's historical analogues were insufficient to establish a national tradition regulating firearms on private property open to the public. Thus, the court upheld the district court's injunction of this provision. Concerning private property not open to the public, the court remanded the preliminary injunction for further analysis.[103]

While the Second Circuit was upholding New York's gun-free zones, a US district court in California was similarly examining that state's recent law (SB2) prohibiting handguns in many of the same venues discussed in the CCIA. Unlike the Second Circuit, the judge in that case, *May et al. v. Bonta*, determined that the statute was "sweeping, repugnant to the Second Amendment, and openly defiant of the Supreme Court."[104] Judge Cormac Carney ruled that all twenty-six categories of the law's "sensitive" places—for example, hospitals, playgrounds, stadiums, amusement parks, banks, and so forth—violated the Second Amendment, and he granted the plaintiffs' request for a preliminary injunction.

In forming his opinion, Judge Carney emphasized the rigorous requirements of California's "carry concealed weapon" (CCW) license—for example, a personal interview, three character references, background checks, 16 hours' mandatory training, and so forth. He noted that the process is specifically designed to insure that individuals receiving a permit are notably law-abiding and responsible. He then observed that the plaintiffs—CCW holders—are clearly part of "the people" covered by the Second Amendment and that the firearms they want to carry in the newly designated sensitive places are clearly arms in common use for self-defense.[105]

Moving from Step One to Step Two of *Bruen*, Carney then stated, "Since the relevant SB2 provisions implicate conduct the Second Amendment protects, they are presumptively unconstitutional unless the government [can] demonstrate that the provisions are 'consistent with the Nation's historical tradition of firearm regulation.' [*Bruen* citation]."[106] Continuing, he observed, "The Supreme Court mentioned in *Bruen* that it is 'settled' that certain, 'relatively few' locations are 'sensitive places' 'where arms carrying c[an] be prohibited consistent with the Second Amendment.' [*Bruen* citation]. These locations include schools, government buildings, 'legislative assemblies, polling places, and courthouses.' [*Bruen* citation]."[107]

Beginning with the category "Hospital and Medical Services Facilities," the judge proceeded to evaluate the state's historical evidence justifying twelve challenged categories of sensitive locations. He noted that, in the first category, SB2 prohibited a CCW holder from carrying a gun in a

> "building, real property, mental health facility, nursing home, medical office, urgent care facility, or other place at which medical services are customarily provided." ... Given the nation's history and tradition of protecting the core right to carry a firearm to those wishing to defend themselves and their families in case of confrontation, it is unsurprising that the government does not offer a single historical prohibition on carrying firearms at hospitals or medical offices, much less one limiting carry by a category of people that is particularly responsible and trained and whom the government has background checked.[108]

Continuing, he observed,

> The government contends that SB2's ban ... "fits within the Nation's tradition of sensitive place restrictions because modern health care facilities exist for scientific and educational purposes and serve a vulnerable population," citing three Reconstruction-era laws: (1) an 1870 Texas law prohibiting bringing firearms to any "school room or other place where persons are assembled for education, literary, or scientific purposes," [Reference provided], (2) an 1878 Mississippi law prohibiting "any student of any university, college or school" from carrying a concealed weapon, [Reference provided], and (3) an 1879 Missouri law prohibiting concealed carry in "any school room or place where people are assembled for educational, literary or social places" [Reference provided].[109]

Elaborating further, Carney stated,

> The government argues these "laws were designed to, among other things, protect vulnerable persons who, because of their age or physical state, cannot easily escape attack, much less defend themselves." ... [But] California's ban ... in facilities

> providing medical services is supported by neither any history or tradition of banning firearms in those locations nor by any analogy to "settled" places. The government provides no evidence that the proffered analogies prohibiting firearms in places where people gather for "scientific" or "educational" purposes are well-established, representative, or consistent with a tradition of banning firearms in places like hospitals or urgent cares. [*Bruen* citation]. Nor are the proffered analogies "relevantly similar" because SB2, which prevents [vetted and trained] people from carrying ... imposes a far greater burden on the right to self defense.[110]

Similarly, focusing on SB 2's public transportation ban, Carney determined that the government failed to show that this regulation was supported by analogy to either historical regulations or to "settled" sensitive places. He rejected the government's argument that the ban comported with the nation's tradition of regulating firearms just because public transit facilities and vehicles were crowded, confined spaces where "'the discharge of a firearm is highly likely to result in severe injury to innocent bystanders....' But spaces do not become sensitive simply because they are 'crowded and protected generally by' the police. [*Bruen* citation]. And densely packed spaces are precisely the types of spaces that malicious criminals target for mass-shootings."[111]

The judge also rejected the state's argument that the ban was consistent with tradition because public transportation "serve[s] vulnerable populations, particularly children."[112] He noted that public transportation was not "densely populated" by children, and "to conclude that public transportation may be considered a 'sensitive place' by analogizing to the 'settled' fact that schools are sensitive places requires accepting the false notion that any place where children may be found, under any circumstances, may be designated a sensitive place. This overbroad reasoning would impermissibly 'eviscerate the general right to publicly carry arms for self-defense.' [*Bruen* citation]."[113]

In a like manner, Judge Carney rejected the state's arguments and analogues offered for the other categories of SB2's sensitive places. Referring to private companies' gun-carriage restrictions proffered to justify the public transportation ban, he noted that a historical statute generally "cannot earn the title 'analogue' if it is clearly more distinguishable than it is similar to the thing to which it is compared."[114] Regarding the state's "closest" analogues used to justify the gun ban in places where alcohol is sold and consumed, he argued, "these [three] nineteenth-century regulations from territories and localities are insufficient to demonstrate"[115] a history and tradition of such regulation. He also rejected the analogues justifying a gun ban for public gatherings and special events as insufficient, both because the cited laws were not long-standing and were repealed and because SB2 posed "a much greater burden than the historical analogues."[116]

After dismissing all the government's arguments and analogues justifying SB2's challenged categories, Carney concluded, "CCW permit holders are among the most responsible, reliable law-abiding citizens. They have been through a vigorous vetting and training process .... The challenged SB2 provisions unconstitutionally deprive this group of their constitutional right to carry a handgun in public for self-defense. Therefore, those provisions must be preliminarily enjoined."[117]

Judge Carney's opinion is not the final word on SB2—the state has already filed an appeal. Additionally, other federal courts (e.g., in Maryland[118] and New Jersey[119]) have also examined the constitutionality of highly similar sets of "sensitive location" gun prohibitions. Given the judicial disagreements among the courts on the appropriate analyses and constitutionality of various "sensitive" places, it seems inevitable that the Supreme Court will address the issue—regardless of how circuit courts rule on appeal.

Handgun Permit Requirements

After the *Bruen* opinion struck down the "special need/may-issue" provisions of New York's handgun licensing approach, that state (and states having similar requirements) revised their licensing regulations, attempting to bring them into line with *Bruen*. However, gun rights activists have challenged the updated regulations, seeing the new provisions as unconstitutional infringements in their own right. The Second Circuit's "sensitive locations" case discussed above also contained a challenge to New York's new regulations. Similarly, a Fourth Circuit *en-banc* court has reviewed a challenge to Maryland's shall-issue licensing procedure, weighing the implications of the *Bruen* decision on the challenged regulation.

In the New York case, plaintiffs challenged four components of the licensing procedure: a "good moral character" provision; a "cohabitant disclosure" requirement; a "social media disclosure" requirement; and a general, "catch-all" disclosure requirement. The plaintiffs argued—and the district court agreed—that these requirements had no basis in the country's historical tradition of firearms regulation, and thus violated the Second Amendment. The circuit court disagreed and rejected the challenges to the character, cohabitant, and catch-all requirements.[120]

The court asserted that the new, specifically defined good character requirement was not (as challenged) *facially* unconstitutional. The court noted some possible applications of the good character requirement would not violate the Constitution, and the requirement was consistent with the historical tradition of preventing dangerous individuals from possessing weapons. The opinion acknowledged that "'good moral conduct' is a spongy concept susceptible to abuse"[121] but argued that permit denials not supported by evidence of untrustworthiness to carry a firearm could still be vindicated in an administrative appeal or in court.

The panel judges further noted, "Similarly, although it is possible that a licensing officer *could* make an unconstitutional demand for information pursuant to the catch-all, we cannot conclude that there are *no* questions a licensing officer might constitutionally ask under that provision."[122] The judges disagreed with the district court's determination that the catch-all provided licensing officials with "unbridled discretion," noting that "it surely does not violate the Constitution for a licensing officer to request … reasonable supplementary information."[123]

Concerning the cohabitant disclosure requirement, the panel judges asserted that the provision was "consonant with the long tradition of considering an applicant's character and reputation when deciding whether to issue a firearm license. … In our view, disclosure of one's cohabitants (in part for the purpose of identifying references regarding the applicant's trustworthiness) is tantamount to the character-reference provision upheld by the district court."[124] The court elaborated by noting that if the character-reference requirement was consistent with tradition, the cohabitant requirement of a few additional references could not be *inconsistent* with that tradition.

In upholding the preliminary injunction against the social media disclosure requirement—a complete listing of all the applicant's former and current social media accounts—the panel judges agreed with the district court. That court had found "the burdensomeness of this modern regulation to be unreasonably disproportionate to the burdensomeness of any historical analogues."[125] The circuit court additionally distinguished between public social media accounts and those maintained pseudonymously. The judges noted, "Conditioning a concealed license on such a disclosure imposes a burden on the right to bear arms that is without sufficient analogue in our nation's history or tradition of firearms regulation."[126]

In the Maryland case,[127] the plaintiffs mounted a facial challenge to the constitutionality of the state's "shall-issue" Handgun Qualification License (HQL) statute. They contended that compliance with the statute resulted in such long wait times that it effectively denied the applicant's Second Amendment rights. They also argued that the HQL was "abusive" in that it was redundant with a second permitting law (77R) which had a similar mandatory background check and other requirements. In district court, the judge rejected these arguments, but on appeal, a panel of the Fourth Circuit agreed with the plaintiffs and determined that the HQL statute was unconstitutional. However, a vote of the full court vacated that decision, and the *en banc* court reviewed the appeal *de novo* (i.e., "from new"—a standard of review where the court need not give any weight to the previous decision).[128]

Referencing *Bruen*, the *en banc* court emphasized that "shall-issue" licensing laws using " 'narrow, objective and definite standards' and [which] do not give authorities discretion with regard to issuing a license, ordinarily do not prevent individuals from exercising their Second Amendment rights. Thus, such laws generally do not 'infringe' the right to keep and bear arms."[129] Citing *Heller*, the court also noted that "certain 'longstanding prohibitions,' such as the prohibitions on the possession of firearms by felons, [are] 'presumptively lawful.' "[130]

Continuing, the court stated,

> So, in accord with the Supreme Court's [guidance], we hold that non-discretionary "shall-issue" licensing laws are presumptively constitutional and generally do not "infringe" the Second Amendment …. And if a plaintiff fails to rebut this presumption of constitutionality, the plaintiff's challenge to the "shall-issue" licensing law fails at step one [of *Bruen*], with no requirement to conduct a historical analysis under step two.[131]

In applying this approach, the court concluded that the HQL statute qualified as a "presumptively constitutional" licensing statute, noting that the law does not allow the state to deny a license if the individual meets the statutory requirements. Elaborating, the court observed,

> Moreover, the very requirements on which the plaintiffs focus their constitutional attack are the same requirements the Supreme Court cited as presumptively constitutional components … namely background checks and firearms safety courses. … Accordingly, the plaintiffs' constitutional challenge … can survive step one … only if they can demonstrate that the law "infringes" or effectively "den[ies]" the Second Amendment right [*Bruen* citation].[132]

The court then considered the three arguments the plaintiffs raised to rebut the presumptive constitutionality of the statute. The plaintiffs contended that the statute "'has been put toward abusive ends' because (1) any 'temporary deprivation' of the Second Amendment right constitutes 'infringement,' (2) the HQL statute imposes 'lengthy' wait times, and (3) Maryland's separate 77R firearm application (the 77R process) renders redundant the background check required under the HQL statute."[133] The court rejected all three arguments.

The court dismissed the first argument that *any* delay qualifies as infringement, noting that "the plaintiffs improperly discount Supreme Court guidance that requirements such as background checks and training instruction, which necessarily occasion some delay, ordinarily will pass constitutional muster without requiring the government to justify the regulation at step two. [Citations given]."[134] Similarly, the court dismissed the "lengthy" wait time contention (i.e., longer than thirty days), observing that in first quarter of 2018, "'no completed HQL applications [were] pending disposition for longer than 15 days' … [and] in some cases, the process … can take only a few days. This time period is far shorter than many of the permissible processing periods cited by the Supreme Court in *Bruen*."[135]

For the plaintiffs' last contention, the court denied that the HQL background check was redundant with the 77R process. The court observed, "unlike the HQL statute, which directs that each *individual* obtain a license before purchasing, renting, or receiving a handgun, the 77R process applies to the purchase, rental, or transfer of every regulated *firearm* … [it is] an application that contains … information regarding the handgun the individual seeks to purchase."[136] The court further noted that the HQL statute also required fingerprinting, absent in the 77R process. Finally, since the temporal sequencing of the required background checks was different, the court asserted that the HQL information reflected the individual's most recent criminal history record.[137]

Citing these distinctions, the court concluded,

> We reject the plaintiffs' argument that the HQL statute's background check is wholly redundant and so abusive as to "infringe" the Second Amendment right under step one of the *Bruen* framework. The plaintiffs have not met their burden to show that the HQL "infringes" the Second Amendment … and, thus, they have failed to rebut the presumption of constitutionality afforded to the HQL statute. … We affirm the district court's judgment.[138]

As these two cases demonstrate, despite *Bruen*'s guidance regarding the characteristics of impermissible licensing schemes, enough ambiguity still exists for serious judicial disagreements to arise. As with the other issues discussed in this section, resolution of these differences appears to require further Supreme Court clarification in some future appeal.

Reflections on the Second Amendment

It seems fitting to end this exploration of the right to keep and bear arms by considering two questions. First, what do all these judicial decisions and opinions imply about the nature and meaning of the Second Amendment; second, what does the Second Amendment imply about American society and culture?

The answer to the first question is straightforward. The contemporary controversy about the nature of the amendment—whether an individual or collective right—is probably best regarded as a judicial misinterpretation of the murky and ambiguous *Miller* (1939) opinion. Despite the misinterpretation's surprising popularity among the federal judiciary, as Justice Scalia noted in *Heller*, mistaking an individual right for a collective right cannot change the nature or meaning of the right. On the other hand, as the historical survey of cases has shown, even as an individual right, the Second Amendment has always had reasonable limits placed upon it. Courts frequently upheld certain restrictions on who might bear arms, what arms they might bear, how they might bear them, and where they might bear them.

Thus, the collective right controversy might best be viewed as a judicial distraction from more demanding Second Amendment issues: What specifically are these "reasonable" limits; and how are they justified in light of the amendment's substantive clause? The collective interpretation allowed the judiciary to side-step these questions and avoid any in-depth consideration of permissible limits. The Supreme Court's *Heller*, *McDonald*, and *Bruen* decisions have changed that and have pushed the judiciary to examine these fundamental concerns more closely.

With "text, history, and tradition" replacing "interest-balancing" in deciding potential infringements, courts must now carefully assess what the Second Amendment meant when enacted, and whether contemporary restrictions reflect this past understanding. As the judiciary wrestles with applying this more difficult evaluative framework, a clearer understanding of the amendment's true nature will certainly emerge.

The second question—what the Second Amendment implies about American society and culture—is complex and difficult. The United States is alone among nations in having an unfettered right to arms specifically guaranteed in a national constitution. Across the globe, this right to firearms is seen as a defining, iconic characteristic of the country. Within the country, the Second Amendment is a divisive topic and easily functions as an informal Rorschach test. A person's position on gun rights and gun control typically predicts a host of the individual's other political, social, and cultural orientations.

This cultural divide among Americans is perhaps most evident in discussions of "gun violence" and how to best address this central societal issue. Gun control proponents emphasize the *gun* in "gun violence" and see a viable solution in limiting and restricting firearm availability. Gun rights activists emphasize the *violence* in "gun violence" and see a solution in expanding firearm availability for armed self-defense. As one novelist expressed it, "An armed society is a polite society."[139] Ironically, both gun factions desire the same outcome—less violent and safer communities—but their means for achieving these goals are diametrically opposed.

As *Heller* and the most recent Supreme Court gun opinions have suggested, the Second Amendment's foremost purpose is to insure that individuals can defend themselves—with firearms if necessary—from dangerous confrontations both at home and on the street. In this light, the amendment implicitly supports the armed self-defense stance of gun rights advocates. This implicit support is not especially surprising. After all, America's first battle in its War for Independence specifically centered on securing guns and ammunition from confiscation—and it was fought by citizens noted for their "rugged individualism." To such people, the notion that firearms—in and of themselves—could be a problem would be mystifying.

Certainly it is impossible to disagree with the alternative notion, that in a world without guns, there would be no gun violence. But that alternative is not an option open to American society. Firearms were and remain an integral part of American life. Impermissible restrictions and infringements on the right to bear arms—promulgated by legislatures perhaps too concerned about the nature of weapons and not enough about the nature of violence—appear to increase safety while not actually doing so. In contrast, by protecting the right to arms from unconstitutional infringements, the Second Amendment reinforces individuals' own self-defense abilities and may, in so doing, make society safer overall.

Notes

1 T. Roosevelt, "President's Address on the Retirement of Mr. Justice Henry B. Brown from the Supreme Court of the United States," *American Law Review*, 40 (1906): p. 548.

2 C. Larson, "Four Exceptions in Search of a Theory: *District of Columbia v. Heller* and Judicial *Ipse Dixit*," *Hastings Law Journal*, 60:6 (2009): pp. 1327–85.

3 For example, see Warren Burger's various critiques of the *Heller* opinion at a January 14, 1990, *Parade Magazine* article (https://guncite.com/burger.html) and a December 16, 1991, MacNeil/Lehrer News Hour Report (https://www.youtube.com/watch?v=Eya_k4P-iEo).
Or see Associate Justice Clarence Thomas's dissent in the *Rahimi* (2024) decision at https://www.supremecourt.gov/opinions/23pdf/22-915_8o6b.pdf.

4 B. Metzger and O. Seddig, "More Than 60% of Americans Say the Supreme Court Is Motivated by Politics, While Just 32% Believe They Rule Based on Law: Poll," *Business Insider*, November 19, 2021. At https://www.businessinsider.in/politics/world/news/more-than-60-of-americans-say-the-supreme-court-is-motivated-by-politics-while-just-32-believe-they-rule-based-on-law-poll/articleshow/87805521.cms.

5 Quinnipiac University Poll, "Americans See Federal Criminal Charges against Trump as Serious, 51% Say He Should Be Prosecuted, 62% Say Politics Is Motivating DOJ's Case, Quinnipiac University National Poll Finds; Supreme Court Job Approval Hits All-Time Low." June 21, 2023. At https://poll.qu.edu/poll-release?releaseid=3874.
6 Ibid.
7 A. Lamparello, "Is the United States Supreme Court a Political Institution?," *Appellate Advocacy Blog*, May 26, 2024. At https://lawprofessors.typepad.com/appellate_advocacy/2024/05/is-the-united-states-supreme-court-a-political-institution.html#google_vignette.
8 Ibid.
9 J. Zeitz, "The Supreme Court Has Never Been Apolitical," *Politico*, April 3, 2022. At https://www.politico.com/news/magazine/2022/04/03/the-supreme-court-has-never-been-apolitical-00022482.
10 Ibid.
11 Ibid.
12 Ibid.
13 S. Lazarus, "How to Rein in Partisan Supreme Court Justices," *Brookings Commentary*, March 23, 2022. At https://www.brookings.edu/articles/how-to-rein-in-partisan-supreme-court-justices/.
14 Ibid.
15 Ibid.
16 K. Whittington, "Is the Supreme Court a Guardian or Player?," *Center for the Study of Democratic Politics*, August 26, 2019. At https://csdp.princeton.edu/blogs/supreme-court-guardian-or-player.
17 Ibid.
18 For a non-Second Amendment illustration of this possibility, see Millhiser's discussion of the rules governing "statutory construction." I. Millhiser, "Why the Supreme Court Just Ruled in Favor of over 300 January 6 Insurrectionists," *Vox*, June 28, 2024. At https://www.vox.com/scotus/357973/supreme-court-fischer-united-states-january-6-insurrection.
19 See A. Lamparello, "Is the United States Supreme Court a Political Institution?," *Appellate Advocacy Blog*, May 26, 2024.
20 See B. Frye, "The Peculiar Story of *United States v. Miller*," *NYU Journal of Law & Liberty*, 3:48 (2008): pp. 61–5. At http://www.law.nyu.edu/sites/default/files/ECM_PRO_060964.pdf. See also Chapter 3.
21 C. Larson, "Four Exceptions in Search of a Theory: *District of Columbia v. Heller* and Judicial *Ipse Dixit*," *Hastings Law Journal*, 60:6 (2009): pp. 1371–86. At https://papers.ssrn.com/sol3/papers.cfm?abstract_id=1347186#.
22 E. Mystal, "It's Time to Repeal—and Replace the Second Amendment," *The Nation*, August 7, 2019. At https://www.thenation.com/articlc/archive/repeal-second-amendment-gun-control/.
23 Ibid.
24 J. Sullivan, "Why We Should Repeal the Second Amendment," *VTDigger*, April 6, 2023. At https://vtdigger.org/2023/04/06/jim-sullivan-why-we-should-repeal-the-second-amendment/.
25 W. Shapiro, "Democrats Need to Start Talking about Repealing the Second Amendment," *New Republic*, May 26, 2022. At https://newrepublic.com/article/166628/democrats-repeal-second-amendment-guns.

26 J. Stevens, "Repeal the Second Amendment," *New York Times*, March 27, 2018. At https://www.nytimes.com/2018/03/27/opinion/john-paul-stevens-repeal-second-amendment.html.
27 W. Burger, Interview. *MacNeil/Lehrer News Hour Report*, December 16, 1991. At https://www.youtube.com/watch?v=Eya_k4P-iEo.
28 I. Goldstein, "Let's Get Serious and Repeal the Second Amendment," *Desert Sun*, May 11, 2023. At https://www.desertsun.com/story/opinion/contributors/valley-voice/2023/05/11/lets-get-serious-and-repeal-the-second-amendment/70183778007/.
29 B. Wittes, "Ditch the Second Amendment," *Brookings*, March 19, 2007. At https://www.brookings.edu/articles/ditch-the-second-amendment/.
30 See Donald Campbell, *America's Gun Wars: A Cultural History of Gun Control in the United States* (Santa Barbara, CA: Praeger, 2019).
31 S. Baldwin, ("Repealing the Second Amendment—Is It Even Possible?," *CBS News*, March 28, 2018. At https://www.cbsnews.com/news/repealing-the-second-amendment-is-it-even-possible/.
32 Goldstein, "Let's Get Serious."
33 Shapiro, "Democrats Need to Start Talking."
34 S. Singer, "Let's Talk about Repealing the Second Amendment," *CT Mirror*, December 12, 2022. At https://ctmirror.org/2022/12/12/lets-talk-about-repealing-the-second-amendment/.
35 G. Newsom, "Governor Newsom Proposes Historic 28th Amendment to the United States Constitution to End America's Gun Violence Crisis," Press Release, June 6, 2023. At https://www.gov.ca.gov/2023/06/08/28th-amendment/.
36 Ibid.
37 Editorial Board, "Don't Touch the Second Amendment," *Florida Times Union*, September 18, 2018. At https://www.jacksonville.com/story/opinion/editorials/2018/09/18/tuesday-editorial-dont-touch-second-amendment/10274982007/.
38 See, for example, the Newsom citation above. Gun rights proponents are highly skeptical of these claims, noting that support for "common-sense" gun regulations dramatically decreases when the specific details of the regulations are revealed.
39 Wittes, "Ditch the Second Amendment."
40 *United States v. Rahimi, 22-915, (U.S. Supreme Court) (2024).* At https://www.supremecourt.gov/opinions/23pdf/22-915_8o6b.pdf.
41 Ibid.
42 Ibid.
43 Ibid.
44 Ibid.
45 Ibid.
46 Ibid.
47 Ibid.
48 Ibid.
49 Ibid.
50 Ibid.
51 Ibid.
52 Ibid.
53 Everytown for Gun Safety, "Which States Prohibit High-Capacity Magazines?" 2024. At https://everytownresearch.org/rankings/law/high-capacity-magazines-prohibited/.

54 *Duncan et al. v. Bonta, 17-cv-1017-BEN (JLB) (U.S. District Court of California) (2023).* At https://www.govinfo.gov/content/pkg/USCOURTS-casd-3_17-cv-01017/pdf/USCOURTS-casd-3_17-cv-01017-4.pdf.
55 Ibid.
56 Ibid.
57 Ibid.
58 Ibid.
59 Ibid.
60 Ibid.
61 Ibid.
62 Ibid.
63 *Association of New jersey Rifle & Pistol Clubs v. Platkin, 18-10507-PGS-JBD, 22-04360-PGS-JBD, 22-04397-PGS-JBD (U.S. District Court of New Jersey) (2024).* At https://caselaw.findlaw.com/court/us-dis-crt-d-new-jer/116445575.html.
64 Ibid.
65 Ibid.
66 Ibid.
67 Ibid.
68 Ibid.
69 J. Cornfield, "Washington Supreme Court to Hear Case on High-Capacity Ammo Magazine Ban," *Washington State Standard*, June 6, 2024. At https://www.courts.wa.gov/content/publicupload/eclips/2024%2006%2011%20Washington%20Supreme%20Court%20to%20hear%20case%20on%20high.pdf.
70 *National Association of Gun Rights v. Garland et al., 4:23-cv-00830-O (U.S. District Court of Texas) (2024).* At https://fingfx.thomsonreuters.com/gfx/legaldocs/zdvxxkdjvx/NAGR%20v%20Garland%20decision%207-23.pdf.
71 Ibid.
72 Ibid.
73 *Garland v. Cargill, 22-976 (Supreme Court of the United States) (2024).* At https://www.law.cornell.edu/supremecourt/text/22-976.
74 *National Association of Gun Rights v. Garland et al., 4:23-cv-00830-O (U.S. District Court of Texas) (2024).*
75 Ibid.
76 Ibid.
77 *United States v. Rare Breed Triggers, 1:23-cv-00369-NRM-RML (U.S. District Court of New York) (2023).* At https://caselaw.findlaw.com/court/us-dis-crt-ed-new-yor/2197172.html.
78 Donald Campbell, *Guns in America: Examining the Facts* (Santa Barbara, CA: ABC-CLIO, 2021), p. 21.
79 *United States v. Price, 2:22-cr-00097, (U.S. District Court of West Virginia) (2022).* At https://www.wvsd.uscourts.gov/sites/wvsd/files/opinions/2_22-cr-00097_Goodwin_10-12-22.pdf.
80 Ibid.
81 Ibid.
82 Ibid.
83 *Vanderstok et al., v. Garland et al., 4:22-cv-00961-O (U.S. District Court of Texas)* (2023). At https://www.supremecourt.gov/DocketPDF/23/23A82/273123/20230727162552428_VanDerStok%20Appl.%20App_.pdf.

84 Ibid.
85 *State of California v. Bureau of Alcohol, Tobacco, Firearms & Explosives, 20-cv-06761-EMC (U.S. District Court of California) (2024).* At https://caselaw.findlaw.com/court/us-dis-crt-n-d-cal/115879120.html.
86 Everytown for Gun Safety, "Which States Prohibit Assault Weapons?," January 4, 2024. At https://everytownresearch.org/rankings/law/assault-weapons-prohibited/.
87 *Miller v. Bonta, 19-cv-01537 BEN (JLB) (U.S District Court of California) (2023).* At https://caselaw.findlaw.com/court/us-dis-crt-s-d-cal/115332562.html.
88 *Association of New Jersey Rifle & Pistol Clubs v. Platkin, 18-10507-PGS-JBD, 22-04360-PGS-JBD, 22-04397-PGS-JBD (U.S. District Court of New Jersey) (2024).* At https://case law.find law.com/court/us-dis-crt-d-new-jer/116445 575.html.
89 USCCA, "Which States Have 'Assault Weapons' Bans?" August 2, 2024. At https://www.usconcealedcarry.com/blog/which-states-have-assault-weapons-bans/.
90 *Bianchi v. Brown, 21-1255 (U.S. Court of Appeals, Fourth Circuit) (2024).* At https://www.ca4.uscourts.gov/opinions/211255.P.pdf.
91 *Antonyuk et al. v. Chiumento et al, 22-2908 (U.S. Court of Appeals, Second Circuit) (2023).* At https://law.justia.com/cases/federal/appellate-courts/ca2/22-2908/22-2908-2023-12-08.html.
92 Ibid.
93 Ibid.
94 Ibid.
95 Ibid.
96 Ibid.
97 Ibid.
98 Ibid.
99 Ibid.
100 Ibid.
101 Ibid.
102 Ibid.
103 Ibid.
104 *May et al. v. Bonta, cv-01798-CJC-ADS (U.S. District Court of California)* (2023). At https://www.courthousenews.com/wp-content/uploads/2023/12/may-v-bonta-prelim-injunction.pdf.
105 Ibid.
106 Ibid.
107 Ibid.
108 Ibid.
109 Ibid.
110 Ibid.
111 Ibid.
112 Ibid.
113 Ibid.
114 Ibid.
115 Ibid.
116 Ibid.
117 Ibid.
118 *Kipke v. Moore, GLR-23-1293 (U.S. District Court of Maryland) (2023).* At https://casetext.com/case/kipke-v-moore-1.

119 *Siegel v. Platkin, 653 F Supp. 3d 136 (U.S. District Court of New Jersey) (2023).* At https://scholar.google.com/scholar_case?case=2920664155641947942&q=Siegel+v.+Platkin,+653+F+Supp.+3d+136,&hl=en&as_sdt=4006&as_vis=1.
120 *Antonyuk et al. v. Chiumento et al., 22-2908 (U.S. Court of Appeals, Second Circuit) (2023).*
121 Ibid.
122 Ibid.
123 Ibid.
124 Ibid.
125 Ibid.
126 Ibid.
127 *Maryland Shall Issue, Inc. et al. v. Moore, 21-2017 (U.S. Court of Appeals, Fourth Circuit) (2024).* At https://fingfx.thomsonreuters.com/gfx/legaldocs/egpboxmmavq/08232024maryland.pdf.
128 Ibid.
129 Ibid.
130 Ibid.
131 Ibid.
132 Ibid.
133 Ibid.
134 Ibid.
135 Ibid.
136 Ibid.
137 Ibid.
138 Ibid.
139 Quote attributed to Robert Heinlein, from the science-fiction novel, *Beyond the Horizon.*

Index